THE PRE-CONQUEST CHURCH
IN ENGLAND

AN ECCLESIASTICAL HISTORY
OF ENGLAND
General Editor: J. C. Dickinson

I. THE PRE-CONQUEST CHURCH
Margaret Deanesly

II. THE LATER MIDDLE AGES
J. C. Dickinson

III. THE REFORMATION
J. R. H. Moorman

IV. THE RESTORATION AND AFTER
(Author to be announced)

V. THE NINETEENTH CENTURY
Owen Chadwick

Illumination from Ælfric's Anglo-Saxon version of
the Heptateuch. (From Cotton MS. Claudius B.iv : *c.* 1050)

AN ECCLESIASTICAL HISTORY OF ENGLAND

THE PRE-CONQUEST CHURCH
IN ENGLAND

BY

MARGARET DEANESLY, M.A.

PROFESSOR EMERITUS OF HISTORY
IN THE UNIVERSITY OF LONDON

NEW YORK
OXFORD UNIVERSITY PRESS
1961

PRINTED IN GREAT BRITAIN
BY R. AND R. CLARK LTD. EDINBURGH

PREFACE

IN trying to deal with so large a subject as church history in Britain from the Roman occupation till 1066, I am very conscious of writing with insufficient knowledge. I have tried chiefly to look at the Celtic and English church from the human angle, so far as the sources permit; I have not aimed at writing a constitutional history of the church, nor an art history. There are already excellent art histories, with fascinating illustrations. As to the constitutional history of the church, there is no modern work on the all-important subject of the relation of synod and witan throughout the period 597 to 1066; where the Anglo-Saxons felt no need of definition and delimitation, I have myself left the subject vague and formless.

This book may perhaps seem to give too roseate a picture of the English church, especially in the later period. One difficulty in arriving at a just estimate is that anti-clericals could not or did not write, and clericals did. Anti-clericals took arms on occasions, but we have no treatise expressing the views of the anti-monastic party about the tenth century reform: though there must have been a certain case for balancing the need of 'defence' against the endowment of monasteries. Among the Franks earlier, themselves like the English under Danish attack, similar conflicting claims had been contested at the assembly of Épernay, 846, and the settlement was not to the satisfaction of the church. Laws for the collection of tithe, again, needed repeated re-enactment: but who has ever liked paying taxes to anybody? Laymen had to be coerced by the king and his officers to pay tithe.

By and large, however, the church and her teaching by 1066 were giving security of outlook, confidence and a good philosophy of life to all men, whatever their rank; and to all men she stood for mercy, for compassion, in a rough, vigorous and brutal age.

For ease of reading, foreign words in this book are not italicised but printed in inverted commas at their first appearance and thereafter without any distinction. Anglo-Saxon proper names and other words are spelt in normal characters, without symbols or accents;

v

for Anglo-Saxon proper names I follow Sir Frank Stenton's spelling in *Anglo-Saxon England*.

I should like to thank for help many more historians than I may specify here; but I cannot omit expressing my gratitude for help over a number of years to Sir Frank Stenton, to Paul Grosjean, S.J., to Professor Wormald, to Professor Wrenn, for quoting his version of Cædmon's hymn, to Mr. W. J. Grisebrooke for liturgical references, and to the Trustees of the British Museum for permission to reproduce an illumination of Claudius MS. B. iv. as a frontispiece.

MARGARET DEANESLY

196 Clarence Gate Gardens
London, N.W.1

CONTENTS

CHAPTER I

EARLY CHRISTIANITY IN BRITAIN

THE history of the early church in Britain rests on slender written
records, and archaeological evidence whose interpretation is comparatively recent. But in tracing the early history of Christianity in
these islands and the foundation and nature of the Celtic and early
English churches, there is another aid to historical reconstruction:
knowledge of the context of early Christendom. The church was one
and recognised as such, though the difficulties of travel made communication between distant local churches difficult. Christendom in
fact extended, at the time of the council of Nicaea, over most of the
Roman empire and in places beyond its borders, as in Persia, Ethiopia
and south India. Christians professed the same faith, made the same
renunciations and promises, received the same sacraments. Because
the church was one, in faith, ministry and sacraments, it is possible to
interpret the slender evidence about the beginnings of Christianity in
these islands in the light of the practice of Christendom elsewhere.

Christianity, however, was never an abstract concept, a pure
philosophy: acceptance implied a new way of life and the incorpora-
tion of Christians into a particular society. The civilisation into which
the Christian faith was introduced helped to shape the forms of
Christian thought, life and worship in different societies, the essentials
in all cases being the same. The background 'culture', in the archaeological sense of the word, produced certain differences in Christian
organisation and notably in Christian art: the old Greco-Roman
Christianity of the Mediterranean had a somewhat different organisation, and very different art forms, from those of the La Tène Celts.
Throughout Christendom, however, bishops were accepted as the
successors of the apostles. As successors of the Twelve they were regarded as ministers of the Christian sacraments and guardians of the
Christian faith.

In the external organisation of the church, the bishop's teaching

I

office was stressed by visible symbol. 'Go ye therefore and teach all nations' had been Christ's final command to the Twelve: and in the Roman empire the sign of the teacher's office was the chair, the 'cathedra' of the rhetor's school. Teaching, both in the rhetor's school and by Christian bishops, was oral, for books were few and expensive and most men illiterate. When the church came up out of the catacombs, at the Peace of the Church in 312, bishops had already been working in the chief cities, the chief population groups, of the Roman empire: the siting of bishops' sees (from 'sedes', Latin for cathedra) followed the provincial organisation of Rome; each city should have a bishop, and the bishop of each mother city of the province should be the metropolitan bishop, or 'primas'.

Archaeology has thrown some light on the pagan temples and Christian churches in Roman Britain, and would have thrown more, but for the successive rebuilding on the sites of Roman cities. The Anglo-Saxons did not use the tumbling ruins of these cities for their own habitation, but they frequently built near them, as sites having some topographical value and as supplies of good, hewn stone; and the near-Roman 'burhs' thus begun by the Anglo-Saxons overspread, in the course of time, the original Roman sites. Moreover, the cells of Christian house-churches, or of pagan temples even, may have been in many cases built with timber posts and lath and plaster filling for the walls: and it is only of recent years that archaeologists have paid much heed to the post-holes of timber work and fragments of painted wall plaster. Nor have builders, excavating old sites for the making of new foundations, been in the past as quick to notify archaeologists of old fragments of pottery and wall plaster.

Objects signed with the chi-rho monogram, α and ω, etc., dated by their associations from before the Peace of the Church, have been found by archaeologists in what was once Roman Britain. Of the remains of churches, the house-church at Lullingstone and the probably Christian basilica at Silchester, both dating from the period between the Peace of the Church and the Roman evacuation, are the most notable.[1] Since down to 312 the various pagan cults of the empire were all lawful, and the cult of the emperor official, while the Christians were a proscribed sect, more small stone altars and inscrip-

[1] For a fuller description of Christian remains found by the archaeologists, see Deanesly, M., *Sidelights on the Anglo-Saxon Church*: which has also some description of the pagan remains.

tions associated with pagan cults have naturally been found than Christian objects or inscriptions. Even after 312, moreover, the Roman army was devout to Mithra or other pagan gods, not to Christ: so that cities based on camps of the legions could not be expected to yield evidence of Christian churches or inscriptions to the excavator. Of all the evidence of pagan cults, however, the small basilica on the Walbrook, the tributary of the Thames, is perhaps the most impressive. The site was disclosed in digging the foundation for new offices on the site bombed in 1940, and severed marble heads and other objects show that offerings were there made to Mithra, and to other eastern gods and goddesses. The site was not a Mithraeum, which should properly speaking be a set of caves: the site here was far too near the water level for a set of caves: but the cult of Mithra seems to have been prominent.

Besides the archaeological evidence, there are also some literary references to the introduction of Christianity into Britain, and to its early character. Such references are few: for papyrus was the common writing material of the Roman empire, and papyrus perishes all too easily, in fires or by damp. Of the hundreds of papyrus letters and memoranda that must have been written in Roman Britain, by officials or private individuals, no original remains. An official schedule like the *Notitia Dignitatum*, which includes lists of the civil and military officers of Roman Britain, must have been compiled from lists written locally, on papyrus, and sent in to some central office, in Rome or perhaps Constantinople: the whole schedule would have been written out on papyrus. But it must have been copied on to parchment before it perished, and on the Continent, not Britain. The damp British climate did not favour the survival of papyrus: and, apart from that, there must have been many fires and destruction of records in the disturbances that preceded and followed the Roman evacuation.

There are very few indications that the earliest writers on the history of Britain had any papyrus writings before them, though one passage in Gildas' 'tearful lament' about Britain suggests that he is quoting an actual letter sent by the provincials of Britain to Aetius, thrice consul: and this would have been on papyrus. But generally speaking, we have to rely on the references of later, not of contemporary, writers, for a tentative history of the introduction of Christianity into Britain.

There is a fair probability that Britain received Christianity early: Gildas asserted that she did so in the reign of Tiberius (A.D. 14-37), but that is a mere guess, an inference indeed from the widely held theory that the Twelve Apostles had divided up the world by lot and proceeded to preach in the parts allotted to them. Eusebius was aware of this theory, and certain passages in his Ecclesiastical History are apparently based on it: and Gildas had read the Ecclesiastical History in Rufinus' Latin translation. The theory, however, was only used by ancient ecclesiastical historians when an early origin of Christianity in a particular region was accepted, but evidence as to who brought it there was lacking (see p. 15). Bede had a copy of Gildas' De excidio et conquestu Britanniae (or at least a part of the tract as printed by Mommsen), but he did not incorporate this statement of Gildas in his own Historia Ecclesiastica.

Christianity had, however, reached Britain in the second century, for Tertullian wrote, c. A.D. 200, that 'parts of the Britains inaccessible to the Romans were indeed conquered by Christ'. The Romans had conquered Britain in A.D. 43, by the campaigns of Aulus Plautius, in the reign of Claudius Caesar, a century and a half before Tertullian wrote that sentence.

It used to be thought that the Roman army brought Christianity to Britain, and though this can no longer be held, it is certain from the scanty evidence about British bishops that Christianity came to Britain in the wake of the soldiers, forming groups of Christian civilians chiefly in the towns guarded by the Roman peace. There was a cross-Channel trade with Roman Gaul, and not only from Gaul to Richborough, where the funds were sent to pay the Roman legionaries, and London, which gained its first importance as a supply port for the army from the time of the Roman conquest. Northern Gaul became Christian much later than the Rhone valley, which had a Greek speaking church in the earliest times: but some Christians must have come across the Channel. There is no evidence, however, about any apostle of Britain.

It is also possible that Christianity followed the trade routes to western Britain, for, besides passages from Gaul, there was a very ancient trade from the east Mediterranean, round the peninsulas of western Europe, and no lack of archaeological evidence of that trade. Carvings of Mycenaean type daggers and bronze axes were, in 1958, found on the stones of Stonehenge, and they must indicate immemorially old contact with the Mediterranean. In the first and second century B.C., again, a great number of Greek coins were brought to Britain by sea and many also from the autonomous cities of Carthage and Syracuse: they were brought to western Britain to be bartered for their weight in exchange for tin, lead and skins. Swords and sword chapes of the same period, the iron age in Ireland, have been found on the banks of the Shannon, objects that show connexion with those of Brittany and Gaul: they must have been brought by traders in their fragile, early boats, round the Breton peninsulas and through the rough Atlantic seas, to Shannon mouth. There is thus no lack of evidence of sea trade between western Britain, Gaul and the Mediterranean, and the possibility that here also Christianity came with the traders cannot be ruled out. There is no evidence as to who brought Christianity to Britain, either in the east or in the west: traders and civil servants and clerics of no exalted station, it would seem.

Bede wrote his *Ecclesiastical History of the English Nation* in 731, and he collected the fullest information possible about the first event he knew of in the history of the church in Roman Britain: the martyrdoms of SS. Alban, Aaron and Julius in the Diocletianic persecution (c. A.D. 304). Bede, for his history, used very great care to get information from such patristic works as referred briefly to Britain, and from the traditions, oral or otherwise, of great contemporary churches like Canterbury, London and Winchester, sent to him by letter or personal messenger. The London priest, Nothelm, searched the Vatican archives and perhaps brought him also an old dossier long preserved at Canterbury. Bede's assertions, therefore, are to be treated with great respect, though it is, of course, recognised that some sources (e.g. archaeological ones) open to us were not available to him.

His earliest reference then (apart from a mistaken assertion about an early king Lucius)[1] is to the teaching of a Roman soldier at Verulamium by a Christian cleric from Gaul. He says that a pagan Roman harboured the cleric in the days of persecution and was won by his continual prayers, vigils and exhortations to wish to imitate his faith and piety, to leave the darkness of idolatry and become a Christian with his whole heart. When the Roman magistrate heard of the hiding-place of the cleric, he sent soldiers to summon him to

---

[1] Taken from the *Liber Pontificalis*: see Plummer, HE. ii. 14.

his presence. His host, however, put on the cleric's shaggy Gallic mantle, took his place and was led before the magistrate, found standing by the pagan altars. The magistrate seems to have penetrated Alban's disguise: for he asked him, as a Roman gentleman, to what family he belonged? Alban answered, 'What business of yours is my family and descent? But if you would know of the true religion, I am a Christian and I study for the Christian ministry.' And when the magistrate still inquired his name, he said 'Alban'.[1] He was adjured to offer incense to the gods, if he desired to live, and, when he refused, was executed, as a Roman citizen; the soldier, who had refused to act as executioner, was beheaded with him and won, unbaptised, the martyr's crown.

In the same persecution, Bede tells us, two Christians, Aaron and Julius, were beheaded: not Roman soldiers, but citizens of the 'Urbs Legionum', Caerleon-on-Usk.[2] Though the names of Aaron and Julius are not to be found in any classical martyrology, or even in Bede's version of the Jeromian Martyrology,[3] there are grounds for accepting that a cult of St. Aaron existed in the fifth and sixth centuries in Wales, and in these early days a cult was always connected with the burial place of the saint. There was certainly a St. Aaron, hermit, who presumably came from Wales, preached at various places in Brittany, and retired as hermit to the isle of Aleth, now St. Malo. He was found there by St. Malo, whose cult eclipsed his own. His name Aihran, Latin Aaron, may have been derived from the 'merthyr' or martyrium to Aaron and Julius, near Caerleon, mentioned in that suspect compilation, The Book of Llan Dâv;

---

[1] There was a gens 'Albana' and also a gens 'Albina', to which some more famous members belonged. It is likely that Bede had the gens right: but that, in the Carolingian period scholars wrote the name 'Albinus' in martyrologies, as better known to them. Alcuin's name, an Irish form of Albinus, and that of the abbot Albinus of Bede's day, are possibly names received on entry to the clerical or monastic order, rather than baptismal names.

[2] Bede calls Caerleon 'Legionum Urbs' and Chester 'Legionum Civitas': see Plummer, i. 21-22 and 84, where Bede adds that the Britons call Chester 'Carlegion', a place name that would be indistinguishable from that used by the Britons for Carlegion, Caerleon-on-Usk. What Bede meant by distinguishing 'civitas' from 'urbs' is uncertain: a civitas should be a tribal centre in Roman Britain, but actually Caerleon was such (Isca Silurum) and Chester (Deva) not. Gildas places the martyrdom of Aaron and Julius at Carlisle: but again, the early Welsh name, Carleol, Caerliwelyd, may have been easily confused in his original MS. with Caerleon.

[3] For the history of Martyrologies, see the Bollandist A.SS. for November, ii. pt. 2, and Père Delahaye in the Propylaeum to December, which deals with the Anglo-Saxon Martyrologies and Calendars. July, tom. i. p. 15 discusses Aaron, Julius and companions as a feast of July 1.

nevertheless there is some evidence of cult at Caerleon earlier than the making of the *Book of Llan Dâv*.[1]

Gildas asserts that there were many more martyrs in Britain, and many martyria erected when the persecutions ceased: but he gives no names. The fact that the known martyrdoms occurred at important Roman towns like Verulamium and Caerleon suggests that most bishops and lay Christians went into hiding in the countryside and that only exceptionally energetic officials sought them out. Some Welsh place names, however, suggest other martyrdoms, and it is possible that 'memoriae' or cemetery chapels should have been erected. Bede says of Verulamium that after the persecutions 'a church of wonderful workmanship worthy of his (Alban's) martyrdom' was built near by, and many cures were made there 'up till this day'.

After the Peace of the Church, A.D. 312, it became possible for bishops as elsewhere to hold property and build churches: the attendance of the three bishops at Arles, only two years later, shows the British church organised with territorial sees in the 'civitates' of London, York and Colchester: metropolitan sees, apparently, as in the mother cities of the provinces of Gaul. The bishop of the senior 'colonia' and first capital of Britain travelled with a priest and a deacon,[2] and it has even been suggested that he was the 'Primas' of Britain.

No British bishops in 325 attended the distant council of Nicaea, though they accepted its decisions. In 347 British bishops attended the council of Sardica in Moesia and supported the council's acquittal of Athanasius, and in 359 some attended the council of Rimini; three of them accepted the emperor Constantius' offer to pay their expenses from the imperial fisc.

The fourth century in Britain saw the gradual increase in the number of Christians, especially in the towns, though the 'prisca religio', the cult of the old gods, continued for long in the countryside. The army, recruited from countrymen, continued notably pagan: Haverfield could write, 'In the legionary fortresses, Isca and Deva, the presence of the Christian religion is almost imperceptible'[3]:

[1] See S. Baring-Gould's *Lives of the British Saints*, 1907, i. 102-103; there are place names, Cae Aron and Cwm Aron near Caerleon, 103.
[2] The third bishop from Britain at the council of Arles is recorded as 'Adelfius episcopus, de civitate Colonia Londinensium': see J. D. Mansi, *Sacrorum conciliorum nova et amplissima collectio*, tom. ii. coll. 476-477.
[3] *Archaeol. Æliana*, 3rd S. xv. 22.

in Britain, as in most provinces, Christianity has left many archaeological tokens in civilian life, but few on military sites. The emperor Julian the Apostate (A.D. 360–363) could claim in the pagan revival he initiated that most of his troops worshipped the gods; the Spaniard, Magnus Maximus, who held high command in Britain before he was emperor, was not a Christian till A.D. 362. It was during the pagan revival in Julian's reign that L. Septimius, 'praeses' of Britannia Prima (one of the five provinces into which Diocletian had subdivided Britain) restored a column erected, apparently about A.D. 300, in honour of Jupiter: the inscription says it had been erected 'prisca religione'. At some point it must have been cast down: it was found at last thrown down a well in Cirencester.

Nevertheless, in spite of external raids, internal disturbances and the gradual abandonment of the towns in the fourth century, Christianity advanced. Pelagius, a notable scholar and heretical teacher, was born in this island c. A.D. 380: he studied and wrote in Gaul, contending against the Augustinian teaching of the complete dependence of man on the grace of God, and his teaching found followers in Britain. From the description of those who contended with Germanus about it, they included upper class officials or officers; it is unlikely, indeed, that any but the small educated class could debate about deep theological issues: but many soldiers and peasants, classes long clinging to the paganism now proscribed, were as willing to follow the Pelagian leaders as the bishops. The danger was sufficiently apparent for the bishops in Gaul to hear of it, and commission Germanus to contend with the Pelagians (see p. 23).

About 390 also, a more famous Briton was born in the north: Patrick who was to convert Ireland (see p. 37). That he should have travelled to Gaul for training is not unlikely: British pilgrims, according to Palladius and Theodoret, visited the Holy Land and Syria in the early years of the fifth century: if the Roman posting system was breaking down, travel was still not impossible.

Between 420 and 430 Fastidius, a British bishop, addressed a book 'on the Christian life' to Fatalis, a devout British widow. In the book, he exhorts Fatalis not to despise the rustic bread he has set before her, for rustic bread can give strength and help to the weary. He explains to her that, as Christ means 'anointed', so Christians are anointed with the oil of gladness. The true Christian is he who keeps Christ's commands and despises earthly things; shall he be called Christian who has never fed the hungry with bread, or given drink to the thirsty, to whose table no guests are invited, whose roof shelters neither stranger nor pilgrim? Let no Christian think it. . . . That man is a Christian who follows the way of Christ and imitates him in all things. About the same time Faustus, probably a Briton, went to Gaul and became abbot of Lérins (see p. 38), and in 461 bishop of Riez.

What kind of a religion then was this early Christianity in Britain, as it appeared to the man in the streets of the Roman town? Judging by the analogy of the continental church from which it sprang, it was a mystery religion, dealing with life and death and their place in a divine purpose: with transcendental forces beyond the boundaries of this world. The pagan Roman gentleman, who had passed through the rhetor's school and been trained in the liberal arts (the branches of knowledge suitable for freemen, 'liberi', to acquire), would conceive of the universe as described by the Greek geographer and astronomer, Ptolemy: with the earth at its centre, and the moon and planets as each a kind of boss or thickening of the crystalline sphere in which it was set: these spheres swung round the earth, and beyond them was the empyrean of the fixed stars. This, as the Roman gentleman was taught, was observed fact, science in the modern sense: there was no indication of any purpose behind the universe. Greco-Roman philosophies, as those of Plato, Aristotle or Epicurus, dealt with abstract ideas, and the relation and duty of the individual to the cosmos and to his fellows: but such matters were the concern of the few mature scholars, they were not taught in the rhetor's school. These schools aimed only at preparing the Roman youth for the life of the magistrate, the civil servant and, incidentally, the military leader.

What every Roman gentleman would have learned, in these schools and by the traditions of family life, was respect for the city, for Rome, for the emperor, and for the 'manes' of the family. This cult of the family, reverence for his own lares and penates, included a tradition of respect for his own ancestors, living and dead: the setting up of their portrait busts in some 'cella' of his home and the making of small offerings in their reverence. But such traditions of the universe and human life, of duty to the state and filial piety for his own family, included no explanation of the universe, no definite moral code in the Christian sense, no expectation of personal survival after death. It is true that the emperors were by now regarded as

2

translated at death 'to the gods': coins were struck at an emperor's death with the legend 'consecratio' on the reverse side, and perhaps a figure of a swanlike bird bearing the emperor's soul aloft: but such an inclusion of the emperor 'among the gods' was no promise of an after life for common people. It is true that the mystery religions of the east, other than Christianity, offered their adherents the hope of an after life, and the Roman gentleman, without specifically adhering to any of them, was not unaffected: he was beginning to interpret the old myths of the gods allegorically in this sense. Persephone or Pegasus might be held a figure of immortality. But, as educated in the rhetor's school, he had no ground for such a hope.

Christianity, on the other hand, meant the acceptance of the Christian faith, set forth in its briefest in the Apostles' creed, and including belief in life after death. Such teaching, as apostolic, had been handed down by a great church of apostolic foundation and therefore of guaranteed authority. What is known today as the Apostles' creed is, in fact, a slight expansion of an old Roman baptismal formula or confession of faith made by the catechumen: local churches had roughly similar baptismal formulas. There was no single verbally identical baptismal creed, universally recited, but that of the Roman church was already widely used in the west. In the form quoted by Rufinus of Aquileia (c. 400) and closely parallelled in a letter to pope Julius of c. 340, this creed runs:

> I believe in God the father almighty; and in Christ Jesus his only son our Lord, who was born of the Holy Ghost and the Virgin Mary, who was crucified under Pontius Pilate and buried, rose again the third day from the dead, ascended into heaven, sits on the right hand of the Father, whence he will come to judge living and dead; and in the Holy Ghost, the holy church, the remission of sins, the resurrection of the flesh.

There is little doubt that this creed goes back to the second century, and it would have been in use for the baptism of early converts in Roman Britain. It offered a very great contrast to the concepts taught to the young Roman gentleman: instead of the Ptolemaic and Aristotelian theory of a closed universe, it offered one created by an almighty father, whom the Christian scriptures identified with love itself, who had broken into his own universe, untying the normal chain of causation, sending his son to be born of the Virgin Mary, redeem the world by his death, and open to his followers the life in the world to come. To the Roman gentleman of the rhetor's school, it seemed a very strange story: but it was part of the Christian faith. To the ignorant, it was very good news: as important in his conversion as the entry into a new family, whose members must give and expect mutual succour, or the adoption of a new way of life.

The origin of Britonnic Christianity in this island lacks recorded evidence, but should be seen against the background of the La Tène culture in western Europe and Ireland generally. The 'Celtic Christianity' of Cornwall, Devon, Somerset, Wales, Lancashire, Westmorland, Cumberland and Strathclyde, like that of Brittany and Ireland, was the same religion as that of Roman Britain and Roman Gaul, with the same faith and the same institutions, but it had been preached against an unromanised, tribal background. It developed institutions to deal with such a background, and the lives of its saints were conditioned by such a background. Its relations with the secular power had to be with the tribal chieftain, not the count of the Roman civitas. Even though it had contact in its border areas with the society of the Roman empire, as in Brittany, Somerset, the borders of Wales and the changing northern frontier of Britain, even though St. Patrick had been trained in the Gallic Christianity of Auxerre, the background culture for long held its own against Roman imperial influence. Petroc and Cadoc and Cyngar, Britons of the south west peninsula of Britain, lived and worked as Celtic Christians; Dubricius and David and Deiniol were bishops, but not territorial ones: nor was St. Kentigern. In Britain, co-operation and communications were maintained with each other by sea, rather than with the hostile English of the fifth century by land. Who will venture to say that in the fourth century there were Welsh bishops of Isca or Deva or Segontium, as there were of York and London?

Tertullian's words that parts of Britain inaccessible to the Romans had been conquered by Christ have a bearing on the origins of Celtic Christianity in Britain. Those origins may have been independent of the occupying legions in Britain, and the foreign civilians they brought in their wake (foreign to Britain). There was a cross-Channel trade between Gaul and Britain, from Brittany right up to Boulogne: in the fifth century and later there is plenty of evidence of the influence of Gallican Christianity on the Celts. There was also a trade from the Mediterranean to Severn mouth, and no reason at all why Greeks and Syrians shouldn't have come to Severn mouth, as they did in Gregory of Tours' time to the mouth of the Loire. But on the whole, while evidence of relations between Gaul and the Celtic Christians is very strong, evidence of relations with Mediterranean Greeks, Jews or Syrians is very slight. It came only with the use of illuminated Gospel books in the sixth century and later. Celtic Christianity on the whole was a transplanted Gallican Christianity.

The whole question of the early church at Glastonbury may be dealt with at this point, not merely as a question of local history, but as involved in that of the historical origins of Celtic Christianity: involved in the question whether the lake villages of Meare and Glastonbury got their Christianity independently of the Roman conquerors of Britain. The tradition of a very early church at Glastonbury is of interest, not because of legends fabricated much later about its foundation, but because of the curious appositeness of the site selected by tradition as that of the oldest church in Britain. When Julius Caesar raided Britain in 55 and 54 B.C., London was non-existent, and Britain's trade with Gaul and the Mediterranean was conducted by way of the Severn mouth and Glastonbury. Economic historians stress the importance of Glastonbury as the focal point of track ways from the Midlands, Wilts and Somerset, as well as the near neighbour of the lead workings carried on in the region of Meare, and the tin workings of Wales.[1] The local chieftains imported wine from Gaul, with the apparatus of civilised drinking in the way of flasks, flagons, cups and strainers (for the wine seems to have been much shaken up in passage), and their wives adorned themselves with the shale ornaments from Kimmeridge in Dorset: and all this in the first century before and the first century after, our era. Early traders do not make their ports at the mouths of great tidal rivers, but in the small streams that flow into the river mouth. The Italian supply ships tied up first a little way up the Walbrook, not by the banks of the Thames itself, with its great tidal flow. Similarly in the west, on the great river that was then the front door of Britain, the small ships of the traders tied up, not at the spot we should now call Bristol, but at Glastonbury, protected by its marshes at the head of the Old Rhyne. Glastonbury was the Bristol of the day.

Both Glastonbury and Meare were lake villages. Meare, like the

[1] *Cambridge Economic History of Europe*, ii. 30.

famous La Tène village on Lake Neuchâtel, had houses built on a timber sub-structure, the houses timber-built and some with super-imposed floors. The villagers lived by farming, fishing and hunting, and they used the crafts of metal working, carpentry, weaving and leatherwork. This old La Tène civilisation was centred in Glaston-bury and Meare, and the local craftsmen produced more beautiful metal work than did the Parisii in Yorkshire, or the later Belgae in the south east. Archaeological evidence shows that at the beginning of our era, Glastonbury as a La Tène trading centre shared in the most advanced civilisation at that time established in the country. Two of the most beautiful objects in the curvilinear style known as Late Celtic,[1] the Birdlip and Desborough mirrors, were found in close relation to Glastonbury. The people of this iron-age culture spread across the Bristol Channel and up the valleys of the Severn, Usk and Wye. The village of Glastonbury itself was raided by Belgic tribes between Caesar's invasion and the Claudian conquest: but the La Tène civilisation of the Cotswolds, Somerset and Dorset lived on and remained independent of its neighbours, though sub-dued finally by the Romans. The Belgic tribes of south east Britain were indeed the chief military opponents of Aulus Plautius: but they never produced objects of so fine an artistic character as the La Tène peoples of the south west and Northamptonshire.

The claim made for the church of Glastonbury to an antiquity beyond memory was, in fact, a claim that the old Celtic, La Tène culture had contact with Christianity independently of the Romans, who brought it to Britain via London and Kent. There is no historical evidence to support the claim except the words of Tertullian, but one or two points can be made in its favour.

The speed with which Christianity spread from eastern Europe to Edessa and Persia along a great trade route, and that in the first and early second century, renders it not impossible that a similar ex-pansion along a trade route should have occurred in the west, through the Mediterranean, Massilia and the Rhone valley to north Gaul and Britain, or round the western promontories to the Severn mouth.

Again, it is strange that early medieval tradition in Britain should have asserted that the church of Glastonbury was the oldest in the land, when the men who made the tradition were without any

[1] Style iv, La Tène.

predilection for a western origin, without the evidence of Glastonbury's economic and cultural importance available to modern
archaeologists, and without the pointer that Glastonbury and the
Severn mouth were indeed the places where a trade-borne Christianity was likely to have arrived in the second or even the first century.
There were no obvious Roman remains in Glastonbury to prompt
the rise of a tradition. No early claim was made on behalf of any other
church in Roman Britain to have been the earliest founded: when
one was made much later, in the twelfth century, by the abbey of
Westminster, it was easily demolished by William of Malmesbury.

Again, the art motifs, interlace and other, of the Celtic Christians,
as used in their illumination later, come straight from those of the
La Tène metal workers, such as those of Meare and the Severn
mouth and Ireland. Whether or not Christianity came to Glastonbury independently, the Celtic Christians got no notable artistic
inheritance from Roman Britain.

Apart from evidence directly bearing on the origin of the church
at Glastonbury, some other points in its history are of interest.

The theory of the quasi-apostolic foundation of the church at
Glastonbury, held in pre-Conquest days, depended on the widely
known (and erroneous) belief that the apostles had taken the known
world as their field of preaching and divided it by lot, each making
his way to the mission field thus obtained. Reference to this belief
appears in Eusebius[1] and in the Jeromian Martyrology, and the
historical importance of the belief in the division of the world by the
Twelve is that to many early scholars the Christianity of certain
regions was believed to be of very early foundation, but the circumstances of the first preaching were unknown. At the same time, it
was held that a very early Christian foundation must have been
apostolic: the first psalm recited in the common of an apostle in the
office of nocturns was the eighteenth (English, nineteenth), with its
fourth verse for antiphon:

In omnem terram exivit sonus eorum: et in fines orbis terrae verba
eorum.

This familiar verse was a kind of warrant for the belief that the
words of the Twelve did indeed reach into the ends of the earth,

---

[1] Bede used Rufinus' translation of Eusebius: see Mommsen's ed. in the MGH.,
Scriptores antiquissimi; see for the Jeromian Martyrology, the A.SS., Propylaeum
Decembris.

and the belief was expressed by Isidore of Seville in his tract, *De Obitu Patrum*:[1] St. Philip, he held, 'preached in Gaul to the barbarous peoples adjoining the dark and dangerous Ocean'. Britain, though he did not mention her, belonged to the praetorian prefecture of the Gauls. The importance of this belief in widespread apostolic preaching, even to the ends of the earth, is that it was invoked to explain the tradition of very early foundation, as of the preaching of St. Thomas in India. It points to the existence of such a tradition.

It was this tradition of early (and therefore allegedly apostolic) foundation that inspired king Ine of the West Saxons to build a great new church at Glastonbury. It inspired Dunstan, when first embracing the monastic life, to make his cell near the 'vetusta ecclesia' at Glastonbury; and it finds its clearest expression in William of Malmesbury's account[2] of the conversation between Godfrey, monk of Glastonbury, and an old monk of Saint-Denis, near Paris, whose monastery Godfrey was visiting:

'Father' (papa), said the old monk to Godfrey, 'does the vetusta ecclesia . . . still stand?'

'Indeed, it is still standing,' he said.

The monk of Saint-Denis was silent for a short space and then spoke: 'This church here of the glorious martyr St. Denis has the same dignity of privilege as that church of which you speak: the one in Gaul, the other in Britain, erected at the same time: each is called "a second Rome"'.

The monk of Saint-Denis believed his house founded by Dionysius the Areopagite, of the Acts of the Apostles, and Glastonbury by some apostle or apostolic man: it was by virtue of their apostolic foundation that they might be called 'a second Rome'.

Again, the series of churches disclosed by excavation at Glastonbury shows that the 'vetusta ecclesia' there was older than the age of St. David, who was said to have visited it, and the Celtic minster which king Ine undoubtedly found at Glastonbury when he had conquered Somerset; this Celtic minster may have been founded from Ireland in the Patrician or post-Patrician period, and it certainly had at least a contingent of Irish monks. But the vetusta ecclesia was older than the Celtic minster.

---

[1] PL. lxxxiii. col. 152.

[2] See Adam of Domerham's ed. of William of Malmesbury's *De Antiquitate Glastoniensis ecclesiae*, 1727, i. 15. The conversation was 'in the days of Henry of Blois, abbot of Glastonbury, before he became bishop of Winchester in 1129'.

The vetusta ecclesia[1] was a wooden building, of wattle and daub with wooden uprights, its structure similar to that of the houses on the lake village at Meare. It was later spoken of as the church of St. Mary, was 60 feet long and 20 wide, and had a square chancel of nearly the same width, believed to have been added by St. David. In the time of king Ine of Wessex (689–728), this old timber church was regarded with great reverence. King Ine built his own church to the east of it, on the same axial line, and beneath the floor of his church has been found some flooring of 'opus signinum', a pink cement used by the Roman builders. Moreover, in 1954, the foundations of another very old building were disclosed beneath Ine's floor: a building not certainly a church, but showing at least that the site was inhabited in the Roman period. The discoveries consisted of a series of post-holes belonging to a wooden building probably with wattle and daub walls, and unfloored. Fragments of pottery trodden into the surface, however, were found, and included pieces of native ware of the first century A.D., a scrap of Samian ware, and some from the fifth and sixth centuries. That is: in the time of the Roman occupation (A.D. 43 to the middle of the fifth century) Glastonbury must have had at least one, if not two, Roman buildings adjacent to, but not coincident with, the traditional site of the earliest church.

These old buildings Ine had cleared away when he built his new basilica, the 'major ecclesia' which survived to the Norman Conquest. His church had a square chancel and 'porticus' beside the nave, as at St. Augustine's, Canterbury; then or soon after a square narthex was built at the west end of Ine's church, enclosing the chapel added by St. David (?) to the vetusta ecclesia.

Bede says nothing of Glastonbury: he was dependent for his information about western England on that supplied from the tradition or records of the see of Winchester, moved about 663 from an original Wessex mother city at Dorchester on Thames. Before Ine's day, the Britons of Somerset were fighting a protracted frontier battle with the West Saxons, and any reference to Glastonbury in Winchester annals is unlikely; Ine's learned bishop, Haeddi, may have guided his building of the new Glastonbury church, as a measure of appeasement to the conquered Britons. Bishop Daniel, with whom Bede corresponded, was naturally more concerned with

[1] See A. W. Clapham's *Eng. Romanesque Architecture before the Conquest*, 1930, p. 49 and fig. 16.

his predecessors in the see, and possibly the passing on of some Wessex annals, than with the Britons.

The first historical study of Glastonbury was made by William of Malmesbury (died soon after 1142), who wrote a treatise *About the antiquity of the church of Glastonbury* about 1125, after spending some years visiting the monks of Glastonbury.

William of Malmesbury was the finest historian of the twelfth century in England; he was librarian of his own abbey of Malmesbury in Wiltshire for a time, and he had access to at least the fine libraries of Glastonbury and Canterbury. He studied Glastonbury's old charters (some of them forged), its complex church with carved inscriptions, and the carvings on the great stone bases of the Celtic crosses in the monks' cemetery. The small crosses which surmounted the bases originally must have perished, for he calls these bases 'the pyramids'. He gives the names carved on these 'pyramids' as he could read them: some of the names of his version are intelligible, some not. His careful description, however, of these and of the old church and its carved tombs, as they survived when he was writing in Henry I's reign, shows that he was familiar with the place and presumably with its monks.

He states in the prologue to his treatise that he has prepared for writing it by long pondering over certain tracts (libellos), including the miracles of St. Benignus, the life of St. Patrick and the passion of St. Indractus, an Irish saint: he has handled the manuscripts and corrected whatever was said in them 'on this side of reason' (citra rationem). All the sources he quotes are written sources, and he makes no mention (as Bede does in his *Historia Ecclesiastica*) of accepting any tales handed down orally. He does not mention any foundation of the church by St. Joseph of Arimathea, nor any association of king Arthur with Glastonbury. The church of Glastonbury, he says, is very old, very holy: he ventures no account of its foundation, though he was ready to believe that the original little wattled church there was the oldest in the land.

Tales about the foundation of Glastonbury date from some sixty years after William of Malmesbury's investigation. A great fire on May 26, 1184, destroyed the monastery of Glastonbury, including the old church and the additions made to it by Ine and Dunstan: the damage was great, and Henry II gave large sums for the rebuilding. Not only was the rebuilding carried out over a period of years, but as part of the effort to rehabilitate Glastonbury, William of Malmesbury's treatise, *De Antiquitate*, was re-edited and additions made to it from various sources. A new first chapter was added after the prologue, and it was there asserted, as on the authority of Freculf, bishop of Lisieux, a Carolingian historian, that when St. James was evangelising western Europe, he sent out twelve companions to convert Britain, under the leadership of his own personal friend, Joseph of Arimathea. (Freculf, while asserting St. James' preaching in western Europe, did not mention Joseph of Arimathea or any voyage to Britain.) The reviser also asserted that Paulinus, the fellow-worker of St. Augustine, came to Glastonbury, and had the old wattled church, the vetusta ecclesia, covered in 633 with wooden boards; this was the old timber church which had survived till its destruction by fire in 1184. The reviser also added marginally many passages deriving from the work of Geoffrey of Monmouth, the romantic historian of king Arthur and his court, and he calls Geoffrey 'the historiographer of the Britons'. William of Malmesbury, though a contemporary of Geoffrey, had not seen fit to insert any of Geoffrey's stories about Arthur in his own grave and serious history. The legends about Glastonbury, that is, date from the rehabilitation of Glastonbury after the great fire: acceptance of its fame as the earliest Christian church in Britain can be ascribed to William of Malmesbury himself.

The proliferation of legend at Glastonbury is a curious and late parallel to the manner of origin of saints' legends in the Celtic church in Ireland. Study of the latter by Dr. Kathleen Hughes has shown that such legends usually belonged to a period of rehabilitation of a monastery, after a raid or catastrophe had dispersed the original monks. When some returned, after a period of years, the elder monks had died and very little was known of the pious founder of the monastery beyond the fact of the foundation. Yet it was desirable to read some account of the founder's life in his office, and also to stimulate the devotion of pilgrims to the shrine: and in such circumstances the meagre information about the acts of the founder were supplemented by borrowings from the manuscript copies of other saints' lives and miracles. At Glastonbury, too, the expansion of the legend was made from written, if unreliable sources; and at a time of re-foundation.

It is certain then that Christianity had penetrated eastern Britain under the Romans, that a provincial episcopate had been established as in Gaul, and that there were martyrdoms in the persecutions, notably those of Alban, Aaron and Julius, but possibly also others, as is asserted by Gildas and supported by certain Welsh place names. It is possible also, though not certain, that Christianity penetrated at a very early period the land of the La Tène Celts in the west of Britain, and the Anglo-Saxon acceptance of Glastonbury as the earliest Christian church in the land reflects the belief in this early origin.

CHAPTER II

CELTIC CHRISTIANITY : THE BRITTONIC CHURCH :
GERMANUS : NINIAN : PATRICK

CELTIC Christianity is a term covering a very wide field, even as applied only to that in the British Isles. The dominant race that the Romans conquered in Britain were, of course, Celts; the majority of the population of Britain when Constantine accepted Christianity were Celts. They were by now, however, Romanised Celts, though they continued to speak their own language, and not a vulgar Latin, as in Gaul. Christianity was strongest in the towns and villas, but the breakdown of Roman government had weakened it in those places. Nevertheless, the fluid Christianity of fifth century Britain, especially in the Lowland zone, was more akin to that of Gaul than was that of the less Romanised western parts of Britain, influenced by its La Tène setting. The Christianity of Britain, as it survived or perished in the fifth and sixth centuries, may perhaps be described as Brittonic, though that term is specifically used of the language used by the Celts in Britain at the time.

Something may be said first of Brittonic Christianity and the visits of Germanus: then of north British Christianity and Nynia (Nynian): then of the Welsh Christians and their leaders, Illtud, Dyfrig (Dubricius) and David; and then of the north British Patrick and his mission to Ireland, and its sequel in Scotland.

Philologists and students of place names and Latin inscriptions have cleared away some of the obscurity about the collapse of Romano-British Christianity in this period. Professor Kenneth Jackson has made some points clear. First, that records were not transmitted because the educated and Latin using class disappeared. The Latin language of the official class in Roman Britain had never become the natural speech of the whole population: it had remained purer and more classical than the vulgar Latin of Gaul, as can be shown from such inscriptions as have survived; purer just because it was never popularised. The Latin used in the Christian liturgy, as in the Roman 'officinae' and military headquarters, as also in the towns and villas, was 'a social accomplishment acquired by mainly upper and middle class youths from generations of conservative schoolmasters', pedagogues, rhetors and notaries.

Secondly: it is certain from place name evidence that, even in many parts of eastern Britain, there must have been substantial survivals of Brittonic speaking people: and that their numbers increased progressively across the Midlands into the west. These people did not speak a vulgar Latin, but the Brittonic language that was the parent of Welsh, Cornish and the Celtic language of Cumberland.

Thirdly: many British or Latin place names must have been transferred into Anglo-Saxon, not in the first flush of the Anglo-Saxon settlement, but by bilingual Britons who had survived and learned the new language; the Anglo-Saxons met very few people who talked any sort of Latin during the course of their occupation of Britain. This reinforces other evidence that the Roman villas were deserted before the protracted Anglo-Saxon occupation of Britain began, or, at least, before it had gone far; and it was these villa owners and occupiers who would have been the most Latin speaking at the outset of the occupation and later: as also, the most Christian. The Christian towns had been deserted even earlier. The Latin using official class, with the church, bishops and clergy, seems to have collapsed with the collapse of towns and villages. They led a precarious life when the villas were no longer used as residences but still as centres of Christian worship; they led a fugitive life during the retreat into Brittany and the west.

In Gaul, on the contrary, the whole population spoke vulgar Latin, and, when the Franks came, bishops, clerics and notaries secured its use for business and administrative purposes. A Romance language evolved and the Christian church survived, whereas in Britain an un-Romanised and largely unconverted peasantry accepted the language and pagan cults of the conquerors, at least where they settled thickly. These peasants were familiar with Latin place names and some of them they taught the Saxons: but they spoke Brittonic, and sometimes the place names as handed on to the Anglo-Saxons had a Brittonic element.

In the west and north the church did survive, and among the clergy some degree of Latinity; but elsewhere the Brittonic speech of the de-Romanised peasantry became the sole alternative to Anglo-Saxon.

Only one language could be used as the language of the moots which held Anglo-Saxon village society together, arranging the communal ploughing and dealing with offences against an unwritten folk custom: and the language of the illiterate conquerors, the Anglo-Saxon language, prevailed.

In the west, the evidence of inscribed stones in Latin shows that the church survived, but with Gallic support, especially in Wales. Their epigraphic convention and formulae derive, not from the pagan epigraphy of Roman Britain, but from the Christian inscriptions of fourth and fifth century Gaul. These inscriptions show that there must have been close contact between the Gaulish church and Britain in the days of St. Germanus of Auxerre (d. 448), though very few of the surviving stones are as early as this. Some inscriptions in the west, however, show Irish influence and indicate that Irish settlers in the western parts of Britain must have retained their own language at least as late as the seventh century.

Another piece of evidence explains our lack of detailed knowledge of church history in Britain during this period: the rapidity of philological change during the years of Anglo-Saxon settlement and early occupation. 'We can be fairly sure that Vortigern around 450 could not have understood Aneirin (the Welsh poet) around 600, though Gildas, living through the first half of the sixth century, would have understood both.' (For Gildas, see p. 4.) Heroic poetry in the Brittonic tongue may have existed in the age of Vortigern; but it would have been 'intolerably archaic, barely intelligible', to the great grandchildren of those who knew Vortigern and Arthur: all the words in the Brittonic language became one or more syllables shorter in the intervening century, and the names of British heroes and saints almost completely perished. Bede knew something of the tradition of the northern church, and he received from Canterbury all that abbot Albinus and Nothelm could find out about this dark period in the south: from them, or from one of the southern bishops he consulted, he received the writings known as Gildas' *De excidio et conquestu Britanniae*, or part of them; but Canterbury itself, or that learned western bishop, Daniel of the west Saxons, could tell him no more of the history of the Brittonic church than could be found in some early form of a *passio* of St. Alban, an early life of Germanus, and the lamentations of Gildas. In Wales, after the sound changes that turned early Brittonic into Welsh, heroic poetry survived in the collections attributed to Aneirin and Taliessin; the genealogies of kings and some knowledge of holy men who worked in the fifth and sixth centuries survived also.

In this first half of the fifth century, when direct Roman government lapsed but British chieftains with Roman names still maintained some appearance of Roman civil life, the missions of bishop Germanus of Auxerre to Britain in 429 and 444–445 are well attested. The story of these missions occurs in the Life of Germanus by Constantius, priest of Lyons, who wrote at the orders of his bishop Patiens, of Lyons, probably in the year 480 or a little later. The Life commands respect as a historical document written not long after the events it describes, for Patiens became bishop a year before Germanus' death, and may have met him as he travelled from Auxerre to Ravenna: indeed, he was scarcely likely to have commanded the writing of the Life unless he had some interest in the great bishop. Moreover, it was published in Auxerre, and dedicated to Censurius, bishop of Auxerre, as well as to Patiens. It was written in the literary and learned see of Lyons, that is, but for circulation in Germanus' own see.

The details of Germanus' career are not without interest for the comparison of conditions in Gaul with those the other side of the Channel. In both Gaul and Britain at the beginning of the fifth century the provincials were disturbed by invaders and orderly Roman government was breaking down: though disorder was far worse in Britain than in Gaul. In Gaul the civil service was still functioning, though the strict separation of civil and military office was relaxed; in Britain, all that one hears of the relics of the Roman civil service are the brief allusions to a 'vir tribuniciae potestatis' or the 'primus illius regionis', both apparently native chieftains retaining the titles and traditions of Roman rule.

Constantius relates that Germanus studied law (no doubt at the rhetor's school) at Rome and practised it at the law court of the prefect of the Gauls. He attained to the high office of dux, which implied the military command in his province, together with that of the fleet which, around A.D. 400, was stationed in ports on both sides of the Channel. His province included Armorica and Nervica (Brittany, Normandy and Hainault), and his command of the fleet, at some point withdrawn to the French ports, would have afforded him information about Britain; Auxerre, his birthplace, was also within his province.

It is uncertain whether he renounced his secular career and lived as priest under Amator, bishop of Auxerre, for a few years before his own election as bishop, or whether his consecration as bishop was demanded by clergy, the ordo or senate of Auxerre, townsfolk and country folk, on Amator's death, while he was still a secular. In any case, he was consecrated bishop on July 7, c. 418. He must have known something of the withdrawal of direct Roman government from Britain and the threat to the Brittonic church from 'bagaudae' and external raiders: but according to Constantius it was the spread of Pelagianism in Britain that occasioned his journey to that country (in the year 429). A British embassy asked for his help, a synod was held in Gaul, and at the command of pope Celestine or the synod itself, the bishops Germanus of Auxerre and Lupus of Troyes were commissioned to bring such help. They started from St. Germain des Vaux, some twenty miles west of Cherbourg, for Frankish advance had already made passage by Boulogne unsafe.

The bishops, according to Constantius, filled all Britain with the report of their preaching: they were daily hemmed in by crowds and preached 'not only in churches but at the crossroads, and in the fields and lanes'. The supporters of Pelagianism, not apparently people of low rank, at length came to meet them in rich robes for a formal debate, accompanied by a crowd of supporters. They opened the debate at some length, but the crowd applauded the arguments of the bishops, who refuted their preaching. This debate must have taken place in a town of some importance, for when it ended 'a man of tribunician rank' requested the bishops to heal his ten year old daughter of her blindness: which they did. All regarded the miracle as a sign of the rightness of the bishops' doctrine. The 'man of tribunician rank' was not necessarily a soldier, for by the Theodosian Code of 432, notaries were accorded this rank.

The bishops, having stamped out the heresy, 'sought blessed Alban the martyr', to give thanks to God through him. The cult of a saint, then and later, always centred at his tomb: Constantius gives no place name, though Gildas, later, spoke of St. Alban of Verulam. Though it has been suggested that Alban's martyrdom was in Wales, and though the bodies of saints were, in the raids of later centuries, carried to places of safety, it is most unlikely that Alban's body, if buried in Wales, would have been later carried to the more disturbed eastern part of Britain. It is therefore safe to follow Gildas in placing his martyrdom at Verulam.

'Meanwhile, the Saxons and the Picts had joined forces to make war upon the Britons.' It is unlikely that the Saxon raids were made other than on the east coast of Britain: and it is known that the Picts had long before made deep raids into north Britain from beyond Hadrian's Wall. In the great 'barbarian conspiracy' of 367–369 the Picts had outflanked or penetrated the legionary fortresses of the Wall, and sacked and burned Corbridge, Piercebridge and Malton, in the north eastern parts of Britain; and in the clumsy and botched rebuilding of the Wall in 369 the 'civitates' of Britain appeared to have contributed corvées: inscriptions on the Wall indicate that the cities of Colchester, Lincoln, etc., repaired their portion. Defence against the Picts was an obligation on all the cities of Britain, not merely on the northern inhabitants of Northumberland, Durham, Cumberland and Westmorland. That a hastily collected provincial force should have marched northwards from Verulam to wherever a joint force of Saxons and Picts had stationed themselves is no improbability: nor is the statement of Constantius that in these circumstances the provincials sought Germanus' help in any way surprising. He had been 'dux' earlier, and 'dux' at the time signified a military leader.

The Britons, in fear, had withdrawn to their camp when they sent this appeal for help to the apostolic 'duces' (which one might translate, 'episcopal generals'). They promised to come, and set out for the Britons' camp: their promise brought such comfort that 'it was as if Christ himself fought through the apostolic duces'. The venerable days of Lent arrived: there were daily instructions and many catechumens were baptised, indeed, a great part of the whole army. On the day of the Resurrection, a church was woven of leafy boughs, on the plan of a city church though actually set up in a camp in the countryside. The soldiers paraded still wet with the baptismal water, and all hoped for help from heaven.

Meanwhile the enemy expected an easy victory over this almost unarmed host, for they had learned of the camp and its appearance and practices by scouts. When the Easter solemnity had been celebrated, and the army, largely newly baptised, began to prepare for battle, Germanus promised to act as dux in the battle itself; he chose out the advance troops, went round the outposts, and surveyed the valley, shut in by steep hills, where the enemy's advance was expected. And in this spot he himself, as leader of the vanguard, drew up his host.

The enemy approached: Germanus, standing by the legionary standard (signum), bade the Britons answer his call with one voice, and when he judged the enemy near enough, the two bishops cried three times the (Easter) Alleluia. If he followed the Easter usage, he would have raised the pitch a tone each time. Then the enemy were smitten with terror and fled, and many were drowned in the river: the victory had been gained by faith and not by force. The bishops, having conquered 'both Pelagians and Saxons', through the intercession of blessed Alban the martyr, returned to Gaul.

As to the site of this 'Alleluia victory', Constantius was uninformed. One tradition places it on the 'Maes Garmon', 'plain of Germanus', in Flintshire, but the emphasis on the Saxon enemy in Constantius' tale renders this unlikely: as does the co-reference to the Picts. Confusion between Germanus of Auxerre and his younger contemporary, Germanus of Man, probably accounts for some Brittonic forms of the name Germanus (Garmon, Harmon) in Welsh place names.

The second visit of Germanus to Britain, accepted by the Celticist, Paul Grosjean, as in the year 444–445, was made in company with bishop Severus of Trier, and again in connexion with the danger from Pelagianism. The bishops would apparently have landed at Southampton or Portsmouth, for in the intervening fourteen years the situation in south eastern Britain had deteriorated. There is reason to believe that the chieftain whom Germanus visited this time, called by Constantius Elafius and described as 'the leading man (primus) of that region' was Elesa, named in the Welsh genealogies as the father of Cerdic of Wessex. The ancestry of the Saxon kings of Wessex has long been suspected as the product of intermarriage with the family of some Romano-British chieftain, for the name Cerdic reproduced the old Latin Caratacus in the vernacular; it is not impossible that in the western lands where the west Saxons later settled, Germanus should have approached Elafius, tribal king of the Belgic lands that stretched from the Isle of Wight to the Bristol Channel and centred in Winchester (Venta Belgarum). The 'region' may have included several civitates, for sacerdotes as well as crowds of Britons greeted Germanus, and 'sacerdotes' as used by Constantius means 'bishops', whose sees, in a countryside still unravaged, would have been in a civitas. Wessex, like Gloucestershire and Hereford-shire (the Archenfield) must have been, like Wales, a relatively secure part of Roman Britain. Germanus' arrival was not made known to Elafius formally by messenger but by rumour: Elafius was not unaware of his coming.

Germanus first inquired about the protectors of the Pelagian error, and condemned them, and immediately Elafius approached and desired him to heal his young son, who was so lame that walking was impossible. The boy was healed, and Germanus returned to Gaul, taking with him the propagators of heresy, so that western Britain was troubled with them no more, and was still orthodox in the faith to the day Constantius was writing (about 480).

Nothing is said by Constantius of any further travels of Germanus after his preaching in Wessex: yet a persistent Welsh tradition as-sociates him with one or two of the earliest Welsh saints, as their master and teacher. Wessex adjoined Gloucestershire, Hereford and Glamorgan, all lands of prosperous Roman villas, and it is not im-possible that Germanus should have travelled through this area on his second visit, and encountered Illtud and even (as one tradition asserts) himself founded the 'llan' or monastery of Llantwit Major; or, alternatively, taken Illtud back with him for training in his own monastery on the Yonne, opposite Auxerre: either would account for the tradition that Illtud was 'discipulus Germani'. In any case, Germanus' activities in Britain would account for any young cleric's going from Britain to seek training under him in Gaul.

The little that is known of southern Britain in the first half of the fifth century is thus connected with the work of the Gallic Germanus: the only Brittonic traditions of this period of Christian collapse come from Welsh genealogies and saints' lives, whence we hear of Christian sub-kings, as ruling in Hereford (the Archenfield), Glou-cester, Wiltshire, Somerset and Cornwall. Gildas knew of the 'martyrium' of St. Alban at Verulam, and wrote that many others were erected in Britain after the age of the persecutions.

Since modern research now accepts life on the northern frontier of Britain, both north and south of Hadrian's Wall, as the link between the old Romano-British Christianity on the one hand and the nascent Christianities of Ireland and south Scotland on the other:

accepts, that is, that northern Britain was the home country of both
Nynia and Patrick, it is worth recounting what is now known of
the north British territories and their history at the time. The modern
study of texts like the *Confessio* of St. Patrick and the Welsh genealogies and also of place names and inscriptions supplement the text
of Bede. Bede says nothing about the Votadini and their employ-
ment by the Romans as federates in defence of the Hadrianic Wall,
or of their chieftain Cunedda; but genealogical, archaeological and
place name evidence indicate that they were so employed, and that a
half-barbarised Christianity survived among their families and those
of the leading tribal chieftains north and south of the Wall. Christianity survived along with the customs of a sub-Roman age.

Bede relates the sending of a bishop by a Gallican synod to this
region. He says that 'Nynia the bishop' (the Brittonic 'Nynniau')
was a most holy and learned man of the nation of the Britons, and
he set up his see at Whithorn. The sending of a bishop and not
merely a priest is a testimony to an existent Christianity in the
region to which he was sent; for pope Celestine, whether or not
he commissioned Nynia as one eighth century source relates, wrote
in one of his letters 'Let no bishop be granted to those unwilling to
receive him. Let the consent and desire of clergy, people and
magistracy (ordo) first be sought': which may be taken as representing ecclesiastical policy at the time. Nynia, Bede says, converted the
'southern Picts, a heathen people': Levison holds from the reconstruction of an early source that they were the Niduarii on the
northern banks of the Firth of Forth: but the see of Nynia was not
among these people, but at Whithorn, far to the south (see below).

Carlisle in the Eden valley, associated in its siting with Whithorn,
was the key point in Brittonic defence in the days of Nynia and
earlier. It had long been a place of great strategic importance for the
defence of northern Britain. In A.D. 71 Cerialis, the Roman general
who subdued the Brigantes of Yorkshire, moved forces northwards
along both sides of the Pennines to converge on Carlisle. Agricola
(d. A.D. 90) completed his conquest of the Brigantes, strengthened
the legionary fortresses of Chester and York, and built roads designed
to hold modern Cumberland, Northumberland and the Scottish
Lowlands. A network of roads was built: that from Chester passed
northwards through Overborough, Brougham and Carlisle; that
from York through Aldborough, Catterick, Piercebridge, Cor-

bridge, High Rochester and Newstead in the north. One link road joined Corbridge, Chesterholm and Carlisle, and another, a road to the sea, joined Overborough to Ravenglass. All these places were military posts, and most had 'vici', suburbs for civilians. All were population groups where Roman traditions and civilisation were to live on for four centuries and some were of great importance in the history of dark age Christianity. Carlisle was a sub-Roman defence centre from the time of Cunedda in the fifth century to that of Urien ap Rheged in the sixth: Ravenglass is accepted by Paul Grosjean as the native town of St. Patrick: at Corbridge Roman building material was used for one of the earliest stone churches of the northern Angles.

In this Romano-Brittonic country north and south of Hadrian's Wall the tribe of the Votadini were early and extensively Romanised. They held the coastal region by the north sea from the Firth of Forth right down to the mouth of the Wear: of their three towns of Coria, Alauna and Bremenium, Coria was probably Corbridge. The Votadini had been brought completely within the province of Britain by the setting up of the Antonine Wall in A.D. 142, and throughout their history they remained a philo-Roman tribe. More Roman finds from the Antonine period have been discovered in their tribal fortress of Traprain Law than from any other Roman site: Traprain Law had, it would seem, the status of the capital of a client kingdom. When in A.D. 196 a governor of Britain transferred the bulk of the Roman garrison of Britain to the Continent, the Antonine Wall had to be relinquished: but for 54 years the Votadini (142–196) had lived completely within the Roman province. The emperor Severus passed the last three years of his life in Britain (208–211), and restored the fortresses of the Hadrianic Wall, making it the frontier; half the Votadini were still left within the Roman province, half were now without. Traprain Law was still their chief town after the Severan reorganisation. The Roman army in the north was losing its alien character by the enlistment of native troops: and beyond Hadrian's Wall the defence of the region between the two Walls from the Picts in the north east was entrusted to the Lowland tribes of the Votadini and Damnonii (to the west on the Firth of Clyde). Both the Votadini and the Damnonii had become client kingdoms.

The frontier troubles at the end of the second century were reproduced at the end of the third: raiders from the north overthrew the

Wall garrison in 296 and pressed southwards: both York and Chester fell. The Romanised 'vici' of the Wall region, either villages or the suburbs of a fortress, had been unwalled and small, usually not more than 12 acres in extent: they were not defensible. Even the walled townships of Catterick and Carlisle were not defended by legionary troops, and their Romanised citizens too were plundered: Carlisle was a large town, some 74 acres within its walls.

Under Diocletian's reorganisation of the empire the legions were, for a time, restored to Hadrian's Wall, but reliance was now placed chiefly on the setting up of a mobile striking force to deal with raiders who outflanked the Wall or penetrated between its fortresses. Such forces were concentrated at points of tactical significance, like Elslack and Piercebridge: but north of Hadrian's Wall the outpost forts, in the lands of the Votadini and Selgovii (immediately north of the Wall) were no longer manned by forces called 'Exploratores', but by 'Areani', who lived in 'areae' or sheepfolds and patrolled the countryside. There was civilian traffic through the Wall, and a special gateway at Housesteads where a limited number of civilian travellers could be shut away at a time and if necessary searched. The Votadini, that is, were not completely cut off from Roman life: in the vicus at Housesteads life was at burgher level, with two-storeyed houses where the ground floor was used as shops and the families lived on the upper floor. Carlisle and Catterick were still walled townships. Roman life went on.

Peace in the fourth century was further disturbed. In 343, forts beyond Hadrian's Wall were destroyed, and not all of them restored. Risingham, which had iron deposits useful for the defenders of Corbridge, was restored, as was Bewcastle; Corbridge's earliest surviving Anglian stone church indicates its importance even after the Anglian conquest; and the Bewcastle cross, the earliest and most beautiful of the 'high crosses' indicates a site once of similar importance. But the refortification of all Britain must have been incomplete for Irish raids into Wales begin at this time.

In 367–369, by a great 'barbarian conspiracy', Franks, Saxons, Atecotti (Irish, or tribes from the Lowlands of Scotland) and Scots (Irish), invaded Britain at the same time. They pinned down the duke of Britain and his forces, and killed the count of the Saxon Shore. They sacked and burned the forts and civilian buildings of the Wall, and behind the Wall they sacked Corbridge, Piercebridge,

Malton and Overborough. In count Theodosius' restoration of the frontier the Areani were abolished as suspected of desertion, and in 369 the before-mentioned rebuilding of the Wall by city corvées was carried through: to the north of the Wall the tribal chiefs were recognised as independent kings. Rome no longer protected them: they protected the Roman frontier. Probably the chieftains obtained imperial commissions, as indicated by the cognomen 'red cloak' (pes-rut) enjoyed by one of the kings of the Votadini. The success of these measures is shown by the continued prosperity of the York-shire villa owners: the signal stations built on the high cliffs of the Yorkshire coast seem to have been effective in giving warning of Pictish and Saxon sea raiders. The building of these stations on the east and not on the west coast seems to indicate the greater danger there from raids: similarly, the Votadini, the holders of the long coast line from the Wear to the Firth of Forth, must long have borne the heaviest burden of defence.

The Irish danger, however, was considerable, and the fort of Caernarvon was now restored to house a new regiment, and re-built with more technical skill than the fortresses of the Wall: its rebuilding was associated in Welsh legend with the Spaniard and Roman general Maximus: Maxen Wledig. In 383 he upgraded his legionary troops to form a mobile force, declared himself emperor (Welsh legend asserting that he was baptised that day) and took them away to the Continent. He fought and killed his rival, Gratian, but was himself defeated and killed near Aquileia in 388. Neither Caernarvon nor Chester could be held against the Irish raiders after this, and they poured in. But among the native kinglets who were, from 388, asserting their authority all over Britain and southern Scotland, the dynasty of Maximus had a prestige rivalled only by that of the chieftain of the Votadini, Cunedda. Both families were Christian, if half barbarian, and it was from the younger sons of these tribal royalties, and the lesser tribal kings, that the ascetic founders of 'llans' (holy settlements, minsters) were drawn. The episcopate was maintained among them, but a tribal not a territorial episcopate.

Maximus married the Welsh Helena, who survived him: his son Constantine ruled in north west Wales, and his Roman tomb, with its inscription, survived for some hundreds of years at Caernarvon; his son, Maximus' grandson, was Ambrose Wledig, described, after 430, as 'king of all the kings of Britain'. His name survived in a place name in Snowdonia, and in the Wiltshire Amesbury (Ambresbyrig). Another son of Maximus, Antonius, or in Brittonic, Annwn, was reputed the founder of the dynasty in Galloway that arose in the lands of the Damnonii, beside the Clyde. He ruled in the Isle of Man, and his reputed rule in Galloway may have resulted from Constantine's expedition into the Lowlands: he is reported to have handled the Picts severely. The indications are that the descendants of Maximus obtained some power in south west Scotland, either by war or intermarriage.

As to the period 388–425 in northern Britain, there seems to have been no general collapse, and at Traprain Law the coins of Arcadius and Honorius still circulated; the Roman sites were still occupied south of the Wall; the Votadinian defence held. In the second quarter of the fifth century (c. 425–450) the Britons endangered by the Irish settlers in north Wales called in the Votadini to defend this region as well, and a large contingent streamed down to Wales and settled there. Whether the legendary sons of Cunedda were actually his sons or grandsons, or merely lieutenants, is uncertain : the name Cunedda appears not to survive in place names.

With a sub-Roman tribal dynasty ruling Strathclyde, and the Votadini under Cunedda and his sons defending the regions north and south of Hadrian's Wall and a large part of Wales, Roman traditions and Christianity lived on. Cunedda's ancestors, in the Welsh genealogies, included men called Aeternus, Paternus and Tacitus, Paternus in the mid fourth century wearing the red cloak and gold-studded belt of a Roman officer. The 'draco', the 'vexillum' of the Roman cohort, became in time the red dragon of Wales. The Roman civil service had by the fourth century adopted with moderate enthusiasm the Christianity of the emperors, and there are indications that a sub-Roman Christianity whose defenders were capable of great sacrifices was transmitted to their sons. The names of Patrick and Nynia stand out as the apostles of this age: both were Britons and there is evidence suggesting that both came from the sub-Roman and Christian region south of the Wall. While Patrick's work in Ireland lasted from 431–462, some modern archaeological opinion accepts Nynia's work at Whithorn and in the Lowlands as dating from the second quarter of the fifth century, though Paul Grosjean would make it later: that is, they were roughly contemporary.

The earliest account of Nynia's work is given by Bede, whose

informant appears to have been Pechthelm, the first Anglian bishop
of Whithorn after the Angles of Bernicia had conquered the Scottish
Lowlands. Pechthelm had for long been deacon and monk under
Aldhelm, bishop of Sherborne: he had been trained under a scholar
versed in the traditions both of the Celts and Canterbury. Pechthelm
found (according to Levison) no written life of Nynia at Whithorn:
but one such was drawn up in his time, and it became the source
both of an eighth century poem written at Whithorn, about Nynia,
and of Ailred of Rievaulx' life of Nynia in the twelfth century. There
is nothing to suggest that Bede ever saw a written life of Nynia, but
when he said 'as they say' of his own account of Nynia, he was
referring to what was said at Whithorn of Nynia in his own day.
Pechthelm corresponded on other matters both with Bede and Boniface. Though Bede's account of Nynia has been challenged as an
attempt to represent Nynia rather than Columba as the apostle of
Scotland, he seems, in fact, merely to have accepted the Anglian reconstruction of the history of the saint described as converting the
Lowlands: it is unlikely that Pechthelm, trained by Aldhelm, would
have had any marked hostility to the Irish.

Bede says, that in the year A.D. 563 there came to Britain from Ireland that notable priest and abbot, Columba, to preach to the
northern Picts: the southern Picts had, long before that time, relinquished (as they say) the error of idolatry and received the faith
at the preaching of the most reverend bishop and holy man, 'Nynias'.
He was of the nation of the Britons and had been taught the faith
and the mysteries of the truth in due order (regulariter)[1] at Rome:
and his episcopal see, famous for the name and church of St. Martin
the bishop, and where Nynia's own body and that of other saints
now rest, the people of the Angles now holds. And that place,
belonging to the province of the Bernicians, is popularly called
'Candida casa' (Whithorn) because he had the church there built of
stone, in a manner unusual among the Britons.

'Long before that time', as a chronological pointer to the dating
of Nynia's work, is now held to cover the middle portion of the fifth
century, when the Votadini still defended the Wall from Carlisle and
Corbridge, under Cunedda or some descendant. Whithorn was
accessible to Carlisle and Uxellodunum (Maryport) by a short sea

---

[1] Paul Grosjean interprets the word as meant by Bede to convey that he had been
properly instructed on the Paschal cycles: not, actually, in question at the time.

journey, and its location can hardly be explained for any other reason. It was too far south to have been chosen as a Christian outpost for the evangelisation of the district between the Hadrianic and Antonine Walls, still less for that of the northern regions beyond; and although the setting up of a minster at the end of a desolate, sandy spit was in accordance with the ascetic practices of the day (and quite common later, in Brittany, Wales and Ireland): yet both in Gaul and Ireland the siting of a head or tribal minster always had reference to access to the secular protector. Whithorn was badly placed for the pastoral care of Strathclyde and even Dumfriesshire alone: it was too far to the south west: but it was well sited for the maintenance of an old but half-barbarised Christianity in a region extending across Britain both north and south of Hadrian's Wall. The most suggestive fact that emerges from the modern study of the founder of Candida Casa is thus the reason for the siting of Whithorn.

That Nynia, using a Brittonic vernacular, should have preached to the Votadinian Celts both sides of the Wall involves no language difficulty: the language of the northern tribes would have differed little from that of the Britons of Bernicia. Even the Picts to the north of the Antonine Wall spoke a Celtic language, though with many aboriginal words: some of their inscriptions cannot be read today. Their Celtic words, in any case, had not undergone the sound changes that turned the p-Celts into the q-Celts. It was not Gaelic. Nynia's mission, in or after his day, would have extended into the land of the Picts without much difficulty.

That Nynia's preaching should have been made in the Votadinian territory from his see at Whithorn receives some small support from archaeological and place name evidence. There is an inscribed stone at Whithorn dating from the mid fifth century with the name 'Latinus', its erector, carved on it in Roman capitals; and in the near and associated site of Kirkmadrine another inscribed stone has the chi-rho monogram encircled by the halo of glory, and, in Roman capitals, 'Hic iacent sancti et praecipui sacerdotes Ides Viventius et Mavortius': the word 'sacerdotes', at the time, signifying 'bishops'. Such a translation is supported by the adjective 'holy and eminent'. The Latinus stone thus attests an early local Christianity, for it begins, 'O praise the Lord': and the three early stones at Kirkmadrine all have the chi-rho monogram. There is some evidence, again, for a survival of Nynia's name in place names. At a Ninianic site at

Brampton, nine miles north east of Carlisle, a church of St. Martin's lies within the lines of a Roman fort, and beneath the northern rampart of the fort 'Ninewells', Nynia's well, adjoins a mass of fallen Roman masonry. Nynekirkes in Westmorland commemorates the saint more probably than the number nine. Though dedications to Nynia throughout Scotland are frequent, and some may indeed date back to the extension of his mission, the dating of these dedications still needs to be established.

The relation of the three fifth-sixth century bishops to Whithorn suggests that at some time the see was moved to the adjacent minster: if indeed, in that area of Brittonic Christianity there was any question of a territorial see at all. The founder of the 'llan' (Gaelic 'kirk'), Kirkmadrine, appears to have been Draigne of Struthair, believed to have been the son of king Brechan of Brecheniauc (Brecknock). Nothing is known of the passing of the see at Whithorn to this nearby site: but such a passage perhaps indicates a break in the Ninianic cult. Philologists suspect such a break also from the fact that Nynia's (Ninyo's) name does not appear in place names north of the Wall in its native, Brittonic form, nor were personal names formed from it. Nynia appears in the Scots 'Ringan' and in the Gaelic 'Truinnean'. While Nynia's work in the Wall region is attested by place names, we have no evidence as to how his episcopal chair passed to Kirkmadrine.

Although Bede spoke of Nynia's evangelisation of the 'southern Picts': modern study of the Pictish symbol-stones and place names has established that the kingdom of the historical Picts lay between the Antonine Wall and the Mounth; the Picts certainly raided deep into Britain, but they never established permanent rule in Strathclyde, Dumfriesshire or Cumberland. Their kingdom lay to the north east of the Antonine Wall, with the 'Niduarii' not far to the north east. Though tradition associates certain sites in the north with Nynia's preaching journeys among the Picts, the evidence is uncertain, though such journeys may, in fact, have been made.

Two minor difficulties arise from early accounts of Nynia: the first, Bede's description of his church as dedicated to St. Martin, the second, the Whithorn statement that he was trained at Rome.

St. Martin died in 397, and though his cult spread rapidly through Europe, it is astonishing to find a church dedicated to him in north Britain by the mid fifth century, astonishing to the point of complete inacceptability. The Celtic Christians made no formal dedication of their llans to saints: even the association of the founder's name with his 'llan' appears to have been only a matter of convenience and custom. The place names of early llans were often geographical: e.g. Llandaff, the llan on the Tavy.[1] Bede's assertion that the body of Nynia rested at Whithorn is impressive evidence that it was indeed his llan, for the early cult of saints was associated with their place of burial: nor is Bede's assertion that the llan was called 'Whithorn' surprising: it was a descriptive, geographical, vernacular name for Candida Casa. Yet Pechthelm found the church of the llan dedicated (? or he dedicated it) to St. Martin. This probably followed from the practice of a clerical, Martinian monasticism at the llan, and the celebration of St. Martin's feast on November 11. Where the day of the founder's death was unknown and could not be celebrated, it happened not infrequently with llans in Cornwall that the annual feast of the llan, becoming in time the parish fair day, was celebrated on November 11, St. Martin's day.[2] At what point the celebration of the feast day led to a formal dedication of the church at Whithorn (if it ever did) is unknown. A formal dedication must have been accompanied by the reception of a relic of St. Martin, and this is not impossible. The relic would have been in the form of dust from his tomb, or a small cloth or veil laid against it.

As to Nynia's training at Rome: the disturbances of the times render a journey thither most unlikely. It is not unlikely, however, that he was of high or even royal birth, and also that he was sent

[1] Cf. also the first dedication of the church of St. Asaph's, *ecclesia Llanelwensis*, from the valley of the Elwy, in which it stood, and Llan Aleth, in Brittany, which was a regional name: see D. R. Thomas, *Hist. of the diocese of St. Asaph*, 1908, i. 6-7; it is suggested, *ib.* i. 8, that the larger of mother churches, llans, were called by the existing names of the places where they were built, and their outlying chapels (or preaching stations) were known by the name of the founder. See also O. Chadwick's 'The evidence of dedications in the early history of the Welsh church', in *Studies in early British History*, ed. N. K. Chadwick, 176 and 186.

[2] These early dedications to St. Martin are of interest, because Bede asserts also that the church of St. Martin at Canterbury was built in the time of the Romans (see p. 42). It may be suggested that impossibly early dedications to St. Martin are to be accounted for by the early celebration of his day as a kind of patronal festival where the founder's obit was unknown: this would be suitable in a house of monk-clerics, following the Martinian usage. In Cornwall the annual parish fair was held on or very near the feast of the patron saint, and the dedication of the church was sometimes changed from the little known Celtic founder, for one reason or another: but the parish fair continued to be held on the original day. A parochial fair day is often a clue to an original dedication. The fair day of the parish of Gulval, or St. Gulval, in Cornwall, for long believed to be the same saint as Gudval, was kept in the middle ages at Martinmas: see G. H. Doble's *Saint Gudval*, 1933, and F. C. Hingeston-Randolph's Register, iii. pp. 1265, 1365.

across the Channel for training. There was no place in northern Britain where Patrick desired to be trained for the priesthood: he went to Auxerre. Nynia may have sought training abroad also.

The only one of the Welsh or Brittonic saints whose written work has survived to us is St. Gildas, canonist, abbot-bishop, and author of the *De excidio et conquestu Britanniae*. That he was of episcopal rank is indicated by the fact that Columbanus, writing to Gregory I between 595 and 600, spoke of him as an author or compiler of canons, though the early calendars do not describe him as bishop; they apply to him the technical word for scholar, 'sapiens'. The *Annales Cambriae* give his death as in 570. Gildas gives us astonishingly little information about the names or work of the Welsh, Cornish or Breton church leaders who preceded him; philologists tell us that sound changes in the Brittonic languages had been rapid in the period and made the handing on even of oral tradition difficult.

The apostolate of Patrick to Ireland belongs also to this age of the collapse of Roman civilisation in Britain. It sprang from the north British church, and was to have unforeseen results on the church of Scotland and northern England later. Patrick was born about 385, in some Brittonic town or village, in which his father Calpurnius was a decurio, a hereditary member of the local ordo, and also a Christian deacon: his grandfather was Potitus, a priest. St. Patrick says this in his *Confessio*: a document which the Celticist, Paul Grosjean, believes to have been, possibly, orally dictated, and which, in any case, would have been first written on papyrus and later copied on parchment. Though there is room for verbal error and scribal mis-copying in these processes, the Patrician authorship of the document is accepted by scholars. In the *Confessio*, Patrick says that he was captured by pirates when sixteen years old at 'Bannaven Taberniae', a place name which P. Grosjean suggests was a mishearing or misreading for some such name as Clannaventa Berniciae: he believes that some form of (?) gloss underlies the mysterious second word in the *Confessio*. Patrick, then, was born in Bernicia, in some small Romanised village that had an ordo or senate, and was therefore more probably south of the Wall, than in the land of the southern Picts, where Nynia was beginning his mission.

Patrick was carried off by the raiders to Ireland: war-captives were slaves, and as such he worked for six years. He escaped (? 407), on a ship taking a cargo of racing or hunting dogs to the Continent, possibly to Bordeaux or Marseilles, the great port of southern Gaul, where the market would be better than in any Breton port. From Gaul he made his way back to his family in Britain, where he might have remained a member of the local ordo; but he remembered Ireland and felt himself called to work there. He returned to Gaul, and joined the familia of Germanus of Auxerre; and he is said also to have stayed at Lérins, where the disciples of Honoratus practised an eastern, Pachomian form of monasticism. Patrick's knowledge of the canons would appear, however, to have been gained at Auxerre: for such knowledge was essential for those trained for apostolic work and especially for the episcopate.

There is no need to suppose that Irish monasticism derives exclusively from that practised at Lérins, and spread by the mission of Patrick. He would have heard of Martinian monasticism at Tours: and there were, moreover, 'Scots believing in Christ' in Ireland before his voyage there, and they also would have heard of it. Admiration for Egypt and monasticism were in the air: Martin had founded his monastery at Marmoutiers in 372; Cassian had lived with the monks of Egypt from about 385 till 399, founded two monasteries at Marseilles c. 415, and before his death in 435 had written the two classics on the interior and exterior sides of the monastic life, the *Collations* and the *Institutes*. Whether the *Institutes*, written c. 420, or the *Collations*, finished between 426 and 429, were known to Patrick before his departure for Ireland is uncertain; in any case, Martinian monasticism was more suited to a clerical apostolate than that provided by Cassian, which had no essential connexion with the clerical order: though monks trained in it in Gaul often became bishops.

Patrick's departure for Ireland was occasioned by the death of Palladius, whom pope Celestine had consecrated and sent in 432 to convert the Scotti of Ireland. Patrick was consecrated bishop, apparently by Germanus, and sent off to Ireland in 432. He landed in Wicklow and preached there and in Leinster and Connaught, the Irish Druids opposing his work; he possibly made a journey to Rome c. 441, and he certainly set up his cathedra in Armagh (c. 444,) thenceforward the centre of his mission. He built monasteries and preached to the tribal Irish kings till his death in 461.

Though Patrick set up his see at Armagh more or less on the model of the sees he had known in Gaul, Irish Christianity was unable to develop on the lines of the territorial episcopate, because Ireland had no civitates. Yet the difference between the territorial episcopate in Gaul and the tribal, monastic clergy under their abbot, in Ireland, can be overstressed. In both cases the head of the clerical order was established near to the secular local authority: in Gaul, the count, in Ireland, some aula of the tribal king. But though the Gallic civitas was focussed in a city ruled by count and ordo or senate, the boundaries of the civitas were ill-defined, and so were those of the episcopal see. In Gaul as in Ireland, Christian rule had a focus, but no exact territorial circumference. The abbot of the tribal monastery was usually of high birth and often a relative of the tribal chief; the connexion between tribal and ecclesiastical rule was close, but the abbot was not necessarily a bishop.

For his clergy, Patrick used volunteers from Britain and Gaul, and his own converts. They used the Latin office and liturgy, and (judging from the quotations in Patrick's Confessio) such Latin scriptures as they could obtain: the old Latin version for the Old Testament, a mixed text for the Gospels and mainly the Vulgate for Acts. The so-called Cathach of St. Patrick, a Latin psalter (Trinity College, Dublin, Ussher MS. primum), is a fifth century book written on the Continent, with one of St. Jerome's versions of the psalter.

None of the Irish annals (annals of Ulster, Innisfallen, Tigernach, etc.) were begun in Patrick's own day, so that evidence about his work has to rely mainly on his Confessio and the Epistola ad milites Corotici (probably Ceretic of Cardigan, son of Cunedda). Patrick's clergy continued to learn and use Latin, while the Druids, who opposed him, had an oral culture. Their oral learning was transmitted by memory, and they and their assistants, the filid, continued hostile to the Christian clergy. The clerics who used writing and were acquainted with the scriptures, and with some portion of the conspectus of Latin learning known as the liberal arts, were designated 'sapientes' when their deaths were noted in the annals, but clerics so denoted were rare. The richer Irish monasteries had a succession of scholars described as 'sapientes', who had charge of the monastic scriptorium for the time being. St. Columba and the Irish monks who accompanied him for the conversion of the Picts (see p. 73) were trained in such scriptoria and took the Irish learning to Scotland; to Iona and, eventually, to Lindisfarne.

To sum up these 150 years of church history in Britain: under the attack of the Anglo-Saxons the Christian faith survived in the western and northern parts of Britain and was transmitted to Ireland. The Celtic Christians were in frequent communication by sea with Brittany, but as the Bretons themselves were usually at odds with the Frankish conquerors this did not mean that the Celtic Christians of Britain had the same communications with Gaul at the end of the 150 years as they had had in the times of St. Germanus. The Anglo-Saxons fought a protracted frontier struggle with the Celts of Wiltshire, Somerset, the Welsh border and Northumbria, and it was unlikely that they would accept the religion of their enemies, which involved conversion across a fighting frontier. Knowledge of the survival of British Christianity in the west was probably very slender in Rome when pope Gregory the Great was considering how to convert the pagan Anglo-Saxons.

CHAPTER III

THE MISSION OF ST. AUGUSTINE

THE sending of St. Augustine by pope Gregory the Great to convert the Anglo-Saxons was an event of great importance in the history of the English church and the western patriarchate. It brought the Anglo-Saxons, still heathen, into touch with the old, Greco-Roman Christianity of the Mediterranean: into touch with what was, at the end of the sixth century, the modern church practice of Latin Christendom: and into a filial relationship with the apostolic see of the west. The Anglo-Saxon church took its place among the provinces of the Roman patriarchate.

There was, as a result of Augustine's mission, a kind of restoration of the old Roman world in the west: for the Roman church had in its library a copy of the old *Notitia Dignitatum*, and was also well aware of the provincial structure of the old empire. There should, it was held, be a bishop in every civitas, and a metropolitan bishop in the mother city of every province. In a list of the cities of Gaul which has survived along with the text of the *Notitia Dignitatum*, certain cities are marked as metropolitan, and, though no parallel list of the cities of Britain with the metropolitan cities noted has survived, yet the Lateran notaries were apparently aware that Londinium was one metropolis, and Eboracum another; of the five provinces of Britain erected in the Diocletianic reconstruction, and their capitals, they had no knowledge. Nor has a certain knowledge of these latter-day provincial capitals survived to us (with the exception of Cirencester for Britannia Prima). But London and York had been the senior cities of Britain for nearly 300 years before the subdivision into five provinces, and of their seniority the Roman scrinium was aware: moreover, the Roman scrinium preserved 'volumina synodalia', and would have known that bishops of London and York had attended the council of Arles in 314. This historical information of the Roman church, and lack of information about the Anglo-Saxon kingdoms explains the Gregorian scheme for the episcopal structure of the new church of the English: there should be two metropolitan bishops, as of old, in the cities of London and York. In practical politics, it was not possible for Augustine to transfer his see from the place given him by Æthelberht at Canterbury to London: the two metropolitans have remained, as established for the Gregorian missionaries, at Canterbury and York (but see p. 51).

For so important an event as the Gregorian mission under Augustine, some discussion of the historical evidence on which our knowledge rests must be excused, especially as part of the evidence for it has recently been challenged as unauthentic. It remains that the most valuable account of the mission is that given by the venerable Bede in his *Historia Ecclesiastica* (henceforth here called the HE.), completed or published ('editum') in 731. Bede was already known to bishops and abbots as a great biblical commentator; he could avail himself of the library of manuscripts which the founder of his monastery of Jarrow had collected: he was in touch with the clergy of Lindisfarne, the cathedral schools of York, the abbot of St. Augustine's, Canterbury, and the clerical *familia* of Christ Church. He had written commentaries on many biblical books, an outstanding work on the difficult subject of dating (*De natura rerum, et de temporibus libros singulos*), and also some historical works. These included some lives of saints, particularly prose and verse lives of the great northern saint, St. Cuthbert, and a careful history of the foundation and abbots of his own monastery. He was well qualified to write a history of the Christian church in the north of England, but he had, apparently, no intention of writing a general history of the English people, for that would have involved the use of materials unavailable to him, especially the records and traditions of the great church of Canterbury. Yet it was to the writing of this general church history that he was incited by the greatest scholar of the Canterbury church: Albinus (Alban), abbot of St. Augustine's monastery at Canterbury. Albinus promised him the use of the Canterbury evidence, and incited him to an undertaking that involved asking the help of other southern bishops and abbots. This is stated in Bede's dedication of the HE. to Albinus, in the following words:

To the most beloved and revered father, Albinus, Bede, the servant of Christ, greeting.

Most gratefully have I received the gifts of your love, which you have deigned to send by our venerable brother Nothelm the priest, and above all I am grateful for the letters, with which you have now for the second time been careful to give me repeated help and instruction in the ecclesiastical history of our race, to the writing of which you have long since instigated me. For which reason I have most rightly sent back to you that same history, as soon as I could finish it, to be copied.

Bede then wrote that he was also sending Albinus another of his works, on the building of Solomon's temple, which also might be copied: and asked for the prayers of Albinus and his monks.

It is clear then, that the desire to have an ecclesiastical history written originated with abbot Albinus and the church of Canterbury: that the HE. is, in a sense, a Canterbury book, and that abbot Albinus sent the London priest Nothelm, not for the first time, with a letter from himself, just before Bede finished the HE., in 731. Bede had been in touch with Nothelm at some time between 716 and 731, for Nothelm propounded to him thirty questions about the books of Samuel and Kings, and Bede dealt with them in a special tractate written, apparently, not long after 716. Bede was in possession before 721 of the nine answers supposedly given by Gregory to Augustine, for he quoted from them in his prose life of St. Cuthbert,[1] which he dedicated to bishop Eadfrith of Lindisfarne, who died in 721. Nothelm may have brought them to him, for he seems to have been the messenger between abbot Albinus and Bede over a number of years.

Now these Gregorian answers (*Responsiones*) may be accepted, in the main, as authentic[2] (see *infra*, p. 44): and Bede's account of the Gregorian mission rests on them and also on another unimpeachable authority, the 28 lettters which Nothelm copied or had copied from the papal registers) 'Nothelm', says Bede, 'came to Rome and searched through the scrinium (writing office) of the holy Roman church, by the permission of him who is now head of that church, Gregory (II), and found there certain letters of blessed pope Gregory

---

[1] Perhaps after 731 ?

[2] See 'The Canterbury Edition of the Answers of pope Gregory I to St. Augustine', M. Deanesly, and P. Grosjean, in the *Journal of Ecclesiastical History*, (1959) 1-49. The tentative theory of the compilation of the separate Answers as a 'libellus' awaits confirmation or otherwise when an edition based on the canonical MSS. appears: it is in preparation by Dom Meyvaert.

(I) and other popes and returned to us, bringing them to us to be inserted in our history, through the counsel of the most reverend abbot Albinus.' Bede inserted these 28 letters in his history: they have been found written in the papal registers not only by Nothelm but by modern scholars: he inserted also another letter sent personally by Gregory to Augustine and not through the notarial scrinium. ⸤The foundation of the HE. on official records for the Gregorian mission and later history of the church lifts Bede's work into a different category from any other contemporary history: and also establishes its position as substantially a Canterbury book.⸥

As to the authenticity of the Gregorian *Responsiones*, sent up at some time from Canterbury to Bede: it has been queried on the grounds that the letters are not found copied into Gregory's register[1] and that one letter contains an obvious anachronism (in a passage now known to be interpolated). Other cases of genuine papal letters having been preserved in local archives, though the letters were not copied on to the rolls of the scrinium, or have not survived in the process of copying and editing of the papal registers, are now recognised. The authenticity of the letters in the 'libellus' of the *Responsiones* can be judged on internal evidence and what is known of its provenance.

⸤The Gregorian *Responsiones*, then, appear in their original form to have been a set of loose 'schedulae', or sheets of papyrus (papal letters were always written on papyrus) preserved at Canterbury.⸥ They are of great interest for the structure of the English church and the origin of the church of Canterbury, and they include one, or perhaps two, lectures on moral theology delivered at Canterbury, probably later than St. Augustine's time. They must have been copied at some time on to parchment, and at some time written out as a single libellus[2]: perhaps when they were sent up north to Jarrow, Bede's monastery. Bede ascribed the libellus to pope Gregory in his list of Gregorian writings in the HE., but as a work for which he was indirectly rather than directly responsible; like the canons of councils over which he presided. The account of Augustine's mission here given is taken from the HE., as supported by the letters copied by the scrinium and these *Responsiones*.

---

[1] See Abbot Suso Brechter's *Die Quellen zur Angelsachsenmission Gregors des Grossen*, 1941, and his article in the Fulda anniversary volume of 1954, *Sankt Bonifatius*, pp. 22-33.   [2] Some writers claim, in Italy.

'In this year,' says the Anglo-Saxon Chronicle for the year 596, 'pope Gregory sent Augustine to Britain with very many monks, to preach the word of God to the English people.'

The Chronicle is here quoting Bede, but Bede's account is much more detailed. He wrote a prefatory letter to king Ceolwulf of Northumbria as well as his dedicatory letter to abbot Albinus, and describes his historical sources in similar terms.

My principal aid and authority, he says, was the most learned and reverend abbot Albinus, who, educated in the church of Canterbury by those venerable and learned men, archbishop Theodore of blessed memory and the abbot Hadrian, transmitted to me, either in writing or by word of mouth, all that he thought worthy of memory that had been done in the province of Canterbury and in the regions adjoining it by the disciples of blessed pope Gregory, as he had learned the same either from written records ('monimenta litterarum') or by the traditions of his predecessors: and those things which he thought memorable he sent to me by the religious priest Nothelm, of the church of London, transmitted either in letters sent to me, or by word of mouth, through Nothelm. . . . For from the beginning of this volume up till the time when the English people received the faith of Christ, we have chiefly learned from the writings of men of old ('priorum'), whence we have collected the matters which we have set forth. But from then onwards to the present time, the things done in the church of Canterbury by the disciples of the blessed pope Gregory and his successors, and under what kings they were done, we have learnt through the industry of the aforesaid abbot Albinus, word being borne to us by Nothelm.

Bede then proceeds to enumerate the prelates he has consulted, at Albinus' advice, for information about the other kingdoms and their bishops.

Gregory I's large scale and apostolic mission to the English is notable as one of the several ways in which he, as pope, undertook an imperial duty, that of converting the heathen as another Constantine. The sending of the expedition was long prepared. In a letter recorded in the Lateran scrinium, but not brought by Nothelm to Bede, Gregory wrote to the priest Candidus, telling him to buy Anglo-Saxon slave boys, to be trained in the monasteries to be future missionaries to their own countrymen (September 10, 595). It is not impossible that Gregory should have seen the blue-eyed, Anglian war-captives in the markets at Rome, for Marseilles was a noted slave market, and merchants may have taken boys thence to Rome for sale; but the story which Bede tells of Gregory's seeing Anglian boys there, and of his famous puns, is of Northumbrian not Roman origin: Bede says he had the story 'traditione maiorum'.

Gregory's choice of Augustine, provost of St. Andrew's monastery on the Caelian, with a band of monks, to be his missionaries to England may seem strange, for the Benedictine rule stresses the enclosure of the monk within his monastery: but it was recognised that a bishop might take a monk out of his monastery and remove him from the monastic to the clerical servitude at need, and Augustine was already designated to be bishop of the English when he should have been received, before the party set out. Gregory moreover was in close touch with St. Andrew's monastery, at which he had himself been trained, and in a position to urge the sending out of so large a body: the individual monks would be bound by their vow of obedience to compliance with their superior's order. No secular clergy, it appears, desired to join them on so precarious a mission.

The monks themselves, Bede says, when they had gone but a short distance on their journey, heard tales of the perils in front of them and sent back Augustine to tell the pope that by their common consent they judged it much safer not to go on. Gregory, however, wrote to these monks a letter in due form, dated July 23, 596, requiring them to proceed, and making Augustine their abbot, to whom they would now owe obedience as to Christ himself: this letter was preserved by Augustine and his successors at Canterbury. On the same day, July 23, 596, Gregory issued a letter commending Augustine and his companions to archbishop 'Aitherius' (Vergilius) of Arles, and the text of this letter, brought to Bede by Nothelm, is inserted in the HE. It was copied by Nothelm from a papal register, because the letter carried by Augustine would have been delivered to the recipient to whom it was addressed.

As can be seen from Gregory's register, this letter of July 596 was one of a batch of eight commendatory letters, to the bishops of Vienne, Autun, Aix, to the abbot of Lérins, and to the secular rulers of the Franks. Most notable of the latter was queen Brunhild, the greatest figure in France, who had married king Sigebert of Austrasia, the district between the Meuse and the Rhine. She was now ruling at Metz or in Alsace, in the names of her two grandsons, Theudebert and Thierry, to whom commendatory letters were also addressed; she led the bitter feud, the forty year long struggle, between Austrasia and Neustria, which had begun in 573. Æthelberht's wife Bertha, daughter of Charibert of Paris, was Brunhild's kinswoman. It was to Brunhild that Gregory wrote, that it had come to his ears that the Angles 'wished to become Christian, but that the bishops in their neighbourhood had no pastoral care for them': a phrase that may well have referred to the neighbouring Frankish bishops: especially as Gregory asks that Augustine may take with him on his mission 'priests from the neighbourhood', clearly meaning Frankish priests.

The reference to the lack of pastoral care of the neighbouring bishops was not unimportant, as the justification for Gregory's sending of the mission: for the Roman church was careful not to intrude on the jurisdiction of subject bishops and archbishops. Britain had once been included in the pretorian prefecture of the Gauls, and when the capital of the prefecture had been removed from Trier to Arles in the barbarian incursions of the early fifth century, the metropolitan of Arles had precedence over other bishops in Gaul, and some kind of pastoral solicitude may have been owed by him to the Christians of Britain, as part of the prefecture of the Gauls. Arles was not, however, adjacent to Britain, and such help as was sent, came from Germanus of Auxerre. Later on, none could be sent: but, in view of the question raised by the conversion of the English, as to whether the see of Canterbury was subject to a Frankish metropolitan, it may be noticed that in the sixth century the great archbishop, Caesarius of Arles (502–542), was the papal intermediary, and his see metropolitan. After his days, however, the position of Arles had declined: the conflicting claims and powers of the Merovingian kings had rendered the maintenance of a single metropolitanate impossible: Arles, Vienne and Aix-en-Provence at different times styled themselves metropolitan. Bede states that Augustine later went to Arles to receive episcopal consecration: no letter quoted by him, or entered in Gregory's register, confirms this, but Bede's statement suggests that his Canterbury informants believed Arles to have had precedence of the other Gallic sees at the time. Otherwise, it is unlikely Augustine would have been said to have made so long a journey to the extreme south of France. The question of Canterbury's independence of a Frankish metropolitan was raised later.

In any case, after presenting we know not how many of Gregory's letters of commendation, Augustine reached Britain, taking with him Frankish interpreters. He landed in Thanet and sent an envoy to Æthelberht, a most powerful king in Kent, whose dominions stretched up to the Humber. Bede elsewhere tells us he was the third of the bretwaldas or over kings of the Anglo-Saxons: as such, he had the right to summon the other kings to battle and to lead their forces.

The bretwalda, moreover, was not unacquainted with Christian practices, for he had married, as long ago as the year 560 (according to Gregory of Tours), and before he was king, the Frankish Christian princess, Bertha. The queen had brought with her as her chaplain Liuthard, bishop of Senlis, and the rites of the Christian religion were celebrated in the little old church of St. Martin at Canterbury. Bede says that it had been built of old in honour of St. Martin, while the Romans still dwelt in Britain. While no part of the extant structure can be shown to be of Roman work, it incorporates Roman material: a dedication to St. Martin 'before the Romans left Britain' is, however, too early for acceptance. Such a dedication may have been occasioned by Liuthard's use of the church as the queen's chapel, however: or may even have preceded it (see p. 35).

To Æthelberht the bretwalda the Christian religion must have commended itself as that of his strong and civilised neighbours across the Channel, with whom the English merchants traded, and who had apparently as good protection in battle as himself, an all-important point. Nevertheless, to adopt the religion of the Franks would be very unacceptable to many of his people: there were many holy places and hill sanctuaries to Woden and Thor throughout his kingdom, and some of the heathen priests and nobles would regard any change of religion as unlucky and undesirable. Though the genealogies tracing the descent of Æthelberht and other Anglo-Saxon kings back to Woden were compiled, probably, later than Æthelberht's day, yet Anglo-Saxon kings were regarded as in some way close to the gods, and Æthelberht, like the rest, had 'scopas' or poets who sang his praises and the stories of the gods at feasts. A little hand-harp, such as the scopas used, was laid among the royal treasures in the ship-burial at Sutton Hoo. However wise and pro- gressive a decision to adopt his wife Bertha's religion might be, the scopas and the heathen priests and the under kings were unlikely to favour it, and Æthelberht hesitated. Nevertheless, Augustine's em- bassy had said he came from Rome, and to Æthelberht, like all the barbarian kings, that was a very great name. He sent word that he would receive Augustine in the open air, and the monks approached him with a silver cross as their 'vexillum' (light, portable, standard), and a picture of the Saviour, an eikon, in the contemporary Byzan- tine manner then used at Rome, painted on wood.

This account in the HE. may well have come to Bede from local tradition at Canterbury: but when Nothelm first visited him, he seems to have had no exact information as to how soon after Augustine's reception in 597 king Æthelberht received baptism. Bede gives no date, but implies that the royal baptism followed quickly. There is reason, however, to believe that an interval of four years followed between the reception and the baptism. The evidence of papal letters registered but unknown to Bede suggests this. They include one sent by Gregory in September, 597, to queen Brunhild of Austrasia, thanking her for sheltering Augustine on his journey, but not mentioning any conversion. In July 598, Gregory wrote to bishop Eulogius of Alexandria, throwing in the joyful news that Augustine has brought more than 10,000 of the Anglo-Saxons to baptism. This was no doubt a round number, and the conversion of Æthelberht is not mentioned. In July 599, however, Gregory sent Syagrius, bishop of Autun, the pallium, in token of thanks for all Syagrius has done to help the mission of Augustine, and at the same time he wrote to queen Brunhild to inform her that he has thus sent the pallium to Syagrius her bishop, and the reason. It may be thought that so notable an honour to Syagrius would only have been accorded when Augustine's work had been crowned by the baptism of the bretwalda: but again, this is not expressly mentioned.

Gregory's letter congratulating Æthelberht himself that, like another Constantine, he has received the grace of conversion both for himself and his people, was not sent till June 22, 601; archabbot Suso Brechter, in his detailed study of the sources of the Augustinian mission, believes that, in fact, Æthelberht's baptism had taken place, probably at Easter, 601.

Bede states unequivocally that Æthelberht gave Augustine the place for a see suitable to his rank in his metropolis of Canterbury: yet when pope Gregory sent Augustine the pallium of a metropolitan on June 22, 601, the accompanying letter from the pope indicated that his see was that of London. Augustine, in the new church of the English, was bidden to create eventually twelve episcopal sees under his jurisdiction, so that the bishop of London should ever have his own synod (of bishops) and the honour of the pallium. Augustine was also to send a bishop to the city of York, so that when that city and the surrounding regions should have received the word of God, its bishop also should have metropolitan honour, and the pallium, and twelve bishops under him, the archbishop himself being subject to Augustine during his lifetime, while later the two metropolitans should have precedence by seniority of consecration.

King Æthelberht, however, had not yet brought about the conversion of his sub-king, Saberht (Sigiberht) of the East Saxons, in whose territory was the old Roman capital of Londinium: nor would it have been practicable to place Augustine's metropolitan see in the capital of an under-kingdom. Augustine therefore stayed in Cantwarabyrig (Durovernum Cantiacorum), where he had set his sedes, his cathedra, in an old church, built in the days of the Romans. The church appears to have had an apse orientated to the west: but this would have been old-fashioned in Augustine's day, and it may have been in his time or soon after that the apse orientated to the east was begun.

For the support of Augustine and his 'familia' Æthelberht provided suitable shelter next the church, and 'different kinds of possessions necessary to them'. In Kent, it seems that the old possessions of the Roman fisc had passed to the Germanic conquerors, and Æthelberht now allocated certain royal villas thus derived to the maintenance of the clergy. Later, he devoted to the support of a monastery for Augustine's followers the site of an old pagan temple of the Romans just outside the walls of Canterbury, with certain villas or food rents.

Once Æthelberht's baptism was accomplished, Augustine sent two of his followers, Lawrence the priest and Peter the monk, to acquaint Gregory with his success, and ask for reinforcements. There is no evidence that Augustine had with him originally any other priest than Lawrence unless any of the Frankish interpreters were priests;

though Peter was later described as priest. A monastery at the date would have very few priests among its members. St. Benedict himself was not a priest, and in the old, traditional beginning of the office of compline, the monk requested his abbot to command that the blessing be given 'Jube, domne, benedicere': a request going back to the day when the abbot, father of all his monks, would yet command one of them, if he had one who was a priest, to give the blessing. Augustine's monks could sing the 'opus dei' in his church, do the work of the house, and look after the boys commended to Augustine by their parents for training. Such monks as had sufficient learning he could now ordain to the priesthood: but in the establishment of the new church of the English, Augustine needed men of weight and experience, men he could, in time, consecrate as bishops. He asked Gregory for more helpers.

Gregory replied to Augustine's embassy by sending a fresh band of helpers, including Mellitus the abbot, Justus, Paulinus and Rufinianus. They brought with them 'all things generally necessary for the service of the church, that is to say, the sacred vessels and altar cloths, the ornaments for churches, vestments fitting for priests and clerics, and moreover, relics of the apostles and martyrs, and very many books (codices)'. He sent also to Augustine the pallium and an accompanying letter instructing him 'how bishops ought to be established in Britain'.

After commanding the future establishment of two synods with twelve bishops each for York and London (see p. 41), Gregory continued:

> But your fraternity shall have subject to you not only those bishops whom you have ordained, nor those whom the bishop of York shall have ordained, but, further, all the bishops of Britain, with the help of our Lord God Jesus Christ: so that they may perceive through your holiness' own words and life both the right faith and the form of good living, and so that, fulfilling their office as regards faith and morals, they may when God wills it attain the heavenly kingdom.

This letter also is dated June 22, 601. Bede made no explanation of the apparent difficulty that, having said that Augustine set up his see in Canterbury, the formal letter of pope Gregory authorises its setting up in London. The church of Canterbury which supplied the historical evidence apparently wished the facts set down without further explanation.

With regard to the four helpers sent to Augustine, they seem to have been men of experience surpassing all St. Augustine's followers except the two sent to Rome. Lawrence succeeded him at Canterbury at his death; Peter was first abbot of the monastery of SS. Peter and Paul at Canterbury, but was drowned crossing the Channel on a mission to Gaul; Mellitus the abbot became the first bishop of London, Justus the first bishop of Rochester, Paulinus of York, and Rufinianus possibly a later abbot of SS. Peter and Paul.

Bede quotes an interesting and properly dated letter of Gregory to the abbot Mellitus (sent four days earlier than the other bunch of letters, brought to Bede by Nothelm and dated June 22, 601). Gregory speaks of his anxiety to hear news of Mellitus, and 'our congregation' which is with Mellitus, and entrusts him with a message for Augustine. Pagan temples (fana idolorum), he says, are not to be destroyed among that people, but the idols within them must be destroyed: 'let holy water be sprinkled in the temples, altars built, and relics set there'. This must be done especially if the temples are well built. People will resort to the temples the more readily if they are used to frequenting them. 'And because many oxen have been wont to be sacrificed to demons, in this matter also there should be some substitution of solemnity: on dedication days, or the feasts of the holy martyrs whose relics have been set there, let them make tabernacles of boughs of trees around these churches which used to be pagan fanes, and keep the solemn day with religious feasting: let them not sacrifice animals to the devil but slaughter them for their own eating to the praise of God, so that while certain external joys are preserved for them, they may the more readily share in internal joys.'

Finally, on the same date, Gregory despatched a letter to the bretwalda Æthelberht, addressing him as 'rex Anglorum'; exhorting him to keep the divine grace he has received and further convert his subjects. Moreover, let him willingly hear our brother Augustine the bishop, who is well taught in monastic rule and the knowledge of holy scripture. He has sent Æthelberht certain gifts, which will not seem small to him since they come from the blessed Peter the apostle, with his blessing.

As to Augustine's further dispositions: Bede tells us that Augustine consecrated Mellitus to preach to the province of the East Saxons, whose metropolis was the city of London, 'an emporium of many nations, coming to it by land and sea', where Saberht, Æthelberht's nephew, was reigning, under the overlordship of the bretwalda. Æthelberht built for Mellitus the church of St. Paul the apostle: not down on the old Roman docks where the temple of Mithra had stood on the banks of the Walbrook, but on the high ground, by the site of the old forum, where the road from the southern bank of the Thames had crossed the bridge of Roman London and run northward up to the basilica and the forum. In the same year Augustine consecrated Justus as bishop for the men of west Kent, giving him a see at Rochester, a church dedicated to St. Andrew, and estates with which to support the bishop and his clergy.

Of Augustine's own work at Canterbury, Bede says that he dedicated his church in the name of the Saviour (Christ Church), Augustine was 'trained in monastic rule', but his chief need, beyond the work of conversion, was to train a familia in the different clerical grades or orders, living with them in his dwelling by the cathedral. Like the bishops in Gaul and Italy, he would need to take such boys as were offered to him, giving them the first tonsure, teach them to sing the psalms of which the divine office was so largely composed, and as much Latin as he could, that they might understand what they sang. They would learn to follow the order of the church's year, and, as they were admitted to the successive grades of the clerical militia, to use the book of exorcisms before the Christian use of any object associated with paganism (the springs or rivers in particular, when their water was needed for baptism); to read or chant in church as a lector: to serve the priest, both in general and at the altar as sub-deacon and deacon: and, as priest, to say the mass, instruct the pagan, bless the sick and bury the dead.

Celtic monks were themselves all in the clerical order, not bound to enclosure, but given to asceticism and the work of preaching. The monks of St. Benedict had been reared in a different tradition, and were strictly bound to the holy rule, which stressed the enclosure of the monk within his monastery, enjoining on him no pastoral work, for which indeed he was neither trained nor commissioned by the bishop. It is true that pope Gregory's apostolic command would have dispensed Augustine's followers from such portions of the rule as conflicted with it, but some of these monks must have been devout men, trained for the enclosed life, and of insufficient learning to be raised to holy orders. It is understandable therefore that, before his death, Augustine obtained from Æthelberht the site and endowment for a Benedictine monastery, where Æthelberht built within the enclosure the church of the blessed apostles, SS. Peter and Paul 'from the foundations'. They used for the small church of St. Pancras, also within the enclosure, the Roman dressed stones of some building on the site: and a recent deep excavation has shown that they built the main church over an old Roman cemetery, almost a catacomb: but the church itself was unfinished at Augustine's death. By Roman civil law, still followed in this respect by the church, burial within a building (except in the case of an infant) was forbidden; but the spectacular heathen cremation rites made some kind of honourable Christian obsequies desirable, especially in the case of kings and nobles, whose kin would expect some funerary honour to be shown. Therefore in the church of this monastery, as in other churches of the date, 'porticus', or side chapels beside the nave, were built, where the noble dead might be buried, yet without offending the old rule against burial in an interior. In the porticus to the south west of the central aisle, Æthelberht, Bertha and the kings of Kent were buried; in those to the north east, Augustine (eventually) and the succeeding archbishops.

As to the question: how far the life of Augustine and his monks in their 'mansio' at Canterbury was in fact 'monastic': it would have been certainly communal, for in Italy and Gaul the cathedral clergy served the 'parochia' and lived together, except in the case of great and well-endowed churches where the higher clergy had separate stipends and lived in separate houses. This is unlikely to have been the case with the newly founded see of Christ Church. Both monks and cathedral clergy would sing an office not yet very different in character from that of the 'secular' clergy at Rome. Gregory's recommendation of Augustine to Æthelberht as 'skilled in monastic rule' supports the view that he would not have lived otherwise than monastically at Christ Church: but it is equally certain that he was there ruling an episcopal familia and training clergy who would not be bound to take monastic vows. There were no cathedral churches in Italy at the time whose clergy were 'Benedictine' monks in the sense that St. Andrew's on the Caelian was 'Benedictine': nor would there have been any need to found the monastery later called St. Augustine's, only a mile from Christ

Church, if the life there were to be in all respects similar.

As to the church order established by Augustine before he died, on May 26th in some year between 604 and 609, the indications are that it followed ordinary continental lines. Only the south east of England had been affected by his mission: east and west Kent, and the land of the East Saxons. These kingdoms had been furnished with bishops' sees, their churches dedicated to the Saviour and his apostles, the 'right faith' taught in them: the apostolic faith as handed down by the Petrine see. The see churches were 'ecclesiae cathedrales', the churches of the bishop's chair, the symbol of his apostolic, teaching function. At Christ Church, Canterbury, subsequent building destroyed Augustine's church, but the foundations of the monastery of SS. Peter and Paul, the church at Rochester and the rather later churches of Lyminge and Reculver show the same plan. They were relatively small, stone buildings, rectangular 'cellae', with semicircular apses orientated to the west, the altar no longer on the chord of the apse as in old Roman Silchester (or the pagan temple of Mithra on the Walbrook), but set within the semicircle, around which, on a stone bench, sat the bishop and his clergy; the chord of the apse was now covered by a triple arcade at Lyminge and probably at St. Pancras. Bede states that Æthelberht was baptised at St. Martin's, but these early Kentish churches, built though they were by Italian or Gallic masons skilled in setting the thin Roman bricks found adjacent to the site, have left no sign of fonts or baptisteries. There are archaeological indications, however, that in late Roman Britain stone lavers or leaden tanks where the neophyte stood while the water was poured over him were in use, and it is possible that some such 'font' was used for Æthelberht's baptism; the Canterbury tradition that he was baptised at St. Martin's is of weight. On the Continent the baptistery was frequently a separate building; possibly Augustine, like Paulinus later, baptised in some cases in the streams. It was barely possible that much preaching could be done in the countryside till the missionaries should have learned English, or indeed till the English speaking boys given to Augustine to train should have grown up.

Augustine's converts would have come to the church of the monastery on Sundays and festivals, and what impressed them was the hedge of the monastic enclosure: 'ecclesia' does not occur in English place names in an English form, as a Welsh form of the word occurs in Welsh place names, but 'minster' became a common English word, from the time of Augustine's mission. Bede speaks, as has been noted, of the laity attending the solemnities of the dedication days of the local churches and the feasts of the martyrs: and he also mentions that the monks of St. Augustine's had an altar dedicated to St. Gregory, in the porticus where Augustine and the archbishops were buried, and where every Saturday a priest of the place made a solemn celebration. But distance and the infrequency of churches must have made lay attendance at Sunday mass small.

In respect of secular life, Augustine's mission had one eventual result: the writing down of the hitherto unwritten laws of Kent. Whereas among some peoples of Germanic origin, murder was punished by the working out of the blood feud, whereby the family of the man killed sought to kill the murderer, a social system that did not make for peace, yet better than one where there was no means of punishing homicide: among Æthelberht's subjects, homicide, theft and other injuries were compensated by a tariff of emendations, adjudicated by a man's neighbours in the moot. The amount of the 'wer', or payment for killing a man, or the 'bot' for injuring him, depended on the social rank of the man injured or killed, and the gravity of the injury. No money was minted in Kent at the time (though a coin minted for the Frankish bishop Liuthard has been found in a hoard at St. Martin's), and it may be said that the only money then circulating in Kent was that brought in by merchants, chiefly Frankish. The wers and bots can scarcely have been paid in coined money. But when it became necessary to protect the new missionaries and their churches by assigning them a social rank, which would determine the tariff of emendations to be made for injuring them, their rank was expressed in the first written recension of the laws by a 'twelve fold', 'eleven fold', etc., amount of the bot, as compared to that paid for injury to a freeman. Now that the instrument of writing was used at Canterbury (for the earlier Runic writing was used only for inscriptions, not literature), the old folk law was written down, the missionaries woven into the fabric of English society, and their persons and goods protected by the penalties commensurate with their rank.

On one matter where Augustine attempted to follow pope Gregory's direction, the obtaining of the Celtic bishops' acknowledg-

ment of his authority with a view to their further guidance in faith
and practice, Augustine had no success. This was not, indeed, to be
expected: for he was the chaplain of the 'bretwalda' of the English,
to the Celts a hated and ravaging race who had installed themselves
in the south east of Britain in the fifth century, and in the century
and a half after their arrival gradually pushed their dominion northwards and westwards by fighting. There was still a fighting frontier
between the Anglo-Saxons and their neighbours, the Welsh and the
Picts. The Welsh still held Devon, parts of Somerset and west Wiltshire: Glastonbury was a great Celtic church. Wales, with its
churches of Llandaff, St. Davids, Caerwent, and the great bangor
(Irish for monastery) in the north, professed an old Christianity, and
in Cumberland and the north west of Britain the Welsh fought and
defended themselves from Æthelfrith, who 'more than all the other
English leaders devastated the people of the Britons'. The Irish missionaries of Iona had converted the Scots in the north. National feeling was all against acknowledging the authority of any Anglo-Saxon
prelate, who had not even converted more than a fraction of the
bretwalda's people; and this was especially the case because the
customs of the Welsh had been those of Gaul, Italy and the western
church when Patrick and Illtud and Petroc and David converted
the heathen and taught their fathers the due practices of the Christian
life, long ago. The Welsh had the catholic Christian's reverence for
the church and the faith as apostolic: but they believed their own
practices, when they differed from those of Augustine's followers,
were indeed apostolic.

Augustine, however, could not leave his relationship with the
British churches undetermined. Using Æthelberht's help (apparently
for the obtaining of letters of safe conduct and the means of travel),
he summoned to confer with him the 'bishops and doctors' of the
nearest British provinces at a spot called in Bede's day 'Augustine's
Oak', on the borders of the Hwicce and the West Saxons. The
Hwicce then held Severn mouth and locations in the Severn valley:
they consisted of one Anglo-Saxon tribe which had advanced south
westward from Mercia, and another which had pushed northwards
from Wiltshire and the Thames. They settled late among the English
tribes, and held the debatable land once thickly planted with Roman
villas: the scene of Arthur's (?) come-back against the invaders in the
early sixth century. They must have settled while the Romano-

5

Britons still inhabited the countryside, for one of their tribes called themselves when settled the Ercingas, from Ariconium, a Roman signal station. In 577, according to the Anglo-Saxon Chronicle, Ceawlin, king of the West Saxons, had fought the battle of Deorham, and thereafter taken over the ruined or half-deserted cities of Gloucester, Cirencester and Bath, extending his dominions over Severn mouth and the lower Severn valley. The bretwalda's safeconduct therefore made it safe for Augustine to travel to this region: but it did not make him welcome to the newly conquered Welsh inhabitants.

In his conference, Augustine tried to persuade the Welsh bishops that, 'entering into the catholic peace with himself, they would join with him in converting the pagan peoples'. Difference of custom, not of doctrine, separated them. 'They did not', said Bede,[1] 'observe Easter day at its due season, but on one falling between the 14th and 20th day of the moon, this reckoning being contained within a cycle of 84 years: and they did other things contrary to ecclesiastical unity.' This difference involved mathematics, not theology: but was of great practical importance, as indicating to which obedience the church thus celebrating the feast belonged. After long argument, the Welsh would not give way, 'prefering rather', says Bede, 'their own traditions to all those which unite the whole world in Christ'. Bede then tells a story, of Canterbury origin, of how Augustine healed a blind man to convince them. They were, however, not impressed: but said they could not withdraw from their customs without the leave and consent of their seniors. They asked that there might be a second synod to which more might come.

This was agreed: and there came to the synod seven British bishops and a great number of very learned men, especially from the noblest of their monasteries, which is called in the English tongue, Bancornabyrig (Bangor), of which Dinoot (Donatus) is said then to have been abbot. And before they went, they sought counsel of a holy and wise anchorite, as to whether they ought to desert their customs at the preaching of Augustine. He advised them, that if, when they entered the synod, Augustine rose to greet them, they should hear him with meekness: if he did not rise, they should show no deference to him. The advice went to the root of the matter: the

---

[1] Bede here appears to be ante-dating the controversy over the Easter date, which became acute when raised by Columbanus in c. 603.

Roman magistrate sat on his curule 'sella' and did not rise at the entrance of those who sought his judgment: the rhetor taught sitting in his 'cathedra', while his pupils stood. To rise on the Welsh bishops' entrance would be to admit equality: to cede beforehand any claim to teach.

'They did, as he had said.' And when they came, Augustine sat on in his sella: and they said they would do none of the things he suggested, nor would they acknowledge him as archbishop. And to their refusal to join with him in converting the English (which would indeed to their own people have looked like going over to the enemy), Bede suggests was due the later slaughter of 1,200 monks of Bangor, in the battle of Chester against the pagan Æthelfrith, when the monks went to pray for their countrymen. It is an instance when Bede's Anglian prejudice got the better of his judgment.

Augustine died before the monastery of SS. Peter and Paul was completed: it fell to Lawrence his successor to consecrate it. He died, indeed, sometime between 604 and 609, and he was buried in the monastery grounds outside the half-built church. As soon as the church was dedicated, he was borne within and buried in the north porticus, the following epitaph written later on his tomb:

> Here rests the lord Augustine, the first archbishop of Canterbury, who in time past was sent here by blessed Gregory, pontiff of the city of Rome. He was aided by God in the working of miracles and he led Æthelberht the king and his people from the worship of idols to the faith of Christ. He completed the days of his office in peace, and died on the seventh day before the kalends of June (26 May), in the reign of the same king.

Of the gifts that came from pope Gregory to king Æthelberht, mentioned in his letter, we know nothing further; but among the codices sent by Gregory to Augustine at the hands of abbot Mellitus one has survived, and has some bearing on the question of what rite Augustine used at Christ Church. It is a beautifully illuminated altar book: but Gregory would have sent it for use, not merely the adornment of the chapel. Augustine must originally have brought a sacramentary with him from Rome: perhaps the only book he brought beside a psalter: but he would, in general, have used the books sent him later by the pope, with such modifications or additions as he saw fit (see p. 154).

The surviving gospel book (Corpus Christi College, Cambridge, MS. 286) is accepted by palaeographers as having been written in Italy in the mid sixth century. It once belonged to St. Augustine's abbey, for documents concerning the abbey were written into the manuscript. It may well have been among the altar books kept with the relics of the abbey, not in the monastic library, for manuscripts thus preserved in the treasury had a better chance of surviving pillage and even the abandonment of the house: the holy relics would be the first things saved in an alarm, and the gospel book with them. The manuscript thus survived the Danish raids, was at St. Augustine's in the eleventh century, and was given by Matthew Parker to Corpus Christi College, Cambridge.

In the manner of gospel books for altar use at the day, this fine vellum manuscript had originally canon tables, a portrait of the evangelist at the beginning of each gospel, of which only that of St. Luke has survived, and a page divided rectangularly and illuminated with small scenes from the gospel. The portrait of St. Luke also has gospel scenes painted into the design: and if all the evangelists' pictures had similar scenes, the gospel book may have had as many as 70 little gospel pictures. One of great liturgical interest is that of the Last Supper, entitled *Cena domini*; Christ in the middle of a group of eight disciples is seated at a round table (those facing him are omitted): the cup is before him and in the centre of the table the paschal lamb of the Passover: he holds the bread in his left hand and blesses with his right, and the three disciples on his right hand copy his gesture. The scene is in fact a representation of the Last Supper as a concelebration, such as took place at Rome on solemn occasions in Augustine's day, and, indeed, ever since. It is a very old picture, very old teaching: Christ himself celebrates what was, in Augustine's day, already colloquially called 'the mass', and with him his apostles.

It is a reasonable surmise that the Roman missionaries, using this Italian altar book, would have celebrated according to contemporary Roman custom on a low square altar. For some discussion of the Kentish church plans, altars and ornaments in the time of Augustine and his immediate successors and the rite used, see Chapter VII pp. 138–141.

CHAPTER IV

THE CONVERSION OF ENGLAND, 604–664

Though the bretwalda, Æthelberht, had accepted Christianity at the hands of Augustine, paganism was still strong at his death in 616, even in Kent. Before his death, Rædwald of East Anglia had defeated him in war and assumed the bretwaldaship: and Rædwald's conversion earlier had been half-hearted and not followed by any conversion of his people. At the East Anglian and East Saxon courts there was a relapse, on Æthelberht's death, to paganism. In the rest of the Anglo-Saxon territories conversion had not even begun. The great pagan ship-burial at Sutton Hoo, in a nominally Christian East Anglia, took place just before the synod of Whitby of 664.

In what kind of a society then, and among what sort of people, had Christian missions, Roman or Celtic, to work?

England in the seventh century was thinly populated, the countryside still largely wooded, and the mouths and valleys of rivers still undrained and liable to flooding. The Wash extended in marshes and fens far to the south of its present boundary. The area of arable land was very small, by present standards, though the Anglo-Saxons were bringing more and more land into cultivation by their heavy ploughs; Anglo-Saxon villagers (and they were practically the whole Anglo-Saxon population) depended on the food they grew, the milk and cheese from their cows, and the bacon from the herds of swine they slaughtered before winter. The women spun the wool from their sheep, and made the cooking pots from clay, not on the wheel. The metal workers could not only provide the spades and the plough-shares, the swords and the shields, but included some skilled craftsmen who could make the cloisonné jewellery of Kent and the astonishingly fine ornaments of Sutton Hoo. The Anglo-Saxons were illiterate farmers, hunters and fighters: but they had discarded the earlier system of maintaining justice by the sanction of the blood feud, and their customary law provided for the compensation for offences by payment in money or goods, according to the nature of the injury and the social status of the person injured, or killed. The pagan villagers whom the missionaries had to convert were simple people, but well aware of the need of law and order within the tribe, and of loyalty to the king who led them against their outside enemies.

The Christianity of the Romano-Britons whom they had locally conquered, or who had fled westward from them, had made no great impression on them. Tribal chieftains of high rank seem to have intermarried with Romano-British ladies, but there seems to have been no general intermingling of the two populations. By the seventh century the Romano-Britons of the 'enclaves', or the Welsh villages up on the chalk downs, had apparently found that life was better with the Anglo-Saxons, and come down to work for them, and eventually join them: but there is no archaeological evidence for a general intermingling of the two races. Only where the Anglo-Saxons did not penetrate till late, as in Somerset, Devon and Cornwall: or, not at all, as in Wales, did Christianity survive.

There is plenty of archaeological evidence of the paganism of the Anglo-Saxons in their cremation and inhumation cemeteries, numerous in Kent and Sussex, and no less numerous and extensive in East Anglia. In the latter province there must have been a great invasion, large enough to establish itself between the forts of the Saxon Shore without any negotiated agreement. The cemeteries are most extensive at Caistor by Norwich, and by Yarmouth and up the rivers flowing into the Wash. Those of Lincolnshire are very little later, and the early ones of Yorkshire show that the first invaders settled round the Malton Gap, on the dip-slopes of the chalk hills north of Humber mouth; they made their way later across the water-logged plain to York. The landings in Bernicia were later still, and these Anglian warriors spread slowly up the Tyne and up the coast to Bamborough: the Romano-Britons fought them all the way. There had been hard fighting too along the coast of Sussex, when the South Saxons outflanked the forts of the Saxon Shore and fought their way back and took Anderida (Pevensey). The Jutes settled in the Isle of Wight and the cemeteries here and in Sussex are early.

The archaeological evidence then, the siting of the cemeteries and the shields and weapons buried with the men, suggests that the Anglo-Saxon invasion was no mere peaceful penetration, but accomplished by piecemeal military conquest. This process lasted for about a century from the traditional date of the landing of Hengest and

Horsa c. 449, with an interval of about thirty years soon after 500, when 'Arthur' held the invaders stationary. In the later stages of the invasion of south western Britain the West Saxon advance was accomplished by 'colonisation' by thegns who took over unploughed land from the 'Welsh' of Somerset and ploughed it; but even this 'peaceful penetration' was made possible by the military campaigns of king Cenwalh and king Ine. It is only in the last stages of the Anglo-Saxon occupation, as in Worcestershire and Severn mouth, that the archaeological evidence points to intermingling of the two races; as at Withington (Worcs.) and with the Anglo-Saxon tribe who settled round the Roman signal station of Ariconium.

The evidence that the Anglo-Saxon advance was, almost throughout, military and hostile, explains the unwillingness of Celtic Christians, descendants of the Romano-Britons, to accept the Christianity of their conquerors later. In the north this racial hostility was lacking: the pagan Angles of Northumbria, who ruled a largely Brittonic population, were less unwilling to accept the religion of the Celts of Iona. Bede wrote with admiration of their saints.

The evidence for the kind of lives lived by the people whom the Christian missionaries hoped to convert comes mainly from their cemeteries, from their poetry (see p. 167), and the laws of the early kings of Kent (see p. 56). The archaeologists have excavated only one village, and that hastily evacuated and abandoned, left to subside into the ground and be grown over, and finally discovered in modern times; this is the village of Sutton Courtenay in Berkshire. Here the houses were built in the form of a Boer lager, round a green where the animals might be driven in for safety at night. The houses were half underground, with timber and mud walls surrounding the four or five foot deep pit: the roofs were thatched and supported by wooden posts, and each house had a stone hearth, and wooden doors that could slide one behind each other. In the hasty evacuation, a woman left a beautiful brooch on the wooden wall beam beside the door; but no children's bones were found in the house: she saved her children, presumably, though she left her brooch behind. Other evidence that the village was an advance post in hostile territory is the fact that there is no cemetery: the place was not occupied long enough. One householder, perhaps a chieftain, died and was laid on his own house floor with an eight inch sheet of pottery clay over him: it was then necessary to build another room to the house. A woman who died was simply laid in the rubbish pit: the skeleton lay on the sloping surface of what must have been the rubbish in the pit. This was not a dishonourable burial, for an ox's head was buried in the pit with her, that she might have food in the far land to which she had gone; the ox would have been killed for her funeral feast. In other houses were found a pit with damp pottery clay, in a kind of basement beneath the main room, and, in the house where the woman's brooch was found, a loom which had had a row of strings hanging from the loom beam and held down by a row of loom weights. When the strings perished in the abandoned house, the loom weights fell in a row beneath; grasses and plants grew on the roof till it, too, collapsed on to the floor, and the house became a low mound, less and less distinguishable.

The site of this abandoned, outpost, village was never built over, but accidentally preserved, as it were, for the modern archaeologists. Most of the invaders' villages were continuously inhabited and re-built and the evidence of early conditions lost. The slight evidence of the early laws does not suggest, however, that the villagers lived mainly in houses half underground, though their walls must have continued to be of lath and plaster or wattle and daub.

There must have been great advance in living conditions and the arts, however, between the days of the Sutton Courtenay abandon-ment and the ship-burial at Sutton Hoo, or the use of the royal villa at Yeavering by king Edwin of Deira, and this advance in the arts can be partly traced in the successive burials in the Anglo-Saxon cemeteries. Early types of brooches and other metal work developed both in their art-forms and their technical skill. A large cemetery would be in use for four generations or more, during which the early practice of cremation burial gave way to inhumation. All these burials attest some belief in survival after death, for provision was made in the pagan period for the needs in the after life of the person buried. In the case of a cremation burial, the cremated ashes and bones were placed in a large pot, and various objects like shell fish, food, etc., in small pots clustered round it, the whole little group being covered with a slate or thin stone, and a low earth mound made on top. In such a cemetery the graves would be in no order and the whole area covered with contiguous burials.

When timber became too scarce quite near the cemetery for further cremations, it was found easier to dispose of the dead by inhumation, with the graves again disposed in no particular order or orientation. In inhumation graves the dead were laid clothed, the men with tunic, belt, buckle and two shoulder brooches, their swords beside them and the lower part of the body covered by their shields: in rare cases, the dead were laid in the grave on the bier on which they had been carried. The Anglo-Saxon lady still had her brooches, belt, and a chatelaine at her belt with keys, in death. In inhumation burials, however, the jewellery buried with the body tends to become smaller and more modest and the cross motif sometimes appears in ornament; food offerings are no longer found for the use of the soul after death, and sometimes many graves are orientated to the east, a sign at the date of Christian burial. In such burials the smaller and more modest jewellery found was in accordance with the teaching of the church, that such objects could do nothing to promote the welfare of the soul after death.

The people who made and used these cemeteries lived by agriculture and occasional hunting. They had horses and held them in high honour; we hear from Nennius that the names of the two federate chiefs who were called in by the Celtic over king to defend Kent were Hengest and Horsa, both horse names, and the horse head appears commonly as the ending of the safety-pin brooch. Oxen were used for ploughing and were too valuable for eating, except at great feasts, such as funeral feasts and those of the pagan gods. An ox's head or a horse's bones were sometimes found at the burial of a chieftain: the skull or bones of an ox were found on a great silver dish near the armour of the king commemorated at Sutton Hoo.

The change from paganism to Christianity is thus indicated in the cemeteries, but not in any striking form. The 'flight from cremation' probably took place before any general conversion, but once a village was converted inhumation would be general, for the church frowned upon cremation burial as associated with pagan superstitions.

The laws of Æthelberht and two Kentish kings who succeeded him, and those of king Ine of the West Saxons[1] (abdicated, 726), show how the complex village society of the Anglo-Saxons was governed and maintained. In political theory, kings were associated with the gods and descended ultimately from Woden; there was a nobility of birth in early Kent and of royal service in Wessex, about a hundred years later. The free peasant (ceorl) had his share in the

[1] See F. L. Attenborough, *Laws of the Earliest English Kings*, 1922, pp. 4–61.

common fields and his wer-geld (compensation for his murder, paid to his kin), and the noble class above him, and the classes of native 'wealh' (Welsh) beneath him, had their appropriate wers. The bishop and his clergy were assigned by Æthelberht their adequate wers. War was of great importance for the defence of the small, local kingdoms, and the 'eorlkund' man, and the thegns later, must follow the king to battle as a primary obligation. The smith who made the weapons (as well as the ploughshares) was a much respected member of society; he repaired the damaged helmets and hammered the bent spears straight again; the war-standard found at Sutton Hoo, surmounted by its grid and the small figure of a stag, was a fine piece of smith's work. It was villagers such as these, and more particularly the tribal kings and their nobles, that the Christian missionaries had to convert. The first approach had always, and necessarily, to be made to king or chieftain.

The death of the bretwalda, Æthelberht, then, allowed the lesser kings, chieftains, nobles and villagers to revert to their earlier paganism: the hill sanctuaries and the groves might be put to their old use. Bede explains that the new bretwalda, Rædwald, had been baptised in Æthelberht's days, 'but in vain'; for when he went home he was led astray by his wife and certain perverse teachers. 'For he had in his pagan fane an altar for the Christian sacrifice, and a small altar to sacrifice victims to demons.' Such cautious deference to two gods appears in Scandinavian folk stories, and must have seemed reasonable when a main object of religious observance was to obtain protection in battle and 'good luck' in normal life. 'King Aldwulf, who is king of that province now,' Bede continued, 'said the fane had remained to his day, and he had seen it in his childhood.' King Aldwulf died in 713 and Bede may have been confusing him with Alfwold, who was alive while he was writing his history; king Aldwulf, who had seen the old fane, would also in his childhood have seen the mound raised over the great ship-burial at Sutton Hoo, where the treasure (including two christening spoons) and armour of a Christian king were placed round the space where his own body, had he been a pagan, would have lain; his body was actually given Christian burial elsewhere.[1] In the second half of the seventh

[1] See R. L. S. Bruce-Mitford, The Sutton Hoo Ship-Burial, 1949, p. 42, and the whole monograph for pagan and Christian burial at the date.

century paganism was still strong in the court circle of East Anglia.

In Canterbury, Lawrence had been consecrated archbishop in Augustine's life-time, a practice still tolerated though uncanonical. He had to live through the dangerous period for the young church of the succession of a half-pagan bretwalda, and in Kent itself of Æthelberht's son Eadbald, who had not only refused baptism, but now married his father's widow (a later wife than Bertha, apparently). Saberht, king of the East Saxons, died too, and his three sons, still pagan, and now open ones, gave licence to their subjects to renew the pagan rites. Yet they apparently still attended when Mellitus the bishop said mass in the basilica, and expected to receive, like the Christians, the white and shining bread of the eucharist: 'You used', they said, 'to give it to our father Saba.' When Mellitus refused to give it them unless they would be baptised, they refused to enter that font (which would seem to have been a metal tank with low sides, as used in Roman Britain, for there is no evidence of the building of special baptisteries in England), 'for', they said, 'they knew they had no need of it', and they expelled Mellitus from their country, and all his familia. Mellitus went to Kent, took counsel with Lawrence and Justus, and decided to withdraw to Gaul: but just then Saberht's sons went out to attack the Gewissae, the West Saxons, and perished in battle. This was a shattering blow to pagan prestige, and prepared the way for the simple Christians to be recalled to Christ: but the Londoners, apparently, rejoiced to serve idols rather than bishops, and it never became possible for Mellitus to return to his see.

In Kent, king Eadbald was so hostile that Lawrence the archbishop almost fled to Gaul himself: but he feared, however great the peril, to leave the sheep of Christ's fold in the midst of wolves, and was able at this juncture to convert Eadbald. He recalled Mellitus and Justus from Gaul: Mellitus remained at Canterbury and Justus returned to Rochester (617).

Mellitus succeeded Lawrence as archbishop in 619 and 'governed the English church with great care and toil'. 'He was noble by birth, but much nobler in mind.' When a fierce fire threatened to consume the whole city of Canterbury and was approaching the bishop's see, Mellitus prayed and the wind, which had been threatening the city from the south, turned round and blew back over the parts already burned and died down; and at other times he prayed and the tempests were stayed. He died in April 624.

Justus, bishop of Rochester, succeeded him, receiving from pope Boniface V the pallium and permission to ordain bishops (by himself: there was no other bishop in communion with the see of Canterbury in Britain at the time); he ordained Romanus to succeed him at Rochester, and he was archbishop three years, dying in 627. But in those three years he consecrated a bishop to send to Edwin of Deira, a mission that eventually led to the founding of the second metropolitan see of Britain.

Power among the northern Angles was divided between the kings of Bernicia and Deira (roughly, Northumberland and Yorkshire). King Edwin of Deira, who had become bretwalda on the death of Rædwald, sent to ask for Æthelberga (the Latinised form of the name: no Anglo-Saxon woman's name can end in 'a'), daughter of Æthelberht and Bertha, in marriage. Her brother Eadbald, on receiving a promise that Edwin would do nothing contrary to the Christian faith, and would allow any of his subjects who wished to become Christian, sent Æthelberga to him, with bishop Paulinus as her chaplain, in 625. The following Easter Saturday night Edwin was preserved from assassination by the courage of one of his thegns, and his wife gave birth to a daughter, called Eanflæd (626). Edwin in thankfulness for protection from the assassin, already granted him, promised to become a Christian if he should further win the victory over the enemy king who had sent the assassin. In pledge of the future performance of his promise, Edwin allowed Paulinus to baptise his daughter, and eleven others of her family, at the following eve of Pentecost (Whitsunday); after which he set out and defeated the West Saxons, and summoned his witan to confer with him about the adoption of the Christian faith.

The story of the witan (apparently held after the campaign in the summer of 626) is one of the finest and best known of Bede's stories. Edwin held counsel with his 'friends, princes and councillors' so that if they agreed with him they might all be consecrated together in the font of life. He asked each in turn how this new doctrine and new cult seemed to him. And Coifi his chief (pagan) priest told him 'there was no truth and no usefulness in the old religion: no man had honoured the old gods more than he had himself, and what had it profited him? If this new faith that was now preached to them were better and stronger, let them receive it.' And another of the king's nobles also assented, saying:

'The present life of man in this world, O king, seems to me, in comparison with that span of time that is to us uncertain, like a sparrow flying swiftly through your hall as you sit at supper with your dukes and thegns in the winter time. The fire burns in the midst, and the hall where you sup is warm, while outside the storms of wind and snow rage; and the bird enters by one door and flies straight out at the other. And while it is within, the winter's storms touch it not: but when it has passed through this small moment of serenity it passes from winter to winter and disappears from your sight. Even so short is the life of man, and of what follows it, and what preceded it, we know nothing at all.'

If the new teaching could bring more knowledge, he advised, let them follow it: and the councillors and the elders agreed. Coifi desired to hear Paulinus further: and when he was thus assured, he asked permission to ban and burn the old temples and the altars, and he asked that arms and a stallion be given him, and taking a spear in his hand he rode off to the temple at Goodmanham, some twelve miles from York. And the crowd thought it a mad deed. But he did not delay, but cast his spear and profaned the temple, and commanded his fellows to burn the temple and all its courts.

Then king Edwin, with all the noblest of his people and very many common folk prepared for baptism. Edwin's home country was on the Yorkshire downs to the east, near Malton: but pope Gregory had commanded that an archbishop's see should be set up in York, the old capital of northern Britain. Moreover, the Roman ruins of York still stood: and in the legionary city north of the river Edwin had built, while he and his people were being instructed for baptism, a small wooden oratory dedicated to St. Peter, and there he was baptised on the vigil of Easter, 627. With him were baptised Osfrid and Eadfrid, his sons by a Mercian princess, and two babies born to himself and Æthelberga since Eanflæd: those both died in their white chrism cloths, and were buried in the church at York.

In York Edwin gave Paulinus his bishop's see, and when he was baptised, he began to build in the same place a greater and more august basilica of stone. He built the foundations 'in a gyre' around the former oratory, and he built the new basilica square. But the stone building took time, and five years were all the time he had. Before the walls were of full height Edwin was killed at the battle of Hatfield Chase (632), fought in the Doncaster region with the combined forces of the Welsh king Cadwallon and Penda of Mercia.

Recent excavation has added to our knowledge of Edwin's court in the north and of an Anglo-Saxon king's vill or tun. Edwin, after his baptism at York, where at least some of his Deiran subjects were baptised, went north with Paulinus to plant Christianity in Bernicia. He went to his royal vill which Bede calls 'ad Gefrin' which was some fifteen miles west of Bamborough, on the little river 'Glene', which flowed northwards into the Tweed; Bernicia, at the time, extended well to the north of Hadrian's Wall. Bede tells us that Edwin and his court went to this royal tun, now Yeavering in Glendale, and remained there thirty-six days; Paulinus worked from morning to night, catechising and baptising great numbers of catechumens in the river.

Excavation by Mr. B. Hope-Taylor in the summer of 1956 has discovered the lay-out of this completely timber-built tun. The foundations were found of the king's hall (aula), and round it a number of smaller halls for his ealdormen and thegns; adjacent to these was the wedge-shaped segment of a shallow amphitheatre, apparently for the holding of some royal moot or witan. The king, standing at the base, could there address his 'sapientes', as a Latin document would render 'witan': the arrangement was designed to enable his voice to carry well to an out-of-door meeting. Among the earliest buildings at Yeavering (i.e. one belonging to the first quarter of the seventh century) was a rectangular hall which appears to have begun as a pagan temple[1] and was certainly converted to a Christian church later on. It gave evidence of periodical feasts, and inhumation-burials were clustered round its southern end. One such burial suggests a conflict between pagan and Christian ritual, in that a full-length, east-west, grave contained a crouched burial occupying no more than its eastern half: an ox-tooth lying on the floor of the western half suggests a token food deposit. This cannot be taken as certain, but towards the end of the pagan period small bone combs and ornaments were put in the grave, clearly as tokens representing the very valuable jewellery earlier buried with the dead, and thought of as for their use in the life beyond. When this converted 'church' had, with all the other buildings, been destroyed in a fire (a fate liable to overtake a collection of timber buildings), the site was abandoned; Bede says the whole tun was rebuilt at Maelmin, not far off, but less

[1] I owe this description to the kindness of Mr. Hope-Taylor.

wind-swept; a new cemetery was laid out, and what was certainly a
church placed in the centre of the area; these burials belonged to the
second half of the seventh century.

Meanwhile, Paulinus worked with Edwin in the remaining five
years in both Bernicia and Deira; he used to baptise in the river
Swale, which flows by Catterick, and in the river Trent, like any
Celtic missionary. In these early days of the church it was not yet
possible to build oratories or baptisteries, though at the royal tun of
Donhead Paulinus built a wooden basilica, afterwards burned by the
pagans. He preached to the Lindissi in the province of Lincoln and
converted Blaeca, the king's reeve, together with all his family; he
built in Lincoln a stone church, for which there was plenty of hewn
stones from the ruins of Roman Lindum, and in this church, when
archbishop Justus died in 627, he consecrated Honorius to succeed
him. He was remembered in Bede's day as an old man, tall, thin and
stooping, with black hair and an aquiline nose: he was very awe-
inspiring to look at. By virtue of his bretwaldaship, Edwin persuaded not only the Lindissi, whom he had just conquered, to receive
baptism, but king Earpwald of East Anglia, shortly before his death
in 627.

There are some indications in Bede that Edwin was not merely a
Germanic chieftain and war leader, born in a northern province of a
race unacquainted as a whole with the Greco-Roman past. He had
spent many years in exile, some of them at the court of king Rædwald, his friend and protector; he would have seen the great silver
dishes with their classical decoration, bought by the king from
merchants in London, or more probably taken as war spoil from old
king Æthelberht of Kent; he would have seen the war standard, a
barbarisation of the war standard of the legions, that was later buried
at Sutton Hoo. He had seen the multi-angular tower at York, and the
ruins of a great civitas. Christianity and Roman citizenship might
well seem to him to go together. The description Bede gives of the
military ceremony with which he insisted on accompanying himself
suggests that some one of his court had Vegetius' *Art of War*, or
possibly the *Etymologies* of Isidore of Seville, where Vegetius'
military information is boiled down. At any rate, he not only had
'vexilla' borne before him, in battle, but in peace time when he was
walking about his 'cities' and tuns, or in the open countryside, he
was always preceded by a standard-bearer; even if he was just walking

across the village green ('per plateas'), he used to have that kind of light standard (vexillum) that the Romans call 'thuuf' carried before him. 'Thuuf' is a word that certainly came from Vegetius, and whatever it meant originally, the Anglo-Saxons connected it with the word 'tuft', from the greenery stuck at the top of the vexillum. Edwin had an inquiring and interesting mind: but the combined forces of the Welsh king and the strenuous Penda were too strong for him. Deiran ascendancy collapsed. Paulinus had to take the queen and flee to Kent by sea, an obvious action when no conversion of the people was possible without the protection of kings and bretwaldas. The pallium that pope Honorius was sending him for his archbishopric of York only reached him when he was a refugee in Kent.

For Æthelberga, her brother Eadbald provided a minster at Lyminge, where she could live as princess-abbess. Assuming that Lyminge was built on the same lines as the minster of Whitby, excavated in modern times, Paulinus and some junior clergy would have lived in a small house within the monastic palisade or hedge; Æthelberga would have lived in a small house with a young nun as attendant, and other buildings would have been provided for the nuns, the novices, the infirmary, and the chapel. Paulinus could never return to York: Penda commanded Northumbria till his death, and then rule passed to the Bernician Oswald: Paulinus remained at Lyminge, which had a kind of pastoral supervision of the people of Romney Marsh, till 625, when he was made bishop of Rochester. He died in 644.

But though Paulinus' work in Northumbria had been so short, it was not without effect. His deacon James remained behind (a musician, incidentally, and able to teach his converts the church chant), and he supported the new Christians in Deira till the synod of Whitby, at which he was himself present, brought the northern Christians into the Roman unity, and ended his isolation.

The history of the Celtic church in Ireland is outside the scope of this book; but it was from the flourishing monastic life of sixth century Ireland that the nation of the northern Picts in Scotland was converted, and it was from the Irish monastery of Iona that Christianity was brought to the northern Angles, and from them to Celtic minsters in Mercia and East Anglia. The work of the Celtic missionaries in Britain was only part of a movement that took them to Gaul, central Europe and Lombardy.

At the time of Augustine's mission, the Anglian kings of Northumbria had extended their dominions northward into Scotland; they held the coast between Bamburgh and the Firth of Forth and they were the hostile neighbours of the southern Picts of Clydesdale, ruled by their king Aidan, whose dynasty was of Irish origin. When the northern Picts were converted by St. Columba, and his disciples pursued the work of conversion in southern Scotland, they were in touch with the most northern of the Anglian settlers, and their language cannot have been entirely unknown. No such language barrier existed between the Scottish monks when they came to the Angles of Bernicia, and the Anglo-Saxons of Mercia and East Anglia, as existed between the Italian missionaries and the men of Kent.

The Irish who came to convert the northern Picts were not peasant missionaries: they were learned men, their leader a prince-monk of royal birth. There was already a connexion between Dalaradia, the land of the northern Picts, and Ulster: St. Comgall, who founded the great Bangor in 555 on the shores of Belfast Lough, came from Dalaradia, and was always reckoned one of its patron saints. A few miles from this Bangor, St. Finnian had founded his monastery of Moville, and both Bangor and Moville were reckoned learned houses, nurseries of scholars in sixth century Ireland. Columba, a son of Niall noi-giallach studied under Finnian at Moville and under the other Finnian at Clonard, learned the writing and illuminating that supposedly caused the trouble which took him to Scotland in expiation for the Irish lives lost in battle over the dispute. At St. Comgall's Bangor, what was then the higher mathematics was studied for the reckoning of the date of Easter: Sinlan Moccu Min, scribe and abbot of Bangor 'was the first of the Irish who learned the computus by heart from a certain Greek'. Afterwards, one of his pupils in this Bangor on Cranny Island in Strangford Lough committed this knowledge to writing, and it is probable that the earliest Irish chronicle was kept in this Bangor, for the study of the computus, the making of an Easter table working out the date of Easter for some years ahead, and the first keeping of an annal in the small blank spaces of an Easter table, were inseparably connected. It was with such men that Columba was associated

6

before he undertook the Pictish mission, and when he worked among the Picts St. Comgall worked with him, probably as an interpreter.

Bede describes briefly the coming of Columba to the northern Picts (in the year 563): they were separated from the southern Picts by ridges of steep and fearful mountains. Columba converted king Bride, son of Meilochon and his people, and received the island of Iona to hold as the possession of his monastery. He had already founded one monastery at Durrow in Ireland, and he now trained the monks of Iona in the clerical, apostolic monasticism he had himself learned at Moville. Durrow, Iona and their daughter house, Lindisfarne, became schools of Irish learning, which involved at the day the writing and illumination of manuscripts. The Durrow and Lindisfarne gospel books, both illuminated altar books, are among the most famous examples of Celtic art. Both Durrow and Iona sent out colonies of monks to form daughter houses, in Ireland and Britain respectively: and over all those in Britain, Irish and Scottish, Iona had the leadership. There Columba himself, 34 years after his coming, died (in 597) and was buried, and there his body rests, says Bede, and there, in honour of its first priest abbot, no bishop rules, but always a priest abbot. Columba's successors, Bede continues, have been men notable for their continence, love of God and regular life, though they made use of dubious cycles to fix the time of the supreme feast, for, since they live on the outskirts of the world, no one has extended to them the synodal decrees governing the observance of Easter. They held to their own Easter observance for a long time, that is, till the year A.D. 715.

Long before the monks of Iona were converted to the Catholic Easter, however, they brought about the conversion of Northumbria. Æthelfrith, hammer of the Britons, died in 616; Bernicia was ruled by Edwin of Deira till 632, and the Bernician prince, Oswald, fled north for refuge. At Iona he was received, baptised and became a good Celtic Christian, attending the monks' offices and admiring their zeal for converting the pagans. While he was there Segene was priest abbot, and Aidan priest and monk.

When Oswald in 633 was able to return to his kingdom, he desired to convert his subjects. He sent to Iona, asking that a prelate should be sent him to teach his people. After the sending of a monk who had no success in this work, the monks made Aidan bishop, and sent him

to Oswald at Bamborough. Oswald gave him the island of Lindisfarne, adjoining the royal fortress of Bamborough, for his monastery,
and from there he taught the northern Angles, travelling on foot over
the northern dales and baptising in the streams. He lived like the
Irish ascetics of the 'second order of Irish saints', accepting no alms
except food, ransoming war captives and training some of them so
that they attained even to the rank of priests. He fed the poor who
thronged the open space outside king Oswald's royal hall, and on one
occasion he heard Oswald order his thegn who brought him the
cooked meat on a great silver dish to take the food to the poor, and
have the dish broken up also and given to them. So far as we know,
no minted money was circulating in Northumbria at the time, and
Oswald's action was no theatrical gesture, but the bestowal of a
royal gift made in a normal manner.

Aidan rejoiced in the king's piety, as Oswald in his bishop's: for
seventeen years, from 634 till 651, Aidan trained his young clergy,
baptised the heathen, and built up the young monastery of Lindisfarne to be another Iona, another Moville: but Oswald had only
seven years to reign, before he was killed in battle at Maserfeld in 641.
Bede wrote indignantly at the impious alliance of the Christian king
of the Britons with the heathen Penda of Mercia, which proved too
strong for Oswald at this battle. Maserfeld may perhaps be identified
with Oswestry in Shropshire, for the place name Oswestry may
reasonably derive from Oswalds-tree, or cross. This would not, however, necessarily imply the actual site of the battle, but rather the
wooden cross set in the ground where Oswald's body rested, on its
way to burial. Back in 448, when Germanus of Auxerre had died at
Ravenna, 'signa crucis' (wooden crosses) had been set up wherever
the saint's body had rested at night, on its journey back from Ravenna
to Auxerre. Oswald, as Bede says, had won his early victory at
Heavenfield (near Chollerford) in 635 by setting up a wooden cross
as 'signum', a legionary standard as it were, in a battle against the
heathen, and it is not impossible that he should have done so in the
battle against Penda: but his enemies at Maserfeld were partly
Christians and the action would have been less appropriate. The
setting up of the cross was, at the time, a kind of exorcism, regularly
used to mark a preaching station or the place of burial.

The veneration for a saint's relics goes back to the early days of
Christianity, to the days of the martyrs in particular. The Christian

teaching that those who died in Christ lived in him was vividly held, so that for the Christian there was no such thing as annihilation in death: the dead in Christ lived on and aided the living by their prayers. Those whom they had loved and helped in life they continued to love and help after death: prayer by their relics, or objects associated with them, was efficacious prayer and would certainly obtain the help of God. Pope Gregory, too, had sent relics of apostles and martyrs to Canterbury, and the Celtic church believed no less firmly in the continued love and intercession of the saints, and the efficacy of prayer by their relics. King Oswald was widely known to have fed the poor and led a saintly life, beside leading the Christian forces against the pagans, and there was great reverence for his relics. One of his hands, Bede tells us, was enclosed in a silver box, and laid up in the church of St. Peter at Lindisfarne, when it was apparently not possible to bring his body thither. When, later, the bones of the first Northumbrian bretwalda were brought on a cart to the minster of Bardney, among the Lindissi, the Anglian monks there, remembering the Bernician conquest of Deira and the Lindissi, were not, at first, willing to receive them: but, they said, they knew king Oswald to have been a saint.

Meanwhile, in Lindisfarne, Aidan lived through the 'hateful year' after Penda's victory, and for ten years after the death of the king he loved, dying on August 31, 651.

The Kentish mission to York was not the only missionary effort from the south in the years between Augustine's death and the synod of Whitby. In East Anglia, king Earpwald had been killed by a pagan soon after his conversion; but he was succeeded in 630 by his brother Sigeberht, whom Bede calls 'a most outstanding and very learned Christian'. He had received the sacraments and been taught in Gaul, and as soon as he became king he took pains that 'his whole province' should share in the sacraments with him. In this zeal he showed special favour to Felix the bishop, who had been born and ordained in Burgundy, but had come to archbishop Honorius (627–653), and on explaining his missionary desires, had been sent by him to preach to the nation of the Angles. And indeed, says Bede, this was very 'felix' for East Anglia, for they were freed from their long misery and iniquity and granted the gift of perpetual 'felicity'. He was given a see in the city of Dunwich (630) and after being bishop for seventeen years, he died there in peace.

The Gewissae, too, were converted in the period, and by another missionary from Gaul, Birinus the bishop. He had sought permission from pope Honorius to work among the Anglo-Saxons, but the papacy was always careful to safeguard the territorial rights of bishops already recognised by Rome. Birinus therefore promised Honorius to go into the interior parts of Britain where the Angles had not yet reached nor any teacher preceded him, and Honorius then commanded Asterius, archbishop of Milan, to consecrate him bishop, though as yet without a see. Bede gives no date, but it appears to have been about 633. Birinus then came to Britain, apparently landing at Southampton or farther west, for the first people he encountered were the Gewissae, ruled over by king Cynegils. The ancestors of Cynegils had originally landed near Southampton Water and been confined to that region for a long period by the pressure of Arthur's Romano-British victory and recovery. The Anglo-Saxons, however, had finally fought their way north, taking Old Sarum and the basin of the small rivers that there flow into the Wiltshire Avon, and had finally expanded north westward towards Severn mouth, and northward towards Oxfordshire, Berkshire and along the Icknield Way that led from the middle Thames to the Wash. There they had encountered and overcome other settlers, who had come from the region round Cambridge to the middle Thames. The mysterious name 'Gewissae', which Bede always used for the people of Wessex, seems to have been no more than a collective name for 'the western people' (like Visigoths for western Goths in Spain): the 'Gewissae' would have included the Saxons who had landed at Southampton Water and the Angles who had come down the Icknield Way to the Middle Thames.

In any case, the royal power of Cynegils was now focussed on the middle Thames, which was more thickly populated than the Wiltshire downs or the pleasant valleys round Old Sarum and Wilton; this focus was nearer also to the fighting frontier with the Mercians and with the Welsh. Dorchester on Thames was in this region which the Angles had long settled and Cynegils now held. Birinus made his way thither to the king from the south, and he found the Gewissae most pagan, nor was any missionary working there. But he was well received by Cynegils, who was consolidating his relations with the northern and Christian bretwalda, Oswald.

Birinus in 636 instructed Cynegils, and baptised him when Oswald came down and stood sponsor for him, afterwards marrying his good-looking daughter. (Bede says she was very beautiful.) The two kings gave Birinus the place for a see at Dorchester, and the same year Birinus there baptised Cwichelm, the king's son, who died the same year. But Birinus built churches and instructed the people, and later he baptised Cuthred, Cwichelm's son, and stood sponsor for him. How he overcame the language difficulty in his work is not known: his name appears of Germanic, possibly Frankish, origin and he may have understood some West Saxon, or taken interpreters to Britain. Frankish and English merchants were certainly trading across the Channel at the time and attending the great fair at Saint-Denis, near Paris. The fact that Felix, Birinus, and later Agilberht, all came from France to do missionary work in Britain suggests that something about English conditions was known to the Frankish bishops, and that there was some memory of the work St. Germanus had done for the British church as in an outlying province of the Gauls.

Birinus worked in Wessex till his death about 650. Cynegils had died in 643, during the ascendancy of the Mercian and heathen Penda. He was succeeded by Cenwalh, still unbaptised, though the Anglo-Saxon Chronicle (henceforth the ASC.) states under the year of his accession, 643, that 'he ordered the church at Winchester to be built'. In 644 Cenwalh was expelled by king Penda: but in 645 he was baptised, well before Penda's defeat at the Winwood in 654.

The long reign of king Cenwalh (643–672) was important in church history in the west. It saw the transference of the episcopal see from Dorchester to Winchester about 663; it maintained Christianity in Wessex till after the overthrow of Penda; it extended the influence of Roman or Gallican Christianity as against that of the Celtic Christianity of Somerset, and it saw the episcopate of another Frankish bishop less able to accommodate himself to a Saxon king than Birinus.

As to the Celtic Christians: the llan of Yniswitrin (Glastonbury) under its Celtic abbots was still held in extraordinary reverence down in the marshes of the Parret, and at the northern tip of the great crescent of the Mendips that encircled those marshes, the llan of St. Cyngar (Congresbury) seems to have been the headquarters of the abbot who became the patron saint of Somerset. Cyngar (Cunocaros) was certainly of royal blood, and according to the genealogies was the great, great grandson of Constantine, who was saluted as emperor in Britain in 408. Allowing thirty years to a life-space in the genealogies, Cyngar would seem to have been founding his llan, travelling and preaching, round about A.D. 530, perhaps some fifteen years after Arthur's victory at Mount Badon (?516). Cyngar lived, that is, in that precious respite from Anglo-Saxon attack that followed Mount Badon; like Cadoc in Brittany and Petroc in Cornwall, he and his monastic clergy kept Christianity alive from his two llans, Llancyngar (Congresbury) and Banwell, and by his preaching journeys. In his days, when every spring was held the property of some enchanting nymph, and every river and stand of trees the abode of some old Celtic god, the missionaries could not baptise or preach without making a kind of visual exorcism by sticking in the ground some rough cross, or the bishop's staff, the sign of his Christian shepherding. The *Vita* of Cyngar tells how, on one occasion, he stuck his staff into the ground and it became a yew tree: yew trees being, as all men knew, very magical trees, associated with the magic of runes, and also with cemeteries and churchyards. The yew tree miracle was, in effect, a symbol miracle: Cyngar's preaching station became a little church.

But the Romano-British respite after Mount Badon was not to last: Cyngar's life must have seen the West Saxon conquest of Salisbury in 552, and from that time Celtic Christianity in Somersetshire was in danger. The British (Welsh) people were on the fighting frontier with the pagans of Wessex, but the peril of West Saxon conquest was deferred while West Saxon forces fought in Oxfordshire, the Middle Thames and along the Icknield Way. King Cenwalh, however, stabilised his frontier in the north and advanced into Somerset, winning a victory at Bradford-on-Avon in 652. By this time, fortunately, the west Saxon court was Christian and the Celtic llans were not plundered: but Saxon settlers pushed into Somerset, and began to call Yniswitrin,[1] Glaestingabyrig and Llancyngar, Cungaresbyrig.

---

[1] 'Ynys' was Welsh for 'island': Celtic llans often had an island site: cf. Ynyspir for Caldey, the first llan of St. Illtud, etc.: Yniswitrin, down in the marshes of the Parret, was then an island site, like the village of Meare (actually built on the Meare Pool). The Latin 'vitrum' means both 'woad' and 'glass': Saxon clerics appear to have taken it to mean 'glass' in this case. 'Island' in these days was used of islands in a marsh: cf. Athelney and the 'Isle of Ely'.

In 658 Cenwalh led another campaign against the Welsh, fighting at Penselwood and driving the Welsh as far as the Parret. The war had come now to Yniswitrin, but the conquerors treated the Celtic llan with respect. Indeed, the widow of Cenwalh, after reigning herself for a year after his death, appears to have been buried in the monks' cemetery there: on the taller of the two high crosses that William of Malmesbury saw on his visit to Glastonbury, beneath a crowned figure, the words 'Here . . . Saexi' are held to refer to queen Saexburg, Cenwalh's queen. Even earlier, a West Saxon sub-king, Baldred, had made the abbey a grant of land. The respect shown by the West Saxons to Yniswitrin indicates acceptance of the belief that the church there was of very early and therefore of apostolic or quasi-apostolic origin. Eusebius in his *Ecclesiastical History* had followed up all the sources known to him in indicating the places where the apostles had preached: but where he had no written source to rely on, he had fallen back on the tradition of 'our fathers' that the twelve apostles had divided up the world by lot into preaching spheres, and departed each to the sphere allotted to him. Isidore of Seville had followed him. While there is evidence that Gildas and perhaps other Celtic scholars had read Rufinus' translation of Eusebius' history and derived thence a belief in the apostolic allocation of preaching spheres by lot, yet such knowledge was not needed when all knew of the apostles that 'their sound has gone out to all lands and their words to the end of the earth'. They accepted from the Celts the tradition of the apostolic foundation of Glastonbury.

Birinus died in c. 650, and Agilberht the Frank succeeded him at Dorchester: his career was to affect the church in Northumbria as well as that in Wessex. He had studied in southern Ireland, where the modern and Roman cycle of nineteen years for determining the date of Easter was followed, and he had been consecrated, probably as a missionary bishop, in Gaul. He travelled to Cenwalh's court, and was given the see of Dorchester on Birinus' death. Cenwalh, however, found his speech unintelligible, for he himself spoke Saxon only, and to rid himself of Agilberht, he divided his kingdom into two bishoprics, without consulting Agilberht. The latter was ordered to remain in his see of Dorchester, and king Cenwalh, by this time ruling mainly from Winchester, 'subintroduced' another bishop ordained in Gaul, by name Wini, in 660. Agilberht was gravely displeased, and in 660 (ASC.) departed from Cenwalh: he was later made bishop of Paris, and there died. Wini remained Cenwalh's bishop for some years and was then driven out and fled for refuge to the king of Mercia, who by this time controlled London: Wini bought the see of London from him, Bede says, 'at a price'. Meanwhile the West Saxons remained for some years without a bishop.

There must, from place name evidence, have been many pagan sanctuaries in Wessex, and many pagans left as late as the synod of Whitby. There must have been also groups of Britons, for Welsh was still spoken in parts of Wiltshire as late as Domesday Book. The Wallops, up on the downs, were Welsh villages, and no one knows when the first Christian church was built at Britford: the fine Saxon church, parts of which remain today, at this once Brittonic village, was built at a much later date. Altogether, Wiltshire, with its great pagan circle up at Stonehenge, its recollections of Thor in Thundersley, Woden in Wednesbury and so many other pagan names: with its groups of Welsh people, and now its episcopal sees at Dorchester and Winchester, must have been difficult to convert in the days of Birinus, Agilberht, and Wini. Cenwalh ended the years when Wessex was without a bishop by mentally connecting his ill fortune in battle with his having expelled Agilberht: and after negotiating with him at Paris, received Agilberht's nephew Hlothere as bishop of the Gewissae.

The difficulties of the Christian converts in the various kingdoms were thus connected with the military predominance at different periods of two pagan chieftains, first Rædwald and then Penda. Bede calls Rædwald, but not Penda, bretwalda: yet Penda defeated various under kings between his accession (?626 or 632) and his defeat on the Winwood in 654. While Christianity in Northumbria was heavily defeated and in Wessex only struggling, in Kent and in East Anglia the kings were Christians and protected its growth.

In East Anglia, Earpwald's brother Sigeberht received baptism while an exile in Gaul, aided bishop Felix to establish in his country those institutions which he had known in Gaul, particularly the training of boys in the school of the bishop's familia, where they had teachers and masters as in the manner of Canterbury: from the slender beginnings of such institutions the Anglo-Saxons, with their oral culture, were made free of the world of Greco-Roman written learning. Sigeberht himself, desiring the service of the heavenly king and entry into the monastic, Greco-Roman world, built himself a minster and became a monk, leaving his kingdom to one who had been under king of a part of it before. When Penda, however, advanced against East Anglia with a great army, Sigeberht left his minster to fight with his countrymen. He and the new king were both killed in battle around the year 634.

Anna, the next king of the East Angles, ruled some nineteen years, dying in 654. Bede praises him as a pious king, with a pious family. Two of his daughters became nuns in France, and his eldest daughter married Earconberht, king of Kent (640–664). In Kent, under their leadership, all idols were ordered to be destroyed and the Lenten fast kept. Meanwhile, under Anna's patronage and with his help, the Burgundian bishop Felix worked at Dunwich, while an Irish missionary, Fursey, worked in a monastery, granted to him earlier by Sigeberht, on the site of an old fort, beautifully situated between the woods and the sea (near Yarmouth), and called by the Angles, Cnobheresburg. Anna and the nobles provided Fursey with better buildings for his monastery and ornaments for his church. Here you had, as it were, a Finnian of Clonard transported to Norfolk, while a bishop like Caesarius of Arles taught his young clerics in Suffolk: and no doubt with different Easters. But to the spatially separate groups of Christians, different Easter dates did not matter much: and both teachers had been set there by the king.

Till the strenuous Penda was killed by the forces of king Oswiu at the battle of the Winwood, in 654, the struggle with paganism was too great for efforts to unite Celtic and Canterbury Christians under the obedience of Rome to succeed. In the ten years following the Winwood, the collapse of pagan military power in the midlands gave Northumbria safety, and made for easier communication with the south of England. Peada, Penda's son, had become Christian without open opposition from his father before Penda's death: that he had some knowledge of continental civilisation is indicated by his issue of the first royal-minted sceattas or pennies. The word 'penny' is now held to be derived from the Latin word for a piece of 'weighed' metal. The impulse to copy the more advanced civilisation of the south was to reach Northumbria under king Oswiu: and to move him to bring his country into line with the Mediterranean, Roman Christianity that already held Canterbury.

CHAPTER V

THE FUSION OF CELTIC AND LATIN CHRISTIANITIES AT WHITBY, AND AFTER

IN the long period before the submission of the Celtic Christians to the obedience of Rome and Canterbury, and in the arguments at the synod of Whitby itself, it is notable that the question of the ultimate obedience of western Christians to the see of Peter was scarcely raised. The Celtic missionaries and the continental missionaries worked in different local areas, and this minimised opportunities for discussion and argument. Moreover, the Celtic doctors, abbots and bishops held the faith as apostolic and the church as one, and reverenced those who went on pilgrimage to holy places, in Gaul, in Rome, in Palestine. Abbot Adomnan of Iona was visited by the Frankish bishop Arculf, who made a pilgrimage to the holy places in Palestine: they compared notes, and Adomnan wrote a book about the same holy places. The monks of Lindisfarne imbued their young guest thegn Wilfrid with a desire to visit Gaul for its places of learning and Rome as the holy, apostolic see: the place of the martyrdom of the apostles, the place where (as St. Leo said) Peter still spoke in Peter's see. There was no wish to keep the young and noble inquirer at Lindisfarne: it was Lindisfarne that sent him away to learn the rules of church discipline where they could best be learnt. There was no hostility, no suspicion, of the see of Peter: the concept of territorial jurisdiction in the church was almost unknown to the Scots: Rome was a place of pilgrimage, very holy, very distant. There was not even, in the north, very great hostility to Canterbury. Young scholars from the northern Angles visited monasteries in Ireland, visited Iona: Bede always wrote with admiration of Scottish saints.

In the south, however, hostility between the Welsh Christians and the church of Canterbury seems to have been acute. Bede, using Canterbury sources, tells how, when the Irish Dagan visited archbishop Lawrence, he would neither eat with him nor enter his 'hospitium': Dagan was an Irish bishop and he seems to have visited Lawrence to confer with him about the manner of life of the Welsh and Scottish (Irish) Christians. Even the story in Bede's history which seems most inspired by anti-Celtic prejudice he seems to have received from Canterbury: for he tells it as evidence that the British bishops and abbots were wrong in refusing Augustine's request that they should co-operate with him in converting the pagans. He says that the heathen king of the northern Angles, Æthelfrith, marched against the Welsh to Chester (616): and fought a coalition of British princes, who had summoned the monks from Bangor Iscoed to come and pray for them. These were quite un-armed, and stayed near the field of battle, flinging their arms to heaven like the old 'orantes' on the walls of Lullingstone. Æthel-frith, presumably, regarded them as dangerous magicians, and had some 1,200 unarmed monks massacred: 'and thus', said Bede, with a complacency derived from Canterbury rather than the northern church, 'was the prophecy of the holy bishop Augustine fulfilled, which he had made long before he was taken to the heavenly king-dom, that those perfidious ones who had scorned to receive the counsel of everlasting salvation offered them by him, should feel the vengeance of temporal destruction'. A comment for which Bede has long been blamed, probably overblamed.

Even in the south, however, hostility between the Celtic and the continental Christians had been abating: in East Anglia in particular, missionaries of both sides had worked without mutual hostility. Open union of the Roman and Celtic Christians could only come, of course, on the initiative of the bretwalda: and the bretwalda was, in 664, king Oswiu, the victor of the Winwood, a well-instructed Celtic Christian. When he summoned a synod, or witan, to meet in the double minster at Streoneshalch (Whitby), he had probably already decided to guide its deliberations towards acceptance of the rulings of the see of Peter: no one questioned that for all Christians the church was apostolic, and one.

The questions connected with the accordance of usage in the churches of Celtic and Roman missions had been ventilated for many years before the synod of Whitby, but not, apparently, as directly one of submission to Rome or Canterbury. The points in dispute were discussed on their own merits, and the authority of the Petrine see invoked, at the synod itself, to end the differences of practice.

As to the points in dispute: the Britons apparently used certain differences in the ministry of baptism, which Augustine urged them to give up for the practice of the Roman and apostolic church: but what these divergent customs were is not known. Augustine, at his second conference with the British bishops, urged only that they would renounce these and co-operate with him in converting the heathen: 'the other things which you do contrary to our custom, we will suffer unruffled (*aequanimiter*)'.

But between Augustine's days and those of king Oswiu, two other points of difference had caused practical difficulty, not for their spiritual significance, but because they were outward signs of a difference of obedience: the shape of the tonsure and the dating of Easter.

The Irish monks, by older custom, obtaining also in the east, shaved the front part of the head, only: while the Romans shaved the top part of the head, leaving a tonsure in the shape of a crown. Large and well-informed houses like Iona had by now conformed to western usage, but the older custom prevailed in many Celtic houses.

The date for the celebration of Easter was of greater importance.[1] Bede explains the Celtic usage on this point, and its divergence from that of Catholic Christendom, with clearness and charity; the Scots, he said, did not, as some say, keep Easter day ever on the fourteenth day of the month, reckoning like the Jews (and therefore to be termed Quartodecimans); but they failed nevertheless to celebrate in the right week. For they knew that Christians always celebrate the Resurrection on the first day of the week, because Christ rose on the first day of the week. They did not lack the grace of charity, but they did this like barbarians and peasants, because they had not learned when that first day of the week should come. Bede was trying to emphasise the holiness of these Scottish monks while explaining their perverse misdating of Easter: but he was wrong in calling them 'barbari et rustici': they were not unlearned men, but they were using dating cycles which the church of Rome had used a century earlier and had discarded.

The dating of Easter had long engaged the interest of mathematicians and astronomers, for it involved the use of an astronomical

[1] See Plummer, 'Excursus on the Paschal controversy', HE. vol. ii, p. 348.

calendar, to be calculated theoretically on the concept of the Ptolemaic solar system, and by observation. Hundreds of years earlier the men who built Stonehenge planned to mark the summer solstice by the casting of a shadow on an altar at sunrise: had the sun gone round the earth in exactly 365 days, they could, by counting the days between one summer solstice and the next, have constructed a calendar. But it did not.

The attempt to reckon the exact length of the solar year was thus a very early problem in applied mathematics, and it appears to have been studied with most success in Egypt. There the whole process of cultivation depended on the yearly flooding of the Nile, which could be counted upon to arrive with some punctuality. It was necessary to know the day on which to expect the flooding, and therefore to have a calendar. As early as the sixth century B.C. the Egyptian priests had worked out the length of the year to within two hours, and their observation of the stars was not unaided. Alexandria became a great school of mathematicians, and when Islam conquered Syria and Persia Alexandria had contact with the Syrian astronomers of Harran, where observation and a cult of the stars contributed to greater precision in the calendar. But for many earlier centuries work had been going on, in the schools of Alexandria, Athens and Rome, to minimise the effects which even a small error in the calculation of the yearly calendar could produce. Various canons and tables were framed to show the period required for the sun, lunar months and phases of the moon to return to the same relative position as they had had when the period began. The determination of the date of Easter involved knowledge of church practice in the past: but whatever the historical practices had been, all involved knowing the date of the spring equinox, and this involved a particular calculation of the solar year, and foreknowledge of the waxing and waning of the moon. Which was a matter of mathematics.

As to the history of the practice of the church: the council of Nicaea, 325, had laid down that Easter must be kept after the celebration of the Jewish Pask, on the first day of the week, at earliest on the fifteenth day of the lunar month after the spring equinox: it condemned the Quartodecimans, who kept Easter on the fourteenth day of the month regardless of whether it was a Sunday or not.

This left the settlement of calendar and equinox to the mathematicians, who evolved successively better 'cycles', which led to difference of observance between churches where communication of knowledge was easy, and distant ones where it was not. In 457 Rome favoured the cycle of Victor of Aquitaine, and about 525 that of Dionysius Exiguus, a Syrian monk who lived at Rome but followed the mathematicians of Alexandria; Gaul continued to use the cycle of Victor. The Dionysian reckoning was based on a cycle of nineteen years and a spring equinox on March 21st, and by this cycle Easter Sunday would fall between the fifteenth and twenty-first day of the month. Augustine brought a table based on this cycle to Canterbury: but the Irish and Britons were still using the older cycle of 84 years, which Rome had long abandoned. This 84 year cycle the Britons attributed, wrongly in fact, to Anatolius of Laodicea, a scholar praised by St. Jerome. By this cycle, Easter might fall between the fourteenth and twentieth day of the month, thus on occasion coinciding with the Jewish Pask: and the equinox was reckoned from March 25. The Irish missionary Columbanus, however, followed loosely at Luxeuil the cycle of Victor of Aquitaine, keeping an Easter Day rather Irish than Roman. His vigorous defence of his right to do so in Gaul brought the whole matter to public notice from c. 603, by which time he had protested to the pope and to the Gallic bishops. The question was academically difficult, and he got no answer.

In 628 or 629, however, the southern Irish were in doubt about their practice of Easter dating: under the learned abbot Cummian they held a synod at Magh-Lene, and sent a deputation to Rome to seek information. The envoys returned after three years, reporting that Greek, Egyptian and Syrian Christians kept their Easter at the same time, while the Celtic Easter was celebrated four weeks later; after which the southern Irish conformed to the Roman usage. The northern Irish and Segene the abbot of Iona (623–652) were convinced, however, either by the letter of Cummian or one of the pope-elect John IV, when the latter reproved them for willingness on occasion to celebrate Easter on the same day as the Jews: i.e. of using the 84 year cycle. It was no new question which was raised at the synod of Streoneshalch (Whitby), nor one causing difficulty only in Britain. Bede states unequivocally that the synod was held in A.D. 664, and the most recent research shows that it must indeed have been held in the first half of the period Christmas 663 to Christmas

664 (in Bede's reckoning the year began on Christmas Day).[1] In that year, Easter fell for the Celts on April 14, 664, and for the Romans on April 21, 664. The eclipse which Bede mentions as occurring in the same year as the death of archbishop Deusdedit, who died in the year of the synod, was on May 1, 664. It was total in Northumbria.

King Oswiu of Northumbria was inclined, apparently, to accept the Roman view of the Paschal question. He summoned a synod of bishops and clergy to meet under the presidency of himself and his court in the double minster of Hilda, great-niece of king Edwin and abbess of Hartlepool (648–657) before she founded the great house of Streoneshalch.

The minster at Whitby has been excavated, and found to consist of many small houses and cells, within an enclosing hedge or wall. The abbess, novices, the nuns, the sick, the old nuns, the monastic clergy in their groups, must have had separate 'cellae': there is nothing, however, to show a rigid spacial division between men and women, or whether or not they used the same chapel. There were indeed, double minsters in Gaul, visited by English princesses, and St. Bridget's monastery at Kildare appears to have been double in the seventh century. Pens, pen-cases and spindles have all been found beneath the surface at Whitby: perhaps the nuns used the pens as well as the spindles. In any case, Whitby had a farm and beasts cared for by peasants: there was food and lodging for a synod, and for the king and his court.

To the minster came Oswiu, baptised and taught by the Scots, his son Alchfrith, under king of Deira, Alchfrith's friend and adviser, abbot Wilfrid of Ripon; and their friend bishop Agilberht of the West Saxons, who after many years still found English an impossible language. There came, too, Colman, bishop of Lindisfarne and his

---

[1] See for an exhaustive discussion of the complex question of dating this synod, coupled as it is with the date of archbishop Deusdedit's death, Paul Grosjean's 'La Date du colloque de Whitby', in the *Analecta Bollandiana*, lxxviii (1960). The confusion as between 663 and 664 has arisen because Bede reckoned the date of Deusdedit's death in years, months and days from the date of his consecration: he used the Canterbury list of consecrations and deaths of archbishops, which did not, of course, use the Annus Incarnationis for the records of early archbishops, but reckoned in years, months and days one from another. Bede apparently miscopied for the date of Deusdedit's consecration that of the archbishop following him, archbishop Theodore: but though such a day could have been held suitable in the year of Theodore's consecration, in the year alleged by Bede for Deusdedit's consecration it fell on a Friday, and could not. Bede's slip explains how he came to say that the synod of Whitby was in 664, and was in the same year as the death of Deusdedit, which apparently conflicts with the Canterbury record of his episcopate.

Scottish clergy, and the venerable bishop Cedd, ready to act as interpreter; James the Deacon, who had remained after Paulinus left, was also there, and Romanus, queen Æthelberga's chaplain from Kent.

King Oswiu opened the synod: Those, he said, who awaited one kingdom in the heavens and served the one God should have one rule of life: and he asked Colman his bishop to explain the Easter rule he used. In the long argument between Colman and Wilfrid, who explained the Roman Easter and its authority, and not without some contempt for Celtic isolation and obstinacy, discussion turned at first on the historical authority for the practice, but finally arrived at the mathematics of the matter: the dating of the spring equinox and the use of the 84 or 19 year cycle. Wilfrid denied that the Celts could, in fact, allege the authority of Anatolius for their cycle: Columba too, whom they said they imitated, he remarked, might well be among those who claimed to prophesy and cast out devils, and to whom the Lord should say in the Judgment: I knew you not. He ended his address less harshly: 'And even though this Columba of yours, and indeed he is ours too, was a saint: how can he be compared with the prince of the apostles, to whom the Lord said: "Thou art Peter . . . and I will give thee the keys of the kingdom of heaven" '.

Nor did Colman, at Oswiu's inquiry, deny that Peter was indeed the doorkeeper of the gate of heaven: and Oswiu, smiling a little, rejoined that never would he contend with such a gate keeper, for he too would some day come to the gates of the heavenly kingdom, seeking entrance: the Roman observance received the royal approbation.

For the bretwalda, and especially his kingdom of Northumbria, acceptance of the practice of the Roman see and amity with Canterbury was a matter settled: but even here the details of the settlement had to be worked out: some bishops and abbots would accept, some would not accept, the new ruling. Away in Wales, the Roman Easter was not accepted for more than a hundred years.

At Lindisfarne, Colman gave up his see and returned to Iona; Tuda, one of Aidan's pupils and ready to accept the new practice, went to Lindisfarne and died almost at once in the plague; after a long vacancy Eata, abbot of Melrose, became bishop of Lindisfarne. Northern Ireland remained conservative till 704, when Adamnan, abbot of Iona and a convert to the Roman reckoning, gained the

7

acceptance of the Irish Bangor: but Iona itself, the house of Columba, could not be entreated to change its usage till 716. Abbot Ceolfrith of Bede's monastery of Jarrow was a great exponent of the Dionysian cycle and the Roman Easter: he corresponded with king Naiton (Necktan IV), who reigned over the Picts from 706–732, and won him over; but great divisions followed in his kingdom. Aldhelm of Malmesbury won over the Britons of Cornwall, and Elfod, bishop in Bangor, won over the south Welsh in 768 and also, before his death in 796, the Gauls who followed Columbanus.

The consequent difficulties of bishop Wilfrid, bishop Chad and archbishop Theodore must all be attributed, at least in part, to the confused situation after the synod of 664. The bubonic plague, which came from Asia by sea, and swept western Europe in the summers of 663 and 664, cleared the stage by ending the life of many bishops and political leaders: but it did not clear the stage of king Oswiu, whose ideas about the sphere of a bishop were still patriarchial rather than territorial. In those dreadful years, when the plague raged like the Black Death of 1349, there died, beside Tuda of Lindisfarne, Alchfrith, sub-king of Deira and Deusdedit, archbishop of Canterbury, very soon after the synod. King Oswiu had now no bishop for his court at Lindisfarne; before his death, his son Alchfrith had desired the promotion of his friend Wilfrid. How far either he or his father conceived of Wilfrid as the future holder of a territorial see, and which, is not clear: landed provision for his maintenance would, of course, have to be made. In any case, Alchfrith had died; Wilfrid went off to Gaul to secure valid episcopal ordination, rejecting that of Scottish bishops as dubious, and was consecrated at Compiègne with great splendour to the see of York. Like Paulinus earlier, he carried out the instruction of pope Gregory about the northern metropolitan see, but Deira was now an under kingdom, and York not Oswiu's capital.

It was, indeed, unlikely that Oswiu would acquiesce in letting the bretwalda's chief bishop take his see in an under kingdom. The bretwalda's bishop must be near his court, the relationship was personal: it can hardly have occurred to Oswiu that his see should not be at Lindisfarne, if, indeed, he thought in terms of territorial sees at all. Before Wilfrid returned, Oswiu designated Chad, pupil of Aidan, brother of Cedd, and abbot of Lastingham, to be his bishop, and sent him to Canterbury for consecration. Archbishop Deusdedit, however, was himself dead and the see not filled: Chad was consecrated by Wini, bishop of the West Saxons, and two British bishops. Wilfrid, on his return, finding the new under king of Deira, Ecgfrith,[1] hostile to him at York, returned to his monastery at Ripon, building up the congregation as abbot and having as bishop episcopal charge of the surrounding countryside, no boundaries yet defined. In Gaul, where no bishop was consecrated without title to a territorial see, he might fairly claim to have been unjustly kept from his see of York: in Northumbria the episcopate was hardly yet regarded as territorial. Wilfrid himself, indeed, had not shaken off the early, missionary, Celtic, concept of the episcopate: at different times he worked among the pagans of Sussex, and, later, of Holland: he consecrated clergy for whatever king asked him.

One of the most moving biographies of the early middle ages is that of Wilfrid by Eddius his priest, surnamed Stephanus. It is biassed, as giving the views of an admiring and devout follower of Wilfrid, and particularly unfair to archbishop Theodore; but it gives an invaluable contemporary picture of church life at the end of the seventh century, both in 'the northern regions of Britain' and at the apostolic see. In it there are casual references to some barbarous events in Anglo-Saxon and Frankish life: and to the old processes of Roman law still distilling in the Roman scrinium, where records are kept, and justice is done before a synod with Roman care and prudence. There are references to saints and miracles, to bishops and their evangelistic work, and to how their nomination and maintenance depend on the will of the Anglo-Saxon kings, often hostile to one another. Eddius is worth quoting: partly because, while he thought himself to be telling the life story of his hero, he was also recounting the long struggle of the Celtic Christians in the north with the continentally-inspired Christians who looked to Canterbury and Rome: a struggle against being knit together as one church in Britain, part of the western patriarchate under the apostolic see.

Eddius then says of Wilfrid that as a boy he was pious and of 'most acute mind'; his stepmother was harsh to him, and he left his

---

[1] Oswiu's children included Alchfrith, Ecgfrith, Ælfwine and Aldfrith, not all by the same mother.

father's hall to serve queen Eanflæd as a thegn. He went to Lindis-farne at her request to look after an old and paralysed noble, who sought the monastic life there: and 'he learned the whole psalter by heart, as well as several books'. After a few years, he desired to go on pilgrimage to the see of the apostle Peter, and his master in the monastery encouraged him. The queen commended him to the king of Kent, who sent him on his way in company with another Anglian pilgrim, Biscop Baducing, the future founder of Jarrow. At Lyons, archbishop Dalfinus found Wilfrid so gentle and intelligent a guest, that he desired to adopt him and marry him to his own niece; for Wilfrid was as yet no clerk: but Wilfrid persisted that his desire was for Rome, the see of Peter. He reached Rome, and prayed in an oratory dedicated to St. Andrew, where the book of the four Gospels rested on the altar, that he might read and teach the gospel among the nations. In Rome at that day, it fell to the archdeacon to instruct the younger clergy and archdeacon Boniface taught him the text of the four Gospels and the true Easter rule, and much else: he taught him as though he were his own son. And Wilfrid set out to return to his own country through Gaul.

At Lyons, however, he was received with such affection by arch-bishop Dalfinus, that he became for three years a member of his familia, receiving from him the clerk's blessing and tonsure in shape of a crown. In 658, however, in the struggles of the Merovingian kings, nine bishops were murdered and one of them Dalfinus: Eddius attributes this wickedness to queen Balthild of Neustria; but, though she was involved in Merovingian fratricidal struggles, she was held in the north of France a very pious lady, the patroness of the abbey of Saint-Denis, and the nunnery of Chelles. She was also Anglo-Saxon by birth, and Wilfrid escaped ecclesiastical massacre and was able to return to Britain. He may have crossed to Southamp-ton, for he became known to Cenwalh, king of the West Saxons, and was commended by him to Cenwalh's friend Alchfrith, as yet under-king of Deira (658). Alchfrith granted Wilfrid a small estate at Stanford, and 30 hides (or family lands) for a monastery at Ripon; in days when information was so scarce, Alchfrith loved to listen to the traveller returned from Rome, and much better informed about the niceties of ecclesiastical discipline than any man in the northern kingdom. When bishop Agilbert visited Oswiu and Alchfrith, he ordained Wilfrid priest.

On the difficult matter of Wilfrid's consecration to York, and the royal obstacles placed in the way of his setting up his see there: Eddius says that the kings chose him to fill 'the vacant see', 'with the advice of their wise men', after Whitby. Whether the 'vacant see' was Lindisfarne, vacant by the death of Tuda, or the now long vacant see of York, Eddius does not state; he says that Wilfrid, when he could not take possession of his see at York, returned to his own abbey at Ripon, and lived there for three years. Wulfhere of Mercia made him many grants of land for small minsters, and he ordained many priests for Wulfhere and not a few deacons. He introduced the Benedictine rule for his monastic familia at Ripon, and brought to the minster masons and artisans of almost every kind; his monks used the church chant, and his singers were named Ædda (Eddius his biographer) and Æona. In these days the chant was still only written as an ascending or descending stroke over the words in the manuscript, and nearly everything depended on the memory of the cantor, for the Byzantine musical notation had not reached western Europe. 'Sounds', wrote Isidore of Seville (d. 636), 'must be held in the memory of man, because they cannot be written.' At Ripon, and in his later minster of Hexham, Wilfrid built stone churches such as he had seen in Gaul and Italy, with crypts, apsidal ends, small stone altars, and illuminated gospel books laid upon them. The Benedictine rule itself provides for the saying of the day and night offices, with appropriate psalms and canticles; but apart from the great feasts, Ripon must have kept its own calendar for saints days, together with the columns of its Easter table, for a Dionysian Easter table was one of the things Wilfrid would most certainly have brought with him from Rome.

As to the small minsters which he was able to found, there is no evidence whether they were clerical or monastic; Wilfrid as bishop was responsible for teaching the faith in the countryside, and making the sacraments available to those baptised. His own large minsters would have kept the Benedictine rule, which stresses enclosure: but it would seem likely that some pastoral work must have been done, both by these monks, and especially by those of the smaller minsters.

'In three years', says Eddius, 'archbishop Theodore came from Kent to the king of Deira and Bernicia, bringing with him the decrees of the apostolic see from which he had been sent.' He deposed Chad, as having been ordained by the Quartodecimans,[1] and installed Wilfrid in the see of York. Eddius was a less learned man than Bede, or less fair, and unable to distinguish between Quartodecimans and those who celebrated Easter from the fourteenth to the twentieth of the moon, therefore occasionally coinciding with the Jewish Pask; he always calls the Celts Quartodecimans, which they were not. Chad in his humility accepted re-ordination, and an episcopal see at Lichfield, to serve king Wulfhere and Mercia.

Eddius then describes with joy Wilfrid's restoration of the church at York (669), begun by Paulinus but now half-ruined and open to the rain and the birds. Wilfrid restored the roof-ridges and covered them with lead; he glazed the windows and washed the walls. He adorned the altar with vessels and hangings, and he endowed the church with land. At the same time he continued the building of the church of Ripon, with its various columns and side aisles: he had a wonderful gospel book made and illuminated, some pages being dyed purple and written in letters of gold; for the altar books he had a golden book-chest made, set with precious stones. The kings Ecgfrith and Ælfwine, with sub-kings, reeves and abbots, came to the great dedication service.

Nor was Wilfrid's work confined to Bernicia and Deira. King Ecgfrith defeated the Picts, who had given trouble on his northern frontier, and Wilfrid was given an estate at Hexham, near the

---

[1] Theodore accepted Wilfrid's claim to the see of York, and re-ordained Chad before sending him to the see of Lichfield, which though not designated as primatial in pope Gregory's scheme for the English episcopate (see p. 227), would be, in fact, a quasi-primatial see for the king of the Mercians. The reason for Theodore's re-ordination of Chad is not clear. Pope Gregory had committed 'all the bishops' of Britain to the charge of Augustine, apparently accepting them as bishops, if uninstructed: 'All the bishops of the Britains (a reference to the five provinces of Britain of the Diocletianic reorganisation, Britannia prima, etc.), we commit to your charge, that the uninstructed may be instructed, the weak strengthened by persuasion, and the perverse corrected by authority'. Similarly, in 640, the pope elect, John IV, wrote to five Celtic bishops, addressing them by name as bishops: there was thus no general denial by the Roman see of the orders of Celtic bishops. Archbishop Theodore, however, had a special problem in the recognition of Chad for the new see of Lichfield: there should be no element of doubt about the consecration of a bishop likely to be called on to consecrate other bishops. It is most unlikely that Theodore was dissatisfied with the rite used by the Celts for consecration; if they used an anointing as well as the blessing by the three bishops, this would not have invalidated the rite. It is much more likely that Theodore (and his notary, Titillus) would have found dangerous the lack of records kept by the ordaining bishops: continental bishops recorded the succession of bishops in their see back to the founder, and his consecration, most carefully. An even further source of doubt would be the occasional plurality of bishops in a monastery: which would be the apostolic bishop? Most of all: how could an apostolic bishop be subject to a priest abbot?

border, for a new minster. There he built a stone church, 'with crypts of wonderfully dressed stone' for the relics, columns and side aisles, high walls, and winding passages with spiral steps: 'we have not heard of any other house on this side of the Alps built on such a scale'. Bishop Acca (he became bishop of Hexham in 705) provided ornaments of gold and silver for the church, and decorated the altars with purple and silk.

Here Eddius breaks off to tell with indignation how Wilfrid was driven from his see of York (678) by the envy of Ecgfrith's new queen (Æthelthryth had by now departed to a nunnery, first Coldingham, then Ely): he says that archbishop Theodore had been bribed by Ecgfrith to humiliate Wilfrid. It was undoubtedly Theodore's policy to set up new bishoprics in the northern kingdoms, and for such a purpose the obtaining of estates for the new bishops was essential; Ecgfrith was now hostile to Wilfrid and willing to co-operate with Theodore, but the allegation of bribery is partisan and improbable. 'In the absence of our bishop he consecrated,' writes Eddius indignantly, 'irregularly and contrary to all precedent, three bishops who had been picked up elsewhere and were not subjects of the bishop's parochia.' He consecrated them by himself. Wilfrid remonstrated about this with king and archbishop, asking for what sin or crime they had, like robbers, defrauded him of the grants of earlier kings? And Ecgfrith and Theodore made him public reply, before all the people: 'We ascribe to you no sin or crime: but we change not our appointed judgments'. Wilfrid exclaimed that he had been condemned through malice: within a year, they should weep bitterly who now laughed. And that day twelvemonth the slain body of king Ælfwine was borne back to York: and Ecgfrith never gained another victory in battle. Wilfrid went off to appeal to the apostolic see, and Theodore installed his new bishops.

Wilfrid, however, did not go to Rome direct. His ship had a prosperous voyage to Friesland, where the people were pagan, but Aldgisl their king was willing to receive him and let him preach the faith. He taught them about baptism and the remission of sins and of life everlasting in the resurrection; his teaching was clearly confirmed in the eyes of the pagans, for the catch of fish was unusually large and the harvest very good; nearly all the chiefs were baptised and very many common people. Wilfrid indeed laid the foundations of the faith there, 'and his spiritual son who was brought up at Ripon,

Willibrord the bishop, is still building upon it, very laboriously'.

Wilfrid then made his way to Italy, by the aid of Dagobert II, king of the Franks, who had been an exile in Ireland, and recalled through Wilfrid's help in 676. When Wilfrid reached Rome, and had been received by pope Agatho at a synod held in the 'Constantinian basilica' (St. John Lateran), he found that an embassy with letters from archbishop Theodore had preceded him. He was admitted to the 'secretarium' of the basilica, and sent in his petition to the pope and synod, lamenting that the archbishop 'and other bishops at that time assembling with him' had robbed him of the see which he had canonically held for ten years: 'they have preferred themselves to be bishops in my church, not merely one but three of them'. He asked that the usurpers be driven out 'from my old sees, over which I have been ruling'; but if it pleased the archbishop and Wilfrid's fellow bishops to increase the number of bishops, 'let them choose such from our own clergy'. To which the apostolic father replied, decreeing that Wilfrid should receive back his bishopric within its old limits, appointing those whom he should choose as his fellow bishops, and seeking consecration for them from the archbishop.

Wilfrid therefore, before he set out from Rome, spent several days going round the shrines to pray there: and he obtained a great many holy relics, 'writing down what each of the relics was and to whom it belonged', and he acquired many other adornments for the house of God. Then he travelled through France, narrowly escaping trouble because Dagobert, whom he had befriended, had been murdered; and when he reached England, he presented pope Agatho's synodal letter, sealed with its leaden bull, to the king (680); but the contents were not acceptable to Ecgfrith, and his adherents execrably questioned the bull, saying the writings had been purchased for a price. Then Ecgfrith despised the writing, and ordered Wilfrid to be imprisoned and allowed no visits from his friends; and the queen took away his precious reliquary and kept it in her chamber or wore it round her neck when she was riding in her chariot. The king's magnates then took Wilfrid to Osfrith, the reeve of the king's tun, to be kept in prison. And so he did: till his wife Æbbe was suddenly paralysed by a stroke, and then he ran hastily to Wilfrid, praying him to cure her: like Peter's wife's mother, Æbbe was healed and ministered to them.

The reeve then sent to Ecgfrith, asking that he might be allowed to release Wilfrid; but the king, enraged, had him sent instead into the charge of the reeve of distant Dunbar, away in Pictland. There he might have remained, but queen Iurminburg fell into an illness when, travelling through the northern cities, tuns and hamlets, she put up at the nunnery of Coldingham, whose abbess was Æbbe, king Oswiu's sister. The most wise abbess saw how ill Iurminburg was, and she warned the king that this calamity was due to his evil treatment of Wilfrid: Ecgfrith was her nephew and she spoke plainly: let him give back the holy relics which the queen had taken from Wilfrid's neck, to her own destruction, and 'carried them about from town to town, as if she were the ark of God'. If the king would not give him back his bishopric, 'at least let him depart from your kingdom with his followers, and go wherever he wills'. And the king obeyed his aunt, the holy mother, and let Wilfrid have back the holy relics and go free (681), and the queen recovered.

Wilfrid went out of Northumbria into exile. First, a friendly reeve of Æthelred, king of Mercia, sheltered him, and gave him land for a small minster: 'his monks possess it to this day'. But Æthelred's queen was sister to king Ecgfrith, and they soon ordered the reeve to drive out Wilfrid, so that they might keep the peace with Ecgfrith; and when Wilfrid went to Wessex, the queen of that king was sister to Iurminburg, and he was again driven out. So he came at length to the kingdom of Sussex, where king and people were still pagan, and at his preaching the king and many of his subjects were converted. The king 'made gentle and pious by God', gave his own estate for an episcopal see, and added to it 87 hides in Selsey, for the maintenance of Wilfrid and his brethren, and not long after (686) a prince of Cerdic's line, till now in exile in the Chilterns and the Weald of Kent, came to Wilfrid and sought his friendship; he won the kingship of the West Saxons in battle, and took Wilfrid as his chief counsellor, as another Joseph to the king of Egypt.

Wilfrid's fortunes had now turned, for king Ecgfrith was dead, killed in battle against the Picts, and Aldfrith, a new king, reigned in the northern parts. Archbishop Theodore had no longer to reckon with Wilfrid's most bitter enemy, and he was himself now old, and, according to Eddius, ill. He sent for Wilfrid, asked his forgiveness for any wrong he might have done him, and wrote letters to king Aldfrith and Æthelred, king of the Mercians, adjuring them to make peace with Wilfrid and fulfil the command of the apostolic see.

First Æthelred received him and restored to him the Mercian minsters he had founded: and then (c. 687) Aldfrith summoned him from exile and gave him, first his minster at Hexham with all its lands, and then the episcopal see at York, and the minster at Ripon: and to do this 'he drove the strange bishops out'. (These were the bishops Theodore had appointed in 678: Bosa at York, Eata for Bernicia and Eadheath for Lindsey. The setting up of all these new sees had been tentative, and involved only the establishment of an ecclesiastical focus: no boundaries to the bishop's parochia were traced. A bishop was appointed to a folk or a king, rather than a territory.)

Peace between Wilfrid and the kings of Northumbria and Mercia was thus re-established through Theodore's efforts in 687: but it did not last. 'Those who had instigated the old quarrel were aroused as though from sleep,' says Eddius, 'they lit the torch of dissension once extinguished.' The primary cause of dissension, he says, was the ancient wrong of the deprivation of the church of St. Peter (York) of its territories and possessions: moreover, Wilfrid's own minster of Ripon had been turned into a bishop's see. Then the third cause was 'that king Aldfrith kept compelling us to obey the commands and decrees of Theodore the archbishop'; so Wilfrid withdrew, c. 691, to the protection of his old friend, king Æthelred of Mercia: nor did a synod held in 702 in Austerfield under archbishop Berhtwald do Wilfrid justice. Theodore had died in September 690, but the synod held that Wilfrid 'must be judged according to the decrees and commands of archbishop Theodore'. So sharp was the dissension in the north afterwards, between the bishops and clergy of Theodore's appointment, who were supported by Aldfrith, and Wilfrid and his clergy, that they would not so much as eat together: 'they utterly abjured communion with us'.

Again, in 703, Wilfrid travelled to Rome, and messengers from Canterbury also sought the apostolic see: Wilfrid petitioned pope John IV to confirm the decree of pope Agatho, and constrain the kings Æthelred and Aldfrith to do him justice. As to the government of the see of York, Wilfrid prayed, let it rest with the pope's judgment: but at least let the two minsters of Ripon and Hexham, which he himself had founded and pope Agatho protected by privilege, be given back to him. The messengers of Berhtwald were then heard by pope and synod: and pope John ordered that the canonical decrees and writings of his predecessors about the dispute should be examined. The scrinium examined its records, and it was found that in the time of pope Agatho, at an Easter synod of 125 bishops, bishop Wilfrid of York had appealed to the apostolic see about his cause and been absolved from all charges: and with 125 other bishops had confessed the true and apostolic faith 'for all the northern parts of Britain and Ireland and the islands, which are inhabited by the races of Angles and Britons as well as Scots and Picts'. The region for which he had confessed the faith is understandable as excluding southern Britain, for which archbishop Theodore was responsible: but it is curious that Wilfrid should have conceived of his responsibility as extending, not only over the country of the Picts, but over northern Ireland as well. The words show how loosely any phrase implying responsibility was used. The examination of Wilfrid personally and of all the documents occupied four months and 70 sessions of the council; and finally pope John addressed a letter to kings Aldfrith and Æthelred, saying that he was saddened to hear of 'the inextricable dissension of certain men': he has examined all old and recent writings about the matter, 'but the principal persons were not present': therefore let archbishop Berhtwald and bishop Wilfrid together hold a synod, together with bishops Bosa and John of Beverley. And if archbishop Berhtwald can bring the matter to a conclusion before the synod, it will be satisfactory for the pope and for the parties concerned; otherwise the matter must be formally dealt with in synod, and each warned to present himself at the apostolic see: may the kings lend their aid and assistance. Then Wilfrid was ordered to return to Britain, bearing papal letters to the kings and to the archbishop; he bore also holy relics authenticated with the names of saints and vestments of silk and purple for the churches.

Wilfrid reached the town of Meaux in Gaul, and was there seized with an illness, in which St. Michael in a vision told him that he would recover through the intercession of holy Mary, mother of God and ever virgin, in whose honour he had as yet dedicated no church, but only churches in honour of St. Peter and St. Andrew: Wilfrid must put this right and dedicate a church in her honour. Wilfrid was now seventy years of age, but he recovered; he set out and crossed the sea, found a harbour in the land of Kent, and sent the apostolic writings to archbishop Berhtwald at Canterbury, at which

he was 'alarmed and trembling'. The two bishops met, and the reconciliation was real. Wilfrid passed on through London 'attended
with a crowd of abbots', and came at length to king Æthelred, his
faithful friend: he presented the apostolic letter, sealed with its
leaden seal, and the king professed his obedience, bowing deeply.
He summoned Coenred, whom he had appointed to be king after
him, and begged him to obey the apostolic precepts.

Aldfrith's reception of the papal letter, however, was quite different: his predecessors, he said, had arrived at a certain decision with
the archbishop sent by the holy see and with his counsellors, and 'as
long as I live I will never change because of writings which you
declare to be those of the apostolic see'. Then he fell ill, and repented
of the evil he had done Wilfrid, and promised amends, as the holy
abbesses Ælfled and Æthelburg heard him declare: but nevertheless
his sickness increased and he died (704). King Eadwulf reigned after
him but only for two months, and he sent a harsh message to Wilfrid;
a conspiracy drove him from the kingdom, and a boy of eight years,
king Aldfrith's son, named Osred, succeeded him. Wilfrid adopted
him as his son.

Then archbishop Berhtwald, in the first year of the new reign,
summoned the northern kings, bishops, abbots and nobles to a
council on the eastern side of the river Nidd (704). Berhtwald and
Wilfrid arrived on the same day. Berhtwald commanded that the
apostolic writings should be read before the council, and then Bern-
frith, second in rank to the king, asked that the letter be translated,
and Berhtwald, remarking that 'the judgments of the apostolic see
are expressed in circuitous and ambiguous terms', explained the bare
sense in English; the prelates in the southern province had two
choices; to make peace with Wilfrid and restore him such parts of
the churches he formerly ruled as the archbishop and wise councillors should settle; or, to go all together to the apostolic see and
'there be judged in a greater council'. Then the bishops asked how
it was possible to alter the decisions of archbishop Theodore and
king Ecgfrith, confirmed by king Aldfrith, archbishop Berhtwald
and the bishops of almost the whole of Britain in the place called
Austerfield?

Then the abbess Ælfled told how Aldfrith had, in his last illness,
enjoined on his heir to make peace with Wilfrid, and Beorhtfrith
too, the chief man in the kingdom whose king was now a child,

told how the northern Angles were besieged (by the Picts) in the city called Bamborough, surrounded by foes, and sheltering in a narrow place in the rock and in great danger: 'we vowed that if God granted our royal child to succeed to his father's kingdom, we would fulfil the apostolic commands concerning bishop Wilfrid. . . . Then our enemies were put to flight and the kingdom became ours.'

Then the bishops took counsel separately: and the archbishop consulted, sometimes with them and sometimes with the wise virgin, Ælfled. And at the end of the council a general peace was made with Wilfrid, which lasted to the end of all their lives; and they returned him the two best minsters, Ripon and Hexham; and on that day all the bishops kissed and embraced each other, and received holy communion together.

Wilfrid lived four years longer in peace after the synod on the Nidd. Eddius tells us that, a short time before his death in 708, he ordered his treasury-chest to be opened by the key-keeper in the presence of two abbots and six very faithful brethren, and all the gold and silver and precious stones to be laid out before them. He ordered the treasure to be divided into four parts: one for gifts to the church of St. Mary (Major) in Rome, and other churches there, to be carried by messengers since he would now never visit them again; one part to be given to the poor; one to the minsters of Ripon and Hexham, 'so that they may be able to purchase for themselves the friendship of kings and bishops', and one to the companions of his exile 'to whom I have given no lands or estates'. To the same witnesses he commended Tatberht the priest as provost of Ripon, and to rule it after his death; and to the whole familia at Ripon he announced his departure to confer with Ceolred, king of Mercia, and his command that, in the event of his death, they should receive as abbot whomsoever the two abbots Tibba and Æbba, the priests Tatberht and Hathufrith, and the master of the school, Aluhfrith, should announce to them. They never, as a community, saw his face again: for he died at his minster at Oundle, among the Middle Angles, desiring that at Hexham his priest Acca should rule the minster after his death.

Eddius' life of Wilfrid then shows most plainly the long struggle after the synod of Whitby between the Scottish-trained Christians and those who sought to change their ecclesiastical ideals and practice. Bede writes of the Celtic saints with sympathy and admiration, though he was a Benedictine monk: Eddius and Wilfrid had no such sympathy. Archbishop Theodore, familiar both with Greek and Latin practice, had sympathy for the Celts, though he would have no future doubts in so important a matter as the ordination of bishop Chad: he re-ordained him. But he was willing to use the service of Celtic clergy who accepted the Roman Easter, especially as the northern kings wished this; when he divided the great northern see, he appointed three bishops all of whom had been trained by the Scots: Bosa, trained at Whitby, Eata, prior of Lindisfarne, Eadhaeth, for Lindsey. Wilfrid complained that none of them had been trained in his minsters.

Moreover, Wilfrid's churches differed in form and material from those of the Celts, which had once been timber churches, and even when they were built of stone, as at Escomb, were small cellae with square ended chancels; the Scots would have gone on building simple churches like them, or like those at Glendalough or in the Irish bangors; Wilfrid reproduced, to the wonder of men, the aisles and the apses, the crypts, the turrets and the spiral staircases of Italian churches.

The life of the clergy too differed: the life of Aidan had conformed to the simple poverty of the 'second order or Irish saints': the life of St. Cuthbert embraced that of the anchorites. Wilfrid, on the other hand, introduced into the northern kingdom the rule of St. Benedict and ordained the following of it in his great minsters. Less emphasis was placed on individual austerity, but more on stability, obedience, and the communal chanting of the office. 'Did I not arrange the life of the monks in accordance with the rule of the holy father Benedict which none had previously introduced there?' demanded Wilfrid at Austerfield: 'Did I not instruct them in the rite of the primitive church to make use of a double choir singing in modes and with assonance, with reciprocal responsions and antiphons?' Not only was this a different monasticism from that of Columba and Cuthbert, but it was a monasticism not intended by St. Benedict for combination with pastoral work, and in some ways less suited to it than the clerical monasticism of the Scots, or the communal, canonical life practised by St. Augustine in Africa. There is no evidence that Wilfrid trained any clergy except as Benedictine monks; and this re-modelling of the whole life of the clergy, interposing a barrier between them and the Celtic clergy trained on an older pattern, proved unacceptable to the Northumbrian king Ecgfrith and his successors. There was no desire to undo the decision of Whitby: but Columba and Aidan and Cuthbert were the holy patrons of Lindisfarne and Northumbria: the kings would have preferred to keep their way of life for the clergy. It is notable that even when Ecgfrith and Aldfrith were most unwilling to upset the arrangements made with archbishop Theodore and restore Wilfrid, they never challenged the authority of the apostolic see: they claimed that Wilfrid had had the letters forged, or obtained them by bribery.

In the end, the wisdom and moderation of archbishops Theodore and Berhtwald found the solution: Wilfrid restored to the minsters he had built up as islands of scholarship, liturgy, art and pastoral work: and the division of Wilfrid's original great see not undone.

CHAPTER VI

THE THEODORAN AGE : THEODORE, BENEDICT BISCOP, CUTHBERT

WHEN pope Vitalian in 668 chose the distinguished Greek monk, Theodore of Tarsus, to be archbishop of the English, he chose a man from a very different world. Whereas in England the energies of churchmen were taken up with spreading the faith in a primitive Germanic countryside and defending the young church from casual extinction at the hands of violent men: Theodore was a Byzantine gentleman, a Greco-Roman philosopher, as Boniface called him, who belonged to the old, civilised, learned Byzantine world. He had been imbued, as Bede says, at the schools of Athens, with secular and divine letters: he was versed in the old Greco-Roman 'artes', and not only in the metrical arts which were a part of rhetoric, but with the mathematical arts, of which so much more was known at Byzantium than in the west. When he lectured on holy scripture he could incidentally deliver to the students the 'disciplines of astronomy and ecclesiastical arithmetic': he well understood the different cycles and the calendar and the movement of the planets in the Ptolemaic universe. 'There are still today', says Bede, 'some of his students who know the Greek and Latin tongues as well as their native language'; and Eddius Stephanus complains that the emissaries of archbishop Berhtwald, in their conflict with Wilfrid before pope John (704), talked Greek among themselves. Theodore had indeed founded a learned house at his cathedral of Christ Church.

No biography of Theodore has survived: so that all that is known of his life before Vitalian chose him, is that he was born at Tarsus in Cilicia, studied at Athens, and was living at Rome when the pope was seeking an archbishop for the English. There was a house of Greek monks at Rome, and he may have been living there: or in view of the recent over-running of the eastern provinces by the Arabs and the crowds of refugees seeking Italy, Theodore may have been a refugee. He had, in any case, lived through times of great danger for the Byzantine empire and the Greek church. When he was born, c. 602, the east Roman empire was threatened by the Persians on its eastern frontier, and by Germanic and Avar tribes in the Balkans: Avars, Persians and Arabs seemed about to submerge the surviving civilisation of the Greco-Roman state: but when the Persians took Antioch, Damascus and Jerusalem, carrying off the relic of the true cross in 614, the emperor Heraclius defeated them and recovered it. September 14 was marked as Holy Cross Day in the calendars of western as well as eastern churches, in memory of the deliverance of 628. But before Heraclius died in 641, the Arab followers of Mohammad had captured Jerusalem, Antioch and Egypt; the new emperor, Constans II, could not stop them: he lived at times at Syracuse, and he had visited pope Vitalian, before he died in 668, the year when Vitalian was seeking an archbishop. Constantinople itself was threatened by tribes in the Balkans, and besieged by the Arab fleet in 670. Theodore lived in perilous times for the Byzantines: the Arabs had taken Antioch before he was thirty, and beyond was Tarsus, his birthplace, and that was taken, together with Edessa and a further border strip between Byzantine Asia Minor and Armenia, by 661, and held thereafter by the Ummayad caliphs. Theodore belonged now to a world of refugees, who brought their eikons and their art-forms, their learning, their silk and purple vestments for the liturgy, their precious relics and their veneration for their own saints, to the west.

The wars in the east had also conditioned Theodore's intellectual background. The emperors, in view of Constantine's work as apostolic, could deal with theological issues, and were, in fact, inclined to do so with a view to conciliating border provinces where frontier defence was urgent. The emperor Heraclius had desired to conciliate Armenia, the border province with Persia, and inclined to Monophysitism; he had issued an imperial edict, the *Ekthesis*, in 638, which affirmed that Christ had, not one nature (which was heresy), but one will or energy; a doctrine hence called Monothelite. It was meant as a possible reunion edict: but it succeeded only in rousing the bitter opposition of orthodox Chalcedonians in Rome and Constantinople. It was a burning issue in Rome and the west, though the provinces it was hoped to win were soon lost, not to the Persians, but to the Arabs.

The choice of Theodore for consecration to the see of Canterbury in 668 was no casual appointment, but an extraordinary instance of a

8

detached and far-sighted decision, made by the Roman see, after careful inquiry. When Deusdedit died of the plague in July, 664, king Oswiu and king Ecgberht of Kent had taken counsel together, and sent off Wighard, priest of Canterbury and chorepiscopus of St. Martin's, to the pope for consecration. So soon after Whitby, it was advisable to have an archbishop under the patronage, not of Columba or Augustine, but of Peter himself; besides, there was a shortage of bishops in the southern province. Wighard, however, died of the plague at Rome: and by canonical custom this left the choice of a fresh candidate to the pope. Vitalian wrote to Oswiu saying that the journey was too great for him to find a 'docile and well qualified' prelate (from among the English), but as soon as he could find a suitable candidate, he would instruct and send him to Oswiu, to eradicate any tares of false teaching.

His first choice fell on Hadrian, abbot of a monastery near Naples and an African by birth; and when he excused himself and asked Vitalian to appoint the Greek monk, Theodore, Vitalian consented with the proviso that Hadrian should accompany him, to be his 'co-operator in doctrine', lest he should introduce any Greek custom or doctrine into the church whose head he would now be. Vitalian must have been aware through Oswiu's letter and the advice of his messengers that a man of wide experience, not too narrowly identified with Latin church custom, was needed; the selection, first of an African, and then of a Greek, may indicate this, and the success of the Byzantine archbishop in dealing with the Scottish-trained bret-walda in the north may seem to confirm it. The Byzantine church whose early missions had lain well outside the Roman empire to the east and south, and where Greek was not a common language as Latin always was in the west, had taught the faith without even insisting on the use of Greek for the liturgy. Greek missionaries taught in Armenian, Persian, Syrian, Indian and African civilisa-tions: some of the Greek churches were very ancient in custom, and a learned Greek prelate, orthodox in faith and instructed as to the right celebration of Easter, might be well able to deal with the ecclesiastical customs of the Scots. Pope Vitalian allowed Theodore four months in which to grow his hair that his tonsure might be cut according to the western manner, and then he consecrated him himself to the see of Canterbury on March 26, 668. It was a remarkably bold and well-justified choice.

Theodore travelled through Gaul with Hadrian, king Ecgberht sending his reeve Rædfrith to escort him on the last stages of his journey. They sailed from Quentavic, and arrived at Christ Church, Canterbury, on May 27, 669. Theodore, in spite of his sixty-six years, proved equal to the hardships of horse travel, necessary when he visited the various kings and held his synods: he worked for some twenty years, and died on September 19, 690. He was the first archbishop recognised by the whole English church, and it was his work that gave unity to the churches in the various kingdoms, while secular union was still in the future. He built up the episcopate of the English; he initiated the holding of synods; he fostered the monastic life; and he made Canterbury a centre of studies in his own and succeeding generations.

As regards the English bishoprics, Bede says that Theodore, making his first perambulation (*perlustrans omnia*), ordained bishops in suitable places, correcting what he found imperfect. He restored Wilfrid to York, the great see extending not only over Deira and Bernicia, but northwards over the Picts whom king Ecgfrith had by now included in his imperium. He re-ordained Chad and sent him to Lichfield, and for Rochester he ordained Putta, a man competent to deal with secular affairs, well trained ecclesiastically and in the church chant. Chad lived a life of great sanctity at Lichfield: he had studied in youth in Ireland, and when he died, in March 672, a vision of his death was seen in Ireland. Chad was a real Irish saint: but Theodore insisted that, for ruling so large a see, he must travel, not on foot, but on horseback.

Theodore's move to increase the number of bishops dates from the holding of his first synod, at Hertford, 672. The place was chosen as on the road to the north, and reasonably placed as between north and south. Theodore had brought his notary, Titillus, with him, for all bishops of the Greco-Roman world had notaries, and he drew up the record of the synod in proper form, whence we know the names of the bishops attending and the canons passed. The bishops, attended by 'many magistri of the church, who knew and loved the statutes of the fathers', included, beside Theodore: Bisi of the East Angles, Wilfrid through his two legates, Putta of Rochester, Leutherius of the East Saxons, Wynfrith (Chad's successor) of the Mercians. The bishops assented to the canonical teaching of the Fathers, and to 10 canons expressly propounded to them by Theodore, most of which referred to matters where Scottish practice differed from that of Canterbury. 'We will keep the Paschal feast', the first canon ran, 'on the Sunday next after the fourteenth day of the first month' (after the equinox); thus excluding any possibility of keeping it on Sunday the fourteenth day and coinciding with the Jewish Pask; 'no bishop shall invade the (territorial) parochia of another; no bishop shall disturb or take ought from any monastery consecrated to God; no cleric shall leave his own bishop and wander at will, or be received by prelates without commendatory letters; no one shall undertake any sacerdotal office, without the permission of the bishop in whose parochia he is known to be; bishops shall take precedence by order of their consecration'; and, as discussed by all the bishops, 'Let more bishops be added as the number of the faithful shall be increased: but for the present we say no more about this matter'. Apart from the possible aversion of any bishop from having his parochia diminished, no new sees could in fact be erected till some king or under king had granted landed endowment to maintain the bishop and his familia.

This canon shows, however, that the increase of bishops was in Theodore's mind five years before Ecgfrith's expulsion of Wilfrid made an opportunity for the division of the Northumbrian see. Before that, Bisi of East Anglia died, and Theodore consecrated two bishops in his stead; Wynfrith of the Mercians was deposed, and Saxwulf, abbot and founder of the great new monastery of Medehamstede, made bishop in his place. For the East Saxons, Theodore gave Earconwald a see in the city of London, the first to have his see there since Mellitus; he was a most holy man, who had earlier founded the monastery of Chertsey, in Surrey, for men, and the nunnery of Barking in Essex, for his sister. For the West Saxons, when bishop Wini died, Theodore consecrated Haeddi in the city of Winchester: he could not as yet divide this great see.

In 678, however, when dissension arose between Ecgfrith and bishop Wilfrid, Theodore was able to consecrate two bishops for the Northumbrians, Bosa for Deira, and Eata, abbot of Mailros, for Hexham: and with them Eadhaeth for the Lindisfari (Lincoln): before this, they had had Seaxwulf of the Mercians for bishop. Bishop Theodore ordained them himself, Bede says. Three years later he ordained Tunberht for Hexham (leaving Eata at Lindisfarne:

see p. 98), Trumwine for the Picts. He moved Eadhæth to Ripon: Mercia had reconquered the Lindisfari. Bishops' sees still, in fact, fluctuated with the advance and retreat of kingdoms; Wilfrid converted a king of Sussex, and was given land for himself and his familia, but all the time Cædwalla and later Ine, princes of Wessex, were fighting to make good their claims, Sussex could have no bishop, nor could the Isle of Wight. Here there was much fighting, and Daniel, bishop of the West Saxons, was the first to have episcopal charge there.

Theodore's care, indeed, extended as much over the north of Britain as the south; he brought about a reconciliation between kings Ecgfrith and Æthelred, after the battle of the Trent in 679, persuading princes and people to forgo a war of vengeance for the killing of Ecgfrith's eighteen-year-old brother, and to accept a large money 'wer': the making of such a peace meant everything to the young church. When Theodore proceeded to the solemn consecration of Cuthbert as bishop (first to Hexham, then Lindisfarne) at York, in March 685, six bishops assisted him at the consecration. No action of Theodore was of greater importance at the time than the watch he kept over the bishops, their increase in number, and the peace he provided for them by the respect and affection he inspired in the various kings.

The bishop's familia in Theodore's day was by far the most important part of the total number of clergy, and, in the north, almost the only clerical units. In Kent there were already mother churches (see Chapter IX): but the development of the non-episcopal parochia had, in Theodore's day, not gone far.

The answer to the question: which of the early English minsters were strictly contemplative and which filled by clergy with a secular charge, must be made with sixth and seventh century conditions in mind. In the Celtic north and west, the only clergy were monastic, and even in Kent, the home of the Benedictine missionaries, the influence of St. Martin of Tours had blurred the line between secular and monastic clergy. It is difficult to say of any of these early minsters that they were strictly 'Benedictine', except SS. Peter and Paul in Canterbury and Monkwearmouth in the north. It is difficult to class Wilfrid's monastery of Ripon with these, for though Eddius says Wilfrid was the first to introduce the Benedictine rule into England, yet Ripon was the monastery of a bishop and provided the clergy and pastoral charge of its adjacent parochia.

Bede does not speak of Christ Church, Canterbury, as a minster: he says that Æthelberht gave Augustine 'the place for a see' within the walls of Canterbury: perhaps the site was too restricted for the word minster to be used. Augustine, he says, rebuilt and enlarged an old Christian church, and it became the church of the Saviour, or Christ Church. A sixth century continental bishop's church might have a square atrium at the west end of the church, round which the clergy would live, but this dwelling place for the bishop and his familia would not be described as a 'monasterium'. The bishop would live in the 'secretarium', the private apartments, the range of small cells alongside the nave of the church. Augustine and his monks must have lived in fairly restricted quarters near the church: they would recite the opus dei and follow the Benedictine rule. How far the rule of enclosure could be followed is not known: but there was pastoral work to be done, and the first duty of any bishop at the time would have been the long training of a native clergy. Augustine must, apparently, have received Anglo-Saxon boys to live with him from the first.

If archbishop Theodore devoted much energy to the establishment (and on occasion, the deposition) of bishops (he deposed Wynfrith, in 675 and Tunberht, in 685): Benedictine monasticism flourished also in his age, at Monkwearmouth—Jarrow, at St. Augustine's, Canterbury, and through Wilfrid's efforts in the north. Any advance in learning and the arts, at the day, depended on monasticism, for the monk only had leisure (schole), and by definition, a scholar is a man of leisure. Kings and thegns spent most of their life on horseback, travelling, hunting and fighting; riding thegns took the king's letters; the 'geburs' guided the plough-oxen, sowed and reaped, and carried the hay, and the herds looked after the sheep and the pigs and the bees. Men worked from daybreak to sunset, and work was hard, for, apart from the plough-ox and the riding horse, there was no power to lift or pull or dig except the power of human muscles. Monks, also, might help with the beasts and the harvests: St. Benedict, indeed laid down that 'if the needs of the place, or their poverty, require them to labour themselves at getting in the harvest, they shall not be saddened thereat', but the Anglo-Saxon minsters had lands where peasants worked on their demesne, as lay thegns had.

All the monks needs must have leisure for the reciting of the divine office: and some had leisure to read and write manuscripts: and it was on such monks that the future of learning depended.

In this respect, the Benedictine form of monasticism was to be of special service in the future. Irish monasticism kept alive a purer form of Latin than survived in Gaul; Irish sapientes studied the liberal arts, Irish scribes were a class held in great honour in the monastery. But where the tribal monastery, or that under the patronage of a local king, had also the pastoral care of the tribe or kingdom, few monk-clerics had leisure to devote themselves to learning. A house like Columba's Iona had a pastoral charge: Bede says in his prose *Life of Cuthbert* that in his familia, the clergy lived communally with him like monks, as Augustine's clergy lived with him at Canterbury: and Iona produced scholars like abbot Adomnan: but Iona was a very great and relatively well-endowed house. Lindisfarne was a wonderful school for the illumination of manuscripts; but it was the Benedictine minster of Jarrow, with no pastoral care, that produced the 'savant' of the age, the venerable Bede.

Bede himself wrote, in his *Historia Abbatum*, the story of his own house, and all the travels and labours involved in setting up the double monastery of Monkwearmouth on the river Wear, and Jarrow, some miles to the north: to make a small replica of Monte Cassino or Lérins in a northern kingdom using timber even for the king's hall, and with only a few clergy able to read and write, was no light task. In one sense, the work of Benedict Biscop, the founder of the monastery, was parallel to that of Wilfrid: but he was a scholar-monk with no vocation to the episcopate or ecclesiastical politics: and he worked, not in opposition to, but in close touch with, Canterbury and archbishop Theodore.

Bede says that Biscopus (whose name points perhaps to a Romano-Christian ancestry, for it cannot possibly be Anglo-Saxon) founded a monastery, dedicated it to St. Peter at Wearmouth, by the help of king Ecgfrith, and ruled it sixteen years 'among innumerable labours of travels and sicknesses'. He was a thegn of king Oswiu, with an estate suitable to his rank, and when twenty-five years old, he despised the earthly warfare and its rewards to fight for the king eternal in the heavens. He left his country (653) to travel and visit the shrine of the apostles in Rome, and, returning, he studied and loved the institutes of ecclesiastical life: and when Oswiu's son

Alchfrith desired also to make the Roman pilgrimage, he planned
to go with him. When Oswiu would not allow Alchfrith to go, he
went alone, and this in the time of pope Vitalian of blessed memory;
and he stayed some months there and then travelled to the famous
monastery at Lérins and became a monk, staying there for two years.
Then he desired to visit Rome a third time: and it happened that a
merchant ship came to the mouth of the Rhone from Kent, bringing
Wighard, who was to be ordained at Rome, with other companions,
and he sailed on that ship; but Wighard died before he could be
made bishop.

Then pope Vitalian chose Theodore 'a man outstanding both in
secular and divine learning, and that in both languages, Greek and
Latin', with abbot Hadrian to be his companion: and Benedict
'whom he knew to be learned, hard-working, religious and of noble
birth' he commanded to give up his pilgrimage, and return with the
bishop and Hadrian as the leader of their journey and their interpreter. In 669 Benedict was placed in charge of the monastery of
SS. Peter and Paul, Canterbury, of which, after two years, when he
had learned English, Hadrian was made abbot (671): for two years
Benedict lived in closest touch with Theodore and Hadrian at
Canterbury, and this was the beginning of the tie that linked the two
Benedictine abbeys together for so many years. In his later journeys
from Monkwearmouth to Rome, he must have passed through
London and Canterbury, and it is unlikely that he, now an abbot,
would have stayed elsewhere than in the abbey he had once ruled.

In 671, Hadrian being now abbot, Benedict was free to visit Rome
again, and he returned with very many books of 'divine erudition',
either bought for money or given him by friends: other friends
at Vienne had been buying books for him, and he brought them
all back. He visited Cenwalh, king of the West Saxons, and when
the latter was cut off by premature death, he travelled beyond the
Humber to king Ecgfrith, making no secret of his desire for the
monastic life. He showed the king the knowledge of monastic life
which he had gained at Rome and elsewhere, and the many volumes
and relics of the Christian martyrs he had brought back: and the king
showed him such kindly friendship that he gave him 70 hides of land
for a monastery at the mouth of the Wear (674). And within a year
from the foundation of the monastery, Benedict sent to Gaul and
obtained masons to make him a stone church in the Roman manner,

which he ever loved: and mass was said in the church within a year from the time the foundations were laid.

He made yet another journey to Rome, and again brought back a great treasure of books and relics, a 'richer harvest of spiritual profit than ever' (see p. 172). Moreover, he brought a written letter of privilege from pope Agatho, securing the monastery from all outside intervention or entrance whatsoever. And king Ecgfrith was so delighted with the use he had made of his earlier grant, that he gave him 40 hides more: and Benedict sent 17 monks under the priest Ceolfrith as provost (under himself) and built a fresh monastery there (Jarrow) on the new land. And he made Ceolfrith abbot, but so that the two monasteries should ever remain united in peace and concord. And when Benedict had need to go to Rome again, he made the priest Eosterwine abbot of Wearmouth: and he himself made a sixth journey to Rome and brought back yet another treasure of books, and no less great a treasure of the eikons (images) of saints. But in the gladness of his return sorrow was mingled, for Eosterwine had died; they had elected as reverend and gentle a monk of the same monastery, Sigfrid, to be co-abbot with Ceolfrith.

And now, after an illness of three years, Benedict knew himself dying: and often bade the brethren keep the rule he had instituted, and the customs: 'and do not think', he said, 'that I have made them up out of my own head: for I have given you to hold the best customs that I have anywhere found out of the seventeen monasteries in which I have stayed in my long pilgrimage'. And the most noble and extensive library which he had brought from Rome for necessary instruction he bade them keep intact, without harming it by neglect or allowing it to be dispersed. And he bade them again and again not to elect an abbot for his noble birth, but for his sound life and teaching: 'for I would rather', he said, 'that all this monastery I have built should become waste for ever, than that my brother after the flesh, whom we know has not entered into the way of truth, should rule this house after me with the name of abbot'. He went on to warn them to exercise the right of election, according to the rule of Benedict the great abbot, guaranteed to them in the privilege: so that they should inquire in the common council of the assembled congregation who should be most fit by merit of life and wisdom of doctrine for the ministry of abbot, and when they had all unanimously found him who was best fitted, through this inquiry of charity, they should at once summon the bishop to establish him as abbot with the accustomed blessing.

Benedict's solemn warning shows that already the Anglo-Saxon thegns regarded an abbacy as a family possession, as Bede was to lament later. And as Benedict's sickness increased, so did that of Sigfrid: and at length he was brought on a stretcher to his dying abbot, and laid with his head on the same pillow that they might speak together, and Benedict summoned Ceolfrith, abbot of St. Paul's at Jarrow, who was no kinsman of his, and assigned to him both monasteries, all judging this the best course. And two months later, Sigfrid died, and four months after that the abbot Benedict died, as the brethren were singing matins, in the night of January 12, 690. He was buried in the church of St. Peter.

Benedict had collected the library in which Bede worked, a library finer, apparently, than any outside Italy in his own day: though Wilfrid and Theodore both sought assiduously for books for their churches. He had, moreover, planted the Benedictine life in the north of England: Eddius claimed that Wilfrid introduced it to the northern provinces, and it may be that he used it in his minster of Ripon before Benedict founded Wearmouth. But Benedict, in his freedom from episcopal office and the pastoral charge, came nearer to the intention of the father of western monks, that a monastery should be a school for beginners in the service of God, in which 'nothing harsh, nothing burdensome' should be instituted, and a monk's first duty should be the recitation of the opus dei. He was, moreover, free to insist that St. Benedict's rule for the election of the abbot should be followed: whereas, the connexion of the abbacy of Ripon and Hexham with the episcopate and the goodwill of the king rendered such an election according to the Benedictine rule precarious. We hear of Theodore's consecrating bishops for Hexham, for the Picts, for Lindisfarne: there is no evidence as to the process by which they were chosen.

The constructive work of Theodore, Hadrian and Wilfrid made possible an efflorescence of learning, manuscript illumination and church building in seventh and eighth century England, which is briefly described in the next chapter. Without the labours of these men in the Latin tradition, there could not have been this efflorescence of the arts: but there was also a Celtic contribution to the eighth century renaissance, and something should be said of the Celtic leaders who made it possible. The names of Columba and Cuthbert should be set against those of Benedict Biscop and Theodore. The austere sanctity of Cuthbert may seem alien to the Latin Christianity which informed the bulk of the Anglo-Saxon people: but it inspired admiration among them. Fifty years after Theodore's death in 690, an archbishop called Cuthbert was elected (or appointed) to Canterbury, and ruled the English church for twenty years; and Cuthbert remained the patron of the great prince-bishopric of Durham throughout the middle ages.

The Celtic abbots and monks in northern Britain included learned men interested in other matters than the determination of the date of Easter. Yet the emphasis in their lives and in their rules was always on austerity and bareness in the tradition of Cassian and the monks of Egypt, and in anticipation, as it were, of the teaching of St. Francis about poverty. In the Columban rule occur the words: 'Be always naked in imitation of Christ and in obedience to the precepts of his gospel'. Columbanus wrote: 'Nakedness and contempt of property (*facultates*) is the first perfection of monks'. Of Cuthbert it was written: 'He consoled the sad, instructed the ignorant, appeased the angry, for he persuaded them all to put nothing before the love of Christ'. The same tradition guided his life and his pastoral work.

So great was the reverence for Cuthbert in the see of Lindisfarne and the whole Celtic church of the north, that on his death in 687 bishop Eadfrith of Lindisfarne enjoined the writing of his life by a Lindisfarne monk (the 'Anonymous Life'), and rather later supplied materials for the same task to Bede at Jarrow. Bede wrote, as he said in his list of his own writings, two lives of St. Cuthbert, 'the first in the heroic metre, the later one in plain speech (prose)'. The Anonymous Life was less concerned with setting forth a chronological account of Cuthbert's life than with collecting together the story of his miracles; Bede's account is the more intelligible, but the Lindisfarne life expatiates on what was, to his brother monks, the more important, his virtues and the signs given by heaven of divine approval.

Cuthbert, as can be gathered from the two lives, was born in the service of a Bernician thegn near the Celtic monastery of Mailros (Melrose). Bernicia extended north of the Wall, and the Anonymous Life tells us that (in 651) Cuthbert was 'feeding the flocks of his master near the river which is called the Leader, in company with other shepherds, and was spending the night in prayer', when he saw the soul of bishop Aidan of Lindisfarne carried to heaven 'as it were in a globe of fire'. The Leader falls into the Tweed two miles below the monastery of Mailros, which Cuthbert must have known well; but for some years he did war service for his thegn, living in camp and fighting with the spear against the enemy (perhaps with Oswiu's army against Penda). He was used to meagre rations and hard living, yet in time he 'arranged to bind himself by the more rigid rule of life in a monastery'. Bede says that 'though he knew the church at Lindisfarne contained many holy men', yet he knew of the virtues of the monk-priest Boisil, prior of Mailros, and preferred to seek admission to this monastery.

Cuthbert, when he made the resolution, had been travelling south to the river Wear: when he had sought shelter with his horse in some dwellings near Chester-le-Street (Kuncacester) used only in the spring and summer, he could find no one to give him food-alms, for it was winter. The hungry horse tried to pull straw from the shelter roof: and pulled out a warm loaf left there miraculously to feed its master. Cuthbert made his way north to Mailros, asked admission, and gave both his horse and the spear he was carrying to the servant who opened to him. He was taken to Boisil the prior, who received him as a guest, and recommended the abbot Eata to receive him as monk, when he returned from a journey. The Anglian boy Eata had been one of the twelve original pupils of Aidan at Lindisfarne: and he now became Cuthbert's abbot, teacher and friend for almost the whole of his life. The Anonymous Life has a long account of Cuthbert's ascetic life as a monk, for a short time at Mailros, and then at Ripon; king Alchfrith gave abbot Eata land in Deira to build a monastery, and Eata took Cuthbert with him and built at Ripon a house having the same rules and discipline as Mailros: Cuthbert was 'at once elected while a neophyte by the community to minister to guests on their arrival'. But in 664 king Oswiu made his decision at the synod of Whitby, and Eata, rather than accept the Roman Easter, left Ripon, taking Cuthbert with him, and returned to Mailros. He was then made abbot of Lindisfarne as well as Melrose, and for a time there was no territorial bishop there; claustral bishops there may well have been in either house.

When Wilfrid of York quarrelled with king Ecgfrith about his support of the queen's desire for the religious life in 677, Wilfrid withdrew from his see, and archbishop Theodore and king Ecgfrith proceeded to divide it. Eata was made bishop for Bernicia, with his see at Lindisfarne; Cuthbert had been provost of Mailros, and was now provost of Lindisfarne. 'He arranged our rule of life,' the monk of Lindisfarne wrote, 'which we composed then for the first time and which we observe even to this day, along with the rule of St. Benedict.'

Cuthbert had been used at Mailros to make preaching journeys: it was while he and two brethren were sailing from Mailros to the land of the Picts, that they found provided for them on the day of the Epiphany three portions of dolphin's flesh on the sea shore, and there are other references to Cuthbert's journeys, baptising the peasants up among the mountains and diligently teaching them. He can have been no stranger to the pastoral work needed at Lindisfarne, as when Hildmer, a reeve of king Ecgfrith, sent to 'our monastery' for Cuthbert to come and heal his sick wife. But by predilection he belonged to the 'third order of Irish saints', the anchorites, and 'after some years' (at Lindisfarne) 'he desired a solitary life, and went to the island of Farne, which is in the midst of the sea and surrounded on every side by water'. Here he dug down 'almost the cubit of a man into the earth and made a space to dwell in'. He raised a wall another cubit around his half underground cell, 'moving by himself great stones that even four brethren and a cart could scarcely have brought along'.

The Anonymous Life has other stories of the years Cuthbert spent on the Farne island, one of a group of small islands and about nine miles distant from Lindisfarne. He was maintained by the monks of Lindisfarne who sometimes visited him, and told their brethren how the holy men's cell was surrounded by a high earth bank so that he could only see the sky: how the sea washed up timber for him when he needed it: the ravens who tore at a thatched roof were banished from the island till they repented and were allowed back. Like the saints of the desert, Cuthbert was the familiar friend of birds and animals: the best known story of the Anonymous Life is of how, when he had been summoned to visit the abbess Æbbe of Colding-ham, and remained several days, he had spent nights in prayer outside the double monastery. He used to walk into the waves up to his waist and then kneel on the sea shore to pray, and once a monk who had followed him saw two little seals come from the sea to lick and warm his chilled feet. Cuthbert blessed them, and they returned to the sea. At another time when he and his fellows were travelling and had no food, an eagle brought them a large fish: Cuthbert commanded that half the fish should be given back to the bird for its own dinner.

The monastery of Coldingham in the far north of Bernicia was that to which queen Æthelthryth first retired before she went to Ely: Cuthbert's friend the abbess Æbbe was the sister of king Oswiu and aunt of king Ecgfrith. Her house, however, illustrates the dangers to minsters which Bede later complained of in his letter to archbishop Ecgberht: scandal arose about the lives of its members, and it has been suggested that Cuthbert's fear of, and hostility to, women arose from his distress at the scandals at Coldingham. The house was completely destroyed by fire in 679, and Bede saw in it a judgment of God. The Anonymous Life is full of references to Cuthbert's normal affection and friendship for women: a widow and nun, Kenswith, brought him up from his eighth year till manhood and he called her 'Mother': he was ready to heal sick women, and to visit Æbbe, and also Ælfled when she was anxious about the life of her brother Ecgfrith. The two met on Coquet island, and Ælfled asked Cuthbert how long her brother should live. He will die, said Cuthbert, within twelve months, and indeed Ecgfrith fell in battle with the Picts at Nectansmere in 685; who would be the king's heir? Ælfled asked, and Cuthbert reassured her: You will find him a brother, he said. She realised he spoke of Aldfrith, her half-brother, who indeed succeeded Ecgfrith. Aldfrith himself had been trained in letters in Ireland and Iona: he was to be both 'tutor and king' (rex et magister) to monks, nuns and scholars.

Cuthbert's life as anchorite at Farne was devoutly admired by all the monk-clergy of the north, and they desired to have him as bishop. Eata, abbot of Lindisfarne, had in 678 been consecrated bishop for Hexham and in 684 the see of Lindisfarne was still unfilled. King Ecgfrith, late in 684, was visited by archbishop Theodore, and the king summoned a great synod to sit at Twyford, near the river Alne, under Theodore's presidency. All chose Cuthbert to be bishop and Theodore arranged for the senior cleric, Eata, to hold the see of Lindisfarne, while Cuthbert should go to Hexham. A distinguished deputation visited Cuthbert, imploring him to submit himself to the will of the synod and accept the bishop's office: they included monks from Lindisfarne, king Ecgfrith, and Trumwine, bishop of the Picts at Abercorn; they implored Cuthbert with tears, drew him from his lurking place, and led him to the synod. Seven bishops, with archbishop Theodore as chief, assisted at his consecration on March 26, 685: and he persuaded Eata to let him hold his see at Lindisfarne, as well known to him, while Eata remained at Hexham. He was no Celtic extremist except in personal austerity; he accepted the Roman Easter, an adaptation of the Columban rule to the Benedictine for his monk-clergy, and his own pastoral responsibility for all the people of his see. Among the few records of his episcopate occur mentions of pastoral journeys and sermons. As bishop, said Bede, he loved God and his neighbour: and when he used to offer to God the sacrifice of the saving victim, he commended his prayer to God not with a loud voice but with heartfelt tears.

When he felt death upon him, he withdrew again to his cell at Farne with a few brethren, and his sickness increased. He desired to be buried on the island where for so many years (like the hermits in the desert) he had fought the heavenly warfare, but he yielded finally to the prayers of the brethren that they should arrange his resting place in the church at Lindisfarne.

Like Benedict Biscop, he feared for his monks in the changes that his death would bring. 'Have no communion', he exhorted them, 'with those who depart from the unity of the catholic peace: either in not celebrating Easter at the proper time or in evil living. . . . Remember, that if necessity compels you to choose one of two evils, I would much rather you should take my bones from the tomb, carry them with you, and, departing from this place dwell wherever God may ordain, than that in any way you should consent unto iniquity and put your neck under the yoke of schismatics.' So he died on the Farne island on March 20, 687.

The brethren took him by ship to Lindisfarne 'and placed him with honour in the church'. They had laid an unconsecrated host on his breast, wrapped him in a waxed shroud, robed him in sacerdotal garments, 'with shoes upon his feet that he might be ready to meet Christ'. They placed his body in a stone sarcophagus in the church of the blessed apostle Peter on the right side of the altar. Then, as Cuthbert had anticipated, the blast of trial beat upon the church at Lindisfarne: for Wilfrid held the see for a year and may have desired changes from the moderate and charitable régime of Cuthbert: some

of the brethren left. These troubles ceased after a year, when Ead-
berht, abbot of Mailros and a monk of great virtue, was ordained
bishop of Lindisfarne (688–698).

But Cuthbert's presentiment of trouble was to be fulfilled in a way
he could not have foreseen. In one of the earliest and most terrible
of the Danish raids, in 793, 'the harrying of heathen men miserably
destroyed God's church in Lindisfarne by rapine and slaughter'.
Alcuin wrote to bishop Hygebeald and the monks of Lindisfarne in
distress and alarm at this desecration of Cuthbert's church; but the
body of Cuthbert had escaped the general pillage and the monks
returned and rebuilt their church and monastery. The storm of
Danish attack passed in the main to Ireland in the next generation.
But in the second half of the ninth century the heathen men not only
raided but wintered in England: the aim was now not merely plunder
but conquest and occupation. In 867 they took York, in 870 East
Anglia, in 871 they invaded Wessex and in 873 Northumbria. In 875
Halfdan the Danish leader rowed up the Tyne and pillaged every
church in Bernicia.

The monks at Lindisfarne heard of the burning of the minster at
Tynemouth, and the raids of Halfdan against the Picts and against
Strathclyde: they were faced with the prospect of no mere raid, but
of being engulfed in a permanent heathen conquest. Bishop Eardwulf summoned to him Eadred, abbot of Carlisle, and reminded the
monks of Cuthbert's dying words, that he would rather they should
take up his bones and flee than live under evil masters. They took the
body of Cuthbert in a light wooden coffin on the bier where it
already rested (for they were accustomed to carry it in procession on
his anniversary and certain great days); they took the relics of Lindisfarne's earlier saints and the glorious Lindisfarne gospel book, and
they took the stone cross of bishop Æthelweald (721–740).

The wanderings of the bishop, the monks and such lay people who
chose to go with them rather than live under Danish masters lasted
for about seven years: from 875 to 883, when they rested Cuthbert's
coffin and set up the episcopal see in Chester-le-Street (Kuncacester).
Seven young clerics were appointed bearers and at first they carried
the saint's coffin and other treasures on their shoulders: later they
placed it in a cart drawn by a bay horse. The full history of the seven-
year wanderings of the cortège is not known, but the coffin seems to
have rested at Whithorn, Hoddom and Mailros in the north, and at

a point so far south as Craike, ten miles north of York. The claim that dedications to St. Cuthbert all represent points where his relics rested cannot be accepted: but Symeon of Durham's story, traditionally handed down in Cuthbert's familia, of a projected flight to Ireland may well be true. He says that when bishop Eardwulf fled from Lindisfarne, he left a monk behind to report on Danish actions there, and this man sent word that the Danes were expecting the monks to return with their relics and precious reliquaries, and were lying in wait for them.

Eardwulf and Eadred therefore despaired of a safe return, or even of finding any safe refuge in Britain. They decided to sail with St. Cuthbert's coffin to Ireland. They came to the mouth of the Derwent, from which a short sea passage would take them to northern Ireland: the great Bangor on Belfast Lough, or Moville where Columba had been trained, would welcome them. Bishop and abbot and the guardians of the relics took ship: but the remaining company stood in despair on the shore and wept. With imploring cries they begged St. Cuthbert not to desert them, and not in vain. A storm arose with waves so violent breaking over the boat that the bishop ordered her return to shore: all took it that the Irish project must be given up.

In 883 bishop Eardwulf found means to halt his familia and set up his see in a church at Chester-le-Street, on the Great North Road not far south of the Tyne. It was indeed far from Lindisfarne: but no coastal site on the North Sea was safe from Viking attack. The familia claimed that Guthred, the successor of Halfdan, endowed them with lands between the Wear and the Tyne, and in time Cuthbert, regarded as the Christian defender and patron of the north of England, received a great patrimony in gifts of land. But the going was at first heavy for all the church in the north, with Danes and Norsemen settled at York, and the Scandinavian gods their natural defenders. Alfred the king, aided by St. Cuthbert, had driven his enemies from Wessex in 878 and received their leader, Guthrum, to baptism: but the Northmen settled in the Danelaw were at first nominal and unenthusiastic Christians, if that. King Athelstan in 927 bettered the Christian position in the north: he came to Penrith and obtained from the kings of Scotland and Strathclyde and the English lord of Bamburgh acknowledgment of his supremacy and a promise to suppress 'idolatry'; in June 934 he came north again in a

9

demonstration against the Scots, and made offerings to St. Cuthbert at Chester-le-Street. His successor, king Edmund, had more difficulties with the king of Strathclyde, who supported the Northmen: he came north in 945, visited the shrine of St. Cuthbert and conquered Strathclyde. Cnut himself made gifts at his shrine some time after 1020: he had enemies across the North Sea and needed a heavenly defender.

The see of St. Cuthbert remained at Chester-le-Street till 995, when bishop Ealdhun transferred it to Durham. The archbishop of York became, in time, as Gregory had intended, the ruler of the northern province of the church of the English, but it was the Celtic saint from Mailros who became the patron of the prince-bishops of Durham.

CHAPTER VII

THE THEODORAN AGE : LEARNING, CHURCHES AND SACRAMENTARIES

In the seventh and early eighth centuries in Britain three 'cultures', the Anglo-Saxon, the Celtic and the Greco-Roman, met and fused in a wonderful age of light and learning. The agents of this renaissance were, for the most part, monks and clergy: those who (as Bede might say) fought the heavenly warfare in the service of the bishop, and those who professed the monastic life, Celtic or Benedictine. Both clergy and monks lived in minsters and most did pastoral work, rarely or continuously, in the countryside. But it was only the clergy who lived a settled life in the minster who had leisure to read manuscripts and practise the arts of writing and illuminating. It was they, at any rate, who employed craftsmen to carve the great stone crosses, glaze the church windows and do fine smith's work on the altar vessels and reliquaries. Kings and thegns must also have employed craftsmen: but their halls and even palaces were of wood, and perishable. Only the church, and she but rarely, built in stone.

The fine flowering of the eighth century renaissance came in Northumbria, but the seed was sown by the work of Theodore and Hadrian at Canterbury. Little remains of Theodore's writings compared with those of Bede, and there is no surviving manuscript written at Canterbury to compare with the Lindisfarne gospels. There are no high crosses in the south to compare with those of Bewcastle and Ruthwell. Surprising as this is, in comparing the learned and artistic works of the northern churches with those of the primatial church of Canterbury, the reasons for the disproportionate achievement in the north are fairly clear. In learning, Bede not only profited by the labours of such men as Theodore and Benedict Biscop, but (according to his own account of his life) he really led the life of a Benedictine monk, giving his time wholly and continuously to reciting the opus dei and to learning, teaching and writing, all within the monastery. He had leisure and he was a scholar; and though Theodore and his familia were learned men, they had the pastoral charge and many things to do beside writing.

There is a more important reason for the greater splendour: the excellence of the renaissance in the north. The bretwaldaship passed to the north with Edwin, Oswald and Oswiu: and with royal power went royal riches and royal patronage. Moreover, the northern minsters received a more direct contribution from Celtic art and learning than those of Kent: Iona and Lindisfarne did more for Monkwearmouth-Jarrow than Malmesbury and Glastonbury at this time did for Winchester. As regards the superiority of stone monuments like the high crosses in the north: there is evidence in charters and place names that some such were set up in southern England, but increased population led to more rebuilding in the south, which militated against survival. As regards illuminated manuscripts: it may be that many such at Canterbury, Winchester, etc., perished in the Danish raids. On the other hand, it is likely that there never were, in southern England, manuscripts as beautiful as the Lindisfarne gospels, because at Canterbury the Latin temperament and 'gravitas' prevailed: this would be a parallel to the contrast between the functional sobriety of the Roman and the comparative elaboration of the Celtic rite. Boniface might write and ask an English nun to send him an altar book written in large letters because his sight was failing with age: we do not know that he or the nun would have desired a book with lovely pages of abstract ornament, such as the Irish scribes produced: or that there was the skill in the minsters of southern England to illuminate such pages. For a monk to spend a lifetime in acquiring and practising such skill was within the Celtic tradition: otherwise, only to be found in houses influenced by such a tradition.

The old Greco-Roman learning, the seven liberal arts, and some knowledge of Roman law, came to the church of Canterbury with Theodore, Hadrian and Titillus: as also to the north with Wilfrid and Benedict Biscop. All these men had been in touch with the old civilisation as it persisted in Rome, Greece and Gaul. Young scholars from outside his own familia sought the teaching of Theodore at Canterbury, and particularly young Celtic scholars. The only written monuments of Theodore's teaching that have survived to us are his Penitential, long published and studied,[1] and the unpublished

[1] A. W. Haddan and W. Stubbs, Councils and Ecclesiastical Documents, iii. 173.

manuscript of his commentaries on the scriptures.[1]

The chief point of interest about the Theodoran commentaries is that they form the link, hitherto missing, between the biblical exegesis of the patristic period and that of the early middle ages. The homilies and *Moralia* of Gregory the Great, and the allegorical commentaries of Isidore of Seville (d. 636) bring the period of patristic exegesis to an end; almost a century elapsed before Bede revived the tradition of biblical study. It has recently been shown, however, that the work of archbishop Theodore in biblical exegesis bridged the gap.

German scholarship has demonstrated that a series of commentaries occur in a Milan corpus of biblical glosses, the relevant part in an eleventh century hand. These biblical glosses must have been put together earlier in a monastery north of the Alps: they include three series of writings on the Pentateuch and two series on the first and second gospels, which must at first have existed in separate manuscripts before their combination in the archetype of the Milan manuscript. The commentaries instance Anglo-Saxon coins and weights, quote the Greek commentators as well as the Latin ones, and have an 'explicit' attributing them to 'Theodorus'. They are undoubtedly quoted by Bede, and appear to have contributed to Bede's occasional following of the literal, critical, Antiochene mode of interpretation, as well as the allegorical Alexandrian school, then more generally used. Gregory the Great had followed the Alexandrian school of interpretation, and it was to be widely so followed by the Carolingian teachers; Theodore and Bede show more critical, historical interest in the text.

There is some evidence also that Theodore not only expounded the text of the scriptures at Canterbury, but gave lectures on moral theology in his *familia* in the traditional manner. Long before medieval theologians were trained in cathedral schools on a collection of important patristic passages called the *Sentences* of Peter Lombard, which became the most commonly used theological textbook of the middle ages, Isidore of Seville had written his own *Sententiarum libri iii* for the same purpose: the instruction (in the first place) of the clergy of his own household. One of the nine *Answers*

[1] B. Bischoff, 'Wendepunkte in der Geschichte der lateinischen Exegesis im Frühmittelalter', in *Sacris Erudiri*, vi. pt. 2 (1954); M. Deanesly and P. Grosjean, 'Canterbury Edition of the Answers of pope Gregory I to St. Augustine', 10, in *Journal of Ecclesiastical History*, x (1959).

(*Responsiones*) of pope Gregory known to Bede, and inserted in the *Historia Ecclesiastica*, is a long *Sententia* about temptation, in which the description of the three modes of temptation is borrowed from pope Gregory's homily for the first Sunday in Lent (*xl Homiliarum libri*). This and another *Answer* may have been composed at Canterbury.[1]

Theodore's *Penitential*, as it stands, appears at first merely a long list of penances for the sins of clerics and laymen, many of them the sins of rough and barbarous men in a rough and barbarous age. His work in connexion with the penitential system was, however, of great importance, and not only for England. He set the seal of his authority on the Celtic system, and wherever the Celtic missionaries went they spread its use. The first penitential books that have survived to us come from Ireland and Britain: the later ones were put together on the Continent. Columba, Columbanus and the Irish-trained Willibrord used the Celtic system: and, since archbishop Theodore authorised it, so did the English missionaries, Boniface and his fellow monks. Whereas the older system of penance in the Mediterranean countries was administered only after grave sin such as heresy and had no essential connexion with the giving of spiritual counsel or the direction of life, the Celtic abbot or priest, regarding sin as a sickness of the soul, not only adjudged penance, but gave salutary counsel. Whereas the earlier penitential discipline concerned the measurement of a long penance, which the penitent must perform before he could be readmitted to the company of the faithful and to holy communion, the final absolution being given in public, in the Celtic penitential system, penance and absolution (now private) became intimately connected with spiritual counsel. The penitent (at first a monk) might admit to his abbot or a priest monk the temptations which assailed him as well as the sins he had, in fact, committed: he consulted his confessor as a doctor and asked him for penance as the medicine for his soul, as well as for the absolution which would reunite him to God. This fusion of the old Greco-Roman with the newer Celtic system, authorised by archbishop Theodore in the first place, was to affect the future administration of penance. A parallel development occurred in the east, also springing from monastic sources.

The penitential books are of importance historically as showing the method of training in the spiritual life used by such men as Theodore, Willibrord and Boniface.

The Celtic books used by Theodore had already undergone some development: various teachers had collected the relevant canons of councils, and the *dicta* of great Celtic abbots, and combined them for their own use in a single roll or tome. The Irish books derived their spiritual teaching from Cassian, who owed his own instruction to the eastern monks and the desert fathers. The eastern monks served in hospitals and were familiar with the theories of Greek medicine, particularly the doctrine of the 'contraries': sicknesses could be cured by the contraries of their causes, as shown in the symptoms. Similarly with sins, which were conceived of as sicknesses of the soul. Cassian wrote that sins like anger, dejection, etc., could be cured by practising their opposites, and the Irish abbot, Finnian, wrote in his penitential that for wrathfulness, especial patience must be used: for depression, spiritual joy; and for greed, liberality. The phrase that appears so often in the prologues of Anglo-Saxon charters, that the donor has made these grants 'pro remedio animae meae', derives from the doctrine of 'the contraries' and may show the influence of the Celtic penitentials. In all these penitential books, penance is asked and given as the remedy of the soul, not as the public satisfaction to be made for a public offence against the law of God.

St. Benedict, of course, was familiar with the *Collations* of Cassian, and the disclosure of secret faults or thoughts by the monk to his abbot, as a means of humility, so that there was nothing fundamentally opposed in the teaching of Cassian and Benedict about the direction of monks by their abbot; but the doctrine of the contraries, and the allocation of specific amounts of penance as remedies for specific sins is not emphasised in the Benedictine rule.

A century after Cassian, the penitential of the Irish abbot Finnian of Clonard (d. c. 550) was used by Columbanus, who in one letter to Gregory the Great stated that Finnian had asked the advice of Gildas about unstable monks. Finnian's penitential is long, begins with advice on the remedy for sins of thought, and goes on to deal with progressively worse sins like anger, bloodshed, fornication, magic, false swearing, murder, and the appropriate acts of penance; these to be lighter for a layman than for clerics. The penitential of Cummian (d. c. 650) probably originated in Ireland and was even longer: its scheme is based on Cassian's doctrine of the eight principal sins, and it appears in manuscripts sometimes as the *Excarpsus Cummiani* (Excerpts of Cummian, implying that he made extracts from older canons and penitentials).

It was probably this book which was used by Theodore, as representing the Celtic penitential system; it deals with rough and barbarous sins, and also with monastic offences like disdaining to bow to a senior, not doing the work imposed upon the monk, not arriving before the second psalm of the office, etc., with those who in error change the words of the sacraments, and with the sins of those outside the minster. 'Good kings should be prayed for: never, evil kings.' Those who furnish guidance to barbarians should do penance for fourteen years, even if this has not resulted in the slaughter of Christians. 'He who despoils monasteries shall fast for a year on bread and water and give everything that he has taken to the poor.' 'But this is carefully to be considered in all penance: the length of time anyone remains in his faults: with what learning he is instructed: with what passion he is assailed; with what courage he stands: with what tearfulness he is seen to be afflicted.'

Another set of Irish canons (the *Canones Hibernienses*) is quoted by Theodore, and seems to date from c. 675: it enjoins the giving of tithes from the flock, but only once, not every year, and from all produce of the ground, every year; if a man has but one cow or ox, he cannot divide it, but he shall divide its value and give one tenth. To the Irishman Adomnan, abbot of Iona from 679 till 704, penitential writings are also attributed; they deal with the hygienic problems of a primitive and hungry age: what sort of pollution or corruption prevents the flesh of an animal or a bird from being eaten? 'Women are not to be in any manner killed by men'; 'If a woman deserves death for killing a man or woman, or for giving poison whereof death ensues . . . she is to be put into a boat of one paddle as a sea-waif upon the ocean, to go with the wind from land. A vessel of meal and water to be given with her. Judgment upon her as God deems fit.'

Very little is known in most cases of the writing down, or even of the authorship, of these penitentials: no doubt partly because they were not regarded as literary works written by particular bishops or abbots, but as the selections they had made from old writers on penance, or even merely as the set of 'iudicia' or 'sentenciae' which they were in the habit of using.

Of Theodore's penitential, however, we know more, from a prefatory note, which says that Eoda the priest obtained these judgments
from archbishop Theodore, and a 'discipulus Humbrensium' wrote
them down. Eoda would have worked in Theodore's lifetime,
before 690, and the young scholar from the north, studying at
Canterbury, not much later. The *Liber Pontificalis*, written in the
latter half of the eighth century, knew that Theodore had published
or edited certain 'judgments on sinners', and archbishop Egbert of
York (734–766) twice quoted from it in his own penitential.

Theodore's 'judgments' cover a wide field. Those who celebrate
Easter on the fourteenth day of the month, with the Jews, shall do
penance. The Greek clergy and laity communicate every Sunday,
and those who miss for three Sundays are excommunicate: 'we (the
English) communicate at will, but those who do not communicate
are not excommunicate'. The bishop only may reconcile penitents
on Maundy Thursday: 'Reconciliation in this province is not public,
for penance is not public'. Churches may be moved, without new
consecration; wood from a disused church may not be used by
seculars, but it may be used in the minsters. A bishop may confirm
in the field if necessary: 'a baptism without confirmation is imperfect, nevertheless, we do not despair'. A priest may say mass in the
field (without altar), 'if a deacon or priest himself hold the chalice
and the oblation'. There is much about monks, nuns and minsters,
and one section implies the pastoral function of the minster: 'If anyone move his minster and set it down in another place, he may do this
with the consent of his bishop and his brethren, and send a priest to
the first place for the ministry of the church'. 'It is in the power and
freedom of the minster to receive the sick into the minster.' Monks
may not enjoin penance to seculars, for that is the special duty of
clerks: nor may women enjoin penance.

Certain clauses deal with those ordained by the bishops of the
Scots or the Britons and who do not keep the Catholic Easter: 'we
have no leave to give the chrism or the eucharist to those asking it,
except they have expressed themselves willing to be in the unity of
the church with us'. Other sections deal with marriage and prohibited
degrees of kinship; the insecurity of life from raids is reflected in the
injunction, 'If a man's wife be violently captured and led captive,
and he cannot buy her back', he shall wait for her five years, and
then take another wife. As to children: a boy up till fifteen years of

age is in the power of his father: after that he may make himself a
monk: a girl, not till she is sixteen or seventeen. After this age it is not
lawful for a father to give his daughter in marriage against her will.
One child may be given to a monastery in place of another who has
been vowed; yet it is better to fulfil the vow. Tribute shall be paid to
the church according to the custom of the province; so, that is, that
the poor be not violently forced to pay tithes, or to do anything
else.

The use of Theodore's penitential by Irish and Anglo-Saxon missionaries, and its copying by Irish scribes, are evidenced by many
manuscripts. The widely-spread *Excarpsus Cummiani*, though an Irish
penitential, contains as many sections from Theodore as from
Cummian.

The history of the *Responsiones*, or answers of pope Gregory to
queries of Augustine, may throw some light on the archive keeping
of the church of Canterbury, from the days of Augustine, through
those of Theodore, Hadrian and the notary Titillus, to those of Bede.
The *Responsiones* may have been received as letters, and the need to
keep important letters, such as the one making Augustine abbot of
his band of missionary monks, or regulating his relations with the
bishops of Gaul and Britain, was obvious. The *Responsiones* have been
attacked as inauthentic on the grounds that copies of them are not to
be found in pope Gregory's register of letters (as printed today), and
also for the incongruity of a pronouncement in one of his answers to
a query about lawful marriage. The *Responsiones* may, however, have
been preserved as a kind of dossier at Canterbury itself, and there are
parallels elsewhere for letters preserved by the recipients and not
found entered in the papal register; the episode is of interest in the
general history of ecclesiastical archives and of Canterbury learning.

The first instance of Canterbury record keeping is the writing
down of Æthelberht's laws. They have come down to us, with later
laws added, as written into a Rochester gospel book. They concern,
in the earlier sections, penalties for theft from a church, and the wers
of churchmen. The knowledge of Germanic folk law hitherto was
handed down orally: but it is not impossible that for a matter so
vital to Augustine's mission, determining clerical status in the
Kentish society, a written record should have been made. Papyrus
was the normal writing material, but it would be copied sooner or

later on to parchment, and in the early days of the mission there were few parchment books except altar books.

The *Responsiones* themselves would have been received as letters written on papyrus, either in a group or singly, for the papal notaries used papyrus exclusively for the letters they issued and the registers they kept in the form of rolls (*volumina*), now and very much later. An East Roman emperor had prescribed its use for all records, when the papyrus industry on the Nile was an imperial monopoly; the notaries, official, legal scribes, used it traditionally, and the papacy deferred to the imperial mandate, as it usually did in all matters not of first-class importance. All bishops in the Mediterranean countries had a notary or two, to write their letters and keep their records, and the papacy had a small body of notaries (the 'scrinium' or 'desk') which continued the use of papyrus even after the Arab dominance of Mediterranean trade routes had cut off supplies of papyrus from the countries of western Europe; these were driven to use the more expensive, and much more lasting, parchment.

Papyrus documents, of which great numbers must have been written in imperial Roman and early medieval times, were relatively fragile. They might last ten or fifteen years, long enough for correspondence, private or that of the imperial tax collector; but they perished easily through damp or through fire. It was this perishability of records that tended to blur the sharp line between an original and a 'forged' document in Europe, for some expedient for supplying a substitute for a destroyed document became necessary, as Roman law required the production of a legal document in due form to prove title to land or to the making of a contract, etc. It was to deal with a possibly lost document that copies of attested deeds were often made at the time, exactly as the original but without the subscription. When an original papyrus was destroyed, the copy sometimes had a subscription added, and this was tolerated. Sometimes again, when an original had been lost or destroyed, scribes wrote a new document, using perhaps fragments of the original, or extracts or references from other sources: or, indeed, simple tradition: 'as the men of old believed'. In short, copies made more or less accurately, or deeds written two or three hundred years later than the contract or gift they purported to record, all came in time to be accepted as originals. Only the exceptional scholar: Eusebius writing his ecclesiastical history: Bede, describing exactly the sources of his statements:

William of Malmesbury, examining the old charters of Glastonbury, distinguished as best they could the authentic from the inauthentic among their written sources. In general, few churchmen saw anything wrong in writing out an old document with minor changes, such as a more modern method of dating: or the insertion of a clause useful at the time of writing though not occurring in the older document; though few, like Daniel of Winchester in a letter to Boniface, would have sought to justify from holy scripture, deliberate deception and forgery, in a good cause. 'I will relate', he wrote, 'what I have extracted from the works of ancient doctors . . . when we read of any deception or even forgery (fingendi) used by them, recourse may be had at need to so useful a deception.'

There is no need, however, to reject the *Responsiones* of pope Gregory to Augustine as deliberate falsifications. They may, indeed, be accepted as authentic on two grounds. The first, that some papal letters are known in other cases to have been written by a clerk in the papal familia and not copied and sent out by the scrinium. They survived among the records of their recipients. When abbot Albinus of Canterbury sent the London priest, Nothelm, to search the records of the papal scrinium, and he did not find these *Responsiones* there (though he found other letters relating to the Canterbury mission), it is unlikely that they were there: archdeacon Gemmulus, who searched also, would have found them. Moreover, the copies of outgoing letters were entered continuously on to papyrus rolls (*volumina*), and not merely preserved as loose sheets (*schedae*), which might have got lost. It is likely that some of the *Responsiones* were sent directly by the pope: that one, dealing with the relations of Augustine with the bishops of Gaul and Britain is a loose version, perhaps compiled at Canterbury, of a genuine letter sent by Gregory through the scrinium and also quoted by Bede.

The other grounds for refusing to reject the *Responsiones* as inauthentic is that the *Responsio* dealing with degrees of kinship within which marriage is lawful has been found in a Copenhagen manuscript without the incongruous passage. The passage may, indeed, have been an insertion of Nothelm himself in the original text, to express it according to the Anglo-Saxon method of reckoning degrees of kinship, which differed from that used by the secular Roman lawyers, the notaries. This insertion in a document attributed to pope Gregory probably struck Nothelm as nothing more serious or dubious than altering the manner of dating in a document to a more modern one; but it gave great difficulty to St. Boniface, and, indeed, to canonists ever since. The Roman notaries, when they reckoned degrees of kinship between two parties, counted generations back to a common ancestor and down the other line to the second party: grandchildren of the same man thus stood in the fourth degree of kinship to each other. The Germanic nations, including the Anglo-Saxons, however, simply counted back to the common ancestor, so that grandchildren were related in the second degree of kinship. Nothelm, wishing to make it clear to Anglo-Saxon lay people, that first cousins could not marry, but the children of first cousins might do so, inserted a passage in the original text of a *Responsio* allowing that those related in the third degree of kinship might marry. To the English, this would mean that the children of first cousins might marry, though not first cousins; to those who used the canonical reckoning, it would mean that a man might marry his aunt or his niece: a proposition impossible to attribute to pope Gregory. Hence the doubts as to the authenticity of this *Responsio*, and of the whole *Libellus Responsionum*.

The school of Theodore and Hadrian at Canterbury was in touch, through correspondents in Monkwearmouth-Jarrow, with the northern renaissance and the learning of the Scots; it was in touch also, through the greatest of its pupils, Aldhelm of Malmesbury, with the learning of the Irish. Aldhelm indeed, in a famous phrase, describes the crowd of Irish scholars at Canterbury who sought instruction of 'archbishop Theodore of blessed memory': he was pressed upon by a throng of disciples 'like a fierce boar surrounded by a pack of Molossian hounds'. They sought to bite him with the sharp tooth of grammatical query, but he always drove back the attacking phalanx, so that they fled to seek shelter in dark, secret caves.

Aldhelm was born about 640, and entered the monastery of the Irish scholar, Maildubh. The watershed between the small rivers running into the Bristol Channel and the English Channel near the Isle of Wight was a ridge of hills then heavily wooded: Penselwood lay at its southern end, separating Hampshire from the Britons of Somerset, and in the woods at its northern extremity Malmesbury had been founded as an Irish minster, at about the time when Glastonbury had received a large contingent of Irish monks or had been refounded by them. When Aldhelm was about eighteen, in 658, king Cenwalh fought the Britons *æt Peonnum* (Somersetshire people still say 'up to Pen'), and swept across to the Parret. While at Malmesbury, Aldhelm studied with the exiled Northumbrian prince, Aldfrith, son of Oswiu, who was later to shelter the northern renaissance. It must have been through Malmesbury that Aldhelm was instructed in the Irish *Hisperica Famina*, for that curious vocabulary was not in use at Canterbury, nor apparently much studied among the northern Scots. Here, too, Aldhelm would have become acquainted with Gildas' *De excidio*.

How long, and when, Aldhelm studied at Canterbury is not known: but it was at a time when some scholars, taught by Theodore, spoke Greek, and certain Roman lawbooks were available. Theodore himself quoted in his Penitential the secular lawbooks of both Greeks and Romans about marriage and the degrees of kinship,[1] and Aldhelm himself alludes in one letter to his studies in Roman law at Canterbury; the Breviary of Alaric was accessible to him there.

Professor Stenton wrote of Aldhelm that he was 'beyond comparison the most learned and ingenious western scholar of the late seventh century, but his ingenuity was expressed in the elaboration of a style which deprives his learning of all vitality'. The style which so unfortunately confused much of Aldhelm's writing was that inculcated by the writers of the tract known as the *Hisperica Famina*. Aldhelm could write clear, direct Latin in the style of the old Latin masters of rhetoric, and such clear, direct Latin was always at the time used for saints' lives and the canons of councils: but Aldhelm belonged to the school of western writers, Celtic writers, who subordinated literary clearness to the need to use the distinguished word: and the stranger, the more distinguished.

The *Hisperica Famina* are themselves 'distinguished words' for 'western speech': Hesper is the evening star, the western star, and 'famen' an extremely rare Latin term for 'word'. In the sixth and seventh century Celtic scholars had access to glossaries but few enough manuscripts of literary masterpieces; in Ireland they had no knowledge of Latin as a spoken language, nor did they hear great Latin verse declaimed: knowledge of Latin quantities faded out. Latin scholarship was a dictionary scholarship, and acquaintance with unfamiliar Latin terms highly prized. The Latin of Gildas in the part

[1] *Canterbury Edition*, 7, n. 2: cf. also ASE., 181, n. 1, and 183.

of the *De excidio* known as 'The Letter' is early Hisperic writing of this type, and shows a preference for unusual words and an involved style, though most of the unusual words are to be found actually in either the Jeromian or Old Latin versions of the Old Testament; Gildas uses, however, one certainly Hisperic word: 'tithica' for 'marina'.

The original version of the tract, the *Hisperica Famina*, was perhaps composed, not in Ireland, but in Brittany, Spain or Great Britain.[1] Then some master composed an edition for the use of his pupils: not merely a list of eccentric words, which would be hard to memorise, but a colometric tract, composed according to certain rules, and with an Irish background. Some of the words are not merely rare Latin terms, but hybrids, compounded of part Latin, part Old Irish or other elements. This manual for scholars was meant for young monks: women are never mentioned, apart from a strange form for 'Cynthia', the moon goddess. The tract shows no knowledge of quantity: the lines have a kind of internal rhyme, and the scansion is neither classical nor Old Irish; it is not a literary masterpiece, but rather a series of short texts enclosing a sufficient number of strange words, rare words, destined to furnish materials for an ornamental style when those who memorised it were writing their own works. The subject of the lines hardly matters: there are no cryptograms, nothing mystical, nothing even religious; passages occur in strange Latin such as the one which may be translated:

The star of Phoebus traverses the high domed arch of the sky and midday approaches. Our stomach at this time is burned up with a devouring hunger. Let us then visit the neighbouring demesnes, so that pasture sweet as honey may be furnished to the hungry.

Which is a Hisperic way of saying 'It is lunch time'.

Apart, however, from the effect of the *Hisperica Famina* in concentrating the interest of Irish scholars on the 'distinguished word', the tract is of great interest in the history of rhyme in early European verse. Each line in the colometric arrangement is constructed on the principle of having either a substantive accompanied by an epithet and a verb or two substantives with their epithet and one verb,[2] and in an immutable order: epithets come first, the verb in the middle, and the substantive(s) last. Epithets and substantives, in the same

---

[1] See for the *Hisperica Famina* the article entitled 'Confusa Caligo', by Paul Grosjean in the Zeuss memorial volume published by 'Celtica', Dublin, 1955.

[2] *Confusa Caligo*, 81–83.

cases, and always in the same places in the line, give rise to a kind of internal rhyme (libosas . . . tricarias; igneo . . . fumo; furibunda . . . discriména). It is a much more complex arrangement than that in the verses sent by English nuns in their letters to Boniface; but both are tentative efforts at writing poetry 'according to the rules' when general knowledge of the quantities in Latin words had lapsed, and a verse arrangement governed by the stressed accent had not yet become general.

It was unfortunate that Aldhelm's Latin prose should have been inspired in some instances by Hisperic teaching: but he was a great scholar who lived at a turning point in the history of Latin literature, and his writings were not without effect.

In the first place, his own Latin verse could scarcely have been what it was apart from his preoccupation with the distinguished word. Miss Waddell's translation of his poem on the thunderstorm is familiar: and she emphasises the rip of the thunder caught in the line:

> . . . baccharentur in æthere.

But who but a Hisperic scholar, fondly bringing out a distinguished word from careful memory, would have thought of bringing the Bacchae into it at all?

Then again, like all monastic scholars, Aldhelm and scholars of the Irish school were at times called upon to write 'charters', records of donations, willed bequests, etc. The body of the grant would follow the protocol handed down by the notaries with the Latin clear and precise; but by custom such grants had a preamble, governed by the rhetoric of the day. To Latinists educated in, or partly influenced by, the cult of the distinguished word, 'basileus' was a better word than 'rex', 'pantocrator' than 'all ruler', 'speculator' than 'episcopus' (Ego Herewaldus speculator aecclesiae dei: Ego, Daniel, dei plebis famulus et speculator). With the use of such aids to scholarship as the Corpus, Épinal, Erfurt and Leyden glossaries,[1] an even richer harvest of distinguished words became available to later writers of charters; it is not necessary to assume that such distinguished words were borrowed to express a particular constitutional significance.

Aldhelm's and other Irish scholars' delight in rare (and obscure) words contributed also remotely to the 'crossword puzzle' element in Carolingian literature, the anagrams, the acrostics, etc. The Old

---

[1] See W. M. Lindsay's edition of three of these early medieval glossaries.

Irish poem written by the scholasticus of a continental monastery about Pangur Ban, his cat, has the suggestive lines:

Hunting mice is his delight,
Hunting words I sit all night;

and, indeed, Carolingian scholars were preoccupied with words; it was part of their inheritance from their Irish forbears and the glossarists.

The churches built by Augustine and his fellow missionaries in Kent naturally followed the plan of the churches with which they had been familiar: they were built for the same liturgical purpose. Bede says that Æthelberht gave Augustine a general licence 'to build and repair churches' and no doubt such were built on the sites of Romano-British churches, for holiness attached to such sites, and in a few cases the old walls of churches may have been standing. But bishops in Roman Britain after the days of Constantine had often used house churches, and since then continental churches had been built in a more distinctive style: the new churches built in Kent followed the continental fashions of the day. The stone churches built were few in number and small in size, by our standards: great effort was needed to find stone masons, in a country where even the kings lived in wooden halls; it would seem that stone masons must have been imported from Gaul.

The buildings used as models by church builders in Gaul and Italy included:

The 'schola' (for small churches): a rectangular 'cella' often with a semicircular (apsidal) end, and often longer than it was wide. The width indeed was governed by the height of trees available for roof-beams: but the length could be prolonged indefinitely. The apse afforded a good speaking place.

The small chapels and 'martyria' in the passages of the catacombs: in the alcoves beside the passages, or in those of the trefoil in which such a passage sometimes ended, were set the flat stone tombs of the Christian dead, sometimes on stone shelves, one above the other. The crypt of Wilfrid's church at Hexham was built for one who had, like Jerome, explored the dark passages of the catacombs, with the quiet dead lying about him under the Christian inscription: just their names and the words 'in pace'. Jerome had been awed here by Christian antiquity; he reflected on the psalmist's words 'they went

10

down quick into hell', the living into the quiet darkness. Wilfrid, like Jerome, saw Latin Christianity as something very old, very heroic, and he desired that his church too should have a crypt for the bodies of the saints, like the Roman churches.

Thirdly, the small square or round churches of the east. In Persia, the land of the Tigris and Euphrates, churches were built while still, in the west, persecution made it impossible, and these small eastern churches were domed. There was no stone for building, and almost no timber: sun-baked brick was used for walls, for arches, and soon for domed roofs. In England there was both stone and timber: but the half dome was used, as in western Europe, to cover the apsidal ends of churches.

Fourthly, for a relatively large church, the secular basilica, or colonnaded building, was used, as it had been in the past for pagan temples. A wider building could be secured if the roof beams were supported on rows of pillars at the side of the central nave. A large basilican church in Italy would, if it had a font at all, have had a separate baptistery: but none are known to have been built in England.

Fifthly, a basilican church with a square, colonnaded court, or atrium, at the end away from the apse. In such a square atrium the bishop lived now with his clergy; Gregory of Tours often refers to this arrangement in the churches of the Franks, and Augustine must have been entertained by bishops in such houses as he passed through Gaul. Excavation has not, however, discovered the remains in England of any atrium built in stone.

The Kentish group of churches, mentioned by Bede, and whose plan is known by excavation, includes eight whose plan is more or less fully known, and of which there are at least fragmentary remains. The churches are much alike in structure, and some can be dated by literary evidence. They were plain buildings of good workmanship, with thin, well laid walls and solid flooring.

The most important, the church of the Saviour, Christ Church, was within the walls of the Romano-British city. Its plan is not easy to describe with certainty, as the site was built over for the churches of succeeding archbishops. If any traces of Romano-British masonry or flooring survived there till the Norman Conquest, they were swept away by Lanfranc in the eleventh century: but Eadmer, precentor of Canterbury, described the church there as it had existed before the fire of 1067. It appears that this church had apses both at the east and the west end: that in Augustine's church the high altar, the altar of Christ the Saviour, was at the east end, raised above a confessio or crypt, and that porticus of his church, on the north and south sides of the aisle, were later crowned with towers. The western apse of Eadmer's church must have been built later than Augustine's day, but may possibly stand upon the site of a pre-Augustinian church orientated to the west. The western altar was, in Eadmer's church, dedicated to St. Mary, and behind it, at the back of the church and facing the high altar, was the bishop's throne. The normal place for the throne in Augustine's day would have been behind or beside the high altar, which may suggest the co-existence for a time of Augustine's church with an older church: but there is no architectural evidence.

For St. Martin's, Canterbury, there is more evidence of Romano-British origin. Its site suggests a cemetery chapel, without the walls, and its form, that of an old chapel to which a Saxon nave was added. The walls of the (old) chancel were largely of Roman brick; the chapel had a small porticus to the south side floored with opus signinum. The form of its east end has not been ascertained, but a small remnant of a foundation buttress suggests that it was apsidal. There is no reason to doubt that queen Bertha and her chaplain used it for mass years before the coming of Augustine, and that a nave was added to the old St. Martin's in the seventh or eighth century.

Of the abbey church of St. Augustine's monastery, dedicated to SS. Peter and Paul, there are more remains. As was usual at the time, it was not the only oratory of the monastery, but it was the chief one, and probably designed also as a royal burial chapel, like that of Saint-Denis outside Paris. It had a nave and eastern apse, with small porticus north and south of the chancel to act as sacristies: this would have made the church cruciform in plan, like St. Pancras, the other oratory in the monastery grounds. But in the main church, side buildings or porticus were continued on both sides, of the same width as the small porticus: they projected beyond the nave at the west end and enclosed the narthex. They were separated from the nave not by a colonnade, but by walls pierced with a door into each porticus: they were, in fact, designed as burial chambers at a date when the old Roman law prohibiting burial within a building was still observed, but when the splendours of pagan burial demanded that some countervailing honour be shown to the bodies of Christian kings and prelates. In St. Gregory's porticus, on the north side, were buried in due course, Augustine and his successors down to Deusdedit (d. 664); in St. Martin's porticus, on the south side, those of Æthelberht, Bertha and Liuthard; at the date, St. Martin was the domestic saint of the kings of Paris.

The church of St. Pancras seems, both from its dedication and form, to have belonged to the days of Augustine or shortly later. It had a nave with a chancel of equal width, its end stilted and apsidal; small porticus were built out at both sides of the chancel. Later, small porticus were built out midway down the nave, and at the west end: but here pierced with an external door to act as 'porch' in the normal modern sense. The walls of this church were built largely from Roman brick, which suggests that they were supplied from the ruins of the old 'fane'. The chancel was separated from the nave by an arcade of three arches, resting upon stone columns, an 'arch of triumph' like that at Reculver. The provision of such arcades, and also of 'stilted' chancels (where the central point of the apse does not spring from a point midway between the ends of the chancel walls) shows that the small, low altar had been moved back from the chord of a semicircular chancel. The clergy would still sit on a stone bench (synthronos) running round the apse: the celebrant possibly might still stand behind the altar. At Reculver, remains of the stone bench have been found.

The third church within the monastery of SS. Peter and Paul was that of St. Mary, built by king Eadbald c. 620, due east of the main church and on the same radial line. Abbot Wulfrid, later, was dissatisfied with his two separate churches, and, to join them, pulled down the east end of the main church and the west end of St. Mary's, joining them with a fine octagonal rotunda, in the Carolingian manner.

Of the other Kentish churches built in the first half of the seventh century, the earliest was that of St. Andrew, Rochester, with nave, stilted apsidal chancel of nearly the same width, and an arch of triumph. The fine church of the double minster of Lyminge was built about 633 for Paulinus, and the Æthelberg who was probably Æthelberht's daughter. It had an apsidal chancel of nearly the same width as the nave, an arch of triumph, and a porticus extending along the junction of nave and chancel on the north side; it could be entered only from the chancel, and must have been used as a sacristy.

There is nothing to indicate any separation of nuns and brothers in the nave.

The church of Reculver, built c. 669 by king Egbert of Kent for Bassa, his mass priest, had a slightly smaller nave than Lyminge, but walls 2′ 5″ thick; it was not the church of a minster, and the fact that it was built for Egbert's court chaplain suggests that it was the church of a royal residence (a 'palatium'). The walls were of rubble composed of Roman brick, and there was a flooring of fine opus signinum, which further indicates that some Roman ruin survived, perhaps the house of a Roman villa estate, now included in the lands of the Kentish kings. The church built at Reculver had a nave and apsidal chancel of similar width, the two separated by an arch of triumph; Bassa must have had under him priests or clerics in minor orders, for whom the stone bench round the chancel was provided. The original church had north and south porticus, covering the junction of nave and chancel, and entered from the chancel: sacristies of some kind, other porticus round the north, south and west end of the nave were added later.

Another church similar in plan, but not in Kent, was built soon after 653 at Bradwell-on-sea (called St. Peter on the Wall). Though continental in form, it was built for Cedd, brother of Chad the Mercian bishop; it was thus the minster of a Celtic missionary, which he chose to build near the ruins of an old Romano-British city, Othona, in Essex, using old Roman stone work. The church had nave, apsidal chancel and an arch of triumph, north and south porticus with doors into the chancel, and a porticus at the west end. As at Reculver, the outer walls were strengthened by small buttresses.

The fine basilican church built at Brixworth, for a daughter foundation of the great Mercian house of Medehamstede, is still, in the main, standing. It was built in the late seventh century, and the architectural style shows an advance upon that of the Kentish churches: it is the most important surviving church of the date north of the Alps. The nave has colonnaded aisles, with four bays; the walls were built of rubble, and the arches turned in two rings of narrow, thin, Roman bricks. Beyond the arch of triumph at the east end of the nave was a square presbytery, indicating that the church was served by at least a small band of 'fratres', and beyond the presbytery lay an apsidal chapel, narrower than the presbytery, and on the outside polygonal in plan. On the small porticus at the west end a tower was later erected: and sacristy and storage space was provided by two small chambers adjoining the presbytery and two beyond the aisles at the west end. Mercia lay between the Celtic north and the continental south; but her great abbey of St. Peter at Medehamstede, and this church at Brixworth, were traditionally southern. Moreover, there was no indigenous tradition of fine stone building in the Celtic north.

Of another of the daughter houses founded from Medehamstede, Breedon-on-the-hill, in Leicestershire, there are no architectural remains, but some most interesting sculpture, including the figure of a bishop with a pastoral staff, who is giving the Greek blessing. Prelates of the training of archbishop Theodore would seem to have given the blessing with the thumb and two middle fingers joined on the palm, and the first and fourth fingers extended. Some fine stone panels have also survived from a great series of friezes in this church, with the Celtic interlace, and small figures including the so-called 'Anglian beast'. All these carvings are early, and accord with the literary evidence that there was a minster at Breedon in 675, that archbishop Tatwin (731-734) had been a priest there, and that the minster was obliterated when the Danes wintered at Repton in 874. It was not one of those restored by king Edgar. The church at Brixworth, these Breedom carvings, and such surviving stone carvings as the Hedda stone at Peterborough, show that fine churches were being built and adorned during the Mercian ascendancy. Central and eastern Mercia were, however, ravaged by the Danes with particular thoroughness.

Within these southern churches, Augustine would have used the Roman rite and ceremonies with which he was familiar, together with such Gallican variants as his pastoral sense told him would be of use 'in the new church of the English'. He was enabled to use an orderly ceremonial, because pope Gregory had sent him, with Mellitus, 'all things necessary for worship and the ministry of the church, namely, sacred vessels and altar cloths and also ornaments for the churches, and priestly and clerical vestments and relics of the apostles and martyrs and, moreover, very many books'.

It is clear from the arrangement of church plans that the Canterbury missionaries used a small square altar built on the chord of the apse, or just within the stilted arch of the apse: over this altar the priest would spread the corporal, a cloth large enough to cover it.

Nothing might stand upon the altar but the cup and the paten: the paten perhaps, as in one Merovingian example, a rectangular metal tray, large enough to hold small rolls or broken pieces of bread much larger than the consecrated wafer of modern times. (The word 'grail' comes from the Latin 'gradalis', dish, used for such a communion vessel.) There might also lie upon the altar the gospel book, regarded as representing our Lord himself.

There is no certain archaeological evidence as to whether, in the small stone churches of Augustine's day, a ciborium was erected over the altar. In the great Roman basilicas, lofty and spacious, the altar was sheltered by a canopy, supported on columns, called the ciborium; this made the position of the small, low altar more conspicuous to a large congregation and veiled the altar when not in use. From the pillars and rods of the canopy curtains or veils were hung, and at the apex of the canopy some ornament, such as a cross or crown, might be set.

It is likely that the ciborium was never actually used in the Kentish churches, because the Saxon arches opening into the chancel were narrow,[1] and partly screened the altar, and an arch of triumph did so even more effectively. Elsewhere in western Europe the disappearance of the ciborium in the west was due, however, to a special circumstance: the desire to place the shrines of the martyrs, or the saints, in very close association with the altar. From pope Gregory's correspondence it is clear that the relics he sent Augustine were buried at the foot of the altar or enclosed within it, with the reminiscence of the verse in the Apocalypse where the saints 'beneath the altar' cry 'How long, O Lord, how long?' But by the end of the eighth century it was becoming customary to raise the bodies of the saints, buried originally in the cemetery outside the church, 'to the altars' within the church; 'relics' might thus consist of small objects associated with the saints, small pallia placed for a time at their tombs, or the actual coffin with the saint's body: or a more honourable chest that replaced it.

A homily once attributed to pope Leo IV, but now known to be of eighth century Gallican origin, has the direction:

Let nothing be placed on the altar but capsae with the relics of the saints, or perchance the four holy gospels of God, or a pyxis

---

[1] The one remaining Anglo-Saxon arch of the four originally beneath the junction of nave and porticus at Breamore, Hants, is very narrow, as was the chancel arch at Bradford-on-Avon.

with the body of our Lord as viaticum for the sick: other things should be stored in some clean place.

The 'capsa' would be a wooden chest or ark, in this case apparently for relics other than the whole body of the saint: but about this time it began to be wished to translate local saints to the altar, and since their bodies were as yet undivided and the capsa holding them too large to be set on a small, cube, altar, the capsa was now set either at right angles to the altar, its end resting upon it, or lengthwise on a low retable, behind the altar. This new arrangement gave the altar a back and a front: it no longer had free access all the way round. The ciborium was now generally dismembered, the canopy being suspended and the posts either abolished or used as standard candlesticks; the altar tended to become longer. The priest had long been accustomed to celebrate facing eastward, with his back to the congregation: the new, Carolingian, form of altar rendered it impossible for him to celebrate from behind.

Some light on the impact of the divine service on lay people can be gained from their use of the Anglo-Saxon word for 'sacrifice' or 'oblation', the word 'husel' (in Middle English, 'housel'). Husel is connected with an older word, the Gothic 'hunsl', and was used for 'sacrifice': the gloss in the Lindisfarne Gospels for 'I will have mercy and not sacrifice' has the Anglo-Saxon words which may be rendered: 'I will have mild-heartedness and not husel'. The Alfredian translation of Bede's ecclesiastical history uses 'husel' twice as meaning the consecrated bread of the eucharist, the oblation: once, when Bede wrote that pope Gregory was buried in the church of St. Peter the apostle 'ante secretarium', the range of private chambers beside the nave where the clergy lived; the translator, not familiar with the structural meaning of 'secretarium' (the English churches were without this provision for the clergy), wrote of Gregory that 'his body was buried in St. Peter's church before the husel porticus'. This shows that in Alfred's day the husel was kept in one of the porticus; from another Anglo-Saxon term, it was kept in a 'husel box'.

The other place where Bede speaks of the sacrament reserved as viaticum is in his description of the death of Cædmon in the monastery of Whitby. He says Cædmon was ill fourteen days before his death 'but so moderately that he could talk all the time and receive visits. Now there was a little house near by, where it was usual to house the sick and those who seemed likely to die. He asked the infirmarian as the evening drew on, the evening before the night of his death, that he would prepare there for him a place of rest; and he was astonished that he asked this, because he seemed not at all likely to die; but nevertheless, he did as he was asked. And when he had cheerfully taken his place there, he talked and joked with those who were there before him; and when it was midnight, he asked if they had the eucharist within? They said: What need is there of the eucharist? You can't be going to die, for you have been speaking cheerfully and mirthfully with us, as a guest.' 'Nevertheless,' he said, 'bring me the eucharist.' And he fortified himself with the heavenly viaticum, and, signing himself with the cross, laid his head upon the pillow and in a short time fell asleep and died. The translator renders Bede's question, 'had they the eucharist (eucharistiam) within?' 'Had they any husel within?'

As to the celebration of the eucharist in the Kentish minsters and the small country churches: there are a few casual references to its celebration in the larger churches, and very little description of its performance in the smaller, village churches. Since the priest celebrating the holy mysteries would have been trained in a minster or a cathedral school (for there were no other places for the training of the clergy), it may be assumed that he would use the rite to which he was accustomed in the minster, but that he would be without the number of clergy in minor orders who would have assisted in the minster or bishop's church. Monk priests sent out from their minster to celebrate in a country chapel would probably be accompanied by a young cleric; a priest sent to serve permanently the church of a thegn's hall would perhaps have a young cleric, or lay altar boys, servers, to assist him: the number of clerks in minor orders in the whole church was large as compared with the number of priests: but occasionally a travelling priest must have celebrated unassisted.

The word used for the Christian mysteries by the clergy in Augustine's time in Kent was in some cases 'missa', in some, 'eucharistia': Augustine, in a letter to pope Gregory, spoke of the 'custom of masses' (consuetudo missarum) differing in the Roman church from that used in Gaul: actually, the 'custom of masses' varied in Gaul itself. Scholars today derive the word 'missa' from

the 'Ite, missa est' pronounced by the deacon, regarding it as signifying the accomplishment of a solemn duty, secular or sacred (see
p. 149). It did not come into general use at first among the Kentish
laity (see p. 148): nor was the popular use of 'missa' known to the
Celts. Judging from Adomnan's Life of Columba, the Celts spoke of
the 'sacra eucharistiae ministeria', the 'sacra mysteria', the 'sacrae
oblationis mysteria', or simply the 'obsequia'.

The most striking ceremonies in the Roman rite used by Augustine
would have been the procession of the celebrant and his ministers to
the altar, and that down from the altar for the reading of the gospel.
To the lay people, the bishop and clergy, or priest and clergy, would
look much like the bishop of Ravenna and his two attendants in the
well-known mosaic of Justinian and Maximianus, dating from
between 546–562. The lay emperor there carries a great gold dish for
an offering; the three clergy wear long white linen dalmatics (the
old form of alb or surplice, with full sleeves and purple bands over
the shoulders: in Latin, the 'clavi'). The bishop wears a dark green
planeta or chasuble and the pallium. The white linen garments, to
the Anglo-Saxons, would be unfamiliar and awe-inspiring.

The lay people would see the entry of the priest and servers from
one of the porticus used as a sacristy and hear the Latin psalm sung,
and the Latin prayers and readings when the priest reached the altar.
The Introit psalm would be the full psalm with the antiphon before
each verse: such an entry psalm had been used on the continent since
about A.D. 430. A litany might be sung between the Introit and Collect: pope Gregory introduced the shorter Kyrie eleison for use on
week days when he celebrated at the stational churches. It is uncertain
whether Augustine himself would have sung the 'Gloria in Excelsis'
in Kent, in his quality as archbishop: his priest followers would not.
Pope Gregory introduced the singing of the Gloria in the Gregorian,
a papal, sacramentary: it did not appear in the presbyteral sacramentaries (see p. 157). Before the Epistle and Gospel one of two or
even three collects might be used, as in the Gelasian sacramentary;
the Gregorian cut them down to one. The people would see the
procession with the gospel book, treated with great honour as Christ
himself: the clergy with lights and incense would sing the gradual
psalm as they walked down to the ambo or pulpit in the nave, and
the standing people would bow deeply to the gospel book, as to
Christ. Possibly, in this newly converted country, the reading of the

gospel would be followed by a homily or sermon: and normally when the bishop was celebrating. Bede wrote a set of homilies for each Sunday of the year, in Latin, of course. He commented on each verse of the gospel read.

There is no evidence to suggest that the gospel was read in the vernacular in the sixth or seventh centuries, either by the Celts or the men of Canterbury. But England at the time was a missionary country, and it is conceivable that the celebrant should have commented on the Sunday gospel in the local dialect. The Greek church was more than tolerant of vernacular gospels and even of vernacular liturgies, and it would be in accordance with the Greek tradition that archbishop Theodore should have commented to a lay congregation on the Sunday gospel: but there is no evidence of any practice of this kind.

No creed would be sung at the eucharist, for its recitation there was first provided for in Gaul by the council of Aix-la-Chapelle, 798; in Rome it was not so sung till 1014; the indispensable place for the recital of the creed was at the profession of the catechumens before baptism.

The offertory in kind was probably made in the Kentish churches, the people passing up with their gifts (bread, oil, wine) to the priest who collected them in a basket.[1] The Kentish churches usually had two 'porticus': chambers with no external door but one opening into the chancel: and porticus of this kind in Syria, Italy and Gaul were called the 'prothesis' and the 'diakonikon', the one for offerings, the other for the use of the clergy. There is no historical reference to the porticus as so named in England, it is indeed unlikely that Greek words would have been so used: but the Gelasean sacramentary provides for an offering in kind, and it would seem that in Kent too, as in Italy and Gaul, the priest would have set aside from the bread and wine offered the portion needed for the eucharist, and the other ministers would have taken the rest of the offerings to the porticus. The celebrant would then wash his hands and proceed to the most solemn part of the mysteries, the great prayer of thanksgiving and consecration, the canon of the mass.

To the lay people, so far as we know, the rest was a high and holy

---

[1] Some liturgical scholars think that the offerings at this period may in practice in many churches have been made before the service, as in the Byzantine and Gallican rites.

mystery: no vernacular words survive to show that they distinguished the different parts of the great 'husel hallowing'. But the vernacular word for sacrifice or oblation was early, and it occurs alone in Anglo-Saxon literature and documents, and in many combinations. To the lay people the hallowing of the 'husel hlaf', the oblation offered to God and given to the faithful, was the heart of the service.

Study in the history of the English language, its native words and its loan words, has shown that direct translations of a Latin word, the substitution of an Anglo-Saxon word for a Latin one, were earlier than the borrowings of church Latin words into English. Thus, the interlinear English gloss of the Lindisfarne gospels translates many Vulgate words, while the slightly later Rushworth gloss, and even more the Late West Saxon gloss, generally use the Latin term in a slightly Anglicised form. Terms that are direct translations, that is, appear to have been used early, when the Latin words would have been quite unfamiliar, and then the Latin terms themselves were gradually adopted into English. This has a bearing on the use of the words 'housel' and mass.

The word mass (mæsse) is a borrowed Latin word, and the word housel (husel) a translation: both occur in the Alfredian version of Bede's *Ecclesiastical History*. Both were probably early: husel, on a priori grounds, the earlier. It meant 'sacrifice', 'offering', and, for that matter, would translate 'oblation': in Augustine's day, 'eucharist' and 'oblation', 'sacred mysteries' would be as much used as 'missa' for the Christian 'servitium'. Later, and perhaps also from the first, husel certainly meant, the consecrated bread. 'Husel eosterlic' is the Anglo-Saxon rendering of 'sacrificum paschale'; sometimes husel translates eucharistia. In an excerpt from a Homily, husel again means the whole eucharist: 'The bread (hlafes) that we taste when we believingly go to the husel is sacramentally Christ's body'; the Alfredian translator equally rendered Bede's 'eucharistiam', husel (see p. 169). In combinations, husel sometimes means eucharist ('baptism, forgiveness of sins and attendance at the eucharist, (husel-gang), are common to all men'), but also, and perhaps more frequently, the consecrated bread: husel-bearn, one who may receive holy communion; husel-disc, the paten; husel-fæt, a sacramental vessel; husel-halgung, housel hallowing; husel-laf, the housel loaf; husel-thegn, an acolyte. If it is asked, 'What did the lay people call the Christian mysteries in Augustine's day?' the answer is: 'They probably called them, "the housel"; to go to mass, was to "go to the housel"'.

The word 'mass',[1] adopted into Northern English as 'mæssa' and midland English as 'messe', though not so early used as housel, is found in a legal document of 831, which enjoins that each mass priest shall sing for Oswulf's soul two masses. The Lindisfarne gloss, using the word for 'religious service' translated 'scenopegia' (feast of tabernacles) 'temples mæssa'. In and after the tenth century renaissance, mæsse is found as often as husel, and in many compounds. Ælfric (see p. 317) wrote: 'Now is the mass a memorial of the Lord's passion' (gemynd Drihtnes throwunge); and compounds like mæsse-æfen (e.g. Christmas Eve); mæsse-boc (missal); mæsse-dæg (mass day); mæsse-hacele (casula, chasuble): mæsse-hrægel (the Alfredian translation of Gregory's 'velamine super-humerale' in the *Pastoral Care*: apparently, the amice). For mass vestment in this later period we get mæsse-reaf; for priest, mæsse-thegn, and, of course, frequently mæsse-preost.

Where church customs or teaching immediately affected the laity, English terms are found which were direct translations from the Latin. To baptise was 'fullian' (to make white as a fuller): where Bede wrote in Latin 'they began to teach and baptise', the translator used 'fullian' for 'baptizare'. The word is regularly used in the English glosses on the gospel, as where John was in the desert, baptising: and he said 'I baptise with water', etc. Fulluht, again, was from the first the lay word for baptism: a font was a 'fulluht-bæth'; a baptismal name, a 'fulluht-nama'; a place of baptism, a

---

[1] The word 'missa', from mitto, mittere, misi, missum, was already in secular use for a dismissal before the church came to use it for the dismissal at the end of a liturgical service, or part of a service. Similarly, 'missio' was used not only for a letting go, a despatching, but for a release from captivity, or a discharge from service, a dismissal. 'Missa', in the secular sense implied some sort of a duty or ceremony accomplished and, in a secondary sense, the dismissal of the people, or the soldiers, following its accomplishment. 'Missum est' is found in a few early cases, and later 'missa', with the singular or plural verb. The phrase was used in palaces and guard-rooms: 'stat miles ad missam' was roughly equivalent to 'dismiss', and in the Theodosian Code of 428 'missam fecimus' means 'we have granted remission'. In ecclesiastical usage, 'missa catechumenorum' and 'missa fidelium' came to mean that part of the liturgy before the catechumens and the baptised were respectively dismissed. Cassian and Cesarius of Arles spoke of the dismissals in other offices as 'missae'. The Benedictine rule, cap. xvii, speaks of the dismissals at the end of each nocturn, and of the offices of prime, terce, sext, none and vespers, as 'missae': 'et missae fiant'. Presumably the abbot in these cases made some signal: no words of dismissal have survived.

'fulluht-stow'; the service of baptism, 'fulluht-thegnung', and the baptism time, the 'fulluht-tid'.

Similarly, the apostles were 'Cristes æthelingas' or his 'thegnas'; disciples were 'leornung-cnihtas'; the altar was the 'wigbed' or 'weofod' (the pagan word for an altar); for candlestick, the early, Lindisfarne gloss has 'light-iron', while the later glosses have the half-English, half-Latin, 'candle-staff'; the penance allotted, and later, the confessor, were the 'scrift'; the paten at mass, the hûsel-disc. The word for psalmist was half-Latin, half-English: 'sealmscop', where 'scop' is the Anglo-Saxon for poet. Martyr was early trans-lated 'throwere' (sufferer); evangelist, 'godspellere'; the word for teach or instruct was 'læran', as in 'I will teach you the fear of the Lord (lære).'

'Preost', from the Latin-Greek 'presbyter', must have been early adopted, judging from the number of compounds found with it. It meant, to the laity, both priest and clerk, all distinguished from lay-men by the white linen vestment they wore at the housel; mæsse-preost was early used for a clerk in the highest clerical order, who could say mass. Bede, monk and priest, described himself as 'beda, famulus Christi et presbyter'; the translator made it 'Beda, Cristes theow and mæssepreost'.

Ecclesiastical terms borrowed from the Latin came into use rather later: e.g. for priesthood, sacerhad; for monk, nun, monastery, munuc, nunna, mynster. The military standard, the 'signum', sup-plied 'segn', the word used, incidentally, for the pillar of fire in Exodus; 'vinum' became 'win'; synod, 'senod'; pinnacle of the temple, 'horn-pic temples'; a visiting of relics, 'relicsocnum'; sheep-fold, 'plett', from the Latin 'plecta', a hurdle. The Greek words for 'angel' and 'devil' have Latin forms in the Vulgate and passed thence into English as 'engel' and 'deofol'; and, though there was no Latinised form in the Vulgate, 'kyriakon', not 'ecclesia', supplied the English word for church, 'cirice'. This may suggest that the meaning of 'Kyrie' in the litany was popularly known.

Beside the stone churches the Canterbury missionaries brought church ornaments, books, and foreign craftsmen who carved stone for the churches, and soon after, for stone crosses such as those set up by the Celts. There are no extant crosses in the south comparable to those of Bewcastle and Ruthwell (see p. 170), but William of Malmesbury's description of the two Glastonbury crosses (see p. 17) suggests that they were comparable. They may have been placed at the head and foot of a grave, like the two that originally marked Acca's grave at Hexham; they were carved with the names of a West Saxon king and queen, as the Bewcastle cross was with those of Oswiu, Alchfrith and Cyneburg. They were set up by West Saxon monks in a minster originally Celtic, just as the Northumbrian crosses were set up by the Angles in territory originally Celtic.

The question whether such carved crosses, and abundant adornment of churches by sculpture such as that of the friezes at Brixworth, were found in the parts of southern England less influenced by a Celtic background is less clear. There are surviving crosses and carvings, but far fewer than in the north, and there is reason for attributing the setting up of at least one of them to the influence of Glastonbury. Italian influence dictated the structural form of Kentish churches and a severe and conservative ritual: there is no evidence that stress was laid on pictorial stone work or sculptured crosses. In a country where Christianity was new and the population of course illiterate, there was a more obvious need for stone pictures of gospel scenes than in Italy, where Christianity was already old. In no county of southern England have such numbers of crosses survived as in Yorkshire and the northern counties.

The standing cross from the church in the minster of Reculver is, however, notable. It has a round shaft carved with many figure subjects, and was set up in, or was anterior to, the late seventh century church; it is set into a pavement of opus signinum. The draped figures, the Italianate scroll work and the human busts in roundels show that it derives from Late Antique art; it must have been set up in the days of archbishop Theodore, but whether the church was built round the cross of a preaching station or whether a specially beautiful cross was set up in the new church as an adornment is not clear.

Surviving stone carvings from Mercia before the Viking raids include those of a colonnaded frieze from a church at Castor, Northants, where haloed apostles carry a gospel book, in the manner traditional to bishops; the Hedda stone, from Peterborough, in the form of an antique sarcophagus, with a gabled roof and a colonnade filled by figures of apostles at the side, where the drapery and inhabited vine scroll derive from Northumbria; the friezes from Breedon-on-the-hill, again with colonnaded figures in the

Romanesque manner; the figures from the church of Fletton, close to Peterborough; from Wiltshire, the carved panels of the arch in the church at Britford, built probably in Egbert's reign, with their vine scroll in the form of a running spiral, their enclosed bunches of grapes and acanthus leaves, showing Italian influence. The Newent cross in Gloucestershire and the tombstone of Frithburga from Whitchurch in Hampshire, belong to the mid or late ninth century, the period of increasing Danish raids, as do other fragments of richly carved cross shafts from southern England. On the whole, the carved stone work from southern England suggests less generous patronage than that of the north.

The art of painting was probably practised in southern England in the seventh century, both in the form of frescoes and the illumination of manuscripts: both would have been of use for the instruction of a newly converted people. But excavation has not been able to produce evidence that the early southern churches had frescoes; no fragments of painted plaster like those found at Lullingstone have been discovered. As to manuscripts: we know that an illuminated gospel book was brought by, or sent to, Augustine (see p. 158); but the earliest surviving illuminated books from Canterbury date from the eighth century. These were not merely southern examples of the more famous Northumbrian style (that of the Hiberno-Saxon school), but of independent origin.

The practice of 'illuminating' Christian books or documents probably started with the Egyptian illustration of papyrus rolls: such work could only become sumptuous with gold and silver and adorned with classical ornament when the writing material employed was vellum. Christian altar books, and particularly the gospels, began to be finely decorated: and since in pagan times a portrait of the writer had sometimes been placed at the beginning of a book, a portrait of the evangelist, in the classical manner, was now painted at the head of his gospel. In the Hellenistic art of the east Mediterranean it was usual to portray the evangelist in the neo-Attic style, as the gods themselves had once been represented, by a typical serene and timeless figure, and an organised, finite treatment of space. It has been suggested that this conservative treatment of figure subjects, with no movement, no intrusion of the outside world into the framed space surrounding the figure, can be associated with the

Christian theological school of Antioch: while the more realistic representations of figures and drapery in movement, a more naturalistic style such as that found in some pen and ink sketches on the margins of scriptural books, belongs to the school of Alexandria. While there are no surviving manuscripts to prove any association of the neo-Attic school with Antioch, it is yet clear that the traditional figures of the evangelists in these early English illuminated manuscripts, with their framed, timeless figures, drapery in the classical manner but not in movement, and their evangelists' emblems as part of the design, owe their inspiration to the east. Painted gospel books came to Britain and to Ireland, and also psalters with an illumination of David at the beginning: and monastic scribes in Northumbria, Ireland and Canterbury followed the Hellenistic inspiration and produced evangelists' portraits in their own decorative idiom: no Irish scribe could have produced an Evangelist's portrait independently, for it was very far from his own traditional abstract ornament.

Though we have no southern illuminated manuscripts quite as early as those of Northumbria, the southern scribes, like the northern, used Italian and Byzantine gospel books, and probably illuminated altar books which have not survived. Those which have survived are not the work of beginners in the art. The scribes produced, in imitation of their east Mediterranean sources, portraits of evangelists, purple pages with the writing in gold or silver (as in some Byzantine manuscripts), and arcaded canons, with the references for scriptures to be read written into the inter-columnar space. These southern gospels are markedly less Celtic in style than the northern, and have less pattern, interlace and barbaric ornament: they keep nearer to the classical inspiration, and show some evidence of Merovingian influence. The figures are more naturalistic and not mere calligraphic decorations.

Three manuscripts are, from their characteristic illuminations, grouped together as belonging to the 'Canterbury School' of the mid eighth century. The Codex Aureus, now at Stockholm, has within a columned arch, a seated figure with a scroll: curtains, which might be drawn across the empty chair, are here drawn back and looped round the pillars on each side in a manner reminiscent of a Byzantine mosaic: the design is somewhat clumsy and solid. In the portrait at the beginning of the Canterbury psalter, however (the

11

British Museum manuscript Vespasian A.1), within a columned arch which has become less architectural and more of a decorative pattern, sits David playing his harp, surrounded by dancing boys and shepherds playing their harps: one figure is, however, waiting with scroll to write down David's songs; it is a very cheerful design, and the ornament is Merovingian rather than northern. The Royal Gospels from Canterbury, perhaps written in the time of archbishop Wulfred (805–832), is a large book with great purple pages in the Byzantine manner and an abundant use of gold; St. Luke is portrayed in a roundel at the top of a decorative arch, and his emblem, the head and forequarters of a bull, against a blaze of colour within the head of the arch; the gospel begins with a great L (Liber) between the columns. In the brightly painted borders of the canon tables and the scrolls and panels with their little leonine creature involved in the ornament, we see not only a mature example of the school of Canterbury, but one influenced by the forms of the Carolingian renaissance.

Apart from the impact of the eucharist on the newly converted laity, the question of the rite used by Augustine at Canterbury and by his followers later, is of interest: though difficult to answer with precision and certainty. Exact knowledge of the rite used by the Irish, by Columba and Aidan and Cuthbert, is equally difficult to attain. Two points may, however, be noted.

First, that the sacramentary used by the men of Canterbury would have been the Gelasian sacramentary, which was a presbyteral sacramentary, and not the old Leonine or new Gregorian, which were pontifical sacramentaries.

Then, that the structure of the 'canon of the mass', as found in the 'ordines Romani' was already fixed when Augustine came to Britain. From the earliest times, and in 'the period of semi-improvisation', which to all intents and purposes ended in the fourth century, the structure, the ritual pattern of the liturgy, the eucharist, was fixed: but a traditional freedom of phrasing was allowed to the celebrating bishop. There was no single, verbally prescribed form of the prayers. There was nothing like, in Augustine's time, a single 'imposed book' of the Christian mysteries; in different churches and localities there were, within the general pattern, recognisable families of the rite.

Augustine would have used the Roman or 'Gelasian' canon of the mass; Columba and his followers some canon of the Gallican pattern.

Both at Rome and in the Rhone valley, the earliest church was Greek speaking: but in neither case is there evidence as to how the Greek canon was changed for a Latin one, or under whose auspices it was changed. At Rome, the earliest version that has come down to us is that found in the *Apostolic Tradition* of Hippolytus, dating from the first quarter of the third century: it is, of course, in Greek. The next evidence is from St. Ambrose's *De Sacramentis*, a set of catechetical instructions, in which the Latin canon used at Milan is either quoted or paraphrased; there is no evidence that the same Latin canon was in use at Rome at the time, nor is this Latin canon a translation of the *Apostolic Tradition*. The Ambrosian liturgy rather later (Ambrose was bishop from 373 to 397) shows important variations from the Roman liturgy and belongs rather to the Hispano-Gallican type (the Mozarabic, of which indeed, according to some scholars, it *may* be the source) or Spanish liturgy, and the Gallican liturgical variants used by the Franks, must have been more akin to the liturgies used by the Irish and St. Columba.

The Roman canon and rite as used by Augustine was substantially that found in the Roman missal of today, and in some manuscripts of the early sacramentaries.[1] Those elements in the modern Roman rite introduced later than Augustine's day include the preparatory psalm and confessions, all the offertory prayers except the secret, the prayers before and after communion, the blessing and the last gospel.

The Gallican rites known to Augustine were sister rites (though apparently newer and more developed ones) of those used by the Celtic church. The liturgies of Ireland, of Iona and her daughter churches, of Wales, Cornwall and Glastonbury, at least till that church came under the patronage of the kings of Wessex, was of the Gallican type: St. Patrick must have taken the liturgy of Auxerre, a Gallican liturgy, to Ireland. Something has been learnt of it from the works and Lives of Patrick, Columba, Columbanus, Adomnan, and the liturgical remains in the Book of Deer, and the Irish books of Dimma and Mulling. It can be stated that the Celtic rite had collects which occur in the Gallican and Mozarabic but not the Roman liturgy; a Gallican form of consecration, various formulae of

---

[1] Cf. also Atcheley, the *Ordo Primus Romanus*, though this is the Ordo of a papal mass in Rome, celebrated in a stational church, with many 'regionary deacons' attending.

thanksgiving after the communion and various biddings or addresses
to the people; and a complicated rite of 'fraction', as found in the
Mozarabic liturgy.

The liturgy of the Anglo-Saxon church from Augustine's time to
the Norman Conquest may be said to have been Roman with minor
Gallican embellishments. No missal of the period before the Danish
raids has come down to us; but it is hardly likely that Augustine
would, for the canon of the mass, have used other than the traditional
form he had used in Rome; for the other parts of the eucharist he
would have used the sacramentary he had brought with him, or the
masses and blessings of the Gallican rite.

The books which he certainly brought with him on his first
coming to England were copies of the scriptures and a sacramentary:
Bede tells us that other choir books were sent to him later. A sacramentary contained a collection of masses for the great feasts and some
of the Sundays of the year; forms for the administration of other
sacraments, and a variety of blessings. No Roman sacramentary had
as yet been officially prescribed, and from the surviving manuscripts
of sacramentaries it appears that new masses were written into old
books as occasion demanded; nor did the use of one sacramentary
preclude the use of another as desired. The difficulty of dating these
sacramentaries follows from this prolonged use of, and additions to,
early material; in no case have we a manuscript of a sacramentary
dating from the time of the pope to whom its issue is usually
ascribed. The celebration of the eucharist according to traditional
form was always the responsibility of the bishop, or such priests as
'ruled' a local church: the calendars and martyrologies would guide
him as to the mass he must say; some bishops may have had collec-
tions of masses on loose sheets (schedae), some may have had local
'sacramentaries' written on a roll, or in a codex, for their church. In
that great church, the Roman church, two sacramentaries were compiled, the Leonine and Gelasian, before the sacramentary of pope
Gregory himself.

The Leonine sacramentary was a large collection of masses,
certainly drawn up for the use of the church of Rome locally, containing the stational masses said by the pope throughout the year.
These are not arranged strictly in order, indeed, as Duchesne says,
'It would be impossible for an official book to exhibit such a state of
disorder'. The dedicatory masses are for churches in Rome, and the

Roman origin of the book is certain. The canon of the mass does not occur. Leo I, to whom the collection is traditionally ascribed, was pope from 440 to 461, but the earliest known manuscript of the collection[1] contains 45 masses composed by pope Vigilius during the siege of Rome by the Goth, Witigis, in 537. Belisarius, the Roman general, defended the city, but great hardships were suffered; the aqueducts were cut, and starvation and plague followed. The masses of Vigilius, pope during the siege, all refer to the dangers and hardships of the siege, and were inserted in the Leonine book on the anniversary of his consecration. The content of the Leonine book was not regarded as fixed.

While the Leonine book was a papal sacramentary, for use when the pope celebrated in the stational churches, the Gelasian sacramentary was a presbyteral book, for use in the Roman churches of title. Many obscurities in the history of the compilation of the Gelasian book, and its relation to the Gregorian and Gallican sacramentaries, have been cleared up recently by a very learned work on the Gelasian sacramentary by A. Chavasse,[2] which has illuminated the history of the three Roman sacramentaries, and their relation with the Gallican and Spanish liturgies. The Vatican manuscript of the Gelasian sacramentary dealt with by the author, our earliest manuscript, was written about A.D. 750; his analysis of the contents and comparison with the Leonine and Gregorian sacramentaries and several Gallo-Roman books supplies a history of liturgical institutions between the fifth and the eighth centuries.

As a result of these researches certain conclusions, long disputed, are established, and have a bearing on the rites used in the English church and the Celtic churches on the fringes of Britain. It now seems certain that the origin of the Gelasianum was Roman, though the Vatican manuscript in question has Gallican additions. It is also certain that in the early middle ages two sets of liturgical formularies were in use in Rome: the papal, stational liturgy, and the liturgy used in the presbyteral, titular churches, which itself varied according to the groups of churches within the 'regiones' into which the city of Rome was divided. The Gelasianum was not a sacramentary for papal use, but for the priests of the Roman titles.

---

[1] See A. Chavasse in *Ephemerides Liturgicae*, vol. lxiv, pp. 170-213.
[2] *Le Sacramentaire gélasien (Vaticanus Reginensis 316): Sacramentaire presbytéral en usage dans les titres romains au VIIe siècle*, 1958. For the text, see H. A. Wilson, *The Gelasian Sacramentary*, 1893.

Hence, it is not possible to fix the priority of Gelasian and Gregorian sacramentaries. The old Gelasian and the Gregorian books were in contemporary use: but they belonged to different places of worship. The Gelasian is a complex book; a compilation in which a series of pre-existent mass formularies fused, though they were of a different type and had had a different origin: it contains examples of an archaic and of a more developed type of mass. The compilation, as in the Vatican manuscript dealt with, dates from the seventh century, and must have originated in a 'parish' church served by a monastic community with a special cult for St. Gregory the Great: a church which was the seat of one of those institutions of charity which were the Roman deaconries.

Unlike the Gelasian, the early Gregorian sacramentary was a papal mass book for the stational churches, with masses for the Sundays and ferias when the pope went to one or other to celebrate. There was still no provision for the series of Sundays between Pentecost and Advent: they were still 'vacant'. The novelty of the Gregorian book was that whereas in earlier books the Sunday masses given were numbered as first, second, etc., after certain great feasts, pope Gregory's book inserted the Sundays and feasts into the Julian calendar, which began on January 1; Aldhelm described his book as 'liber sacramentorum anni circuli'.

Returning to the Gelasian book, with its larger variety of blessings, occasional offices and votive masses for use on 'vacant' Sundays or times of special emergency: Augustine must undoubtedly have brought this book to England, even if he also brought a copy of the new Gregorian book,[1] or of parts of it. The Gelasian book he brought must have been already an orderly collection of masses and blessings, though earlier than the manuscript analysed by A. Chavasse. This had the masses and offices for the ecclesiastical year, beginning with the great feast of Christmas; masses for saints days, for divine aid against plague, famine, enemies in the field and enemies to the faith, and for the dead, and many blessings and exorcisms; it must have had also prayers for catechumens, blessing of the font and the holy oil, and the rite for the ordination of priests and deacons at Rome, for the ordination of a bishop and for the consecration of a virgin.

---

[1] See the Rev. Klaus Gamber, *Wege zur Urgregorianum*, Beuron, 1956, who believes the Gregorian book to have been compiled in 592, but doubts Augustine's taking it to England as inappropriate.

It may now be said of the relation of the two Roman sacramentaries (Gelasian and Gregorian) to the oldest examples of the
Gallican missal (the Bobbiense and the Gothicum): that neither is
directly descended from the other, nor that both had a common
ancestor in the Leonine.[1] It is now held by some scholars that there
must have been an intermediate book between the Leonine, and the
two later books, Gelasian and Gregorian: itself sharply distinct from
the Leonine book. From this intermediate source, now perished,
were derived, on the one hand the pre-Gelasian and Gelasian books,
and on the other, the pre-Gregorian and Gregorian. Each of the two
groups had a double development, the one 'Roman', the other
'Gallican'.

As to its development in England between the coming of Augustine
and the catastrophe of the Viking attacks, manuscript evidence is
lacking. By Aldhelm's day, however, the new Gregorian arrangement of the Sunday masses according to 'the circle of the year', had
reached England, for he mentions having a book with this arrangement, which must have been the new Gregorianum.

By his day, the learned clergy studied the old liberal arts as a
secular preparation for theology, and the text of the scriptures in the
patristic manner. And the laity were made Christians at the great
'whitening' service, and went to the housel at times, and knew that
when they did crimes of violence they would not only have to pay
the wers and bots, but confess to the priest and have their 'scrift'
allotted to them. They would pay church scot at Martinmas: at least,
the king had ordered so. The saints and the martyrs would come to
their rescue if they went to the shrines and prayed: and if they were
sick and prayed devoutly, they might well be healed. And after this
life, which, as all men know, is very precarious, they would go to
the heavenly country with Christ; the door of heaven would be set
open, and within would be fair fields and great forests spread
beneath the skies; there neither rain nor snow nor blast of fire nor
fall of hail should do any hurt: that noble land is all abloom with
flowers.[2]

[1] See Chavasse.
[2] Cf. for this description, the poem 'The Phoenix', in R. K. Gordon's *Anglo-Saxon
Poetry*, 1954, 240: the poem is later than the Viking period, but seems to express, as
does a passage in king Alfred's works, the Anglo-Saxon idea of heaven. Bede speaks
of heaven as 'patria nostra'; of death as 'ascending to the heavenly kingdoms'.

CHAPTER VIII

THE NORTHERN RENAISSANCE : BEDE, ADOMNAN :
THE HIGH CROSSES : THE ILLUMINATED GOSPELS :
THE GALLICAN RITES

THOUGH the renaissance of learning and the arts came to southern England first with Theodore, its fine flowering came in the north. The greatest importance attaches to the work of Benedict Biscop, who brought the great store of books, the stone masons and the craftsmen to Northumbria, and to the name of Bede, his pupil; as also to that of Wilfrid, who brought the Latin rule of St. Benedict and civilised Byzantine traditions to the Celtic north. He brought no less sculptors from Gaul and 'caementarios' to build his churches: the Orontes had long ago flowed into the Tiber, and now the Tiber began to flow into the Tyne and the Solway Firth.

We have an account of the life of the venerable Bede (d. 735), the great scholar of the Northumbrian renaissance, from his own lips, from the time when he was a little oblate of seven years, offered by his parents to the most reverend abbot Benedict. The account shows how closely all his life and work was connected with the divine office and scriptures; learning them and then teaching them. He called his ecclesiastical history, in its last chapter, *Historia Ecclesiastica Brittaniarum et maxime gentis Anglorum* and ended it by saying that:

I, Bede, the servant of Christ and priest of the monastery of the blessed apostles Peter and Paul, which is at Wearmouth and Jarrow, have digested this history . . . either from ancient writings or the tradition of our ancestors or from that which I could learn of my own knowledge. I was born in the territory of the same monastery and when I was seven years old was given by my relatives to be educated to the most reverend abbot Benedict, and, following him, to Ceolfrith. And I dwelt all my life from then onward in the same monastery and I gave all my labour to meditating on the scriptures, and between the observance of regular discipline and the charge of the daily singing of the office in church, I ever held it sweet to learn or to teach or to write.

He was ordained, he said, in his nineteenth year to the diaconate, and in his thirtieth to the priesthood (703), by bishop John (of Beverley) at the request of abbot Ceolfrith. From the time of receiving the priesthood up till his fifty-eighth year he laboured, for his own needs and that of the community, to annotate briefly holy scripture, or to comment on its literal meaning and its interpretation (Bede's earlier work dealt with secular subjects, the liberal arts, chronology, etc.: it would not be considered fitting that he should teach the scriptures till he had been made priest, in the year 703. He had finished his work, *De temporibus*, by 703).

Bede then gave a list of his works: commentaries on Genesis, the first part of the book of Samuel, 'thirty questions on the book of Kings' soon after 716: about this tract he had a correspondence with the priest Nothelm; commentaries on Proverbs, the Song of Songs, Isaiah, Daniel and the twelve minor prophets (excerpts from Jerome), Ezra, Nehemiah, Habakkuk, Tobias, the Pentateuch, Joshua, Judges, Kings, Job, Proverbs, Ecclesiastes, Isaiah, the gospels of Mark and Luke, homilies on the (Sunday) gospels, certain expositions of saint Augustine on Acts, written out in order, an exposition on Acts, which he finished before 716 and dedicated to bishop Acca of Hexham; a book each on the Catholic Epistles, and certain other tracts on the New Testament and the Epistles and passages of the Old Testament. The Leningrad manuscript of the *Ecclesiastical History*, an early and authoritative manuscript, adds to this list of scriptural commentaries other commentaries.

Besides these examples of his work as a 'Lector', in the classical sense of commentator and expounder (of scripture), Bede includes his other works:

On the Tabernacle, its vessels and the priestly garments.
On the building of the temple: an allegorical exposition.
On the equinox, according to Anatolius.
On saints' lives: a metrical version of the life and passion of St. Felix, which he translated from prose to verse; a book of the life and passion of St. Anastasius, badly translated from the Greek, and worse emended by some unskilled person, which he corrected according to the meaning of the text, as best he could; the life of

the holy father of monks and prelate, Cuthbert, which he narrated first in the heroic metre and afterwards in prose. (The prose life he dedicated to bishop Eadfrith of Lindisfarne before 721.)

'The history' of this monastery, in which I serve, in the joy of heavenly piety': the house of Benedict, Ceolfrith and Hwaetberht. The ecclesiastical history of our island and people.

The martyrology of the saints: where he included not only the day of celebration (natalicia) of all the holy martyrs he could, but the nature of their martyrdom and under what judge they suffered. Bede used the so-called martyrology of St. Jerome (Martyrologium Hieronymianum), actually composed, not by St. Jerome, but in Columbanus' cloister of Luxeuil between 615 and 629. This compilation from the oldest calendars of eastern, the Roman and western churches became the foundation of most of the martyrologies of the west.[1]

Bede then listed the treatises that dealt with the different branches of the liberal arts: two books on metres, a book 'de natura rerum', and his two most important books on chronology, which would, as involving the movement of the heavens, rank as astronomy. Then for 'grammar', a book on spelling, for rhetoric, a book dealing with the art of metre and, added to it, a pamphlet on figures of speech and metaphors.

Bede's writings cover, that is, the whole field of sacred and profane learning of the day, nor was there any scholar in the Latin west to be compared to him. Further, the school at Monkwearmouth-Jarrow was in touch with that at Lindisfarne, and the instructress of that at York, through Bede's pupil, archbishop Egbert. For encyclopaedic learning, Bede is at the head of the line of scholars that runs through Egbert to Alcuin, trained at York, and through him to Hraban Maur and the other great Carolingians. Yet it is as what Bede calls a 'verax historicus' that he must have his chief title to scholarship. His mathematical studies had prepared him to cope with the historian's chief problem at the date: the fixing of a scale of time by which events occurring in Britain and the Continent, and in the different kingdoms within Britain, could be correlated. Dionysius Exiguus had worked out the year of our Lord's birth in relation to the consular lists of the Roman empire (and not accurately, according to the findings of

[1] See the Bollandist A.SS. for November, ii. pt. ii, p. x, published 1931.

modern scholarship): but he had given early medieval Europe a scale of chronology. It was Bede's use of the 'annus incarnationis' in his *ecclesiastical history*, however, that popularised this scale.

Bede's three tracts on chronology were important as laying a foundation for his historical writings, though he must have written these tracts as part of the instructions on the liberal arts which he gave to the young monks of the monastery. He had behind him, in writing his *Ecclesiastical History*, the work of Eusebius of Caesarea (c. 264–340), the first great writer on Christian history. Eusebius had collected together his historical material in his *Chronographia*, and in his *Canones* had shown the history of the great monarchies in parallel columns, so that contemporary events came side by side. He had used the years since the birth of Abraham as a general time scale, setting them in another column. He wrote also a general *Ecclesiastical History*, which Rufinus translated c. 395, and which Bede used: as also a chronicle of Jerome running up till 378, and the Consular lists and Roman Fasti. Bede used also the time scale of Dionysius Exiguus. He wrote three works on chronology: the *De temporibus libri* (in which he says in error that the council of Nicaea ordered the use of the nineteen year cycle), the *De Paschae celebratione liber* (to brother Wicredo the priest), and the *De temporum ratione*. Here he explains at length the use of the nineteen year cycle, saying that 'Dionysius, the venerable abbot of the Roman city, using the nineteen year cycle, chose to reckon time, not from the memory of men who were impious and persecuting, but from the Incarnation of the Lord Jesus Christ'.

In this book also he refers to certain English customs:

The English from of old have reckoned times by the moon's changes, that is, in months. The moon with them is called 'mona' and hence 'monath', month. April is Easter-monath, which now means for us the paschal month, but of old it used to be called after one of their goddesses, Eostre; the custom observed of old has acquired a new and solemn joy. May was called Thrymylchi, because in this month the beasts were milked thrice daily: such was the fruitfulness of Britain in times past, or of Germany, from which the nation of the English entered Britain. November is called blood-month; or month when they vowed the beasts to be sacrificed to the gods: thanks be to thee, O Jesu, who hast delivered us from these vanities and granted us to offer thee the sacrifice of praise!

As a church historian again, Bede's labours in collecting information from the best living authorities places him in a class by himself; Isidore of Seville and Gregory of Tours were both learned men, but they attempted (as far as we know) nothing like it. Not only did Bede correspond with abbot Albinus, but at his suggestion he obtained information about Wessex and Sussex from bishop Daniel of Winchester, and from the brethren of Lastingham about the preaching of the faith in Mercia and Essex by Cedd and Chad. Abbot Esi related to him the history of the East Angles, and bishop Cuneberht and others that of the Lindissi (in Lincolnshire). With the history of the church of Lindisfarne he had special acquaintance through the communications of the brethren in his preparation of the Life of Cuthbert.

Bede's simple and unassuming account of his own life is that of a good Benedictine monk, who takes it for granted that his life will be spent within the monastery, in obedience to his abbot and the rule, and with his day completely filled by the recitation of the opus dei and such work as is enjoined upon him; in his own case the charge of the singing of mass and office, teaching, study and writing. Like his contemporaries, he believed that holiness of life and nearness to God might be attested by miraculous signs from heaven, either at the saint's prayer, or simply at the divine will. With this belief in the efficacious power of holiness went the firm belief in the saint's power after death, if prayer was made near his tomb, or even some object associated with him in life. It would not have seemed extraordinary to Bede that the seals should warm the feet of St. Cuthbert, or that St. Aidan's oil should still the storm at sea, or that the plague which afflicted the South Saxons and the monastery of Selsey should be stayed through the intercession of St. Oswald. He recounts these and many other miracles, many of them miracles of healing.

The northern renaissance, whose fine flower was the scholarship of Bede, extended, however, to the Celtic monasteries of Iona and Lindisfarne. Here the influence of continental learning and art was less great, for the houses were directly or indirectly Irish in origin and looked for inspiration to their mother country; but some continental influence there must have been, for the Lindisfarne gospels have the illuminated portraits of the Evangelists, not a native Irish adornment. Some manuscripts written on the continent probably

penetrated to Iona. The work of the learned abbot, Adomnan of
Iona, preceded that of Bede, though it was narrower in scope. This
Irish monk, who was born about 624 and died in 704, was remotely
related to Columba himself, entered Columba's monastery, and
became its ninth abbot in 679. In 686 and 688 he made visits to
Aldfrith, king of Northumbria, who had been educated in Iona, and
at Aldfrith's court and at Lindisfarne he seriously considered the
arguments for the Dionysian cycle and the new dating of Easter. He
was won over, and on his return to Iona he tried to convince his
monks, who found his abandonment of the Columban dating startling
and rather shocking. He converted only a minority. From 692 onwards he corresponded with and tried to convert the northern Irish.

At some point he took over the duty of writing a better life of the
patron of his house, some form of which must have existed from the
time when the monks began to celebrate his annual feast day. Such
an early 'life' would amount to little more than a recension of his
miracles. Adomnan's predecessor as abbot, Cuminus Ailbe, had set
in order a life of Columba, and Adomnan rewrote and extended it.
Though he relates something of Columba's birth and training under
bishop Finnian of Moville, and how, when he was forty years of age
'he sailed as a pilgrim from Scotia (Ireland) to Britain', and how for
thirty-four years he carried on the heavenly warfare on the island of
Iona, the Life is not arranged with primary regard to chronology.
The first of its three books deals with his prophetic revelations, and
throughout the Life the intention is to give evidence of divine
approval of Columba's holiness, not only by the blessing on his work
but by miracle.

It is of interest that Adomnan narrates that holy order, among the
Celts, could be conferred by one bishop only, though normally
three bishops conferred it. Though the abbots of Iona, in memory of
Columba, were always priest abbots, yet claustral bishops there must
have been: as the consecration there of Aidan, Finan, Colman and
others shows. It appears also in the Life that the diaconate was given
younger among the Irish and Scots than on the Continent; for when
Columba was studying under Finnbarr the bishop, it states, 'while he
was still a youth' in deacon's orders, there was a shortage of wine
for the holy mysteries; Columba heard the servers at the altar lamenting the shortage, and, as deacon (for in those days he was serving in
the grade of deacon), he went to the spring and drew water: and the

water became wine. He came back from the spring and entered the
church and placed the water made wine upon the altar: and the holy
bishop Finnbarr and the servers gave thanks to God.

Bede, in his account of Adomnan as 'sapiens' (skilled in the liberal
arts) and 'most nobly instructed in the scriptures', mentions that he
'wrote a most useful book' on the holy places in Palestine. He wrote
it after conferring with Arculf, the bishop of a city in Gaul, who had
made a pilgrimage to Jerusalem and travelled throughout all the
Holy Land, and visited also Damascus and Constantinople, Alexandria 'and many marine islands'. He was returning to his own land
by sea, apparently round the promontories of western Europe, and
he was driven by gales up the Irish Channel and carried to the
western shores of Britain; and at length he arrived at Iona, and found
Adomnan well taught in the scriptures and well acquainted (by
book) with the holy places. Adomnan welcomed Arculf to Iona,
and whatever in his account of the holy places he deemed worthy of
remembrance, he wrote down. He wrote a book, 'as I said, very
useful to many, and chiefly to those who knew only by reading of
those remote places in which the patriarchs and the apostles lived',
and he sent the book to king Aldfrith.

Another product of the northern renaissance of learning, and one
about which there is little certain knowledge, is the keeping of
'annals' in some northern house. From the time that Easter tables
came into use (see p. 87), it was possible to record in the column for
the 'annus incarnationis' events of great importance to bishops'
minsters or abbots' minsters: the accession and death of kings, the
blessing of abbots, the consecration of bishops, and the days of
their deaths, with such outstanding events as battles or years of the
plague. The keeping of annals seems to have begun first in Ireland,
in the latter half of the sixth century: a set of Irish annals would seem
to lie behind the Welsh annals, the *Annales Cambriae*,[1] as do also some
North British annals, as indicated by certain North British entries.
No written records have survived from the North British area: but
a consistent body of later traditions represents prominent Irish fifth
and sixth century saints as receiving their education at Whithorn,
and it has been suggested that the original annals of the 'Men of the

---

[1] For the Irish and Welsh annals, see Wade-Evans, A. W., Nennius's *History of the
Britons*, 31: the subject is complicated, but the prior keeping of annals in Ireland is
likely from the study of the computus at Bangor (see *supra*, p. 73) and *Studies in
the Early British Church*, Chadwick, N. K., 56 and passim.

North' were compiled at Whithorn; bishop Pechthelm, whose see was at Whithorn, was a learned man, in touch with both Aldhelm and Bede. An alternative theory makes Hoddom in Dumfriesshire, the monastery of St. Kentigern before he became bishop of Glasgow, the home of these lost North British annals: but the keeping of a set of northern annals in some house, and their passage to north Wales, seems indicated. Some such annals were used not only in the *Annales Cambriae*, but in the *Historia Brittonum*, associated with the name of Nennius, and perhaps compiled at Bangor Fawr in Gwynnedd.[1]

Besides the growth of learning in the northern minsters, there is evidence that the Christian account of the creation of the world, and many passages from the Christian scriptures, were being taught to the laity. Bede has many stories bearing on the impact of Christianity on the laity, and these take the shape of the recounting of the preaching journeys of the Celtic and southern saints and their miracles of healing; these occur also in the earliest saints' lives. But besides this indirect evidence of impact, it is clear that the instrument of oral culture, the memorising and singing of verses to the harp also began to be used at this time by Christian teachers. The only surviving poem of Cædmon, and the lines from the *Dream of the Rood* cut in runic letters on the Ruthwell cross (see p. 170), are both in the Anglian dialect of the half-century round about the year 700. They are the earliest forms of English Christian poetry that have come down to us: they belong to the golden age of Northumbria and Mercia: they are in the language of the layman. In the eighth century Boniface took English Christianity to Germany, and some English monk had knowledge of the poetry which Cædmon the herdsman made in his own tongue, and this was recalled when an early ninth century clerk wrote the *Heliand* (Saviour) in Old Saxon. Eventually, part of an Anglo-Saxon version of the *Heliand* was interpolated into an Old English paraphrase of Genesis. The tradition of vernacular paraphrases of scripture and vernacular verse about the cross as the instrument of salvation started in seventh century Northumbria and was handed on.

It would seem that in the days of abbess Hilda of Whitby (d. 680) the rhythm, metre and alliteration of the scops' songs must have been familiar, not only to the nobles but to peasants: not only to the

[1] EBC., 92.

ealdormen, gesiths and thegns in the king's hall, for whom the songs were sung, but to the servants who waited and the poor who crowded into the back of the hall, hoping for a food-alms. The scops' songs were rule-governed and stylised: but some freemen and servants with a good ear may have caught their swing and poetic sequence, for Bede's story of how songs of some kind, possibly in the old heroic metre, were sung at the 'convivia', the ale-drinking, of the peasants who worked the land for the abbess of Whitby, seems to point to this. But the songs dealt with the old heroes and the old kings. Bede, in the well-known story, tells how Cædmon had never been able to sing when the harp was passed to him at such a feasting, 'when one was ordained for the sake of joyfulness'; so he retired to the cow-stall to sleep there, because he could not sing. When commanded by an angel, however, he found he could sing 'in praise of God the Creator'. Seventeen manuscripts of the *Ecclesiastical History* have an Anglo-Saxon version of what Bede tells us Cædmon sang inserted into the Latin text.

In the lines recorded in the manuscript, acknowledged by scholars as those of Cædmon, the technique of the scops is followed. The hymn is in the classical run-on style, with every line but the eighth ending with a pause, and every sentence ending with a line. Where the scop used royal epithets for his hero, Cædmon used them of God; God is the ruler, the lord, the keeper, and his divinity is shown by the adjectives coupled with the epithet: he is the almighty, the eternal, lord and king: he is the ward or guardian, not of a folk or tribe, but of all men: he is the 'heaven-realm's keeper', the 'glory-father', the 'keeper of mankind'. Cædmon sang of the glorious works of God just as the scop celebrated the heroic deeds of his royal patron.

A modern version of Cædmon's hymn to the creator runs:

> Now must we hymn the Master of heaven,
> The might of the Maker, the deeds of the Father,
> The thought of his heart. He, Lord everlasting,
> Established of old the source of all wonders;
> Creator all-holy, he hung the bright heaven,
> A roof high upreared, o'er the children of men;
> The king of mankind then created for mortals
> The world in its beauty, the earth spread beneath them
> He, Lord everlasting, omnipotent God.[1]

[1] A. S. Cook and C. B. Tinker, *Translations from Old English Poetry*, 1926, 77.

A fine prose version[1] renders the lines thus:

Now ought we to praise heaven's kingdom's guardian, the might of the Creator and the thought of his mind, the works of the Father of glory. How he, the Eternal Lord, set up a beginning for every wondrous thing. He who is the Holy Creator designed heaven as a roof for the children of men. Then mankind's guardian, Eternal Lord, All-mighty ruler, afterwards made the earth for men.

No version reproduces adequately the alliterative force of Cædmon's hymn, for such attention to alliteration would involve poor translation of the sense of the words. But the alliteration is there and would help to fix the hymn in the memory of the illiterate (always much better than that of those who have learned to read books!) A single phrase, 'the might of the Maker and his mindthought' is an inadequate rendering of the original; and for the final line

firum foldu frea allmectig

with its three alliterative hammerstrokes leading up to the final 'Almighty' there is no alliterative modern rendering at all.

After Cædmon's song about the Creator, Bede continues, the abbess Hilda bade that he should become a brother in her monastery, and that scholars should recount to him 'the series of sacred history'; and Cædmon 'ruminating upon them like a clean beast', turned them into sweet song and sang them most sweetly to those who had taught him. Bede says that others among the people of the Angles attempted like Cædmon to make religious poetry: but there were none who could equal him. Apart from Cædmon's work as the father of English verse, it is clear that he had initiated an instrument for vernacular teaching.

That he, and the church using his talent, had indeed found a means to teach lay people of God the Creator and various stories from the scripture is evidenced by the history of his first hymn. The two oldest manuscripts of the *Ecclesiastical History*[2] and two others, have the hymn in the Northumbrian dialect, eight others in Late West Saxon speech, and there are five more in Late West Saxon in king Alfred's English version of the *Ecclesiastical History*; from certain minor differences in the text it is clear that the Alfredian translators

---

[1] See *The Poetry of Caedmon*, Wrenn, C. L., p. 6 ; *Proc. of the Brit. Acad.*, vol. xxxiii, 1946.
[2] The Moore MS. and the Leningrad MS.: see Wrenn, *supra*, 6 and 7.

12

were using a traditional form of the hymn, different from that in the Bedan manuscript. That is, the hymn was passed down orally, as well as by manuscript.

Moreover, the Cædmon poetry, produced after the Whitby priests had recounted to him the stories they wished to have in verse, was written down at once, and gave rise to a school of scriptural verse not meant to be sung to the harp, but to be read in the refectory of minsters. Such a collection is found written in the famous Bodley MS., Junius xi, which contains paraphrases in Anglo-Saxon verse of portions of scripture, and also paraphrases of non-scriptural material (see p. 264). None of this poetry is Cædmon's: it is later in poetic style, and begins with a poetic paraphrase of the Vulgate Genesis; it consists of long poems meant to be read aloud, not of short poems to be sung to the harp. But its subjects suggest that later writers, clerical writers, followed the school of Cædmon, of whom Bede wrote:

> He sang about the creation of the world, and the origin of mankind, and the whole tale of Genesis; about the exodus of Israel from Egypt and entry into the promised land; about many other tales of holy writ; about the incarnation, passion, resurrection and ascension into heaven of the Lord; about the coming of the Holy Ghost and the work (doctrina) of the apostles. He made many songs too about the terror of Doomsday and the horror of hell-fire but the sweetness of the kingdom of heaven; but also many others about divine benefits and judgments.

The lines from the *Dream of the Rood* (see p. 171) inscribed in runic letters on the Ruthwell cross (see p. 181) show that this Anglian version of the poem can be no later than the cross itself, now accepted as having been erected about A.D. 700. The whole poem survived in a Late Saxon version, probably half as long again as the earlier form in the Anglian dialect. The dialect of the lines on Ruthwell shows that the author was a Northumbrian, and the poem itself belongs to the early stage of the run-on style. The lines inscribed on the Ruthwell cross must have formed part of an early version of the poem, now lost, and are the better understood in the context of the whole poem, actually surviving in Late West Saxon, where the cross itself speaks as follows:

> It was many years ago—I remember it still—
> that I was felled, afar, at the forest edge,

borne off from my roots. Evil men took me; . . .
When I saw the ends of the earth shaking
I dared not bow or break, against
the word of God. All at once I might
have struck his foes down, but I stood fast there . . .
I quaked when he clasped me, but I could not bow to earth,
nor fall to the ground; it was my fate to stand.
As a rood I was raised; I bore my Ruler up,
the king of the skies; I could not bow down.
They pierced me with dark nails; the places are on me still,
the wicked wounds are open. Not one of them dared I harm.
They railed at us both. I was all running with blood,
as he gave up the ghost, with gore from his side.
A heavy burden I bore on that hill,
My lot was hard . . .[1]

The opening lines from the Ruthwell cross run:

(Un)clothed Himself God almighty when he would mount the
cross, courageous in the sight of all men; bow . . . I, the powerful
king, the Lord of heaven; I durst not bend. Men mocked us both
together. I was bedewed with blood, shed from . . . Christ was on
the rood . . .

The silverwork made at the end of the tenth century as backing
for a large relic of the wood of the true cross (now known as the
Brussels cross) has inscribed upon it words also reminiscent of the
Dream of the Rood:

Rood is my name. Once long ago I bore
Trembling, bedewed with blood, the mighty king.

The devotion to the holy cross, which had swept from the east to
the west Mediterranean, affected the church's calendar and her liturgy
on Good Friday, as well as expressing itself in verse, and the raising
of stone crosses. The feasts of the Exaltation of the Holy Cross,
September 14, and the Invention of the Holy Cross, May 3, are both
found in early calendars and pontificals.

Eusebius himself relates the story of Constantine's vision of the
cross before the battle with Maxentius, October 28, 312: of how he
saw with his own eyes the 'trophy of a cross of light' in the heavens,

[1] See A. S. Cook and C. B. Tinker, *Select Translations from Old English Poetry*,
1926, 94: for the runic inscriptions, 100-103, and Bruce Dickins and A. S. C. Ross,
1934, *The Dream of the Rood*, 5 and 14.

bearing the inscription 'Conquer by this sign': it is this event commemorated in the feast of the Exaltation, though it was not imperially prescribed till after the recovery of the holy cross by Heraclius from the Arabs in 627. The Invention of the Holy Cross commemorated the empress Helena's finding of the true cross on Mount Calvary. Both feasts were celebrated by monks and bishops' clergy, and spread the devotion like the carrying of relics of the true cross, generally as precious gifts to kings, in the west. The emperor Justin II sent a reliquary with the wood of the cross to the pope, and in 569 he also sent a fragment of the true cross, enclosed in a magnificent reliquary, to the princess Radegund, now abbess of her monastery of Poitiers.

The wood of the holy cross was venerated on Good Friday with the triple prostration, made at the imperial Byzantine court before the enthroned emperor: but the accompanying words of devotion were always made to Christ, suffering but also reigning on the cross. In England, as in western Europe generally, the 'rood' or cross was the symbol of Christ and the 'rode tacn' (the rood token). Devotion to Christ and the cross were not separated. When a cross was set upon an altar, it was nearly always plain (without figure), but of rich materials, the colours of which had a mystical interpretation. The prayer for the blessing of such a cross in Egbert's *Pontifical* has these words:

> Let the splendour of the divinity of thine only-begotten Son shine forth in the gold, the glory of his passion shine in the wood, our redemption from death glow in the crimson and the purification of our life in the brightness of the crystal.

Similarly, the office in the same *Pontifical* for the consecration of churches directs that the bishop shall make the sign of the cross with the chrism in various places.

That devotion to the holy cross as a 'signum' in the Christian warfare and therefore also an exorcism had reached Britain early there is plenty of evidence, and Bede mentions that among the many pictures brought by Benedict Biscop from the Continent were a pair, the one representing the serpent raised up by Moses, the other of the Son of Man 'in cruce exaltatum'. His wording recalls the feast of the Exaltation, and implies a figure of Christ crowned and reigning.

It has been pointed out that, in the *Dream of the Rood* a delicate balance is kept between the mental image of Christ, the young hero, reigning from the tree, and the suffering Christ, whose blood the cross bedews. To adore only the suffering Christ, neglecting his impassible godhead, would be to fall into the error of the Nestorians; to adore only Christ triumphant on the cross, to err with the Monophysites, to whom the body that suffered was but a phantom. The human Christ, the young hero, willed to ascend the cross: no yielding here to the Monothelites.

Since the whole life of the monastic clergy of Lindisfarne and Iona, Ripon and Hexham, Monkwearmouth-Jarrow and York, was governed by the recitation (singing) of the opus dei and the liturgy, it followed inevitably that the new learning and the new arts should be inspired by monastic needs and sources. Studies in chronology and history, mathematics and astronomy were needed for the establishment of the church's calendar and saints' days. Devotion to the relics of the holy cross inspired poetry and sculpture, as well as the offices of veneration and adoration which sprang up, spontaneously as it were, to mark, in the first place, the reception of such relics. The finest hymns for use in such offices and processions were those of Fortunatus (d. 609): but the erection of the high crosses in Great Britain were no less an outcome of the devotion.

Similarly, it was the portraits of evangelists in continental gospel books that inspired those in the Lindisfarne Gospels and the more primitive and Celtic ones in the Book of Durrow. Even more important for Northumbrian figure carving were the 'pictures' painted on canvas and brought over to adorn churches in Northumbria with scenes from the gospel histories, and even portraits of the apostles, martyrs and saints of the Egyptian desert. Speculation has sought in the past to account for the sudden rise of a school of figure carving in Northumbria by finding its inspiration in the carved work of reliquaries or the small figures sketched into the design of illuminated manuscripts: but it is now held likely that the rise of this school was due to teaching by foreign craftsmen and the large-scale pictures brought from the Continent. These were painted on canvas and could be brought rolled. Hundreds of years earlier the designs for Roman mosaics had been so brought.

Bede in his *History of the Abbots* (of Monkwearmouth-Jarrow) relates how Benedict Biscop brought books, relics, altar furniture and craftsmen from Gaul to adorn the churches of the twin monastery. He sent for masons from Gaul to build him a stone church in the Roman manner. When the church was nearly built, he sent for glass-makers, to glaze for him the windows of the church and its porticus and the dining-halls of the monastery: they made also for him glass lamps for the church and many vessels for various uses, and not ignobly. 'And all those things which they needed for the ministry of the altar and the church, holy vessels, and vestments, this religious purchaser took care to have brought him from abroad, for they could not be found at home.'

And moreover, those things which could not be obtained even in Gaul, ornaments or church furniture, he brought from the distant church at Rome: not only an innumerable store of books of all kinds, but a great number of relics of the apostles and martyrs . . . and 'pictures of the likenesses of saints' for the adornment of the church of St. Peter the apostle which he had built; the likeness namely of the blessed mother of God, the ever-virgin Mary and also of the twelve apostles, with which he adorned the middle vault of that same church, stretching the painted canvas from wall to wall; the like-nesses of the gospel stories with which he decorated the south wall of the church; the likenesses of the visions of the apocalypse of blessed John, with which he adorned the north wall, so that those entering the church, even if they could not read, 'in whatever direction they turned might behold the ever lovely aspect of Christ and his saints, although in picture only, or recollect with a mind more alert the grace of the Lord's incarnation, or seeing the last judgment as it were before their eyes might remember to examine themselves the more strictly'.

From Bede's careful account there were actually foreign pictures of gospel stories, and the rest, hanging on the walls, and fastened to the vaulted roof of the church at Monkwearmouth. The craftsmen who carved the figures of the Bewcastle and Ruthwell and other crosses must have been Angles or Irishmen, for their tendency to fill vacant spaces with the Celtic interlace or Anglian runes renders it all but impossible to believe they were themselves from Gaul or Italy; but they would seem to have learned to carve in stone from the Gallic stone masons, and to have adopted for the panels of the crosses the figures from the pictures of Christ and his saints and the stories from the gospels of the pictures (picturae). The likenesses of St. Anthony, or Paul the first hermit, would not have been found in an illuminated gospel book.

Considering first, the stone churches of the north, where the native guides were the wooden, thatched churches such as that set up by Aidan at Lindisfarne, and the remains of Roman masonry on the Wall and in the ruins of Roman towns like Carlisle: there are very few early churches surviving, at least in the Celtic tradition, with square-ended chancels. These apparently reproduced in stone the plan of earlier, wooden churches, and the halls of kings. At Yeavering, excavation has discovered not only the wooden halls of the king and nobles, but another building, surrounded by a cemetery, which was apparently built as a wooden fane, and later used as a Christian church.

Of the early northern stone churches, those of Corbridge and Escomb are of special interest. Corstopitum had been a place of great importance when Cunedda and his people had guarded the Wall, and Roman work at Corstopitum and Binchester seems to have been still standing when the Angles built the church at Corbridge: they re-used Roman material for the arch between the nave and western porticus. As the Roman stones were of different sizes, the wall has an uneven appearance, but the Anglian masons built a solid and workmanlike church. Only the nave and this western porticus remain: but they show that the nave was lofty and had a very high pitched roof.

There are no literary records to date the building of the church at Escomb, Co. Durham, but the remains show that it was early.[1] The long, lofty nave had a small, square chancel; the windows are both square and round headed. The doorway in the west wall and the stones of the chancel arch have early examples of 'long and short work'. The stones of the arch may actually have come from the Roman station of Vinovium, five miles distant, and have been taken down and rebuilt at Escomb.

The two churches built by Benedict Biscop for his twin monastery of Monkwearmouth-Jarrow were slightly later in date, and larger. A considerable portion of the Monkwearmouth church, built c. 675, remains; though not the chancel. The long, narrow, lofty nave has

[1] For illustrations of Anglo-Saxon churches and Anglo-Saxon art at the period, see A. W. Clapham, *English romanesque architecture before the Conquest*, 1930; for more detail, the classical G. Baldwin Brown, *The arts in early England*, 6 vols., 1926 *seqq.*; T. D. Kendrick, *Anglo-Saxon Art to A.D. 900*, 1938.

walls of rubble with roughly squared stones at the angles; the western porticus, with an external round-headed doorway, had a barrel vault, a second storey, and a stone figure at the gable of the high pitched roof above it (the present upper storeys of the western tower were added later). There was also a carved frieze above the doorway. The room above the porticus must have been used for some purpose: it has a doorway at first floor level opening on to the nave, possibly suggesting access to a (?wooden) gallery. The church had the normal north and south porticus, but these have now disappeared.

Only the square chancel of the church at Jarrow, Bede's own monastery, is still standing; it has small, round-headed windows and an original, round-headed doorway. Bede, in his *History of the Abbots* of his own monastery, relates that abbot Benedict brought stone masons from Gaul to build these churches 'more Romanorum', and certain half-barbaric carvings of the churches do indeed suggest Merovingian workmanship.

Of the four churches built by bishop Wilfrid in Northumbria there is literary evidence, and in two cases the crypts still remain. In architectural form they were, like old St. Peter's at Rome, both martyria and basilicas. In the church of St. Andrew at Hexham the crypt was in the form of a confessio; it is not known that any Romano-British martyr suffered in the north and it is unlikely that Wilfrid would have sought to commemorate such: but he certainly brought relics of the martyrs from Rome: the confessio and passages adjoining are reminiscent of the catacombs, not burial chambers for future use, like the porticus at St. Augustine's, Canterbury.

The plan of the church of St. Andrew at Hexham, as shown by the crypt, recalls that of the church built by Constantine's architects over the traditional burial place of St. Peter, which Wilfrid must have regarded with particular awe. When pope Julius II commanded Bramante to build the present great church and piazza of St. Peter at Rome, he had to clear away the great basilica and atrium which Wilfrid had seen on the slopes of the Vatican mount, and which remained throughout the middle ages. St. Peter had been martyred, according to Roman tradition, in the gardens of the Vatican mount, outside the walls of Rome, and buried in the cemetery adjoining. There was as yet no traditional form for a great Christian church for Constantine's architects to follow: the persecutions had only just ceased and churches were only beginning to be built above ground: the bishop could celebrate the mysteries before a low, portable altar in buildings of many types. There were, however, 'memorials' of martyrs, where their bodies rested and their help was invoked, often in the shape of niches where offerings could be made: or their burial place might be marked by a small, open-ended chapel. But the martyrium of St. Peter, like that of St. Paul on the road to Ostia, was to be a very great, solemn martyrium.

The architects planned it with the traditional site of the burial as the focus of the building. They cleared away the old 'red wall' which had been built across the cemetery, leaving only a section with two niches, built to mark a burial beneath or adjacent to it. They built a stone basilica with five colonnaded aisles, orientated to the west: it had a transept whose arms projected beyond the nave, and in the centre they set a small apse, covered by a half-dome. On the chord of the apse, and projecting beyond it into the transept was a square platform, raised a step above the floor of the church and covered by a monumental canopy, carried on four beautifully carved columns. Near the west end of the platform and now covered with a box-like edifice, was left the section of wall with the two niches, above and below: this shrine, now covered with slabs of porphyry, was known as the 'little dwelling', the 'aedicula'. A golden lamp was suspended from the centre of the canopy, and when the liturgy was celebrated a portable altar must have been used. In this splendid church, for centuries, pilgrims prayed before the shrine, gazing at the arched opening left in the covering.

Wilfrid built at Hexham a similar church: colonnaded, with three aisles, short transepts and a small apse in the centre of the transepts: the confessio, where presumably Wilfrid deposited his treasured relics, was built, not on the chord of the apse, or in any relation to an altar, but before the apse and at the eastern end of the nave. The proportions of the church and position of the confessio recalls old St. Peters. The church, like that at Ripon, is described by Eddius; he says of the church at Hexham, that it had a lofty stone crypt with separate chambers (*cum domibus*), and above ground a 'multiplex' chamber set about with varied columns and porticus, of great length and height and decorated walls and passages leading from one storey to another with spiral staircases. Eddius mentions moreover that 'bishop Acca of blessed memory, who by the grace of God is still alive, provided for this manifold building splendid ornaments of gold, silver and precious stones, and decorated the altars with purple and silk: who is sufficient to describe it all?' The purple and silken hangings for the altars suggest that at least the main altar had the kind of canopy known as a ciborium (see p. 144), as it would have had in an Italian basilica.

Eddius mentions also the fine stone church at Ripon, whose crypt survives; there are no traces of the stone church Wilfrid restored at York, or the second church he built at Hexham and dedicated to St. Mary. This is the earliest known instance of a centrally planned church in England: Wilfrid had it built as a tower, almost round, and with porticus on the four sides.

Though comparatively few of the churches built in northern England have survived, there is evidence of a remarkable renaissance of carved stone work, which apparently originated in Northumbria and spread to the south. The free-standing crosses (the high crosses particularly) have survived in some cases, partly from veneration through the centuries for the beauty of their workmanship. There are also carved stones that once formed part of friezes or panels in churches that have perished. The rise of this school of stone carving in a society using almost entirely wooden buildings in the second half of the seventh century is remarkable, and due to the imperious demands of church leaders that their dead should be commemorated and their churches adorned with beauty such as they had seen in Italy, or in the stone crosses of the Irish monasteries. The inspiration behind the particular art forms of the crosses and friezes can be traced: the sudden acquirement of masterly skill in a new art is more astonishing. Celtic art had been almost purely a linear art and pagan Anglo-Saxon art exercised almost entirely in metal work: Christian art, stimulated after the synod of Whitby by intercourse between Britain, Gaul and Italy, and the bringing to England of illuminated manuscripts, vestments, ivories and reliquaries and foreign craftsmen, expressed itself in the native production of illuminated manuscripts, embroidered vestments like the stole of St. Cuthbert, and an astonishing school of sculpture. Foreign craftsmen must have taught their skills to Englishmen. The East Mediterranean was a focal point of art and culture in the sixth and seventh centuries; Greek art and liturgy were admired and studied even in Italy itself, and through the influence of Benedict Biscop, Theodore and other nameless churchmen they now reached the remote isles of the west.

The new Christian art of the Anglo-Saxons flourished naturally under the patronage of the church. The northern series of superb stone crosses are the oldest of their kind in the world: the Mediterranean countries produced nothing of the sort, though Constantius' Life of Germanus mentions that a 'signum crucis', apparently a wooden cross, was erected at every stage where his body rested, when it was brought back from north Italy to Auxerre, for burial. The 'signum' was the Roman military standard, the standard of the legion, and the setting up of a cross (as by Oswald before the battle of Heavenfield) was, as it were, the planting of a standard in the Christian battle.

The free-standing crosses of the Celtic north illustrate the spread of Irish influence: the lives of many Irish and British saints of the sixth and seventh centuries refer to the raising of such crosses. Tirechan's Life of St. Patrick, written c. 664–668 and using older material, mentions that when Patrick came to a cross-marked grave he used to stop and pray, which shows the earliness of the custom of using the cross as a kind of exorcism of the powers of the old gods at the site of a Christian burial. Crosses were raised also to mark places of prayer, as by St. Kentigern (d. 616) wherever he made a group of converts; one such, in a wild, remote valley, was replaced later by a church. They were raised, too, as votive monuments: St. Finnian of Moville is said to have raised one such to St. Bridget of Ayrshire. Sometimes these crosses were of wood: but the pagan Irish (and perhaps the pagan British) associated megaliths or pillar stones with pagan worship, and Christianised them by placing small stone crosses upon them. The shape of the high crosses, with their tall, tapering bases and small equal-armed crosses at the top, is thought to have been thus remotely derived.

On the other hand, the Irish crosses may have been influenced by the Romano-British flat pillar stones, with the Greek cross in a circle engraved at the top, like that at Kirkmadrine (see p. 34). There was plenty of intercourse between the minsters of Strathclyde and northern Ireland even in St. Patrick's time, and the pillar with Greek cross and circle appears early in Ireland, as that at Arraglen which commemorates 'Ronan the priest, son of Comgall'. To the severe design of the Kirkmadrine pillar, the Irish soon added their luxuriant spirals and old La Tène patterns. The Irish influence on the Christian stones of Scotland and northern Britain is very clear; it was transmitted by Columba and his followers to Iona and her daughter houses, and Kentigern, a great raiser of crosses, was for part of his life bishop at Hoddom on the Arranwater. By the time king Ecgfrith died in 685 at the battle of Nectansmere, the English had settled Lothian, Berwick, Dumfries and Selkirk and the link between the Celtic and Anglian churches was close.

The Anglo-Saxons adopted the standing crosses for the same purposes as the Celts, to mark Christian graves, to commemorate the dead, and to Christianise some spot in the open for preaching, and the celebration of the liturgy 'in the field'. We hear of Acca's cross, to mark his place of burial, and of the two high crosses at Glastonbury in the monks' cemetery, with their names of old abbots and West Saxon prelates and royalties. William of Malmesbury mentions that Aldhelm died some thirty miles from Glastonbury, to which his body was carried for burial; at every stage of seven miles, at which the body rested, a cross was erected. The Life of St. Willibald states that in eighth century Somerset it was customary for visiting priests to preach and pray by the cross set up outside a thegn's hall, and there are references to crosses set up to mark, or as being used to mark, the boundaries of estates. A very large number of crosses or parts of crosses survive, nearly all richly carved. They are of local stone, locally carved, though all have a family resemblance.

The ornament on these crosses derives from both pagan and Christian sources; from Celtic, Latin and the Byzantine cultures. There is much geometric ornament on the side panels of the crosses, or separating the panels of figure sculpture on the high crosses. The commonest of patterns, the interlace, is a legacy from late Roman art, and appears in nearly every monument as plait-work, fret work or a chessboard pattern. The Celtic spiral is rare, and the marigold ornament, a Roman legacy, common in Scotland.

Of the art forms derived directly from the Mediterranean or from Roman Britain, the naturalistic plant or animal motifs are among the most beautiful. The vine scroll appeared in the mosaic floors of Roman Britain, and was much used in sixth century Mediterranean art. Sometimes the vine leaves and bunches of grapes formed the sole pattern: sometimes the vine was 'inhabited' by birds and beasts, at which cupids or boys shot arrows; both forms are found carved on the crosses.

Representations of the human figure are the great innovation in Anglo-Saxon, Christian art: a single figure, or at most two figures, appear on the crosses, presented under a canopy: the most beautiful appear on the Bewcastle cross, and its sister cross at Ruthwell. The dating of these northern high crosses can be fixed in two cases, showing that fine figure sculpture in stone was being produced first towards the end of the seventh century; for the other crosses, earliness or lateness can only be suggested by a comparison of styles. Bishop Acca of Lindisfarne was Bede's friend, and they both corresponded and, at times, conversed together; he was a very learned man, who had made the pilgrimage to Rome. He outlived Bede, died in 740 and was buried outside the church at Hexham, with a cross to commemorate him. This large and famous cross is accepted as having been raised soon after his death. The Bewcastle cross is earlier, with a barely decipherable runic inscription which includes the names of Alchfrith (Wilfrid's patron), Oswiu and Cynieburg, the daughter of Penda who married Alchfrith; since Oswiu died in 671 and Alchfrith did not succeed him, Alchfrith must have been already dead. The most likely commemorators of Alchfrith would have been Wilfrid at Hexham, or perhaps Acca at Lindisfarne: Wilfrid died in 709: the Bewcastle cross was probably raised before his death. The ornament of the Ruthwell cross appears earlier still. The Ruthwell cross, the Bewcastle cross of c. 700 and Acca's cross of c. 740 would all have been erected during the ascendancy of Northumbria. This historical evidence as to the dating of the crosses is in agreement with the conclusions of art historians.

The siting of the Ruthwell and Bewcastle crosses is of interest, if only as a subject of speculation. They belong to a time when the northern Angles held the region north of Hadrian's Wall and 'Reged', the district north of the Solway Firth. To the Celtic church, the Irish sea was a Mediterranean lake, and the Solway Firth was but an arm of her home waters. Round the Solway Firth the old Romano-British tradition had been transmitted to the Celts: at the head of the Firth was Carlisle (Luguvallium), with its impressive Roman ruins, and while Hadrian's Wall led away to the east, through Cambo-glanna and Corbridge, the coast line to the west, the southern bank of the Firth, was studded with Roman forts; Clannaventa, from which port Patrick was abducted by Irish pirates, lay just to the south. On the northern bank of the Solway lay Whithorn and

Kirkmadrine: the Ruthwell cross, not a mile from the sea, and near the famous church and minster of Hoddom on the Arranwater: Hoddom, where Kentigern had been for a time bishop, and where many Irish crosses have been found; the Bewcastle cross, set up near the Roman fort of Banna, at the end of a Roman road that ran south through Camboglanna to Bravoniacum (Kirkby Thore) and Catterick. Carlisle had been a Roman road centre: from Ribchester and Brougham a road ran through it, northward, nearly to the Antonine Wall; and the road joining the forts of Hadrian's Wall passed through Carlisle and ran southward to Moresby on the west coast. The Isle of Man stood in the mouth of the Solway Firth, and across the North Channel from Whithorn and the Mull of Galloway lay Belfast Lough, the Irish Bangor and Moville. There was plenty of movement down the Solway Firth to the minsters of northern Ireland.

As to Bewcastle and Ruthwell: the crosses were not erected in the cemetery of a known minster, but apparently as votive crosses in places easily visible to travellers. Ruthwell stands but a mile from the northern shore of Solway, on the sea route from Carlisle to Belfast. Bewcastle, visible from the hills around, and sited near a Roman fort at a road's end, lies just north of the Wall, quite near Camboglanna and not far from Hexham. The siting of both should probably be regarded, like that of Whithorn, as lying along the main line of communication of the Hiberno-Saxon church: the crosses were meant to be landmarks.

The naturalistic ornament, the birds and animals of the 'inhabited' vine scroll on the Ruthwell cross is near to classical ornament in feeling, and less a patterned space filling in the Celtic manner than that of Bewcastle; it is held to be earlier. The figures, carved in deep relief on the panels of the red sandstone shaft at Ruthwell, are partly scriptural (St. John and St. Matthew with their emblems, the Annunciation, the Crucifixion, etc.) and partly chosen as patrons and emblems of the monastic life: the desert life as practised in Egypt, and by Cassian. Ruthwell has St. John Baptist, the desert saint, Christ with St. Mary Magdalene, the saint of penitence and contemplation, St. Paul the first hermit, St. Anthony, and the Flight into Egypt. It has also, as has Bewcastle, the figure of the divine protection in the desert, Christ treading upon the lion and the adder:

> Super aspidem et basiliscum ambulabis:
> et conculcabis leonem et draconem.

The Bewcastle cross, as the later, has panels of abstract ornament, like those of the Lindisfarne gospels.

The illuminated manuscripts of Northumbria are of peculiar beauty, and combine figure work and naturalistic ornament in the classical tradition with the most beautiful and intricate interlaces and abstract ornament of the Celts. There is clearly a relationship between the Northumbrian books (the Lindisfarne gospels, the Codex Amiatinus, etc.) and those illuminated in the Irish minsters (the Book of Durrow, the Book of Kells, etc.), but it is not, as was once thought, one of filiation. The Northumbrian books are not simply the product of Irish scribes, or Irish taught scribes, developing their own tradition in Lindisfarne or Iona. The study of the Latin text in the Irish and Northumbrian books, as well as the study of the art forms, suggests rather that the Northumbrian books slightly preceded the Irish, and influenced their text and ornament: though it is possible that the Irish minsters received illuminated gospel books from the Mediterranean countries independently of Northumbria. The abstract art of both the crosses and the manuscripts is termed Hiberno-Saxon, and there is no doubt that this came to Northumbria from Iona and across the Solway Firth.

The first reference to the early illuminated manuscripts of Northumbria comes from Eddius' Life of St. Wilfrid. He says that Wilfrid built a great church at Ripon (671–678), 'adorning the bridal chamber of the true Bridegroom and Bride with gold and silver and varied purples', and he also 'provided for the adornment of the house of God a marvel of beauty hitherto unheard of in our times. For he had ordered . . . the four gospels to be written out in letters of purest gold on purpled parchment and illuminated. He also ordered jewellers to construct for the books a case made of purest gold set with most precious gems . . . all these things and others beside are preserved in our church until these times.'

Of the surviving Northumbrian illuminated manuscripts, dating from c. 700 or soon after, the most famous is the Lindisfarne Gospels. All these books, like the sculpture, have panels of Celtic, interlaced work, attenuated animals, the classical human figure (specially those of the Evangelists and St. David), the vine scroll, and various rectilinear patterns. The Lindisfarne Gospels, which apparently accompanied the relics of St. Cuthbert to Durham and are sometimes known as the Book of Durham, bear a statement by 'Aldred the sinner' to the effect that they were written by Eadfrith, abbot of Lindisfarne (698–721): and that they were bound and covered by his successor, bishop Æthelwald (d. 740), and adorned with a gold cross and gems by an anchorite, and finally glossed by Aldred himself (in the ninth century). These most beautiful gospels have four portraits of the evangelists, five cruciform pages of pure decoration, sixteen pages of arcaded canons, and six pages with beautifully illuminated chapter openings. The design is varied, intricate and done with marvellously sure brushwork, and makes use of long necked birds like the cormorants that haunt the Farne islands, and conventionalised, elongated dogs; the trumpet pattern and spiral ornament are freely used. The colours are soft and harmonious, with blue, red, green, yellow and purple used in delicate contrast. The text is that of the Vulgate, written in beautiful half-uncials, and enriched throughout with coloured initials and ornament. The Neo-Hellenic figures of the Evangelists are set in framed spaces tinted pale violet, without conventional ornament; they are described in a kind of Latinised Greek: 'O agius Marcus', etc., and each has an emblem, with the words peculiar to Latin iconography, 'Imago hominis' (for the emblem of St. Matthew).

The Lindisfarne Gospels have also a sister manuscript, whose history is known: the Codex Amiatinus, now in Florence. This is believed to be the codex written at Jarrow by the order of abbot Ceolfrith (d. 716) and carried by him on his last journey to Rome in 716, as a gift to the pope. Bede tells us this in his *History of the Abbots*. Codex Amiatinus has a text of the Vulgate: it has a picture of a monk in a scriptorium evidently closely related to the St. Matthew in the Lindisfarne Gospels. The attitude, etc., is the same, but the picture in Codex Amiatinus is of superior design and workmanship, which suggests that the Lindisfarne Gospels' St. Matthew was the prototype, and of earlier execution than 716. The portraits in Codex Amiatinus are somewhat crudely drawn, but the composition, flow of drapery, naturalism of hair, etc., clearly follow Italo-Byzantine tradition. In the Lindisfarne Gospels, that is, the scribe has gone further into transforming a naturalistic scene into a calligraphic exercise: the Celtic influence is much more apparent than in Codex Amiatinus.

The Durham Cassiodorus is another famous Northumbrian manuscript of approximately the same date: it is a copy of Cassiodorus' commentary on the Psalms and is enriched by two full-page miniatures. They represent king David as a harpist and as a warrior; in the one, king David, in classical drapery, sits upon his throne-chair, playing a small harp which rests upon his knee: around the enclosed space is a heavy border, with varied panels of interlace, some with elongated fish and animals. The face of David the warrior is almost calligraphic, with the hair in stiff, spiral curls. This is a choir book, not a library book: perhaps to be set in choir on the desk of abbot or cantor. Some other manuscripts in the hand of the Durham Cassiodorus but not illuminated also survive: the Épinal Glossary, the *Liber Vitae* of Durham (a list of benefactors) and some manuscript fragments.

These Northumbrian manuscripts, like the sculptures, bear witness by the nature of their ornament to derivation from three cultures. The elongated animals in both crosses and books are almost certainly connected with those in the metal work of the pagan, Anglian period. From an Italo-Byzantine source come the figures in both, in their enclosed, timeless background, and, in the Lindisfarne Gospels, tables of lessons for festivals, some proper to the calendar of the church of Naples. The Celtic patterns and interlaces speak for themselves; but it has also been suggested that the Northumbrian manuscripts derived their whole inspiration from Ireland or Iona, on the strength of the affinities between them and the Irish gospel books, particularly the Book of Durrow.

The Book of Durrow has a colophon attributing its writing to St. Columba himself who died in 597: but it is accepted that the manuscript can only be a copy written in the seventh or eighth century of a book, possibly connected with Columba. It was written in the Columban monastery of Durrow, near Tullamore, in central Ireland. It is a small manuscript, with five full pages of decoration, one with the emblems of all four evangelists, the others with the separate emblems and an elaborate initial for the beginning of the gospel; the image of the calf has curious, spiral scrolls on the thighs, and little boots: that of St. Matthew, a full-faced man with feet sideways, and a conventional, embroidered mantle. There are thus no portraits of evangelists and nothing naturalistic in the ornament.

In the Book of Kells, probably written in the eighth century, the high water mark of Irish illumination is reached. The four evangelists' portraits and three full pages of abstract ornament show incredibly

13

sure and beautiful draughtmanship, and strange and beautiful designs, unsurpassed for intricacy and variety. Elongated animals, tiny pictures of birds, horses and dogs adorn the text with lovely colour and a great play of fancy: at the bottom of the canon tables cats and kittens play with mice: in the full page illumination of Christ's temptation on the Temple the head and shoulders of Christ appear above a curious, shrine shaped building: a majestic, Byzantine Christ repels a dark, elongated, Celtic devil. The evangelists' portraits are fantastically stiff and bizarre; in a full page picture of the madonna and child, the madonna is stony-eyed, and the child has an old man's face. This manuscript may have been written and illuminated in Iona, before the two Danish raids which drove the Columban monks to cross the sea and seek refuge at Cenannas (Kells), in Meath; after various efforts to restart the monastery on the island of Iona, the community settled permanently at Kells in 849.

Irish missionaries certainly carried their own traditions to the Continent, and for two or three centuries Irish monasteries both at home and abroad produced illuminated books with the same odd, attractive, colour scheme and the same lovely, flat designs and crude figure work. No such Irish manuscript dates from before the eighth century, and they afford no proof of the priority of Irish to Northumbrian work. Some books illuminated in Ireland also found their way to England, like the eighth century Rushworth Gospels, and the Lichfield Gospels of St. Chad.

The close relationship between the designs of Irish and Northumbrian manuscripts is not, after all, surprising, when there was so much intercourse between travelling monks of the monasteries of Ireland, Strathclyde and Northumbria. In which country the characteristic school of illumination originated is difficult to decide: there is no historical account, and the evidence is circumstantial. The fact that the Northumbrian church was an offshoot of Iona, and some of the monks of Lindisfarne Irishmen, does not settle the matter, for the figure work of the Northumbrian manuscripts is plainly derived from southern models, not Irish ones. Nor does a study of the Latin text of the two sets of Gospels support a Northumbrian filiation to Iona; the British and Irish churches used a mixed text of the Bible, an old Latin version, earlier than the Vulgate.[1] The Kentish church seems to have had the Vulgate from the start, and Benedict

---

[1] See F. C. Burkitt, *Antiquity,* ix (1935), p. 33.

Biscop brought the Vulgate from Rome to Northumbria. The Codex Amiatinus, thought to have been copied from a book brought by him, has the best text of the Vulgate in the world. Codex Amiatinus, or its sister manuscripts, introduced the Vulgate text to Lindisfarne; it appears in the Lindisfarne Gospels, though with some passages in the Old Latin. The Book of Durrow has the Vulgate text, more widely interspersed with the Old Latin: and the Book of Kells follows Durrow, with rather more Vulgate readings. The Irish monasteries, that is, at the end of the seventh century, still relied largely on the Old Latin text, while those of Northumbria normally used the Vulgate: but the priority of either school of illumination cannot be deduced from this.

It would seem then, that at the time of Aidan's mission to Lindisfarne, 'there must have been in existence an established method of illumination in the Columban church', an Irish style, 'frank in its barbarism and total rejection of the classical, figural style'.[1] To this style was added, in Northumbria, the evangelists' portraits and other classical details; the Irish, too, were influenced by continental gospel books, perhaps those seen in Northumbria, perhaps brought to the Celts directly. They, too, introduced evangelists' portraits, not merely evangelists' emblems as at Durrow, into their illuminated gospels, but with much less skill in the naturalist manner, or even doubt of the lawfulness of its use in the scriptural texts. The portraits of St. Mark in the Lichfield Gospels or the Gospels of St. Gall: the figure of Christ in the St. Gall Crucifixion are designs, calligraphic exercises in paint, rather than studies of a human figure.

Finally: in matters liturgical, the Celtic church in Ireland and Britain followed the Gallican rite, under its various forms, and as it must have existed written in local sacramentaries. No single local Gallican sacramentary of very great antiquity has survived. The Gallican liturgy has been reconstructed from Letters attributed to the St. Germanus who became bishop of Paris in 555,[2] but the attribution cannot be sustained. A manuscript known as the Bobbio Missal and representing liturgical practice in upper Italy in the seventh century

---

[1] T. D. Kendrick, *Anglo-Saxon Art to A.D. 900*, 1938, 104.

[2] A translation of the Gallican mass so reconstructed is printed by E. Kovalevsky as 'La Sainte Messe selon l'ancien rite des Gaules', in the *Mélanges de l'Institut Orthodoxe français de Paris*, 1956: it contains a translated text of the mass of the catechumens and mass of the faithful.

has, however, been impeccably edited and commented on;[1] it is a sacramentary rather than a missal, and it appears to have come either from the monastery of Bobbio or Luxeuil, both houses founded by the Irishman, Columbanus. The liturgical contents are accompanied also by Irish penitential canons. As in the Gelasian sacramentaries, there are masses for the Sundays in Advent, Christmas and the saints after Christmas; none for the Sundays between Epiphany and Lent; masses for the Sundays from the first in Lent till Pentecost (here called Quinquagesimo); then masses for various saints, for special purposes as a mass of requiem; for five 'Sunday masses', and various blessings.

But though the structure of the various Gallican sacramentaries followed the course of the ecclesiastical year much as did the Gelasianum (no masses being assigned for Sundays 'after Epiphany' and 'after Pentecost'), yet the prayers of the mass varied, and the Gallican books were earlier to introduce anointing the hands of the priest at his ordination with oil than the Roman sacramentaries.

Among the characteristics of the Gallican rites occur the following: collects and anthems found in the Mozarabic rite but not in the Roman liturgy; various formulae of thanksgiving after communion; frequent biddings or addresses to the people in the form of (Gallican) prefaces; a prayer called the post-Sanctus, leading up to the words of institution; a complicated rite of 'fraction', as described in the Irish treatise at the end of the Stowe missal; and, in the earliest Irish baptismal office, the presence of the Pedilavium.

The question as to how early the anointing of the head of the bishop or king with oil was practised in the Celtic churches has been much discussed;[2] a passage in Gildas' *De excidio* was once thought to indicate the practice at least as early as his time, but it is now held that he was only quoting a verse in Leviticus, and that his words are not evidence for an ordination sacring in the sixth century Celtic church. Nevertheless, one Gallican service book known as the *Missale Francorum*,[3] which is probably from Poitiers, and shows marked signs of both Visigothic and Irish influence, has the first sure

---

[1] As *The Bobbio Missal: a Gallican Mass-book: MS. Paris Lat.* 13246, the text edited by Dr. E. A. Lowe, and the comment by Dom A. Wilmart.

[2] See G. Ellard, *Ordination anointings in the western church before 1000 A.D.*, Med. Acad. of America, No. 16, 1933, chapter 1. Gildas' phrase, 'benedictioni, qua initeantur sacerdotum uel ministrorum manus', seems to be a paraphrase of Leviticus xvi. 32, 'Expiabit autem sacerdos, qui unctus fuerit, et cuius manus initiatae sunt ut sacerdotio fungatur pro patre suo'.   [3] See *ib.* 18-24.

witness to the ceremonial anointing of the hands of the candidate for orders. It was written probably between 700 and 730, when Aquitaine still had memories of the Visigoths (and, at the death of Charles Martel, desired to be Visigothic again). The anointing of the dying had been, of course, much earlier; but this is the first known rite with the anointing of the hands of the priest. It may have had a double ancestry: there is, at any rate, an alternative prayer for the anointing of the hands, one with a reference to the anointing of David by Samuel. In the rite for the consecration of bishops in this manuscript, there is no anointing.

As to the anointing of kings: here, too, Gildas' words were once taken to mean that Celtic kings were anointed in his day, but this is now held to be mistaken. Gildas wrote that:

> Kings have been anointed, not by God, but by those who are even more cruel than the rest: and shortly after and without a just judgment they were butchered, and others even more atrocious were elected.

Gildas here is no more than referring to the ease with which kings were elected, inaugurated and removed: kings at the time were blessed, not anointed. Cummian, in his Life of Columba (see p. 73), says that Columba, in obedience to a thrice repeated angelic warning, ordained at Iona king Aidan: 'he laid his hands upon his head, ordained and blessed him'. Columba was himself of royal birth and acquainted with Celtic practice. In short: neither kings, priests nor bishops were anointed in the sixth century Celtic church.

When Boniface, however, desired to consecrate a new dynasty to the rule of the Franks, in place of merely blessing Pepin the Short in 751, he anointed him in the abbey of Saint-Médard, and with him his sons. Such an anointing recalled the transfer of the monarchy from Saul to David: and was in line with the anointing of priests at their ordination, in at least one of the Gallican sacramentaries. Ceremonial splendour in any rite tended to spread from one church to another, and in Gaul the anointing of priests, as perhaps that of kings, led on to the anointing of bishops. Anointing was not used in the oriental churches in the patristic period: it appears indeed to have emanated as a ceremony from centres in Aquitaine and Neustria in the eighth century, to have crossed with the Gallican service books to England, to have spread in southern France without crossing the

Pyrenees: to have crossed the Meuse, the Rhine and the Alps and thence to have reached Rome. Eventually, stamped with the Roman mark, it passed out to the farthest corner of Latin Christendom (see p. 280).

It should be noticed that the Gallican service books both in Gaul and Britain were influenced and interpolated by prayers from the Roman sacramentaries, especially the presbyteral Gelasianum, which penetrated Gaul by way of Marseilles soon after 500. In 494, indeed, a collect from the Gelasianum was quoted by the priest Vincentius from a monastery in southern Gaul; bishop Honoratus of Marseilles (492–496) corresponded with the pope, and may have been the channel of communication. The great Caesarius of Arles, archbishop for forty years (502–542), was papal vicar in Gaul from 513, and active in promoting Roman liturgical usages. The use of her grave and severe liturgy was never in any way pressed by the Roman church, and knowledge of it spread only gradually from the south to the north of France; evidence that it was known at Tours appears only in 567, and at Reims in 620. But Marseilles was the cradle of Cassian's monasticism, and Tours that of Martin's clerical and pastoral monasticism: both must have been centres where the scarce and valuable manuscripts of sacramentaries could be obtained. Every service book of the Gallican rite known to us contains formularies unquestionably Roman in origin; local Gallican usages were overlaid constantly with Roman ones, and these adapted to suit a non-Roman mentality. Peculiarly Gallican rites, however, such as the blessing of the Paschal candle, were not yet carried over the Alps and adopted in Rome. Till the reign of Charlemagne, liturgy in Gaul and Britain developed locally unchecked; the Gallican books with some adopted Roman formularies: the Roman sacramentaries often copied in Gaul and Britain with supplementary Gallican blessings and ceremonies.

CHAPTER IX

MINSTER AND PARISH

FOR the understanding of the work and organisation of the Anglo-Saxon church before the Danish invasions, the concept of 'a church in every village' should be discarded. It was far in the future. The parish church was not normally, as in nineteenth century England, a village church, but the church of the bishop. It was not till the Carolingian age in Europe that bishops, as shepherds of souls, aspired to have churches or chapels wherever a small group of people in the countryside needed them. England, in this matter, had accomplished no more than the Franks. After Augustine's day the word 'parochia' appears in the canons of councils, or episcopal letters, as meaning the modern 'see' or 'diocese', and also as meaning the area lying in the pastoral jurisdiction of some minster; in Bede's day, it first appears for the area in the spiritual charge of a single priest, the mass priest of a thegn or of the bishop himself. Such a priest served a church in a village, assisted perhaps by one or two boys or young men in minor orders. Paganism lingered long after Augustine's day, partly from the belief that the old gods might be stronger than the new, but mainly because the royal endowment of bishops' sees and large minsters could only bring the Christian faith to peasants and thegns who lived near at hand. Bishops, clerics and Irish monks travelled and preached and baptised; converted country people walked many miles to hear mass at the great feasts; but, by and large, churches were very few, even in Kent.

The Christian church then, as the unconverted or newly converted heathen encountered it, in the days when Augustine planted the faith in Kent or Aidan planted it in Northumbria, was seen embodied in the minsters, and in the churches of the very few 'cities'.

The pagan Anglo-Saxons, like all primitive people, were accustomed to a traditional belief in a god, or gods; they were used to priests and temples and sacred groves. Temples were often hill-top sanctuaries: there had been a Roman hill-top sanctuary at Lydney, near the Bristol Channel: there was one at Harrow. The king of the Cantwara had a 'fanum', his private pagan temple, just outside the walls of Canterbury. Anglo-Saxon heathen priests were maintained by double the holding of the Anglo-Saxon freeman or ceorl. The Anglo-Saxon then was very well used to religion and priests and temples.

What struck him about the new Italian teachers and their Frankish interpreters was their minsters: the hedged or stockaded enclosures round the pieces of land the king had given them. The pagan might go inside the minster if he decided to go along with king Æthelberht and be progressive and risk having Thor with his thunder strike his house and catch his thatched roof afire, and take the risk also that the old gods would not support him in battle: well, if he risked all this and let the black-eyed, hook-nosed Italian teacher dip him in the river in the name of his god: then, if he lived nearby, he would go inside the minster to the sacrifice, the husl, in the little church of the minster. He would go at the great feasts, and on Sundays if he could, and watch the black-eyed Italian, now dressed in very fine golden garments, stand behind the altar, while the teachers chanted: see him bless the white bread of the sacrifice. This would be all in the small, rectangular, thatched 'ecclesia' within the minster, where he himself stood all the time, watching, till the priest blessed the white bread. Then he would bow deeply, and the women on the other side of the church hold up the children to see and be blessed. When it was over, they all streamed out and through the little houses of the Christian brethren and sometimes the village reeve caught him and one or two senior villagers as they left, and they had a village moot; for it was a convenient time for the reeve to get them, and no ploughing to keep them away. His wife hurried the children home and got on with preparing the dinner.

From the time of king Earconberht of Kent he had to keep the Lent fast too, and all the idols, for the first time, were rooted out of the kingdom. The minsters were the only places of religion in the Kentish countryside from Earconberht's reign, which ran from 640–664: Earconberht was the grandson of the bretwalda Æthelberht. There had been trouble for the Christians in the reign of Æthelberht's son, Eadbald, at least at first, when king Eadbald had chosen to go along in religion with the new bretwalda, Rædwald of East Anglia; but things had improved and Eadbald declared himself Christian, and now Earconberht was outstripping his grandfather in the Christian pieties. No doubt one must move with the times.

Minsters in this period are understandably prominent in Anglo-Saxon land grants, in Bede's *Ecclesiastical History* and in place names. If kings alienated lands to anyone not their thegns, it is understandable that they did so to support groups of clergy, consisting of a few priests, and clerics in the minor orders from exorcists upwards: such a group, besides exercising pastoral care of their region, trained boys who after many years would become their own successors. They would also supply, eventually, councillors and scribes for the king. The grant of land for a minster brought the king no fighting soldiers, but it was not without future usefulness to him. Moreover, a pious king frequently provided endowment for a minster of nuns of which his daughter or relative should be abbess; the nuns needed a staff of monastic chaplains, who, again, provided pastoral care for the countryside and trained young clerics. The endowment of such a nun-minster could be made from estates that would have gone to his daughter on her marriage, and produced as useful a reward to the royal donor as the loyalty of a thegn or the alliance that would have come from his daughter's marriage.

On the Continent, where Christianity was older and organisation more developed, more is heard of bishops' cathedral churches, and mother churches served by a group of clergy not headed by a bishop; monasteries, minsters, were relatively few. But in Anglo-Saxon England little is heard of any churches except the minsters: whether double minsters, minsters of nuns, with clerics saying the office and exercising pastoral care, or the relatively few minsters of monk clerics, where the obligation to recite the opus dei and remain within the minster was primary, and pastoral work incidental and subsidiary.

Since what struck the Anglo-Saxon peasant about the minsters was the hedge or palisade around them: and since 'tuns' were hedged or stockaded villages: and 'chesters' the ruins of Roman camps or walled towns: Sir Frank Stenton suspects that the Anglo-Saxons sometimes used minster and chester and tun interchangeably: e.g. Tunna's chester, which was Tunna's minster. Bede tells us about Tunna's minster, which was Towcester in Northamptonshire: he says that when Æthelred of Mercia defeated the Northumbrians and won back Lindsey from Northumbria in 679, one of the

Northumbrian king's thegns, Imma, was left for dead on the field. He was eighteen years old. His brother was priest and abbot of a minster called Tunnacæster. When Imma was captured and kept bound in prison, Tunna, believing him dead, said mass for him every day, that his soul might not be bound in hell: and, as he prayed, every day some of his earthly bonds fell off from the living man.

The Anglo-Saxon peasant's vagueness as to the nature of the life lived within the hedged enclosure of the minster illustrates the difficulty of describing Anglo-Saxon minsters in general as either secular or Benedictine. The word itself, monasterium, minster, was undoubtedly used originally of the enclosure containing the oratories and dwellings of solitaries, men living the ascetic and contemplative life and without any pastoral obligations. But, in France, St. Martin had lived monastically while bishop of Tours, and the Celtic Christians had used a monastic clergy though not one bound to enclosure; the Frankish bishops lived communally with their 'familiae', until by seniority certain members might attain to be granted a separate church within the see city, or a rural parish, and go off to rule their own endowments and serve their churches. Founders who endowed a monastery of ascetics did not, for the greater part of the seventh century, bind the monks to follow a particular rule: rather, they collected various monastic rules and bestowed them on the monks as aids in following the life of perfection. Still, the distinction in France between minsters of ascetics and minsters of clergy living communally together was fairly clear: in England as a missionary country it was not clear at all.

Turning for a moment, then, from the effort to see the Anglo-Saxon church as most Anglo-Saxons saw it, to the constitutional meaning of certain ecclesiastical terms, as used in charters, and by the ecclesiastical writers of the day: it is clear that words such as parochia, diocesis, abbas, provost (and some others) had a different significance then and now. Parochia has been explained: it meant a regional sphere of spiritual authority, normally the bishop's, with territorial boundaries roughly known, but often in dispute. Diocese, as in Gaul from the fifth to the eighth century, meant, not the modern see, but the outlying, rural parts of the see: a Gallic bishop was spoken of as 'riding through his dioceses', and when Offa's setting up of a metropolitan see at Lichfield was put right, a papal letter described the act as the wrongful detaching of certain dioceses (rural territories) from the see of Canterbury.

Abbas, again, and 'abbatissa' were used in the early sense of 'father', 'mother', and not exclusively of the heads of Benedictine or Celtic monasteries. Abbas was a title of general and affectionate respect, used of a spiritual person of rank: generally of the head of a community of monks or clerics, sometimes of the senior members of such a community. An abbas would normally have a familia of clerks living under him: but he might be the archipresbyter of an urban or rural basilica. The word 'abbacy' in Gaul was first used of the headship of a clerical familia, and only later spread to the headship of communities of monks; in seventh century Gaul the headship of the clergy serving the royal chapel was called an abbacy, and the senior cathedral clergy who elected the bishop of e.g. Cahors, might be spoken of as the 'abbots of Cahors'. What would now be called 'five of the senior cathedral clergy' of another city were termed 'five of the senior abbots'. Similarly, in England before the Danish invasions 'abbas' was as readily used of the head of a large minster of clerics living in common, like Chertsey, or of a quite small clerical minster, or of the clergy living within the minster of an abbess, as of a Benedictine minster like Monkwearmouth or St. Augustine's. Abbas again, though it means head of a community either monastic or clerical, does not of itself imply possession of the priesthood. Headship of a community might depend upon kinship to some royal or noble family; documents of the period carefully state whether such a head was 'abbas' or 'abbas et presbyter'. Hæddi, before he was bishop of Wessex (670), is described as 'abbas et presbyter'.

Provost (praepositus), again, is a word occurring in the Benedictine rule with the specific meaning of a second-in-command, set in his position by the abbot, or by those who appointed the abbot; St. Benedict advised that, since such officers often took upon themselves to be 'second abbots' and to tyrannise over others, it would be better for an abbot to rule his monastery through deans (decani): a word that in his time signified a kind of non-commissioned officer: 'so that, the same office being shared by many, no one may become proud'. Nevertheless, if the brethren humbly demanded it and the abbot judged it expedient, the abbot might himself appoint a provost: 'who should do reverently whatever was enjoined him by the abbot and nothing against his will'. 'Provost' was thus a Benedictine term for the second-in-command in the monastery: but again and again in Anglo-Saxon sources it is used of those set at the head of monastic or secular minsters usually by the king. Praepositus and praeposita are terms sometimes used of the abbots and abbesses themselves. The word emphasises that the abbot or abbess has been set there by king or bishop. When Cuthbert of Melrose spoke of Boisil as 'provost of the monastery of Melrose under abbot Eata', he used the word in the sense of the Benedictine rule: Boisil, he also said, had been his own 'magister' or teacher, and 'nutritor', the guardian of his youth in the minster as an oblate. In later Anglo-Saxon and Norman history the word provost is used of the lay officer in charge of the husbandry and estates of an abbey, and is rendered in Old English as 'reeve'. About 833 Abba, the praepositus of Christ Church, Canterbury, made his will in Old English as that of 'Abba the reeve'. It was witnessed by archbishop Ceolnoth and contained a bequest to the familia (hiwan, higan) of Christ Church.

The conversion of Anglo-Saxon and Celtic England was undoubtedly carried out by the minsters, and had little to do at first with the foundation of rural parishes. The minsters were a focus of Christianity for the region or the tribe: they had a church served by Benedictine monks, by monastic clerics in the Irish tradition, or by priests and clerics in minor orders living together, as in Gaul, Italy and western Europe. They were at first royal foundations, endowed to serve the king and his court, or his relations, and to provide a church and home for the missionary who converted the king. Minsters were next founded for royal princesses (in this case, double minsters), for the king's mass priest, or for the service of the sub-kings and ealdormen. It was unquestioned that the conversion of the king's subjects had to proceed from the top downwards: the minster as founded would serve as a Christian centre for the countryside, but no statement that the minster was founded to convert the countryside is found in any early source. The minster was founded to the glory of God and in honour of the holy apostles, or St. Peter, etc., in the south; for the Celtic north, foundation charters have not survived, nor were formal dedications early practised, but various references show that the intention of the abbot to go preaching and baptising was more explicit. There were, in the Celtic areas, no other clergy than the monks.

The apostolic intention of all minsters then being assumed, though not stated as primary: the manner in which they gradually evangelised the countryside differed, as did the point at which they established rural parishes or daughter minsters. Some minsters were from the first the see of a bishop, like Christ Church, Canterbury; some minsters of clerics, as in Gaul; some princess-minsters with a familia of clerics; and, in the Celtic regions, minsters of monastic clergy, on the Irish and Martinian pattern. Some were minsters of Benedictine monks, like St. Augustine's, Canterbury, and Monkwearmouth-Jarrow.

The share of the strictly Benedictine minsters in the evangelisation of the countryside would seem to have been limited to the building of a chapel or oratory on their more or less distant lands. This would be served by a clerk or priest from the abbey, when such could be spared. There is no evidence that in the south the cure of such a small, local chapel was spoken of as a 'parochia': the region was still part of the abbey's parish. In the Celtic north, however, with its tribal and pastoral monasteries, the small cells founded to replace preaching stations by the tribal abbot were said very early to have a parochia (fairche). It is significant that the earliest known case in England in which 'parochia' apparently means a rural parish occurs in the Anonymous Life of St. Cuthbert, where Ælfled, abbess of Whitby, is said to have been sitting one day at a meal with St. Cuthbert 'in her parish which is called Ovington'. The saint told Ælfled that one of the brethren of her minster had just died, and the abbess inquired diligently in her minster as to whom this might be. She heard at length that brother Hadwald had been killed, falling from a tree: and next day, when Cuthbert was saying the mass of dedication for the new church at Ovington, she came breathless into church and asked Cuthbert to include the name of 'my Hadwald' among those prayed for as departed. If the estate at Ovington were the Ovington between Carlisle and Lindisfarne, for which there seems some support, it would have been worked by such peasants as Cædmon, and the church would have been served by some frater from the monastery in priest's or some clerical order.

The use of the term 'parish' for a rural church with cure of souls, built by abbot or abbess on abbey lands, does not occur so early in the south, less influenced by Celtic practice. But oratories and small chapels, served by one of the brethren of the abbey, seem to have been built on the lands of St. Augustine's: in the case of Monkwearmouth we have no evidence. St. Wilfrid of Ripon was both bishop and abbot: he was professed at Lérins, but his biographer speaks of his being the first to spread the use of the Benedictine rule in the north. He founded many small minsters on his abbey lands; their small familiae may have said the Benedictine office and in other respects kept the Benedictine rule: but the foundation of these small minsters would seem to have been primarily for pastoral reasons. Thus even the more strictly Benedictine houses did apostolic work by small foundations and outlying oratories.

The great Mercian monastery of Medehamstede was closely associated with the Benedictine rule, but also involved in pastoral activities. It was built on the edge of the fen country: according to Bede, by Peada, king of the Midland Angles, and Oswiu, brother of king Oswald, for the nobly-born abbot Saxwulf. This would have been no later than 657, and in a region barely Christian, the purpose being evangelisation as well as the recitation of the opus dei. The great plague of 664–665 can scarcely have left the house unscathed, and some ceremony of further endowment, or even reconsecration, may have taken place under king Wulfhere, the brother and successor of Peada: an insertion in the Peterborough version of the ASC. lists those present at the consecration of the minster, probably confusing those present at two ceremonies. It says the minster was consecrated by archbishop Deusdedit, bishops Ithamar of Rochester, Wini of Wessex, Jaruman of the Mercians, Tuda (who succeeded Colman at Lindisfarne in 664) and Wilfrid the priest. Saxwulf the abbot was made bishop of Mercia by archbishop Theodore in 675, and when the diocese was divided into five sees, in 679, Saxwulf retained the see of Lichfield. He thus had a general pastoral care for Mercia and he continued to care for and protect his old minster. It was, in such circumstances, natural that Medehamstede should send out daughter houses, whose abbots exercised pastoral care for the countryside. They fetched the chrism from the bishop in whose see they were situated, for use in baptism and the anointing of their parishioners; no such rite could be administered without the chrism.

A twelfth century register of Peterborough abbey contains some anomalous records founded on early Medehamstede charters, or records of oral grants accompanied by the placing of a turf from the land given on a gospel book. They, and the chronicle of Hugo Candidus, monk of Peterborough, deal with the foundation of

Medehamstede and its daughter houses, among them Breedon on the Hill in Leicestershire, Brixworth, Bermondsey and Woking. Friduric, a religious ealdorman of king Æthelred of Mercia (abdicated 716), is stated to have founded the minster of Breedon, stipulating that the brethren at Medehamstede should appoint from among themselves a good priest as abbot: one who should be able to afford the grace of baptism and sound teaching to the people entrusted to him, and should himself remain one of the brethren of Medehamstede. Whether the clause about baptism and preaching was actually in a record made in the time of Saxwulf is doubtful: no such clause occurs in Bede's account of the foundation of any minster: yet that Breedon was actually intended by Friduric to be a focus of evangelisation is likely. The monk Hæddi was appointed abbot, and he later bought more land from king Æthelred for his minster at a price of 500 smillings, paying the price, not in money, but in gifts that included beds and bedding, a man and a woman slave (war captives), a handsome, florid, square-headed brooch, riding horses and hunting dogs. Bede states that when archbishop Berhtwald of Canterbury died in 731, he was succeeded by Tatwin, a monk of the Mercian Breedon.

The remains of a large eighth century church have been found at Breedon: and at Brixworth, another daughter house of Medehamstede, there survives a very fine Anglo-Saxon basilica, such as would have been the church of a considerable minster. The evidence of the foundation of other Medehamstede colonies at Bermondsey and Woking consists of a grant of protection by pope Constantine, which Sir Frank Stenton accepts as genuine. The canonical rights of the bishop and the monastic rights of the abbot are carefully defined and secured: but the intention in procuring the grant was primarily to safeguard minsters distant from their mother house, and in the small sub-kingdom of Surrey, at that time passing rapidly from the power of the king of the West Saxons to that of the rulers of Kent and Mercia. The minster of Hogh or Hoo in Kent was also founded in a time of political insecurity as between Wessex, Kent and Mercia: but it appears also as connected with Medehamstede.

The 'double minsters' also must have been a force in the evangelisation of the country: and to them especially the indefiniteness of the term 'minster' applies. Did either the nuns or the monk clerics or their chaplains keep the Benedictine rule? A strict observance of the rule would, at the time, have excluded monks from having the parochial charge of the countryside; yet this was clearly not the case, for a charter speaks of the people of Romney Marsh as belonging to Lyminge minster, which was a double minster. The monk clerics there and in other double houses must have gone through the clerical orders and been part of the clerical militia: some were eventually promoted to the episcopate. Yet it is not unlikely that copies of the Benedictine rule were available to nuns and clerics, and, since that rule lays down in many chapters the psalms and versicles to be said in the divine office on the different feasts and ferias, it is not unlikely also that both nuns and monks said the divine office thus, and may, by virtue of this, be termed Benedictine. How strictly the rest of the rule was followed is unknown. The minsters in Kent, most of them double, took the place of what were known in Gaul as 'mother churches'.

The existence of double minsters, however, was regarded as un-canonical in the Christian east and the Mediterranean world, where both the clerical hierarchy and the monastic life were already old and well organised. In the more newly Christianised regions of northern Gaul, and of Anglo-Saxon England, however, such minsters economised royal endowment, and provided both for a monastic life and the pastoral care of the region. Archbishop Theodore was hesitant about sanctioning the existence of minsters for men and women, living together, but said that as it was the prevailing local custom, he allowed it ('It is not lawful for men to have women as nuns, nor for women to have men as monks; nevertheless, we for our part do not disallow that which is customary in this country').

The origin of these double minsters, found at the time both in northern France and Anglo-Saxon England, must have been con-nected with the need for finding landed endowment for bases of Christian expansion in a newly converted country. In southern Gaul Christianity was old: it had expanded slowly, from thickly populated centres. The Christianity of the Rhone valley and Provence was very old, and here the bishops had been able to send out members of their familia to serve chapels and oratories, and then to give such rural churches a separate endowment and a priest or deacon of their own. But in the north, rural chapels came only with the conversion of Clovis, and landed endowment for clergy had had to be found by kings newly converted themselves. The situation was in some respects parallel to that of Kent in the time of Æthelberht and other of the Anglo-Saxon kingdoms. While the first need was for provision for a bishop and his familia, it was, on both sides of the Channel, found possible to use land that might have been given in marriage with a king's daughter to found a minster for her. Such a religious house would need a staff of clerks as chaplains, clerks who would join the minster as boys, proceed with due training up the ladder of the clerical orders, afford pastoral care to the local countryside and supply their own successors and in some cases future bishops. The double minsters of northern France had a direct connexion with those of England: but the same missionary conditions account for their existence: as, indeed, in a few cases in Ireland.

Bede himself shows that monasteries benefited from the patronage of royal princesses, provided places of refuge for them and were sometimes double. Anglo-Saxon ladies, in the early days, were sent to French minsters for training. The Benedictine rule was no more than one of the rules they studied: the influence of Columbanus was, for a time, stronger than that of Benedict. Among the notable Frankish patronesses of monks may be counted Chlotild (d. 544), a Burgundian princess who married Clovis, the Merovingian king who took Paris from the Gallo-Romans. They built the church of the Holy Apostles in Paris (it later became the church of St. Geneviève), and, when Clovis died in 511, Chlotild retired to live at the abbey of Saint-Martin at Tours. Radegund, married to king Lothar of the Franks in 529, escaped from the court and founded her famous nunnery at Poitiers. Balthild, said to have been an English war captive, was married to Clovis II and became the particular patroness of monasteries, especially that of Saint-Denis near Paris, and of the nunnery of Chelles. There was a cross-Channel trade of English merchants between the Solent and the fair of Saint-Denis, and there must have been some knowledge of Frankish conditions at the courts of the English kings: but the references to the training of English ladies at Frankish minsters is specific. Bede says that when Earconberht became king in 640, his daughter Earcongota was a virtuous virgin then serving God in the monastery built by the Frankish princess Fara (Faremoutiers en Brie). 'For at that time not many minsters had been built in England and many were wont to seek the grace of the monastic life in the minsters of the Franks or of the men of Gaul;

14

moreover, they used to send their daughters to be taught and pre-sented to the heavenly bridegroom there, and chiefly to Brie, and to Chelles and to the monastery of Andely.'

'And chiefly to Brie' (Faremoutiers). Bede tells us how no less than three Anglo-Saxon princesses were successively, and in spite of their foreign origin and what he calls their 'pilgrim' status there, made abbesses for their virtues. These were Saethryd, stepdaughter of Anna, king of the East Angles; Æthelberga, his natural daughter; and Earcongota, his grand-daughter (she was the daughter of Seax-burg, Anna's eldest daughter, married to king Earconberht of Kent). Faremoutiers en Brie was certainly a double minster, for Bede men-tions the 'fratres' of the minster in connexion with Earcongota's death. He says that when she knew death was near, she went round all the little houses (casulae) where, within the minster, the sick, the old and those of special monastic virtue were housed, and told how she had seen a crowd of men in white robes, who had told her they sought to bear away with them that 'gold coin' which had come from Kent. That night, at dawn, she died, 'and many of the brothers of the monastery, who were in other of the little houses, said they had heard the sound of angels singing, and the sound too of a great multitude entering the minster; and they hastily came out of the little houses, to learn what was happening.' Chelles, founded on the demesne of the king of Paris, and Andely, were also double minsters.

The Frankish institution of double minsters may thus be said to have been transplanted to Britain: double minsters there soon in-cluded Bardney, Barking, Ely, Whitby, Coldingham, Wenlock and Wimborne and several in Kent: but even without Frankish influence the needs of a newly converted country would probably have been met in the same way. The partial care of a princess and her nuns could be combined with that of the neighbouring peasants. Some of the 'fratres' would be well educated, some not; the 'fratres' at Brie apparently shared the work of building the new chapel, and found the plan desired by the abbess Earcongota over large.

The Kentish minsters must have played a large part in the con-version of Kent, as supplementing the familia of the archbishop of Canterbury and that of the bishop of Rochester. There were at first no other local churches. Their siting depended on that of the king's estates, for all were endowed by royal grants, and these estates had a natural connexion with the roads and ports. The old Roman road which ran from London to the Channel passed through Rochester and branched at Canterbury, running thence to Dover, to Lympne, and to Reculver and Richborough, at either end of the Channel dividing the Isle of Thanet from the mainland. Folkestone was by now also a Channel port, with no Roman predecessor: the king had lands there and founded a minster.

The minster of Lyminge, near Lympne, was founded for Æthelberga (Æthelberht's daughter) and her chaplain Paulinus, after they were driven from Deira in 633; king Eadbald gave the land for the minster. Later, Romanus, chaplain to the abbess Eanflæd, Ethelberga's daughter, gave land to the minster, and his name survives in the place name, Romney Marsh. Cuthbert, abbot of the familia of Lyminge, became successively bishop of Hereford (736–740), and archbishop of Canterbury (740–760). We hear of marshland as given to the minster of Lyminge by ealdorman Oswulf at the synod of Clofeshoh in 798, of an abbess Saethryth of the minster c. 804, and of a bequest of ewes and cows, by Abba the reeve before 835: the exact date of the destruction of the house by the Danes is not known.

The minster of Dover was early founded, where the Watling Street reached the Channel. This house became possessed of some of the estates of the said ealdorman Oswulf: it was a house for clerics.

Folkestone was founded c. 640 by king Eadbald as a minster for his daughter Eanswyth and her nuns and chaplains; Abba the Reeve bequeathed it oxen, cows, ewes, swine, and a considerable sum of money, and the payment each year from the man to whom his own estate should pass of six ambers of malt, six of barley, and a certain weight of spices, cheese, 400 loaves and a sheep. The minster was wrecked by the Danes, and in 927 king Athelstan gave the lands of the desolate house to Christ Church: St. Eanswyth's burial place was still known.

Reculver (Raculf) was founded c. 669 by king Egbert of Kent as a clerical minster for Bassa, his mass priest. Its most illustrious monk was to be Berhtwald, who became archbishop of Canterbury on the death of Theodore; he was consecrated on 29 June, 693. King Hlothere of Kent made a further grant of land to him in Thanet and at Sturry. Bede said of Berhtwald that he was well trained in the scriptures and in ecclesiastical discipline 'but by no means to be compared (in learning) with his predecessor'. Like Theodore, he was buried in the central part of the church of St. Augustine's, the side porticus for the archbishops being now full, and the force of the old Roman law against burial within a building further diminished. King Cenwulf of Mercia, while maintaining the archdiocese of Lichfield at the expense of Canterbury, seized the minster of Reculver and held it till his death.

Two other great minsters were founded at about the same time as Reculver: Minster in Sheppey and Minster in Thanet. The foundress of Minster in Sheppey was Seaxburg, the daughter of king Anna of East Anglia. She married king Earconberht of Kent, who died in the plague of 664, and acted as regent till their son Egbert was grown. She then founded her minster in Sheppey, where the road from Maidstone crossed the Watling Street and reached Sheppey and the sea passage across Thames mouth to East Anglia. It was a natural place to select for her retirement: but Seaxburg as abbess desired the life of a simple nun. She left her minster to her daughter Ermenild and went to the monastery at Ely where her sister Æthelthryth was abbess: yet here also, when her sister died in 680, she was elected abbess. It was she who, after her sister had been dead some years, and buried outside the church, according to normal practice, desired to translate her bones within the minster; to find an honourable coffin she sent her 'fratres' from Ely to an old, desolate little city called Grantchester, where they found near the walls of the city a white marble coffin, with a beautifully carved lid, which they brought back to Ely to be Æthelthryth's sepulchre. Even so, more than a hundred years later, they found for Charlemagne an old Roman marble coffin with a figure of Proserpine (Eurydice) carved on it: no one knows in what way the marble from Grantchester was carved, but Seaxburg judged it suitable. A tent or pavilion was set up over Æthelthryth's grave, and while the 'fratres' and the 'sorores' chanted psalms on either side, Seaxburg went within and found her sister's body incorrupt. She clothed the body in new garments, had it laid in the marble sarcophagus, and carried within the church. The scene described by Bede well describes the common practice where it was desired to venerate the remains of a holy founder, buried as usual in the open ground. Æthelthryth had been so buried sixteen years; it is not said that the sarcophagus, when placed within the church, was associated with an altar, though Bede says that miracles occurred and

the shrine was held 'to this day' in great veneration. In the Carolingian period, some two hundred years later, the sarcophagus would
probably have been placed in some association with the altar, still a
small, square pillar; the coffin might have been placed behind it with
its foot to the altar or, as more commonly, behind it with the length
extending sidewise. The process would have been termed 'raising to
the altar', a manifestation of canonisation by local and episcopal
acclaim: and such a process would end in changing the dimensions of
the altar itself from a low, square altar, to a long one, with perhaps
raised carving at the back. The earlier placing of relics within the
altar had been effected by laying cloths (pallia or vela) against the
tomb of the saint, and then placing them within the small altar.

The foundation of Minster in Thanet is not noticed by Bede
nor recorded in the ASC.: Thomas of Elmham, a chronicler of St.
Augustine's, using doubtful material, attributes its foundation to
king Egbert, the son of Seaxburg who founded Sheppey. He gave
land for its endowment to his sister Domneva (? domina Æbbe?),
elsewhere called Earmenburg, who built her church on the south side
of the island, and was consecrated abbess by archbishop Theodore.
She was succeeded as abbess by her daughter Mildred, trained as a
nun at Chelles, who certainly became the chief Kentish saint after
St. Augustine. Eadburg succeeded Mildred as abbess on her death,
and under her the South Minster was prosperous and learned. Not
only were two dependent minsters built in her time near by, one
consecrated by archbishop Cuthbert (before 758), and another a mile
to the east of the original Minster: but Eadburg corresponded over a
period of years with St. Boniface, who wrote to her with affection
and respect. In 716 he recounted to her the visions of a monk in the
minster of Wenlock, the minster of Milburga the abbess, and said he
had been told the visions by abbess Hildelith of Barking. In 735–736
he thanked Eadburg for sending him books (see p. 242); he wrote
again between 742 and 745, and Lull, his successor, wrote in 746.
When Eadburg died in 751, her successor was consecrated by archbishop Cuthbert, and in her time the Danes first raided the abbey.
In 797 the abbess Selethritha and her nuns perished when the Danes
again burned the abbey. The minster was, from its position, peculiarly
subject to Danish attack, and, though restored, was again burned in
980: in 1011 the abbess Leofruna was captured by Swein, after which
the nuns deserted the place.

After the Christian mission to Kent had been settled at Canterbury, the sub-kingdoms adjacent to Kent were converted and endowed with minsters. The small sub-kingdom of west Kent had the see of Rochester; beyond it, to the west, Earconwald, son of Frithwald, sub-king of Surrey, founded the clerical minster of Chertsey and became its first abbot. The over king of Frithwald is shown (by rather late evidence) to have been Wulfhere of Mercia: the foundation was later than the plague of 664 and probably c. 678. Earconwald became in 675 bishop of London: travelled to Rome and brought back a charter of privilege for Chertsey from pope Agatho (678–682).[1] Subsequent kings of Mercia made grants to the abbey. No other minster appears to have been founded in this small sub-kingdom.

In Essex, whose conversion had originally been provided for by the establishment of the see of London, Earconwald, abbot of Chertsey, founded the minster of Barking for his sister Æthelberga, before he himself became bishop for the East Saxons. The chief endowment for the minster came, however, not from Earconwald, but (as stated in a probably authentic charter of 692–693) from the East Saxon princes, notably a certain Hodilred. Earconwald died at his sister's minster in 693, his body being taken back to Chertsey. Æthelberga was eventually canonised, as was Hildelith, who had first taught her the rule and who succeeded her. At one time Hildelith had under her as nun Cuthberg, daughter of Ine of Wessex, who became 'mistress of the rule' at Wimborne and trained Lioba, the friend of Boniface. Both these ladies were skilled in embroidery and could write Latin verse: the minsters, clerical and double, fostered the best learning of the day. The minster of Barking survived till its destruction by the Danes in 870: a hundred years later it was restored by grant of king Edgar. The late Saxon minsters were then, however, of less importance to the pastoral care of the countryside, for rural parishes had been founded by thegns, and on the lands of bishops.

The history of the other Essex minster, that of St. Osyth's of Chich, is confused. According to a partly legendary account, Osyth was the daughter of king Frithwald and grand-daughter of Penda, king of Mercia; she was married against her will to the king of the East Saxons, but escaped and founded her minster on the estuary of the Blackwater.

---

[1] BCS. no. 56: as elsewhere, the pope speaks of a bishop as a 'speculator'.

In the kingdom of East Anglia, the foundation of only one great double minster is recorded: that of Ely. East Anglia was a land where paganism lingered; it had been the scene of a great settlement of pagan English, and under the Christian bretwalda Æthelberht, king Rædwald had adopted Christianity half-heartedly. A strong pagan opposition had caused the erection of the great pagan burial mound at Sutton Hoo as late as c. 654–670. Bede, however, describes Anna, king of the East Angles, as 'a good man and happy in a good and saintly offspring', and he had daughters and grand-daughters who embraced the religious life. For one only, however, was a minster founded in East Anglia: for Æthelthryth, who married first the ealdorman of the south Gyrwas, and secondly Ecgfrith, king of Northumbria, who appears to have been much younger than herself. Leaving him to become a nun, she was trained for a year under abbess Æbbe of Coldingham, and then founded her own minster on the isle of Ely, on land which she may have taken with her as dowry to her first husband. Her sister Wihtberg joined her there as nun. Ely became the great minster of the fenlands; but Anna's other pious daughters took their dowries, and founded minsters, in foreign parts, outside East Anglia. Seaxburg founded Sheppey and Æthelberga became abbess of Faremoutiers en Brie.

The kingdom of the East Angles had but one bishop, from the time of bishop Felix till Bisi, who died in 673; Theodore then provided sees at both Dunwich and Elmham. While supplementary pastoral care was provided by Ely in the fens, in Norfolk the bishop was aided by the Celtic monastery of Cnobheresburh (Burgh Castle).

So far, the evidence for the pastoral care of the countryside is indirect and inferential, except in the case of the daughter houses of Medehamstede. There is, however, direct evidence of the building of rural churches by lay thegns in the seventh century, and earlier evidence of such building by lay thegns than by bishops. Whether the foundations of lay thegns or bishops, however, such rural parishes centred often in privately owned churches. The priests in charge of them were appointed by and maintained by the lay thegn who built the church, or the abbot or bishop who built it; in time it was laid down that the lay thegn who appointed the priest must present him to the bishop and seek his approval and confirmation. The earliest mention by Bede of such a thegn's church occurs in his account of the miracles of bishop John of Beverley, stated by the

ASC. to have become bishop of Hexham in 688 and to have died in 721: Bede says that abbot Berchthun of Beverley told him that a certain gesith, Puch, whose village was 'about a mile from our monastery' had a wife who was sick. During her sickness Puch summoned the bishop to dedicate his church; when he had done this and said he must now return to his minster, Puch implored him to stay, dine at his house and give the blessing. The bishop sent the sick woman some of the holy water which he had blessed for the consecration of the church, and she was at once cured. Puch's church was a private church, as was that of the abbess Ælfled of Whitby.

The letter of Bede to bishop Egbert of York (732?–766) throws much light on the pastoral care for rural districts at the time, and also on the abuses in the minsters where endowment by a royal or noble founder had led to control of the house by the founder's relations, regardless of personal merit or due regard for religious order. He exhorted Egbert diligently to read the scriptures and Gregory's *Pastoral Care* and homilies on the gospels. Since Egbert could not in so large a diocese by himself preach in all the villages and hamlets, even in the course of a whole year, he must ordain priests to help him preach, say mass, and above all baptise: they must teach the apostles' creed and the Lord's prayer, in Latin, or, for those who speak only their own language, in English.

Further, with the help of the pious king Ceolwulf, Egbert must seek to consecrate more bishops: Gregory ordained that the bishop of York should be metropolitan, with twelve bishops under him, but by the slackness of earlier kings, or the foolish misdirection of endowments, the number had not been completed and it would not be easy for Egbert to find a place for a new see. He should, by the consent of a great council (witan) and by episcopal and royal edict, select some minster to be the seat of a bishopric, and cause the monks to elect the new bishop, who should have charge both of the minster itself and the surrounding region for a diocese. And if such a minster, by reason of becoming a bishopric, needed further places or possessions, there were numerous places, as all men know well, most foolishly styled monasteries (minsters), completely without the monastic way of life, which should be recalled to continence and piety by synodical authority and added to the episcopal endowment.

'Since there are many great minsters which, as common folk are wont to say, are useful neither to God nor man, because neither is the regular life lived there, nor do they maintain knights nor counts of secular power, able to defend our people from the barbarian: if a bishop's see, according to the needs of the time is set up in such a place, this is no wrong doing but meritorious.' Bede goes on:

There is a yet worse abuse, when laymen, with no intention of establishing the regular life or of being called to the fyrd as thegns, buy land from the king under the pretext of founding a minster, and then live at their own pleasure and have the place confirmed to them in hereditary right by written deeds, which they have signed by bishops, abbots and nobles. These villages and hamlets which they have usurped they hold free of all divine and human service. They even fill the so-called minsters with married men and women, and their children.

For about 30 years now, since king Aldfrith's death, our province has been distracted by this evil custom, so that there is scarcely any man set over it (as prefect) who has not obtained for himself this sort of a minster, and even king's thegns do this: so that there are some young men who call themselves both abbots and secular prefects: they know nothing about the regular life and have been taught nothing. Yet suddenly, as you know, they receive the tonsure at will and become, not merely monks, but abbots. You must correct such evil customs, if necessary by visiting the minsters in your parish, to see what good and what evil there is in them, so that neither abbot nor abbess shall be ignorant nor despisers of the rule.

You must be solicitous also for lay people, who in our province, for lack of teaching, go to holy communion only at Christmas, the Epiphany and Easter: though there are numerous boys and girls, young men and virgins, old men and old women, who without any scruple of controversy may well do so every Sunday and on the holy days of apostles and martyrs. Married people, duly taught to live virtuously, may do the same.

Bede's advice to archbishop Egbert shows clearly that the convenience of converting land by written deeds from folkland to privately possessed land held by hereditary right, had not escaped the Anglo-Saxon ealdormen and thegns, and had led to abuse. Such a transfer of folkland, or of a royal estate, by 'booking' had the additional incentive that land so booked, as to a minster, was not subject to fyrd service nor the customary food rents.[1] The secularisation of minsters had even earlier been held an abuse in Gaul, and the councils of the seventh century passed canons seeking to restrain it.

Seen against this background, it is not impossible that the learned and able set of clerics left behind him by archbishop Theodore should have sought to deal with the evil in the kingdom of Kent, where pastoral care as well as the monastic service of God had devolved upon the two bishops' sees and the minsters. The position of the Kentish minsters is defined in a spurious privilege, said to have been granted by king Wihtred of Kent (696–716), and confirmed at the Kentish synod at Bapchild, and the Mercian one of Clofeshoh, 716. The earliest surviving manuscript containing it dates from no earlier than 1220, but a note states that it was copied from a very old charter or land book: which may have been the source from which the privilege was copied into the late, Canterbury version of the ASC. It was there placed, undated, near the beginning of Wihtred's reign. The form of the privilege is undoubtedly spurious, the work of Anglo-Norman monks at Canterbury desiring to uphold the archbishop's original rights over the minsters of Reculver, Upminster and the South Minster (both in Thanet), Dover, Folkestone, Lyminge, Sheppey and Hoh (Hoo): but even such a document is of interest as showing that these minsters had come to be regarded as the old 'mother churches' of Kent. In the course of years, they built dependent chapels or oratories on their lands, and such as survived the Danish raids appear as parishes in the *Domesday Monachorum*, which was a survey of the lands of Christ Church, Canterbury, made when sworn evidence was being collected in Kent for the royal Domesday of 1085.

[1] See, for a rather different view on the effect of 'booking', E. John, *Land Tenure in early England*, 34; it is not disputed that such 'booking' to thegns was desirable, in reward of service.

CHAPTER X

THE EIGHTH CENTURY CHURCH : ROYAL AND SYNODAL GOVERNMENT

BEDE says he finished his *Ecclesiastical History* in 731; thereafter we lack his fine narrative of the history of the English church. But by this date other scribes were recording grants and even keeping annals, so that information is not completely lacking. Provision had been made for the English bishoprics and for the great English and Celtic minsters (see Chapter IX): provision also to keep the small minsters and the rural priests of bishops and ealdormen, out in the country-side, in some subordination to their diocesan bishops. Communica-tion was difficult, but the church was recognised as one. Though a village church seemed isolated, or dependent upon the lay thegn who had built it, yet no village baby could be made a Christian, and no old villager should die, without the chrism and the holy oil: the village priest anointed, but only the bishop blessed the chrism. At the synod of Clofeshoh, 746, it was laid down that bishops must make annual visitations of their parishes; and, at some time later, a diocesan bishop is found requiring priests and abbots to attend his own diocesan synod. All these links between the bishop and local churches were old, and preceded the struggle of the bishops to control their see by requiring rural priests to be licensed, before they could take over the cure of souls round the village church to which the ealdorman or thegn had presented them.

As to the machinery of the eighth century church, which pro-duced men willing to give their lives for the conversion of the heathen, like Willibrord and Boniface, the bishoprics were now as follows: for the southern province, the sees of Canterbury, Rochester, Selsey, Winchester, Sherborne, London, Leicester, Worcester, Here-ford, Lichfield, Lindsey, Dunwich, Elmham; for the northern, York, Lindisfarne, Hexham and Whithorn (for Galloway). The sees were maintained by an original landed endowment as were the minsters; but when a bishop built an oratory on his estate, or a church where there had been but a preaching station, and when such rural churches attained independence (with the priest having cure of souls and fetching his chrism in Lent): still some part of the church revenue had to be paid to the bishop. 'Church scot' (church 'sceattas': later a penny from each hearth) is first mentioned in king Ine's laws of c. 690:[1] the payment is mentioned as well known, and king Ine laid down that it was to be paid at Martinmas (when the harvest should all have been gathered). No rural parishes existed at the time, so presumably the money went to an old minster, or to the bishop. The priest of the village church lived later on his own strips of land in the common field: his share being double that of a villager; or he was maintained by the thegn who built the church. The offerings of the villagers should rightly go to the priest and also 'soul scot', or the offering made at the death of one of his people: but the thegn who built the church sometimes claimed to take these offerings, or the greater part of them. Synods sometimes condemned thegns who thus built churches for the sake of gain. The payment of tithe, a tenth of a man's income from whatever source, is sometimes recommended in sermons of this period as a pious act: but it had no legal sanction.

The most important institution in the life and growth of the church in these centuries was the episcopal synod, usually held concurrently with the king's witan, or meeting as a single body with the witan under the presidency of the king. It was especially important as ratifying or recording donations from king or nobles, or as making remonstrances to the secular power about abuses; though declarations about doctrine were made, and disciplinary canons passed, yet, on the whole, the synod (or synodal witan) was chiefly important as the meeting-place of church and state for executive purposes. The synod was as much a vehicle for royal action as the witan for secular, and royal sanction, royal endowment and royal confirmation of the land grants of others were all necessary for Christian expansion of all kinds.

It is often difficult from the scanty evidence to determine whether a meeting were strictly a synod or a witan. Willibald, in his Life of Boniface, mentions that king Ine held a synod of great ecclesiastics (a primatibus aecclesiarum), but 'with the council of the king's

---

[1] In Ine's laws the payment must be made, apparently, in proportion to the house and the season's produce from the land (healme).

servants': it was addressed by the king himself, and was not exclusively an episcopal and abbatial synod. Yet, though an archbishop and a bishop or two were often present at a witan, and though an archbishop may well have assisted at the redaction of secular laws, which often included clauses dealing with ecclesiastical matters: yet some distinction between secular laws and canons remains. The king's laws, if written, were recorded in Anglo-Saxon, and new canons, as yet, in Latin. In the case of canons, drafting by any other than the archbishop and his household is most unlikely, and there is no positive evidence to show that the king and laymen were present when the archbishop's draft of the new canons was first read out and discussed; the notarial record of canons was careful, indeed, to say that the canons were enacted by the consent, not only of archbishop and bishops, but of the king, queen, royal princes, ealdormen and thegns, who had all confirmed and attested them.

The difficulty of distinguishing between witan and synod in pre-Conquest history, especially at this early date, is the less surprising in view of two facts.

The first is, that the relationship of church and state was a working partnership and one as yet not theorised over: it was undefined, unsuspicious, friendly. The heathen Anglo-Saxon king was officially the descendant of the gods, with a right to sacerdotal supervision and decision among his folk, which made the Byzantine attitude of the Christian clergy to the king all the easier and more natural; they were prepared to accept him as a providentially sent protector. In Bede's day the Hildebrandine concept of church and state, as set in a perpetual antithesis one over against another, was three hundred years and more ahead. Nor were strictly Byzantine contacts needed to make the English clergy well-disposed towards kings, and particularly the over king (though they read Greek easily in Theodoran Canterbury): for all clerics who recited the office knew of the emperor Constantine, at least from the lessons of the Invention of the Holy Cross, on May 3. They knew that Constantine had seen the sign of victory, the Lord's cross, in the sky, and then won the battle over Maxentius whose winning meant the conversion of Europe. Celtic clerics knew well the name of Constantine, for among them there was no more frequent and honourable name for a king.

Secondly, the boundaries between synod and witan are little known and probably non-existent, because so little is known about the witan itself. It was a meeting of the king's wise men, his 'sapientes', but how often they met, or precisely who met, historians cannot say. In Theodore's day, the Anglo-Saxon kings were not crowned, so that there cannot have been, precisely, the three 'crown wearings' of Easter, Christmas and Pentecost; there may well, however, have been feastings at such times, at courts as well as in humbler homes, right from the time of pope Gregory. In any case, witans were not held as often as three times a year, at Christian feasts when only the king's family and household were necessarily present. The curious amphitheatre or audience place, wedge-shaped on plan, at Yeavering, was set up in timber to hold more than the king's household: this, indeed, was meant for the holding of a witan.

The difference between a witan and a seasonal court feasting was that the king's princes, ealdormen and perhaps bishops attended, all of whom must have been summoned from some distance, by messenger. The king summoned to a witan whom he wished, when he wished and to where he wished. It is likely that the king's chief bishop, or archbishop, should have attended many witans, when the business dealt with was purely secular, for he owed the king counsel; moreover, at many witans some land grant to a minster might be made, or come up for confirmation. If important decisions about minsters were to be made, or disciplinary canons to be passed, the king seems to have summoned all the neighbouring bishops, or even all the bishops, north and south of the Humber; this appears from their subscriptions to canons and land grants. The initiative in desiring an assembly of bishops (and the word 'synodus' means no more than an assembly) for the purpose of getting measures passed specifically for the good of the church must have lain with the archbishop: but he worked through the king and the royal summons. The great purpose of witan and synod was publication, and it was often as needful that new *acta* should be published to the lay thegns as to the clergy through their local bishop.

The relation of Anglo-Saxon synod to the witan was thus very close, even in the time of archbishop Theodore who inaugurated the first synod. Theodore lived in the 'Byzantine centuries', when Christian philosophy assumed that the emperor, or indeed any Christian king, was God's agent for the protection of the church or the conversion of the heathen; he had the means of summoning councils of bishops, and of finding them a lodging when assembled.

It was appropriate that he should, if he wished, preside over them.

Visigothic procedure is of interest as compared with that in England at the time. After the conversion of the Visigothic kings of Spain, a country always in close touch with Byzantium through its Mediterranean seaports, the council of Toledo, comprising lay nobles and bishops, and presided over by the king, legislated on matters both secular and sacred. Similarly in England, it was not felt derogatory to the spiritual power that the king should preside over councils of bishops, or that the royal family and the great lords should be present at them. It was not till the time of Hildebrand (Gregory VII) that the supreme worldly and spiritual power were felt to be set, one over against the other, and that it was necessary to fight for the final supremacy of the spiritual.

In view of the importance of synodal action between the days of Theodore and the general ravaging and destruction of sees and minsters by the Vikings, some of the most important meetings and their enactments may be noticed. In nearly all cases the councils are better described as synodal witans than as 'synods', for if the king met his bishops and ecclesiastical business was done, still he, his family and the thegns of his household would be present to attest and confirm, together probably with the ealdorman of the shire in which the meeting was held.

When Theodore held his first episcopal synod in 672 at Hertford, there was no single over king or bretwalda, and Bede, in his account of the synod, makes Theodore its sole convener, 'in the third year' of king Ecgfrith of Northumbria. The seventh canon laid down the old canonical rule that synods (of bishops) ought to be held twice a year, but for various causes, it was agreed that they should be held only once a year, 'in the place called Clofeshoh'. They all knew where this place was: Theodore, Putta of Rochester, Lothar of the West Saxons, Wynfrith of the Mercians, and Wilfrid's legates from Northumbria. It is unlikely that it was a meeting-place in the open fields, like those of early shiremoots and some later hundred moots, and it was surely centrally placed for bishops from all quarters. Later synods of Clofeshoh occur in the ascendancy of the Mercian kings, and though Clofeshoh has not been identified in spite of much research, it is reasonable to assume that it was a hall or estate of the Mercian kings, possibly near London, like Hertford and Hatfield. A king's hall would be of wood, with some sort of farm buildings, and the possibility of lodging the bishops: it may well have been destroyed in the complete destruction of south east Mercia in the Danish wars. Since the discovery of the king's hall at Yeavering, so long unsuspected, this complete destruction cannot be held impossible.

Yet Theodore himself did not convene his second synod at Clofeshoh: Bede tells us that he summoned it at the command of Ecgfrith, king of the 'Humbrenses', Æthelred of Mercia, Aldwulf of East Anglia and Lothar of the Kentish men. Since the matter to be dealt with was doctrinal (the Monothelite heresy), it is clear that the real initiative was Theodore's own. He held it at Hatfield, in 680.

A local Mercian synod at Burford in Oxfordshire was also attended by Theodore in 679: a sub-king of Æthelred of Mercia made a grant of land to Aldhelm of Malmesbury. The prologue of a questionable document calls the meeting a synod, but the term could cover a meeting of the witan. Bede mentions also a Northumbrian synod to confirm a papal privilege for the monastery of Monkwearmouth, and Theodore's presence at the synod at Twyford which unanimously elected Cuthbert to the bishopric of Lindisfarne. At this date it would seem that provincial or English synods were summoned not for the passage of general or disciplinary canons, but for the publication of some royal grant or appointment.

The holding of a Kentish synod a few years after Theodore's death is indicated by some confused evidence in a (much re-written) form of the 'privilege of Wihtred' (see p. 210). This states that the 'privilege' was confirmed at the council of Bapchild (698), in Kent, over which king Wihtred and archbishop Berhtwald presided. Another dubious memorandum, which follows the 'privilege' of Wihtred in the Canterbury Cartulary, states that the privilege was further confirmed at the synod of Clofeshoh, 716; abbot Albinus appears among the signatories, and the names of three 'praepositi' or provosts. The post-Conquest and forged forms of the privilege sought to turn it into a general synod and to strengthen the 'dominion' of the archbishop of Canterbury; but the earlier form of the privilege speaks only of a local, Kentish synod. As the danger from the secular control of minsters was already evident among the Franks, it is not impossible that some kind of a decree was passed about the Kentish minsters as early as the last years of the seventh century, though Bede's letter to archbishop Egbert was written only in 734. He there speaks of the abuses in secular or feigned minsters as widespread and well known.

The division of the bishoprics of the West Saxons between two sees held respectively at Winchester and Sherborne seems to have been planned by Theodore, but deferred till the death of bishop Hæddi in (?) 705. Opposition to the division appears to have been made by the West Saxons and reprehended in a canon of the annual synod of that year, held perhaps at Clofeshoh; a West Saxon synod then accepted the division and appointed Aldhelm bishop of Sherborne. This may or may not have been at the same synod as one held 'near the river Nodder' in Wiltshire, where Aldhelm's right to retain his abbacies of Malmesbury, Frome and Bradford on Avon while holding the bishopric of Sherborne was maintained: such a concession would help to finance the new bishopric, always a matter of anxiety.

About 706, again, a synod confirmed the grant of Æthelweard, sub-king of the Hwicce, of land at Evesham to found a minster. King Cenred of the West Saxons and archbishop Berhtwald were present. Bede states that in 709 a 'general synod' was held at Alcester (ten miles from Evesham), the endowment of the new minster was confirmed, and bishop Wilfrid of York was commissioned to consecrate the church in the new minster.

The next period of synodal activity in England is covered by the life of St. Boniface, and forms part of a great reform movement of which he was the author and prime mover. This synodal activity, an outcome of monastic fervour both Celtic and Benedictine, manifested itself in efforts to evangelise the pagans (particularly in Germany), to acknowledge subjection to and commission from the see of Peter, and to reform abuses connected with the worldly conduct of bishops and abbots among the Franks, and the lay ownership of minsters in England. Boniface wrote of the splendid, worldly and sometimes evil life led by the Frankish bishops and abbots, but the accusation of prelacy or evil life was not brought against the English bishops and abbots by the reformers: at the worst, monks were forbidden to go hunting with falcons and hunting dogs. Even so, when flesh meat was practically never eaten even by the gentry who depended upon wildfowl for any dishes at all savoury, the monks who joined the minster servants in taking out dogs or a hawk were

15

probably not engaging in any very splendid pursuit. Still, it was one held unsuitable for monks. Denunciation in England of sham minsters, however, and of scandalous conduct of lay nobles with nuns was fairly frequent, and canons were passed to deal with the evils reprehended in Bede's letter to archbishop Egbert.

The eighth century reforming synods in England should be seen as promoted largely by the letters of Boniface, and as contemporary with the reform he was carrying through in the Frankish church. Boniface (see p. 124) sailed first for Frisia in 716, was consecrated bishop in 722, archbishop in 732 and by 741 had founded bishoprics for the lands he had converted in Germany, all with the aid of Charles Martel and many helpers from English minsters. He had founded his great abbey of Fulda, in Hesse. When his protector, Charles Martel, died in 741, he found Charles' two sons, Carloman and Pepin the Short, anxious that he himself should undertake a reform of the Frankish church.

Accordingly, Boniface left the bishops and abbots he had appointed in Germany to deal with their own cures, and spent most of his energies in the years 742 to 747 inspiring and seeking to enforce reforming canons passed by Frankish councils. The problem of the confiscation of church lands by kings and nobles, which was in fact that of equalising the contribution to defence made by minsters and sees whose lands had been confiscated, with those which had not suffered this deprivation, was dealt with; and disciplinary matters like the worldly and irregular conduct of Frankish bishops, abbots, clergy and monks, surviving pagan customs among the laity, the observance of a uniform calendar of church feasts, and regular monastic observance were regulated by canons.

This programme of Frankish reforms was begun by two synods of 742, the one presided over by Carloman, mayor of the palace in Austrasia, the other by Pepin, mayor in Neustria. Carloman's council was a mixed assembly, and the canons issued as royal capitularies: those for Pepin's council of Soissons, 742, have not survived. In 743 a general, reforming council of the Frankish church was held, and another in 745 when Boniface presided and declared aberrant and heretical two Frankish bishops: he was also occupied in these years in trying to get the reforming canons carried out, and in writing to English ecclesiastics urging reform there. Another general Frankish council in 747, attended by Boniface and his German bishops, summarised earlier reforms: Boniface wrote to archbishop Cuthbert in 747, stating that he has decreed in synod his acceptance of the catholic faith and subjection to St. Peter and his vicar, and enacted that synods shall be held yearly, and the sacred canons and the 'norm of regular life' read out annually at them. Hunting and coursing moreover shall be forbidden to the clergy: each priest shall in Lent give an account of his year's work to his bishop, and bishops shall preach, confirm and teach, etc. He has reported all this to pope Zacharias.

Boniface had been found useful by English abbots while he was still only a learned and devout young monk at Nursling, six years before he started his missionary work in 716. We are told in his Life that after he had been made priest in 710, while Ine was reigning over the West Saxons, a new emergency arose (we are not told what, but it must have been connected with the monks), and a synodal council of church leaders was held 'with the advice of the king's monks and priests (servorum dei)'. The expression probably means the abbots and bishops of Wessex: the subject of contention was discussed by those in the sacerdotal order, and they deputed legates to go to Berhtwald, archbishop of Canterbury, lest their decision should be held presumptuous if made without his advice. Then 'the whole senate and clerical order' (i.e. the mixed witan) consented, and the king asked the monks whom he should send as messenger? Then the chief archimandrite (head abbot), Wynberht (of Nursling), and Wintra, abbot of Tisbury, and (another) Berhtwald who ruled the minster called of old, Glastonbury, suggested Boniface as messenger. The king laid this duty upon him and sent him off, with companions. Boniface set forth in order to the archbishop the message imposed upon him by the king, and receiving an immediate answer, reported it to king Ine and the aforesaid 'servi dei'.

While Boniface was working in Frisia, Thuringia, Bavaria and Hesse, he had little leisure to urge reforms in England, but he kept in touch by letter with English church leaders, abbots and abbesses. Ine of the West Saxons resigned his kingdom in 726, and a general leadership of the Anglo-Saxon kings then passed to the vigorous and able, if not virtuous, kings of Mercia. It was the over king of Mercia (not called bretwalda by Bede) who would need eventually to be won over by Boniface to countenance any general measure of reform in England.

At some time between 744 and 747, while he was occupied with Frankish reform, Boniface wrote formally, with his five co-bishops, to king Æthelbald of Mercia, commending his generous almsgiving and the law and order and good peace which he kept in his kingdom, but reproving him for never having been lawfully married and leading an irregular and scandalous life. He blamed him even more for his disregard of the charters of minsters and theft of their property, and for his own and his thegns' scandalous conduct with nuns. Boniface wrote also to archbishop Egbert of York, to the priest Herefrith and others, exhorting them to persuade Æthelbald to give heed to the admonitory letter he had directed to him.

This effort of Boniface was responsible, as far as one can tell, for the holding of the great reforming synod of Clofeshoh, 746,[1] at which Æthelbald and his nobles were present. Just as among the Franks, the question of secularised minster lands in England was dealt with, and some kind of a settlement reached, and one not entirely favourable to the church. Bede's letter to Egbert implies that the secular use of minster lands, or sham minster lands, was connected with the needs of military defence, and the bishops at this synod were compelled, apparently, to accept the situation in the case of some secularised minsters and even to visit them.

The bishops present in 746 included archbishop Cuthbert and Dunna of Rochester, two bishops from Mercia, two from Wessex, and one each from East Anglia, Essex, the Hwicce, the Lindissi and the South Saxons.

The acts of the synod of Clofeshoh, 746, appear to have been made in correct notarial form, beginning with the words 'Regnante in perpetuum Domino nostro Jesu Christo', a phrase used many years earlier in Gallican councils, and adopted by pope Hadrian when, in the Iconoclast dispute, it was undesirable to quote the year of the reigning Iconoclast emperor, as if acknowledging him. The bishops stated as being present at the passing of these synodal acts at Clofeshoh, starting with archbishop Cuthbert, are named with their sees, and the episcopal list agrees with those bishops known to have held the sees in 746: there is some probability, that is, that the redaction of these canons was made at the time, though a less formal account may have been notarialised later. There is no reference to king Æthelbald of

[1] The synod of Clofeshoh, 742, is mentioned only in ASC. F, and seems a mere confusion with that of 746.

Mercia as presiding over the synod, as would have been usual earlier: but the prologue, after the list of bishops present, dates the proceedings by the year of grace, and the thirty-second (?) year of Æthelbald, king of the Mercians 'who was there present with his princes and dukes (war-leaders)'. This dimidiating reference to a royal presidency accords with Bonifatian notions, as does the relation of how proceedings were opened by the production of the letter of 'the pontiff venerated throughout the whole world, the apostolic lord, Zacharias', which was read through first in Latin, and then translated into English, for better understanding. This proclamation of apostolic presidency was Bonifatian in spirit, but aroused no opposition in England, where the conversion by pope Gregory was yearly devoutly remembered, in which tradition Boniface had himself been trained.

The prologue further stated that the synod was held 'concerning the unity of the church and the state of the Christian religion, and to arrange and confirm a peaceful concord' (presumably about the secularised lands of minsters, and the residence of seculars in them).

Canons then laid down that each bishop be firm in enforcing the sacred canons within his cure, well ruling and teaching his people; that sincere charity be preserved among 'all men of ecclesiastical religion, so that although sees are divided for different regions, yet all may serve God united in mind and spirit'; that each bishop visit his parish once a year, calling the people together and teaching them, and forbidding, among other sins, pagan customs, that is, diviners, fortune-tellers, auguries, phylacteries, incantations and all other pagan wickedness. Moreover, that bishops shall admonish abbots and abbesses in their parishes to live regularly, and the 'praepositi' and 'praepositae' of minsters faithfully to dispense minster goods, and never to steal from them.[1]

The next canon dealt with secularised minsters and was passed only after discussion: some members of the conference would seem to have urged that bishops should altogether refuse to visit such minsters. The canon as passed, however, ordered bishops to visit 'those minsters, if it is lawful to call them minsters, which in whatever place and for whatever length of time cannot, because of tyranny and avarice, be recalled to a Christian religious status, but which are, through human invention, everywhere held by seculars: such

---

[1] Praepositi and praepositae may here mean the monk and nun provosts of minsters.

minsters, none the less, shall the bishop visit, for the souls' good of them that dwell there, and specially to warn them lest anyone should perish in sickness without the ministry of a priest, the secular possessors allowing this'.

Some twenty-four other canons dealt at some length with the provisions for study in minsters; and ordered that priests on the estates of laymen, duly appointed by the bishop, should diligently preach, baptise and visit, and teach the people to understand in their own tongue the words of the creed, the Lord's prayer, the mass and baptism; that priests 'shall not garrulously babble in church in the manner of secular poets, nor corrupt and confound with the intonation of tragedy (tragico sono) the form and distinct pronunciation of sacred words: but they shall use a simple, holy melody according to the custom of the church; feasts of our Lord and the nativities of martyrs shall be uniformly kept, according to the martyrology of the Roman church, with the appropriate psalmody and chant; priests and abbots shall ever say mass on Sundays, putting away secular business; and moreover all people on that day and on the greater festivals shall be frequently invited by priests to assemble in church to hear the word of God and the sacrament of the mass'. The seven hours of prayer shall be observed in minsters with psalms and melody, according to the custom of the Roman church, and ecclesiastics and monks shall pray, not only for themselves but for kings and the whole Christian people. The greater and lesser litanies of Rogation shall be observed, and not with the vain custom of games and horse-racing and feastings; the feasts of Saints Gregory and Augustine shall be observed by both clerks and monks. Monks and nuns shall be humbly subject to their superiors and clad, not in splendid garments, but a simple habit suitable to the monastic intention. Bishops shall keep watch in their parishes that minsters be, as their name implies, places of silence, quiet and work for God: and not receptacles for those practising mirthful arts, such as poets, citharists, musicians and scurrilous jesters; nor should seculars have leave to wander inside minsters at will and to talk inside the little houses of the minsters. For familiarity with lay people is a harmful custom, and chiefly in minsters of nuns living with little regularity, from which cause divers suspicions and infamies arise. For the houses of nuns should not be cubicles of feasting, drunkenness and luxury, but dwelling places of those living continent and sober lives, studying, and making psalmody: rather let nuns give heed to reading books and singing psalms, and not to weaving and embroidering many coloured clothes for their own glorification. Lay children shall be urged to go to holy communion often, as also those older people, celibate or married, who are not sinners. Any secular desiring to become a monk shall not receive the habit or the tonsure without proof of his life. Bishops appointed to a see shall hold a synod with priests, abbots and provosts: any bishop who finds he cannot emend what needs correction in his diocese shall expose all this in open synod before the archbishop.

All these provisions are similar to the canons passed by Carloman and Pepin for the reform of the Frankish church. That some effort was made in England to deal with the needs of minsters is indicated by William of Malmesbury, who says that at a synod of Clofeshoh, 749, Æthelbald 'pro remedio animae' freed minsters and churches from all public payments, and all public services except bridge-building, and the defence of strongholds against enemies.

Whatever the success of the Bonifatian reform in England, the news of his death in 755 was received with sorrow. In a synod held soon after, it was decreed that the feast of his martyrdom (June 5) should be everywhere observed, as archbishop Cuthbert wrote to Lull, his pupil and successor in the primatial see of Mainz.

The next landmark in English church history after the Bonifatian reform was also a sign of Mercian supremacy: the legatine mission of 786–787 and the establishment of an archbishopric for Lichfield. King Æthelbald of Mercia died in 757, murdered, apparently in private vengeance, by one of his own bodyguard. He had ruled London as a Mercian town and exercised some kind of superiority over all the Anglo-Saxon kings south of the Humber; he played no part, however, in the politics of western Europe. After a short Mercian civil war in 757, Æthelbald was succeeded by his relative Offa, whose coin legend described him as rex totius Anglorum patriae. He reigned till 796. He was a great warrior, like Æthelbald, but not merely a soldier and a tyrant: he had a learned court, negotiated on equal terms with Charlemagne, crushed the sub-kingdom of Kent, alienated its arch-bishop for the exaltation of Mercia, and seemed to the papacy a ruler who must be drawn into closer relationship with Rome: such an im-pression he made on that far-seeing statesman, pope Hadrian I (772–795).

The English church conceived of itself as the child of pope Gregory I, and of its episcopal hierarchy as mapped out by him; it had acknowledged its spiritual parentage in 746. No papal messengers, however, no legates, had visited the country since the days of Gregory and Augustine. The initiative in sending such a mission was taken by pope Hadrian, who seems to have received reports that Offa was personally ill-disposed to him: he wrote to Charlemagne that rumours of that kind had reached him, but of course he did not believe them. He thought fit, however, to despatch George of Ostia, an old bishop experienced in papal business, and Theophylact, bishop of Todi, to England. Their formal business was to inquire into the state of the English church by synod, to enact such canons as were needed and to report to Hadrian. To Offa their visit was welcome, for he desired the setting up of a Mercian archbishopric, as befitted a kingdom where a secular primacy was exercised. Moreover, he had defeated Kent in war, and detested Jænberht, archbishop of Kent, whose loyalties were entirely Kentish. In modern times, Jænberht was the spiritual leader of the Kentish resistance. For Offa to upset pope Gregory's arrangement of provinces, papal sanction was necessary, and the matter was discussed by the legates, though surviving records do not mention the setting up of the new province as a legatine enactment. The pallium, however, was at once sent to Hygeberht, bishop of Lichfield, when the new metropolitan see had been set up, in 788.

The two legates' report of their actions to pope Hadrian fortunately survives, though it was either sent before the end of the mission, or some part of it has been lost. They reported that they had been received by archbishop Jænberht at Canterbury, 'where the body of St. Augustine rests', had admonished him in such matters as were necessary, and travelled thence to the hall of Offa, king of the Mercians. 'He received both ourselves and the letters from the holy see with great joy.'

Then Offa and Cynewulf, king of the West Saxons, met in council; 'to whom we delivered your holy pact' (the canons which the English kings and synods were expected, after discussion, to subscribe). 'They forthwith promised to emend their faults.' 'Then, taking council with the aforesaid kings, bishops and worldly rulers, reflecting that this England (angulus ille) stretches far and wide: we allowed the veneral bishop Theophylact to go to Mercia and north Wales. I (George) however, taking with me Wigbod the priest abbot, whom your son the most excellent king Charles sent with us, travelled to Northumbria to king Ælfwald, and Eanbald, archbishop of York.' 'A council was summoned, to which came all the princes of the region, secular and sacred (787: at Finchhale?); we heard that many things needed correction, for, as you know, from the time of Augustine, no Roman bishop has been sent here, except ourselves. We wrote all these things in order, in capitular form, and read them aloud, and with all humility and good will they accepted and promised to obey them.' 'These are the capitula which we delivered to them to keep.'

Twenty canons follow in the letter, some of them long, and most of them already covered in the canons of 746. Among those making new dispositions may be noted:

> Can. 4. All canons shall live canonically and monks shall live according to their rule (regulariter).

(This distinction between monks and canons was notable and novel in Anglo-Saxon England, where the old Martinian, clerical monasticism had not been sharply distinguished in popular estimation, from Benedictine monasticism. Monks shall wear the monastic habit, as in the east, and canons that of western canons, and not cloth dyed with Indian dyes, or expensive materials. Bishops, abbots and abbesses shall set their subjects a good example in this.)

> Can. 10. No minister at the altar shall wear short tunics, showing bare legs.
>
> Can. 12. Kings shall be lawfully elected by bishops and princes of the people, and only those of legitimate birth.
>
> Can. 16. Only children of legitimate birth shall share in inheritance.
>
> Can. 17. Holy scripture commends the giving of tithes, and beyond that, of alms. Usury is forbidden. Just weights and measures shall be used.
>
> Can. 20. We admonish all to confess their sins (for if we say we have no sins we deceive ourselves); according to the judgment of the 'sacerdos' (bishop or priest) and the measure of the fault, receive ye the Eucharist and bring forth fruits worthy of repentance.

'These decrees, O blessed pope Hadrian, we presented publicly before king Ælfwald and archbishop Eanbald and all the bishops,

abbots and princes of the people of that region: and we have signed
them in your place with the sign of the holy cross, even as they are
diligently subscribed on papyrus later on this sheet.' Among the list
of signatories occur bishop Æthelberht of Whithorn, Aldwulf of
Mayo in Ireland; and (?) the legate of bishop Elfod of Bangor.

It is probable that in 787, after this Northumbrian synod, a general
English council was held at Offa's hall at Chelsea. The ASC. records
under the year 787: 'This year there was a stormy synod at Ceal-
chythe and archbishop Jænberht gave up some portion of his
bishopric, and Hygeberht was elected by king Offa (to the new archbishopric of Lichfield), and Ecgfrith was hallowed to king'.

Hygeberht was already holder of the see of Lichfield. The anointing of Offa's son Ecgfrith was a sign of his association with Offa in
the kingship, and probably copied in the anointing to kingship in
781 by pope Hadrian of Charlemagne's two sons. Though the ASC.
is silent, it is likely that such an anointing would be the work of the
two legates. The storminess of the synod would have been occasioned
by the objections of Jænberht and perhaps other southern prelates to
the setting up of the new province. The actions of the legates in 786–
787 were a triumph for Offa, and brought cordial relations between
him and pope Hadrian. Offa is thenceforward found signing as over-
lord the granting away of Canterbury lands, and using the Canterbury mint for the issue of his new coins. Even his grant of lands to
the protomartyr St. Alban, and the entrusting of his relics to a new
minster to be set up at the old Verulam, would have had some
reference to the exaltation of Mercia: his kingdom had no apostolic
church like Glastonbury, no tomb of St. Augustine or St. Cuthbert:
but it would now have a very old, very holy, place, duly marked
and reverenced.

The continuance of synods, or witans with a substantial attendance
of bishops, from the legatine mission onwards is attested by occasional reference in chronicles and charters. A claim made by king
Offa against the church of Worcester was conceded by Hathored,
'humble bishop of the Hwicce', in a synod held at Brentford, presided over by king Offa, in 781.[1] Synodal councils continued, even
though the year 787 was not only the year of the mission, but the
beginning of the Danish raids. These became ever more serious and
frequent till the danger reached its climax in the reign of Alfred.

[1] EHD., 466.

There is no reason to suppose, however, that in the first half of the ninth century bishops ceased to visit their parishes and hold diocesan synods; and at times some grant of land to a minster was published and confirmed by king and archbishop in synod or witan.

In the remainder of Offa's reign, there is evidence that Offa granted lands to a thegn in synod at Chelsea in 788, and that another synod was held at Oakley in Surrey, where he had been campaigning. But Offa died in 796 and the Mercian position deteriorated. His son Ecgfrith reigned only five months and was succeeded by a distant cousin, Cenwulf. His position was weaker, though he remained probably the strongest of the English kings till the end of his reign.

On Offa's death revolt had at once broken out in Kent and Wessex against Mercian overlordship: in 802 Egbert, the son of one of Offa's enemies, succeeded as king in Wessex. The erection of Lichfield into a metropolitan see was still widely resented. Archbishop Jænberht, though he died in 792, before Offa, had yet protested in synod against the wrongs done to the church of Canterbury; his successor, the Mercian abbot, Æthelheard, had naturally favoured Offa, but when the men of Kent revolted in 796, he abandoned his see. King Cenwulf, recognising his own lack of support, in 798 began a correspondence with pope Leo III about the archiepiscopal see of Lichfield; he still hoped to prevent the return of the primatial see to Canterbury.

The correspondence is of interest as showing Cenwulf's political needs, and also the ability of his ecclesiastical councillors to study Bede's *Ecclesiastical History*, and to make political capital from Gregory's letter there quoted, where he provided for two provinces in the English church, at London and York (see p. 51). London was now a Mercian city, and Cenwulf would have been willing to give up the archbishopric of Lichfield if the primatial see of the whole southern province could be accepted as at London. He admitted in his letter to pope Leo that Offa's establishment of a third archbishopric was contrary to pope Gregory's plan, stating that some wise men wished Canterbury, where Augustine was buried, to take precedence of London, but emphasising that this was not the Gregorian plan.

Pope Leo was kept informed of the set-up in England; he knew the archbishop of Canterbury was a fugitive, the see of London vacant, and Cenwulf and his successors likely to dominate the holders of a Mercian primacy in London. He tried to conciliate Cenwulf by censuring the Kentish rebels, but avoided giving a decision about the archbishopric. He was himself attacked in 799 in Rome, was restored by Charlemagne in 800, received archbishop Æthelheard at Rome, and in January 802 gave him letters confirming his authority over all the sees which had, before Offa, been subject to Canterbury. In 803 Æthelheard held a synod at Clofeshoh and proclaimed the annulment of pope Hadrian's grant to Offa, as obtained through misrepresentation. Archbishop Hygeberht appears to have resigned his see before the council, which he attended. It is clear that the decisive factor in obtaining the assent of the Mercian clergy to the reversal of Offa's arrangements was the 'reverence of individual bishops for the traditions of Augustine's church'.[1]

One outcome of this Mercian-Kentish quarrel over Canterbury was the rise of the practice of making a written profession of faith and promise of obedience to the metropolitan by each newly elected bishop in the southern province. The first written profession that has survived was made by Eadwulf, bishop of the Lindissi, to Æthelheard; it was probably written in 798, when Æthelheard had returned to Canterbury and before the synodal declaration of Clofeshoh, 803.

Another sequel to the quarrel, in which Offa had granted away many estates of the church of Canterbury, was the struggle over their restoration, or partial restoration, between Cenwulf and archbishop Wulfred, who had succeeded Æthelheard in 805. Peace between king and archbishop was kept till 817, Wulfred attending Cenwulf's witans and attesting his charters between 805 and 817: he held an important council at Clofeshoh in 816, with Cenwulf present and authorising the issue of new disciplinary canons. But from 817 till 821 Wulfred attended no witans, or, at least, attested no charters, and Cenwulf made certain charges against him to pope Paschal I: Wulfred could not exercise his office for that four years. When a reconciliation took place between king and archbishop in 821, in a witan at London, Wulfred was forced to surrender an estate of 300 hides and pay a fine of £120: otherwise, the king threatened, he should be despoiled of all his possessions and banished from the country. On these terms, Cenwulf agreed to withdraw the charges made against him to the pope; but, the record continued, for three years after the archbishop was deprived of money and food rents from the South Minster and from other places in his parish.

[1] Stenton, ASE., 227.

No clear distinction between synod and witan appears during this period, but the influence of the Bonifatian reform and the Carolingian synods across the water is shown in the wording of English charters: the record of an important ecclesiastical event, such as a grant to church or minster, the scribe records the meeting in question as a 'synodal council'. A dispute between the church of Worcester and the abbey of Berkeley over the minster at Westbury was settled at a synod of 824, thus described:

> In the year . . . 824 A.D., in the reign of Beornwulf, king of the Mercians, a pontifical and synodal council was held in the place which is called 'Clofeshoh', the aforesaid king presiding there and the venerable man, archbishop Wulfred, directing and guiding the meeting. There were assembled and present all our bishops and abbots and all the ealdormen of the Mercians, and many of the wisest men. . . . If anyone attempts to remove this estate from this church in the city (Worcester), let him know that he is acting against the decrees of the holy canons, because the holy canons decree that whatever a holy universal synod with its catholic archbishop has adjudged right is not to be made null and void in any way.[1]

Among the signatories, Beornwulf's name comes first: then that of Wulfred the archbishop who 'corroborated this synodal judgment', then those of 10 bishops, 4 abbots, 9 ealdormen, the king's brother, a papal messenger and a few others.

[1] EHD., 476.

CHAPTER XI

ENGLISH MISSIONS AND DANISH RAIDS

THE great break in the growth and development of the English church comes at the Danish invasions of the ninth century, just when the greatest of all her missionary enterprises, the conversion of the Germans, had been accomplished.

This enterprise, the work not only of Boniface, but of all those men and women from the English minsters who came out to help him, or his successors, could only have been carried through at a period when the English church had solved some of her old problems, and was organised, fervent and relatively prosperous. As to the old problems: the awkward relations with the Celtic church: the need of material provision for sees and minsters, without which the national flowering of the liberal arts, Latin literature, and the visual and plastic arts would have been impossible: were now solved. Large and small minsters of clerics, large minsters of monks, shepherded souls and studied the old Greco-Roman learning; Christian influence accompanied the writing down of codes of laws. Malmesbury co-operated with Canterbury, and the tree of English religion, firmly planted, was to bear fruit in missions abroad.

This development, however, was interrupted. It had been made possible not only by religious fervour, but by the maintenance of a relatively peaceful society at home. Battles between kings, rivalries between provinces, indeed, had not been lacking, but serious danger of conquest by an outside enemy had been absent, ever since the Britons of Carlisle had held the northern frontier against the Picts, and king Æthelfrith and his Angles had defeated them but taken over their charge. The Angles then defended the northern frontier from any outside enemy.

At the end of the eighth century, however, an enemy from over the sea threatened northern Britain, and soon, the whole island. In the ninth century Anglo-Saxon independence and English Christianity might well have collapsed together. The valiant and precarious safety which king Alfred gave his country could not in his time restore the ravaged minsters, towns and bishoprics, and the English church seemed broken and defeated. Its restoration belongs to another chapter. Here, something should be said of the English missions in the splendid period before the raids: and a little of the raids and their consequences.

Both Christianity and the best learning of the age were sent by the English church to Germany in the eighth century. Though this flowering of Christian art and letters in hitherto pagan lands was at its most splendid in the hands of Boniface, yet he had predecessors, helpers and successors, both from the Celtic and the Anglo-Saxon church. Columbanus (d. 615), who had founded monasteries and spread the teaching of Cassian over western Europe, had expressed the Irish apostolic zeal and desire for the pilgrim life; his fellow pilgrims were mainly Irish; but now, in the eighth century, when Celtic and Anglo-Saxon Christianity had been fused by the work of Theodore, the work of Columbanus was carried on by Englishmen. They were Englishmen, however, who had gained apostolic fervour from the Celts; they had been trained in minsters where the Celtic penitentials were held as guides to the spiritual life, and they in their turn took manuscripts of the penitentials abroad, and used them in the conversion of the heathen. Their religion was the mainspring of their work, and it was fed from Celtic as well as Benedictine sources.

As to the early use of penitential books, it may suffice to say that archbishop Theodore had had experience of the absolution of sinners after the performance of a penance among the Greeks and Romans; specific periods of penance after grave sin had been laid down by early councils, and absolution had been public and by the bishop; only when absolution had been given was the sinner re-admitted to holy communion and the company of the faithful. Early councils had divided the lapsed and other grave sinners into four classes of penitents, none of them admitted to holy communion; public confession of sin was required at that early date, but was gradually dropped, though public acknowledgment of the state of penance was still required in the wearing of a special dress. Pope Leo I in 459 wrote to certain Italian bishops, forbidding penitents to be compelled to read publicly a detailed confession of their sins: but he declared public confession of sins before the church 'praiseworthy'.

Reconciliation continued a public act: when archbishop Theodore (see p. 126) compared the penitential practice of Greeks, Romans and Celts, he noted that the Greeks absolved 'in the apse of the church', i.e. the bishop, sitting on his chair or throne in the apse, reconciled the penitent publicly.

Penance under the ancient system thus concerned those who had sinned publicly and gravely, though by pope Leo I's time penance was also given for grave sins done secretly. The Celtic system of penance, however, had developed in a land where ignorant and near pagan peasants needed instruction in the Christian life, and received it individually from the priest or bishop to whom they confessed. The Celtic penitential books spread over all western Europe, through the work of the Celtic and Anglo-Saxon missionaries. They had been trained under the Celtic system themselves, recognising the confessor not only as the spiritual judge of the gravity of the sins confessed, but as 'the soul's friend' who directed them on the road to heaven.

The lives of the Irish and Anglo-Saxon missionaries would fill a book in themselves. Notable among them were the Irish brothers, Fursey, Feuillen and Ultan, who began their 'pilgrim' life of preaching and baptising in East Anglia, continued it in north France, and were associated with the monastery of St. Gertrude of Nivelles (d. 659), near Brussels. Fursy had died at Péronne: but St. Gertrude received Foilanus and Ultanus, and gave them for a monastery the villa later known as Fosse.

St. Wilfrid of Ripon, when banished from Northumbria (see p. 95), sailed across the North Sea and preached for a year in Frisia in 678, baptising many heathen chiefs and their people.

Willibrord, who had been trained first in Wilfrid's minster at Ripon, in a sense continued his work in Frisia. He had been offered as an oblate to Wilfrid, and when his bishop and abbot was deposed by king Ecgfrith in 678 and went off to Frisia, Willibrord withdrew to Ireland and there spent twelve years in 'pilgrimage' and study. He had as his master an Anglian nobleman, Egbert, who had since 664 been leading in Ireland a life of voluntary monastic exile. Egbert desired to convert the heathen who lived beyond the territories of the Franks, who remained, after the short success of bishop Wilfrid's mission, as heathen as ever. Egbert sent first a single disciple, Wihtberht, who preached in Frisia for two years before 690, but with little success. Egbert then collected twelve volunteers for the pilgrim life, the only priest among them being Willibrord, and sent them off to Frisia; though sent from an Irish house, the names of some of Willibrord's associates show that, like him, they were Angles: they include Suitberht, Theutberht, the two Hewalds and Lawrence, who later wrote charters for the community at Echternach. Echternach became Willibrord's monastic headquarters and a famous literary house.

Willibrord preached at the Rhine mouth under the protection of Pepin, the Carolingian mayor of the palace; at his suggestion, he made two journeys to the holy see, to secure relics for his Frisian churches and the papal blessing. On his second journey, in 695, he was consecrated archbishop for the Frisians by pope Sergius, receiving the name of Clement. Pope Clement I was at the time reverenced as a martyr who had converted the people of the Crimea. To the learned Roman clergy, outlandish names like Willibrord and Wynfrith seemed unsuitable for bishops. Willibrord became Clement, and a penitential book ascribed to him was headed in the manuscript, *Iudicium Clementis*.

While Willibrord was absent in Rome, his companions chose Suitberht to be their bishop, and sent him back to England, where he was consecrated bishop in 692 or 693 by Wilfrid. Suitberht, however, set up his see at Wijk bij Duurstede, on the northern bank of the Rhine and near its mouth; he was under Frankish protection, but perhaps too near hostile Frisian forces. He departed to preach in Westphalia, but when the Saxons invaded the country, founded a monastery on an island at Kaiserswerth on the Rhine. His withdrawal to Westphalia had, in any case, left the country to be evangelised by Willibrord, as unquestioned head of the mission. Pope Sergius had himself invested Willibrord with the pallium, which gave him metropolitan rank over the missionary province west of the Rhine, as over the independent Frisians to the north east, when they should be converted.

Willibrord made many dangerous missionary journeys beyond the Rhine, explaining the Christian faith to Radbod, king of the Frisians, who regarded him as the emissary of their enemies, the Franks. He baptised converts in the springs of Heligoland and even preached to the Danes: but his main achievement, accomplished by forty years' work, was the planting of the church in Frankish Frisia. Pepin gave him the place for a see near Utrecht, so near to the independent

16

Frisians that for three years after Pepin of Heristal's death in 714 it had to be abandoned. It was recovered, however, by Charles Martel, and Willibrord in his later years worked mainly from this Christian outpost, founding minsters and churches. But the learned centre of his work, where manuscripts were written and scholars trained, was at Echternach. He died in 739.

The greatest name, however, in all this missionary movement is that of Boniface, born in Devonshire and given the Anglo-Saxon name of Wynfrith. From time to time monks or clerks visited his father's house (apparently, the 'aula' of a thegn), and he desired, like them, to serve God as a monk. He went as a child oblate to the minster at Exeter, and then, with his abbot's consent, to the larger and more scholarly house at Nursling, near Southampton. He became 'magister' of the monastic school there, attracted pupils from other houses, studied the liberal arts as well as the divine scriptures, admired the genius of Aldhelm and was not unacquainted with the delights of Greek and Hisperic Latin. As one who was to spend his life as a missionary founder of monasteries among the heathen, as bishop, archbishop and reformer of the canonical practice of most of western Europe, he had no time to write original treatises in classical or Hisperic Latin, like Aldhelm: and for the writing of canons and liturgy Hisperic Latin was always held unsuitable. Boniface's Latin remained that of the classical rhetors, like Bede's.

Boniface was ordained priest at thirty, and was well known to his bishop, the learned Daniel of Winchester. News of Willibrord's venture in Frisia reached him, and he besought his abbot's permission to join him: with a few companions he sailed from London for Wijk bij Duurstede in 716. He arrived just when the pagan prince, Radbod, had laid waste the country in a campaign against the Franks: he had burnt and plundered Utrecht and Willibrord's other minsters, and driven him into exile. Wynfrith had to return to Nursling, but only temporarily.

Bishop Daniel came to his assistance, and supplied him with a commendatory letter to pope Gregory II, whose protection and sanction Wynfrith was now anxious to seek. In 718 he sailed again, reached Rome, was granted many interviews with the pope, and commissioned to go preaching, as 'the devout priest, Boniface, (the martyr Boniface's feast was kept in Rome the day before the papal letter of commission) in heathen parts'. He went through Bavaria to Thuringia in May 719.

There, the news reached him that Willibrord had been able to return to Utrecht, and to Utrecht Boniface went, and worked for three years under the elder missionary. When Willibrord desired, however, to make him his coadjutor bishop, Boniface still wished to work among the unconverted pagans, as the pope had commissioned him, and Willibrord let him go, with his blessing.

Boniface now worked among the pagans of Hesse, a frontier province of the old Frankish kingdom of Austrasia, held now only by a few Frankish garrisons. The Frankish bishop of Mainz could not cope with the heathen in this part of his diocese: there were no churches, no preaching stations. Boniface's companion Willibald, who was to write his Life later, tells us, however, that Boniface soon gained converts, but had all too few helpers to preach to all the tribes; he wrote to Gregory II for advice, and was summoned to Rome for counsel and direction. In November 722, Boniface was received by the pope in St. Peter's, was asked for a profession of faith and made it in writing, in excellent Latin, and on St. Andrew's day, November 30, was consecrated by pope Gregory bishop for all Germany east of the Rhine. No place for a see was as yet assigned him: but he was not placed under the jurisdiction of any metropolitan: his oath of obedience was taken directly to the apostolic see.

On his way back to Hesse in 723, Boniface visited Charles Martel, no friend of monks but favourable to the conversion of pagans in his frontier province. He granted Boniface a letter of protection, commending him to Frankish officials, and Boniface returned to the work of conversion. To demonstrate the powerlessness of Thor before Christ, he hewed down the sacred oak of Geismar and used the timber to build a small chapel dedicated to St. Peter: the monastery of Fritzlar was later built near by. From Hesse he pressed on into Thuringia, destroying pagan cult centres, and now aided by the helpers his letters to English abbots and abbesses had brought out to Germany.

Boniface's work among the pagans was complicated by a certain opposition from Frankish bishops who claimed he was working in regions under their jurisdiction (as did bishop Gerold of Mainz), and by the earlier missions of Irish monks in some regions. Were the orders given by an Irish claustral bishop valid, and what of the sacraments of travelling monk priests whom they had ordained? How strictly should marriages within the prohibited degrees of consanguinity among his own or the Irishmen's converts be enforced? Boniface took much trouble to clear the consanguinity question up, writing to pope Zacharias, to the head of the papal secretariat in Rome, and to archbishop Nothelm of Canterbury. The matter was not made easier in that Roman notaries calculated degrees of consanguinity in one way, and all the Germanic nations, in matters of inheritance, another (see p. 133). Boniface received and read a copy of Bede's *Ecclesiastical History*, and found that a supposed letter of pope Gregory dealing with the matter used the Germanic calculation when he should, if he spoke of degrees of consanguinity at all, have used the Roman method; as a result, he appeared to say that a man might marry his aunt or his niece, which Boniface knew was canonically nonsense! The question of lawful marriage affected inheritance, and Boniface pressed archbishop Nothelm, who had searched the papal archives to send copies of documents up to Bede for his history, about this Gregorian (and quite impossible) letter. Whether Nothelm admitted to him that he had modified the passage in question, using the Germanic calculation, to make matters clearer to English laymen, we do not know: no answer to Boniface's query has survived. The same thoroughness, intelligence and learning is shown in all Boniface's dealings: the same administrative ability in using the helpers he inspired for the setting up of bishoprics and the planting and staffing of minsters.

A hundred and fifty years earlier, Augustine, under papal commission, had come to the heathen Saxons, founded two bishoprics and one minster, and converted the small heathen kingdom of Kent. Boniface, before his death in 755, had been made archbishop for all the Germans east of the Rhine, refounded bishoprics in 739 for Bavaria (Salzburg, Regensburg, Freising and Passau), three more by 742 for Hesse and Thuringia (Würzburg, Buraburg, Erfurt), and planted the newly converted territories with minsters. He had more effective military protectors in Charles Martel and Pepin the Short than had Augustine in Æthelberht; he had had a more effective training for mission work at Nursling than had Augustine at St. Andrews on the Caelian, and he was working among people less far removed from himself in race and language than were Italians from the Anglo-Saxons of Kent. The ground had been, in Boniface's case, to some extent prepared by the Irish monks, even though a legacy of minor difficulties was left by their work. Finally, Boniface's own drive, energy and ability would seem to have much exceeded those of Augustine: his success was even more remarkable in collecting helpers and some measure of material support than in the actual conversion of the heathen. What he could not have accomplished alone, the bishops of his province and the men and women in the minsters did for him; and the access of helpers continued after his own death. It is of interest that among the minsters planted for the conversion of these regions, two were double houses on the English model, headed by abbesses of noble birth: Heidenheim, under Walpurgis, and Tauberbischofsheim, under Leofgyth (Lioba).

Boniface's Life, written by Willibald his friend, represents his martyrdom at the hands of Frisian freebooters as rather inspired by the desire for plunder than pagan hatred of the missionaries.[1] Boniface with his clergy had travelled to Dokkum, on the northern coast beyond the Zuyder Zee, bearing with them, as usual, a wooden chest with the holy relics, texts of the scriptures and a linen sheet to wrap Boniface's body for burial. Boniface fixed a day when he would confirm all the neophytes and those recently baptised, and they pitched a camp by the river. But when the day for the confirmation arrived, a band of heathen warriors came rushing up, instead of the neophytes: they brandished swords and spears, and the attendants at the camp prepared to defend themselves and the clergy. Boniface exhorted his followers to lay down their arms; but the heathen mob came on and slew them with swords and other weapons. What they desired, says the Life, was the spoils of victory: they plundered the camp, stole the chests in which the books and relics were stored, thinking them to be full of gold and silver, and carried them off, still locked, to the ships that had accompanied Boniface's expedition. 'They broke open the chests containing the books and found, to their dismay, that they held manuscripts instead of golden vessels; pages of the sacred texts instead of silver plate. In their disappointment, they threw the books about the field and some of them into the reeds and marshes.' A long time afterwards, the books were found and returned to the monastery. The bodies of Boniface and his companion martyrs were brought by boat, after a voyage of many days, to the city of Utrecht; they were buried there first, but bishop Lull sent a ship to bring them to the

[1] See C. H. Talbot, *The Anglo-Saxon Missionaries in Germany*, 1954, 56-60.

monastery of Fulda, which Boniface had built. King Pepin wished the body to remain in Utrecht: but the bell of the church rang by no human hands, and the citizens of Utrecht were warned that they must let the saint go. With psalms and hymns they accompanied the body to the river, and for thirty days it was rowed upstream to the city of Mainz, where Boniface had had his see. And without any arrangement, a great crowd of the faithful arrived from all parts, and Lull, who had been visiting Pepin, came to Mainz almost at the same hour; and they laid the saint's body in a new sarcophagus in the church at Mainz, with the customary rites of burial; and many blessings followed. He departed to the Lord with the palm of martyrdom on the 5th day of June, in the year of the incarnation, 755.

One of the most touching of Boniface's letters sought to provide, as early as 752–753, that his monks and clergy, some of them now old, should have some protection and maintenance after his death. He wrote to his friend Fulrad, abbot of Saint-Denis and one of the royal chaplains to the Frankish court, asking him to report to king Pepin his anxiety for the future. His own disciples were nearly all foreigners to the Franks and Saxons, some were priests, spending their lives in the service of the church and people; some monks in cloisters or oblate children learning to read. Some were elderly and had been his companions and helpers for many years. Boniface feared that, if he died, they would be as sheep without a shepherd and be scattered abroad, unless they had Pepin's support and patronage; he feared, too, that some of his converts near the pagan border might lose their faith in Christ. He prayed that Lull, his auxiliary bishop, might be appointed in his place: he would be a good master and teacher to clergy and monks: Boniface had a special reason for writing this plea for support, 'because the priests living near the border lead a very bare existence': they could procure food to eat from their people, but they had to have clothing and help from elsewhere; so far, he had given it them.

Boniface's Life was written by the priest Willibald, at the command of bishop Lull and the bishop of Würzburg. He was one of the most learned of Boniface's disciples, and had made a great pilgrimage to the holy places of the east before he joined Boniface. His own Life, and an account of his journeying, was written by an Anglo-Saxon nun of Heidenheim, whose name is known to us because she inserted it in the form of a cryptogram between the Lives of Willibald and his brother Wynbald in the manuscript: she was called Huneberc. She must have taken down notes of his journeyings from his own mouth, and been enormously interested to learn what places he had been to. She called her Life of Willibald the *Hodoiporikon*, apparently preferring a Greek word for 'pilgrimage', 'wayfaring' to a more usual term; she must have had some knowledge of the aims of Hisperic Latin, for *Hodoiporikon* is surely a very distinguished word! Willibald had made a pilgrimage to the Holy Places, like the Frankish bishop, Arculf, earlier; she may have got the Greek word from him.

Huneberc gives no dates in her *Hodoiporikon*; she wrote before the diffusion of Bede's work had made dating by the year of the incarnation widespread. Some dates can be supplied from other sources. Willibald, a relative of Boniface, was educated at the minster of Bishops Waltham in Hampshire, and in 720 he set out on pilgrimage, with his father and his brother Wynbald, from the mouth of the river Hamble: they were making the pilgrimage to the shrine of St. Peter at Rome. At Lucca, the father fell sick and died; but the two brothers made their way to Rome, climbed the Scala Santa, and reached the basilica of St. Peter. Though Willibald was already rigorously observing the monastic rule, he desired a yet harder life and to go on a more distant pilgrimage.

With two companions, he made his way to Gaeta, and crossed over the sea to Naples, and there their fondest hopes were fulfilled and they found a ship that would take them to Egypt. They went to Catania in Sicily, where the body of St. Agatha rests, and is carried out by the peasants to stay the flames and lava when Mount Etna is in eruption: and the flames and the lava cannot pass her. They went to Syracuse, crossed the Adriatic and sailed to Chios, leaving Corinth on one side. They came to Ephesus, and on to the spot where the Seven Sleepers rest; they saw the tomb of St. John, in a beautiful spot near Ephesus. They passed through Hierapolis and Patara and Miletus, where they saw two 'stylites', ascetics living on columns. They suffered from hunger and sailed to Cyprus, and by now it was Eastertide again, a year after their setting out from Rome. They saw a Greek bishop and joined in a Greek litany.

They set sail again, and crossed to Emesa, in Syria, land now held by the Saracens. Willibald now had seven companions and they were all arrested by the pagan Saracens, who said they must be spies; but they took them to an old man who questioned them as to where they came from, and said: 'I have often seen men who come from these parts of the world, their fellow-countrymen; they cause no mischief and desire only to fulfil their law'. But the Saracens kept them in prison, withholding permission for them to go on to Jerusalem; yet almighty God wonderfully preserved them from harm, for there was a merchant there who would have wished to redeem them all, for the good of his soul; and since he could not do that, he sent them dinner and supper every day as alms; and Wednesday and Saturday he sent his son to take them out of the prison for a bath, and take them back again. Every Sunday he took them to church, going through the market place and buying for them anything he thought would give them pleasure. A Spaniard also came and spoke to them in prison, and he had a brother who was chamberlain to the Saracen emir, and he spoke with the emir about these men who came from the west, where the sun sets. And the emir said: 'They have done us no harm. Let them depart and go on their way.'

So they made their way to Damascus, near which St. Paul was first converted, and then to Galilee, where Gabriel first came to our Lady and said: 'Hail, Mary'. They saw Nazareth, and Cana, and mount Tabor where our Lord was transfigured, and there is a monastery dedicated to our Lord, Moses and Elias. They came to Bethsaida and the springs of Jordan: and the shepherds gave them sour milk to drink, and they had great herds of cattle, long in the back and short in the leg, and all dark red in colour. They came to the place in the Jordan where our Lord was baptised, and on the very place where stands a little wooden cross. A rope is stretched over the Jordan, tied at each end: and on the feast of the Epiphany the sick and infirm come there and hold on to the rope and plunge into the water; and Willibald the bishop (of Eichstätt) bathed himself there in the Jordan.

They said many prayers, and visited monasteries, and at length came to Jericho, and to the monastery of St. Eustochium, midway between Jericho and Jerusalem, and then to Jerusalem itself and the very place where the cross of our Lord was found. They saw the place Calvary, and the three crosses outside the church which Helena set up as a memorial, within Jerusalem. They saw the garden tomb of the Saviour, and the slab on which his body lay; they saw a great stone by the door of the sepulchre, a replica of the one the angel rolled away. Willibald reached this spot by St. Martin's day: and he was ill, and when he recovered he went up to the church called 'Holy Sion', which stands in the centre of Jerusalem: for on that spot in the centre of Jerusalem our Lady passed away, and the eleven Apostles bore her to the gates of Jerusalem, and the angels came and took her away from the hands of the Apostles and carried her to Paradise.

So Willibald saw mount Olivet, and the hill of the Ascension, where there is a church with no roof, in remembrance of the two men who said: 'Men of Galilee, why stand ye gazing up into heaven?' and he saw Bethlehem where our Lord was born; and many other places. He saw Jerusalem four times: he was imprisoned again by the Saracens and again set free. He had many adventures and perils: and when he returned to Constantinople after a four months' voyage, he stayed two years, and then went back to Rome. He had been away ten years (720–730): and his voyage reads like a commentary on the gospels.

For the next ten years he lived in retirement at Monte Cassino, and in 740 pope Gregory III ordered him to join the Anglo-Saxon missionaries in Germany. Boniface ordained him priest, and in 741 he was consecrated to the see of Eichstätt. His brother Wynbald had joined Boniface earlier, and his sister Waldburg came out to him soon after from England: her name, as abbess of Heidenheim, was fortuitously associated with the witches' festival, the Walpurgisnacht. Willibald died, a very old man, in 786.

When Boniface had first started on the life of pilgrimage, he had taken with him a few helpers from Wessex, and, through his correspondence with ecclesiastics, men and women, increasing numbers came out to him. Many were monks, 'readers' (in the sense of theological lecturers), writers and students of the liberal arts: they came out from English minsters and many became the heads of German ones. From Glastonbury came Wigbert, to be the first abbot of Fritzlar; from Malmesbury, Lull, the first abbot of Fulda and Boniface's successor in the see of Mainz, and Burchard, whom Boniface made bishop of Würzburg. Other Englishmen were made bishops and abbots: for the minsters, as in the early days of the English conversion, became mission headquarters and schools whence not Christianity alone, but the best learning of the day was diffused in Germany.

Women no less than men came out: Leofgyth or Lioba, Cunihild and Berta (Lull's relations), Cunitrude and Thecla. The letter in which Leofgyth wrote to Boniface, her kinsman, offering herself for work under him and modestly setting forth her qualifications, survives:

I beg your mercy, that you would deign to remember the old friendship with which you were of old joined to my father Dynne, in the western parts (of Britain), who died eight years ago ... and I commend to your memory my mother Æbba, bound to you, as you know, by ties of kinship; she is still alive though weighed down by infirmity. Would that, unworthy as I am, I might account you my brother, for there is no man in whom I place so much hope and confidence. I have taken pains to send you this small gift, not as worthy of your gentle regard, but to make perpetual the bond of true love.

Leofgyth then explained that she is enclosing some (Latin) verses composed according to the poetical discipline, in a desire to exercise a very slender talent. She has learned the art from her mistress Eadburg, who ceases not to render the divine scriptures into rhyme.

Leofgyth and Eadburg remained close friends and helpers of Boniface all his life. Leofgyth came out to him and was made abbess of a double minster at Tauberbischofsheim, thirty miles from Würzburg: Eadburg, the daughter of a West Saxon king, remained abbess of Thanet all her life, corresponding with Boniface and sending him manuscripts of the scriptures which she studied so assiduously. Leofgyth's Life was written by Rudolf, a monk of Fulda and pupil of the most learned abbot in Carolingian Germany, Raban Maur: Leofgyth herself had been in close touch with Boniface's abbey of Fulda, and her body was taken there for burial. The links between the two abbeys were close and Rudolf states in the Life that he got his materials from the nuns who in youth had been pupils of Leofgyth, giving their names. It is likely then that he was well informed: and he says that Leofgyth was sent by her mother to the princess minster of Wimborne under the abbess Tetta: a natural choice for a West Saxon nobleman's daughter. Since it is indisputable that Leofgyth learned the poetical discipline, part of the art of rhetoric, from the learned lady Eadburg, it would seem that she must have been sent on from Wimborne to Minster in Thanet, like Boniface himself from Exeter to Nursling.

Boniface himself was writing letters to Eadburg in 716; he had not yet sailed for Frisia, and she was not yet abbess but perhaps 'magistra' of the young nuns: he addresses her as 'the norm of religious conversation' and sends her an account of a miracle at St. Milburg's abbey of Much Wenlock in Herefordshire: he refers to Hildelith, abbess of Barking. In 735–736 he wrote to thank Eadburg for sending him books, and in 742 to implore her to pray for the poor pagans. In one letter he asked her to have copied out for him in large letters, letters of gold, the Epistles of St. Peter, his especial guide in the preaching of the gospel. At another time he wrote to an abbess Bugga, asking her to get hold of a Martyrology for him: but Bugga could not procure one: she sent him 50 shillings and an altar frontal.

Boniface was not only the apostle of Germany, but the builder of a German church that embraced territories of such different character as Hesse, Thuringia and Bavaria. While in the first two regions the only different Christian tradition resulted from the work of Irish missionaries, in Bavaria Frankish bishops had come with the Frankish conquerors and there were now some missionary centres of their foundation, but no territorial dioceses: bishops were either attached to minsters, as with the Irish, or were wandering preachers. When Boniface arrived in Bavaria in 739, the Bavarian duke Odilo was looking for an opportunity to regain his independence from the Franks: nevertheless, he was ready to support Boniface, the Frankish protégé. Boniface was able, under the terms of the papal mandate of 739, to instal Willibald in the Bavarian see of Eichstätt: and set up territorial sees in Regensburg, Salzburg and Freising, all in Bavaria. He summoned, as apostolic legate, a plenary council of the Bavarian church, initiating the practice of synodal government. Some hundred minsters were established in the Bavarian church.

Over all this new church, Boniface ruled as archbishop, since Gregory III has sent him the pallium in 732. No metropolitan see had then been assigned to him: no place was specially indicated by circumstance, and the papal scrinium well knew that this signal honour could of old be bestowed on whom the pope willed, even on a simple bishop. Boniface's status is shown, however, by the papal permission to consecrate his own followers bishops. It was not till 747, in the course of his reform of the Frankish church, that Boniface was given the see of Mainz, earlier held by Frankish bishops, and not till 780, long after his death, that Mainz became itself a metropolitan see. Boniface's authority throughout his life rested on his position of papal legate. After his coronation of Pepin in 751, he used the novel title of archicancellarius to authenticate documents, but this was a notarial title.

Boniface's death at Dokkum in 755,[1] at the hands of a heathen band, brought grief to his friends in England and a sheaf of letters of commiseration to his disciple, Lull, at Mainz. That from archbishop Cuthbert of Canterbury rendered thanks to God that the English people had been found worthy to send forth this student of the heavenly learning and noble soldier of Christ: and informed Lull that the English church had recently decreed by synod that June 5, the day of the saint's martyrdom, should be celebrated annually, and ranked Boniface with Augustine and Gregory as one of the three patrons of the English church.

The danger to the English church and nation from the northern sea raiders had been long foreshadowed when Lindisfarne was wrecked, as recorded by the Peterborough Chronicle, in 793: 'Terrible portents appeared over Northumbria and miserably frightened the inhabitants: there were exceptional flashes of lightning and fiery dragons were seen flying in the air. . . . And a little after that, in the same year, the harrying of the heathen men, miserably destroyed God's church in Lindisfarne.' To the compiler of the ASC., the raiders were not 'Vikings', but always 'the heathen men', 'the heathen army', or occasionally 'the pirates'.

The Norsemen and Danes had long ago learned to cross the North Sea in their clinker-built ships (their boards riveted with iron nails). Their axes felled a tall tree, which they fastened as mast into a square platform in the middle of the ship; they hung a great sail on the mast, and let down a deep keel in the ship's centre, to secure stability. When wind-becalmed, the ship's crew, themselves the sea warriors, drove the ship forward with oars. Young men were trained in sea-camps for the profession of pirate or sea-trader (for the one merged easily into the other), and when peace between the Scandinavian kings narrowed the demand for their fighting services at home, they crossed the sea for plunder or settlement. Sea raiding was dangerous but profitable; settlement offered lands in a milder climate than that of Norway or Denmark.

---

[1] There is some uncertainty in reckoning the date: the Germans hold that it occurred in 754, the English church in 755.

In northern and western Scotland indeed, many bands settled. After plundering the wealth of Irish kings and minsters, the northern pirates settled there too, and from Ireland and the Isle of Man they crossed to Cumberland, Westmorland and Lancashire and settled, often intervening later in the affairs of the Danish kingdom of York when such had been set up. But by and large, the long-continued raids for plunder were of more acute importance to the Anglo-Saxon church than the early settlements.

The northern raiders were of course heathen, acknowledging Odin as All-Father and the war-god Thor as almost their national champion. How much this made them crueller enemies than, say, Northumbrians to Mercians, cannot be demonstrated: but certainly their exploits are recorded with peculiar bitterness by the Anglo-Saxon chroniclers, and certainly they not merely plundered the minsters (as was indeed natural, for the minsters had much portable plate and other loot) but brutally maltreated such monks and bishops as they captured. The Saxon chroniclers' account of the killing of king Edmund of East Anglia and bishop Ælfheah of Canterbury by the heathen Danes represents them as deliberately brutal, and may well be true. In any case, while all classes of the English suffered from the plunder of the raiders and the gelds levied by kings to buy them off, it was the English clergy, both pastoral and monastic, who suffered peculiarly.

The words of king Alfred about the lack of learning in the English clergy, and the apparent need of reform in the English church in the period immediately preceding Dunstan should both be seen against the background of the Danish raids on, and partial conquest of, England. The raids were dangerous from 793 to the near-conquest of England in 870–871, and Alfred's division of the country with king Guthrum by the treaty of 878; by the end of Alfred's reign the church had been revived and encouraged at his court, and a respect for learning there demonstrated; but the king's resources were too few to maintain the military defence of his kingdom and also re-endow the minsters, the schools of learning of the day.

The ASC. itself supplies evidence enough of the blow dealt to the English church; not only was Cuthbert's church at Lindisfarne destroyed, but 'Northumbria was miserably ravaged by the heathen, and Ecgfrith's monastery at Donemuth (Jarrow) was looted'. Most of the raiders at this time, however, passed from Scandinavia north of Scotland, either settling in Shetland, the Orkneys and the Hebrides, or passing on to the plunder and conquest of Ireland.

The raids on England were so much the lighter for forty years: but in 835 the ASC. records another devastating raid. 'In this year the heathen devastated Sheppey': one of the earliest of the Kentish minsters was looted. In 840 king Egbert of Wessex fought 25 ships' companies at Carhampton, for it was the custom of the raiders to row silently as far inland as river or creek permitted, gather horses, and raid the countryside. King Egbert's fyrd would have been foot soldiers and they were defeated: for the enemy held the place of slaughter. In Lincolnshire, in 841, another ealdorman and many with him were defeated and killed by the Danish host. There was no means of getting English forces to the right place at the right time.

The south west of England was plundered at the same time, by raiders coming from Ireland, or down Channel from Denmark. In 838 a great pirate host joined the Britons of Cornwall to fight king Egbert of Wessex: but he put them both to flight at Hingston Down. In 840 a Wessex ealdorman fought 33 ships' companies at Southampton and won the victory, but the same year a Dorset fyrd, led by ealdorman Æthelhelm, fought the Danes at Portland and the ealdorman was killed and the battle lost. In 848 the ealdorman of Somerset and bishop Ealhstan of Sherborne and the ealdorman of Dorset fought against a pirate host at the mouth of the Parret, the landing place for Glastonbury: but they made a great slaughter and won the victory: Glastonbury was saved, for the time. In 850 again, the ealdorman of Dorset defeated a Danish host at Wigborough.

In 851, however, the peril increased: the summer raiders began to build camps and winter in the island. In 850 Athelstan, a son of Egbert of Wessex and sub-king of Kent, and the ealdorman Ealhere had destroyed a great host off Sandwich in Kent; but nevertheless the heathen men stayed over winter in Thanet. In 851 350 ships sailed to the mouth of the Thames and stormed Canterbury and Rochester and put to flight the king of Mercia, who had marched with his levies to defend London; three of the greatest English churches were plundered. Then the Danes went south over Thames into Surrey and were heavily defeated by king Æthelwulf and the fyrds of Wessex. In 855 for the first time the heathen men wintered in Sheppey, farther inland than Thanet; and in face of so great a danger king Æthelwulf pledged himself by charter to give one tenth of his land to the glory

of God, and made his way to Rome to pray for the protection of the
saints. He died, however, and his body lies at Winchester; and his
son Æthelbald reigned over Wessex and Surrey, and died, and his
body lies at Sherborne. And in 860 his brother Æthelberht succeeded
to the entire kingdom, and a great pirate host came and stormed
Winchester, though the ealdorman of Hampshire and Berkshire
defeated them later.

In 865 the Danish host again wintered in Sheppey: and the Kentish
men made peace with them and promised them money; and under
cover of this peace the host went secretly inland by night and
ravaged all the eastern parts of Kent. That same year another Danish
host wintered in East Anglia and took horses: and they made peace
with them (at a price). In 866 worse followed: the host from East
Anglia went north and over Humber mouth to York, which they
seized. The fyrds of Northumbria, under two kings, fought desper-
ately to regain the city, fighting both within the walls and without,
with immense slaughter. 'Both kings were slain, and the remnant
made peace with the host.' The Northumbria of Bede and Cuthbert
and bishop Egbert, Bede's friend, perished in the battle: the Danes
settled and, in Sir Frank Stenton's words, 'a culture was wiped out'.
The next year the Danes invaded Mercia and settled in Nottingham.
Mercia, with two great river mouths to defend, those of the Trent
and the Thames, and with the Trent a great waterway into the heart
of the country, was strategically impossible to defend against such
enemies; except for her western territories, with Worcester in the
land of the Hwicce and Hereford in that of the Magonsætan. Elsewhere, she was completely ravaged.

In 869 king Edmund of East Anglia perished. The host had ridden
across Mercia into East Anglia, and the king fought against them.
The Danes overran the entire kingdom 'and destroyed all the
minsters to which they came'. 'At the same time, the host in Mercia
came to the minster of Medehamstede (Peterborough) and burned
and demolished it, and slew the abbot and monks and all that they
found there, reducing to nothing what had been a very rich foundation.' Kent, East Anglia, Northumbria and Mercia were now at their
command: and in 870 the host rode to Reading in Wessex, building
themselves a camp there. It was a year of desperate battles for Wessex:
king Æthelred and Alfred his brother fought at Englefield and
Reading and Ashdown and Basing and 'Meretun'; many thousands

perished there: and there bishop Heahmund of Winchester was slain, and many good men. After Easter king Æthelred died, presumably near Wimborne minster, where his body lies; and a fresh army, 'a summer host', came to reinforce the Danes.

In this year, 871, Alfred the king fought nine desperate battles and innumerable forays 'which were never counted' and still was driven back. He fought with a small force the whole host of the Danes at Wilton, near Salisbury: in his nine battles nine Danish jarls and one king were slain: but the West Saxons had to buy peace with the Danes.

In the years following, the ASC. records the Danish host at London, Torksey in Lindsey, and Repton in Mercia, whose king, Burhred, now also made his way to Rome, hoping for the help of the saints: and the Danes again ravaged Northumbria and the Strathclyde Britons; three Danish kings then came south and sat for a year in Cambridge. In 875 the host got Wareham, a considerable port with two churches: Alfred made peace with them and they swore him oaths on the sacred ring (the heathen priests wore it in their assemblies and it was kept on the altar in their temple): but they broke their oath, eluded Alfred and the fyrd, and got into Exeter.

In 878 the host went secretly in midwinter to Chippenham and rode over all Wessex and occupied it, some of the inhabitants they drove overseas and most they made subject to them: 'all except Alfred the king'. He and a small company moved through woods and into inaccessible places and marshes, to the marshes of the Parret: and they made a small fort at Athelney. And in the seventh week after Easter they rode east of Selwood, and fought the great battle of Edington and defeated the whole host and put it to flight. Three weeks later, under oath of peace made after the battle, king Guthrum came among a band of thirty honourable men of the host at Aller which is near to Athelney, and Alfred stood sponsor to the king at his baptism, and the ceremony of the loosing of the baptismal fillet was at Wedmore.

It was a great landmark, this royal baptism and a first beginning of the conversion of the Danes; but that baptism was accepted as a condition of peace after defeat and little else. The host moved in 879 from Chippenham to Circencester and then to East Anglia, where they divided up the land and settled. Many went off to Normandy: and some bands at times attacked southern England. In any case,

Alfred had saved and defended only part of England: Wessex, the country south of the Thames including Kent, and the small, south-western part of Mercia. All northern and midland parts of the country were under Danish rule, and at first after the peace of Wedmore, under heathen rule.

For the church, the wars had been tragically destructive: the great minsters, the towns with their churches, had all been burned and plundered. Lindisfarne and Whithorn, Jarrow and York, Ripon and Medehamstede, London, Rochester and Canterbury, Selsey, Wimborne and Malmesbury; all had gone. The Welsh minsters had occasionally been raided from Ireland, but had suffered less severely: as had the minsters of western Mercia.

Of the bishops' sees, plundered and overrun by the Danes, the most notable was St. Cuthbert's see of Lindisfarne; the bishop and his familia led a fugitive life till, in 883, he could set it up again in Chester-le-Street (see p. 122).

As to the other bishops' sees in the times of the Danish raids, so far as we know there was no complete breakdown of pastoral care. The lists of bishops can be traced with few vacancies, though Dorchester on Thames had no bishop, apparently, from c. 896–909. But in all the sees in the worst part of the fighting, though the list of bishops can be reconstructed, there is no certainty when one succeeded another: East Anglia was raided and overrun, and the times of accession of the bishops of Dunwich and Elmham are quite uncertain: either no Easter table and annal was kept, or the book perished. Of bishop Cunda, consecrated in 836, it is uncertain whether his see was Elmham or Dunwich: of bishop Ælfred, consecrated c. 934, whether his see was Elmham or Lindsey. Nor are the names of any other bishops of Elmham known for the hundred years between 836 and 934, though after this there was a continuous episcopal succession down till the Norman Conquest. The succession years of the bishops of Hereford are uncertain in the second half of the ninth century, and the see of Leicester drops out with bishop Ceolred, who died sometime between 869 and 888. The succession years of the bishopric of Lichfield are quite uncertain in the same half century: and there is the same lack of record for the bishops of Lindsey and even those of London, Rochester and Selsey. For Winchester, the years of the bishops' consecrations are unknown between 871 and 900.

17

Few bishops perished in battle with the heathen host, but the cathedral minster and small, thatched houses of the bishop and clergy were burnt and plundered: the relics and perhaps an illuminated altar book might be saved, but the manuscripts in the wooden chest that constituted the library: who was to save them when the roof was burning, and heathen men stood with swords ready to cut down the monks and priests as they sought to escape? The bishop's lands were plundered too, and the bishop, with the remnant of his familia, must have led a meagre and fugitive life for many years.

For Canterbury, though plundered more than once, the obits (records of the day and year of the archbishops' deaths) were kept: Ceolnoth was archbishop nearly forty years, up till 870; Æthelred nineteen years, from 870 till 899; Plegmund from 890 till 914, covering the worst years of the raids.

In the uncertainties of the Winchester succession, it was yet remembered that St. Swithun (see p. 336) died on July 2, 862; while in Worcester, more central and less open to attack, the deaths of Eahlhun were remembered as in 872 and Wærferth as in 915. The minsters as schools of learning perished, though enough monks and priests survived to keep the faith alive even in the parts of England occupied by the heathen Danes. There is plenty of evidence of the co-existence of Danish paganism and the Christian faith in the Danelaw, and the extreme poverty of the see of York even after the reconquest of the Danelaw by Edward the Elder of Wessex: but there is no evidence that any general new evangelisation of the Danelaw or East Anglia became necessary: no new apostles were needed.

It appears then that, as a result of the raids and Danish settlement, an impoverished English church lived on, her episcopal churches and her minsters no longer adequate for the instruction of the clergy, her landed endowment largely given by the kings to lay thegns and earls for the pressing needs of military defence. If Alfred found it necessary to invite learned bishops from Wales and western Mercia to his court, like Asser and Plegmund and Wærferth, it is because there only could they be found.

CHAPTER XII

THE ENGLISH RECOVERY UNDER ALFRED AND EDWARD THE ELDER

THE English church under Danish attack had suffered great loss: but it had not been wiped out. The bishops' sees, and their endowments, or some of them, remained. The glebe or the patron's stipend was still there to support the priest of a rural parish. What had been lost was the cathedrals and their libraries, and the minster libraries. Not only were the actual 'families' of bishop or abbot dispersed, and with them the store of learned clerks who had hitherto educated the younger clergy, but with the monastic and clerical families gone, the lands that supported them had been taken into the king's hand. They had, in many cases, been granted to the thegns, or leased out to them.

Alfred, by his treaty of 886 with the Danish king Guthrum, had set a boundary between his own kingdom and the north eastern part of England, now ruled by the Danes. Kent and Wessex were Alfred's, as was London, which he had just occupied; from London the boundary ran up the Lea to its spring, then in a straight line to Bedford, and along the Ouse to Watling Street. From here, Watling Street itself formed the boundary between English and Danish territory. This left the sees of Chester-le-Street (where St. Cuthbert's bones rested from 883 till 993), York and Elmham in the land of the Danish settlers, their position precarious and impoverished; the great northern minsters like Ripon, Beverley and Medehamstede had been plundered and not restored. Their landed possessions had gone to the conquerors.

The Danish wars in some cases ended or interrupted the tenure of episcopal sees in northern Britain. Hexham had no bishop after Tidferth's death in 821; Whithorn or Candida Casa no bishop whose existence is certain after Baldwulf, who was alive in 803. In spite of the raids there was an unbroken succession of English bishops at York till the appointment of Osketel, c. 957; and the succession of bishops of Lindisfarne was unbroken though bishop Eardwulf wandered with

St. Cuthbert's relics till he found the place for a see at Chester-le-Street in 883, and finally at Durham at the close of the tenth century. The raids extinguished also the sees of Dunwich and Elmham in the years following 870, though Elmham was revived c. 950. The English population of East Anglia remained Christian though the Danes conquered and settled in it: possibly the bishop of London exercised some episcopal care, and Hoxne was in the eleventh century an episcopal see for Suffolk; Bury St. Edmunds is mentioned in Domesday Book as having once been an episcopal see. Sidnacester seems to have been extinct for the first half of the tenth century, and the see at Leicester was moved to Dorchester on Thames.

Even in Alfred's own kingdom the needs of defence had been, and were, so great, that no large scale restoration of the minsters could be undertaken. Across the Channel, the Franks, to deal with the surprise attacks of the Danes, had passed the Edict of Pistres in 864, to provide defence for the coast and river mouths by means of the building of forts and the raising of cavalry forces. In England the danger had been as great, but no reorganisation of defence had been made till Alfred's reign. The fyrd of the shire, summoned to fight by the ealdorman, was an infantry force, whereas the first thing the Danish raiders did when they rowed up a river and landed, was to gather horses and ride afield. Alfred eventually turned his fyrd into mounted infantry, requiring the shire thegns who composed it to ride to his summons. Whereas the ASC. says in 870 that king Æthelred and Alfred 'led great levies to Reading', while the Danish jarls 'rode up-country', it says in 876 that 'Alfred the king rode after the mounted host'. Alfred the king was at length at the head of a mounted army: and one much more expensive to maintain than the old, unmounted, fyrd. To maintain the thegns who rode with his court, and the shire thegns who rode at the summons of the ealdorman, it was necessary to keep the lands of derelict minsters in the king's hand, and to make many land grants to thegns and ealdormen. Alfred had a desire to found minsters and foster learning as strong as that of Oswiu and Aldfrith of Northumbria: but military needs were paramount. They continued paramount in the great military reigns of Edward the Elder and king Athelstan.

As to the reassertion of English power over the Danelaw: this was achieved in the reign of Alfred's son, Edward the Elder. Edward's sister, the Lady Æthelfleda, had married Æthelred, ealdorman of

Mercia, or rather that part of the old Mercia that remained outside the Danelaw. Unrest along the frontier of the Danelaw was chronic, and in 910–911 the Yorkshire Danes broke the peace treaty and harried English Mercia and the Severn valley. Edward and Æthelred met and defeated the Danes at the battle of Tettenhall, and the reconquest of the Danelaw began. Fortified 'burhs' were built along the frontier at strategic points, and when ealdorman Æthelred died, his wife succeeded him in 912 as ruler of Mercia. She had to help her the young warrior Athelstan, her nephew: and with his help she proved as effective a leader against the Danes as her husband had been.

Edward's enemies included some Norse Vikings from Cumberland, who had landed there from Ireland, now conquered by the Northmen. The Yorkshire Danes had elected Ragnald, one of the Norse settlers in Cumberland, as their king: but by 920 Edward forced Ragnald to renew his homage. King Constantine III of Scotland, also harried by the Northmen, now came to Edward and 'took him for father and lord'. Ragnald had been raiding the Isle of Man, the Waterford region in Ireland, Dunblane in Perthshire, and the Yorkshire Danelaw: the Danes had found Ragnald as dangerous a warrior as Edward, and they had hoped his other enemies would defeat him. The 'submission of the north' to Edward in 920 was really the formation of an anti-Norse coalition; but Ragnald was forced to accept the submission too. He held York: but under the supremacy of Edward. The Danelaw was reconquered: at least nominally. Moreover, the Danes were now settled on the land and at any rate partially converted to Christianity.

In 925 Edward died and was succeeded by his son Athelstan, who ruled till 939, and was succeeded in turn by his two brothers, Edmund and Eadred. The reign of Athelstan was notable, not only for the continuance of his father's sucesses against the Danes, but by his further organisation of them as his subjects. They were never his feudal vassals, because feudalism in England had not yet come: but he maintained an overlordship over them.

He prevented the setting-up of an independent sub-kingdom of York. He annexed the kingdom of York on the death of Ragnald's brother: but Anlaf, the brother's son, hoped to regain his uncle's kingdom. In 933 king Constantine took up his cause, and Athelstan marched to Scotland and defeated him; when, in 937 the situation was repeated, Athelstan marched through Westmorland and Cumberland to the Solway Firth, round its extreme eastern inlet, and along the northern coast of the Solway Firth to Brunanburh, and there he won the victory made famous by the Anglo-Saxon poem. He broke the strength of Constantine and his helpers, the Strathclyde Britons, Vikings from Ireland, and the Norsemen and Danes from Cumberland and Yorkshire. Constantine had wanted a Danish buffer state between himself and the king of England: but Brunanburh defeated his hopes.

Athelstan, after this victory, used on his coins the old coin-legend of overlordship:

Rex totius Britanniae,

and as a result of his victories England became again a west European power. Of Athelstan's sisters, one married Charles the Simple, king of the West Franks; one, Hugh the Great, count of Paris and father of Hugh Capet; and one, Otto the Saxon, who became the emperor, Otto I. England was brought within the Carolingian orbit, and communications with the Frankish courts and Frankish monasteries brought Carolingian styles of illuminating manuscripts to England, and, eventually, echoes of the Cluniac and Lotharingian reforms.

Though the whole of Britain was now reunited under the kings of Wessex, a large Norse and Danish population had settled in the northern Danelaw and East Anglia, where Danish jarls and their warbands were now the ruling class. Social custom was affected by Scandinavian influence; the streets of York, then and much later, had Norse names. Though the invaders had accepted Christianity, Scandinavian paganism lingered, and the northern bishops were poor. Scandinavian art forms replaced Anglian ones when carved stone was used, as in the ninth century Great Beast in the Jellinge style, carved on one of the faces of the cross from St. Alkmund's, Derby, and the confused, interlaced beasts and serpents found on minor ornaments. It is characteristic of the figure scenes found on stone carvings and metalwork of the period, and this both in Norway and the English Danelaw, that pagan and Christian subjects are often found combined. On the side panels of the later Yorkshire crosses representations of the Norse gods and the stories about them were carved, indicating a marked degree of tolerance for pagan culture and even religion in the north. As in the newly converted Northumbria of about 700, the craftsman who carved the figures of the Franks casket in whalebone combined Christian figure scenes, like the Adoration of the Magi, with that of the pagan archer, Egil, defending his home: so, in some of the northern crosses set up after the Danish settlement, pagan figure scenes appear on Christian monuments, e.g. the Gosforth cross (see p. 180). Northumbria had once been a focus of light, learning and Christianity; after the Danish settlement the driving power of Christianity was focussed in the south.

The reign of Alfred, from the point of view of church history, was notable for the repulse of 'the heathen men' and the preservation of a Christian society in England; and it was no less notable for the renaissance of vernacular literature to be effective later in Christian education. In western Europe the very language had developed from a popular Latin; and it was no great intellectual hardship that the language of government should continue to be Latin. In Britain, Latin had never become the tongue of the people: government, from Anglo-Saxon times, had been in some dialect of the Germanic invaders. The songs sung by the scops at their banquets had given rise to a genre of Christian poetry: it was Alfred's work to extend the use of English from poetry to prose, always a later-developed and more civilised vehicle of communication, and to use it as a general means of education for lay people. English had been in use for the orally-transmitted laws from the time of the Anglo-Saxon landings, and the laws of Kent, Mercia and Wessex had been written and handed down, in that tongue. Alfred now desired that the local ealdormen should be able to read English, to read his laws, and, if need were, to read his sealed writs if he should send them. More than that: English, as the language of lay people, should be used for translations of those books on which, as Alfred held, civilisation rested. There was small possibility of endowing minsters where clerks should read Latin and write books; but Alfred's own court should be a learned one, and clerks who had drunk at the springs of Latin learning should teach himself and his thegns in their own tongue. He and they would write the great books of all time in English.

Alfred, it should be remembered, had seen as a child the monuments and the old civilisation of Rome. When he was five years old, he had been sent by Æthelwulf his father to make the pilgrimage and visit the pope, Leo IV, and a letter from Leo to king Æthelwulf assured him of Alfred's safe arrival. Leo said that he had affectionately received him and 'invested him as a spiritual son with the insignia and robes of the consulate', a parallel to the bestowal of the patrician dignity on the sons of Pepin the Short when he was anointed king of the Franks. The bestowal of the patrician rank was in some sort a recognition of their royal right to succeed their father: and the bestowal of the consular rank also recognised a future right to rule. The writer of the Anglo-Saxon Chronicle roundly put it that Leo 'hallowed Alfred as king and took him as his bishop's son', implying that Leo also confirmed him. Again in 855 Alfred visited Rome, this time in the company of his father, remaining for a year in Rome; in 856 he saw his father honorably received by the emperor Charles the Bald, and married to the Emperor's daughter Judith, a child of twelve or thirteen. Alfred, that is, saw in his childhood the splendours of an imperial and a papal court, and Charles the Bald's court was both learned and splendid. Alfred saw something of the Frankish royal palaces and the figures of the Carolingian renaissance before the worst of the civil wars and attacks of the Northmen had wrecked them.

The chief source of our knowledge of Alfred's own love of learning, and determination to diffuse it, as much as possible, among lay people, is the Latin Life written by Asser the Welsh monk of St. Davids, in 893. Alfred constrained Asser in 885 to spend half the year with him, returning for the other half to fulfil his obligations in Wales. Only late copies of the Life have come down to us, and in these a few later additions once caused doubts as to whether the work were, indeed, the work of a contemporary of Alfred; but it is now recognised that the Life is authentic, and the more valuable as Asser used a version of the Anglo-Saxon Chronicle earlier than any that have survived to us. Asser came to spend his whole time eventually in Alfred's service, especially after the king had, by bestowing on him St. Cyngar's two monasteries of Congresbury and Banwell (see p. 79) provided him with a monastic home in place of St. Davids. He seems indeed to have placed him in spiritual control of a large area in Cornwall, with a minster at Exeter from which to carry on episcopal work (Exeter was not erected into a territorial bishopric till the see of Crediton was removed there in 1046); and Asser received the see of Sherborne on bishop Wulfsige's death at some time between 892 and 901. The uncertainty as to time indicates that no annal was kept, or that one perished in a raid or fire. Asser himself died in 909.

Asser states, in his glowing description of Alfred's character, that he was not taught to read and write till he was twelve years old, though he listened attentively to the old Saxon poems that he often heard recited and which, having a good memory, he memorised himself. This would indeed be the normal education of a young prince of the day, who would be trained in the whole business of riding, hunting and fighting. Writing was for clerks. The West Saxon court rode from one royal hall to another, as the exigencies of feeding what was, for the day, a large body, demanded; and one or two 'capellani' would accompany it. The paramount duty of the chaplain was to guard the king's 'halidom' or chest of relics; but he could also write, at need, land books or letters; it is of interest that the notary's 'scrinium' or desk, in which he kept his feathered pens and writing material, became in English the word 'shrine', which may suggest that the chaplain kept the king's relics in his desk. A little later, the Anglo-Saxon form for scrinium was regularly used of a relic box: Ælfric wrote c. 1000 of the 'sacerdos that beareth the scrin (Vulgate arcam)'. The chaplain at this time was not necessarily expected to say mass every day (though later Alfred himself heard mass daily): his charge was the holy relics and the business of writing. Lay princes and thegns did not learn letters.

In another place Asser wrote of Alfred's learning of Saxon poetry by heart, in the well-known story of how his mother showed him and his brothers a book of Saxon poems with a beautifully illuminated initial letter. When Alfred could recite the poems by heart, she fulfilled her promise to give him the book.[1] Asser speaks also of Alfred's continued regret that in youth he had no masters to teach him learning, 'he never ceased from studying to the best of his ability'. 'He was zealous in the habit of hearing the divine scriptures read by his own countrymen (which seems to imply the hearing of some English paraphrase, for Alfred learned Latin late): and if by any chance anyone arrived from abroad, he would hear prayers in company with the foreigners.' He instructed the sons of ealdormen and nobles, bred up in the royal household, in literature, day and night; he lamented that Almighty God had made him ignorant of divine wisdom (the scriptures and theology) and the liberal arts.

[1] EHD., 266.

In a sense, Alfred's yearning for the better instruction of lay nobles and even the children of any freeborn man, was a reflexion of the Carolingian renaissance of learning across the Channel. Charlemagne (d. 814) and Charles the Bald (d. 877) had maintained learned courts; and though it is objected of the Carolingian scholars that in spite of this royal patronage they produced few or no masterpieces of literature, it is admitted that the royal efforts produced a great democratisation of learning in the church: the cathedral and country clergy became much better educated, the Benedictine abbeys busy with scholarly activities. Alfred had no Benedictine abbeys to patronise and few learned clergy: but he made his own court a school of English learning.

Asser states that God, hearing Alfred's complaint of the intellectual darkness around him, sent him certain shining lights: Wærferth, whom he made bishop of the church of Worcester (probably, indeed, his own church, in the unharried, western parts of Mercia), and Wærferth translated for him 'clearly and elegantly' the *Dialogues* of pope Gregory; Plegmund, a Mercian, who became archbishop of Canterbury in 890; besides two other learned clerks, Mercian by birth: 'he never suffered himself to be without one of them'. Having collected around him men of learning, Alfred himself learned Latin from them: set them as his chaplains to make translations of books which he believed essential for priests and laymen, and even undertook the work of translation himself. The different dialects in some of the manuscripts of translations attributed to him make it more probable that Alfred dictated or suggested phrases to his accompanying learned clerks than that he wrote the translations himself. It was not at the time held that translation involved any work of authorship: whether you read the psalms in Latin or English, it was king David who wrote them; and whether Alfred's translations were merely instigated and watched over by him, or whether all the English sentences were actually his own, would not to contemporaries have seemed a matter of importance. It was Alfred who was responsible for the translations.

Alfred's letter to bishop Wærferth of Worcester, sending him his translation of pope Gregory's *Pastoral Care* (which, he says, 'I translated into English'), is often quoted for the description it gives of the ravaged minsters in Alfred's day, and the decay of learning, consequent on the loss of libraries.

It has very often come into my mind [wrote Alfred], what wise men there formerly were throughout England, both of sacred and secular orders, and what happy times there were then throughout England . . . how zealous the sacred orders were both in teaching and learning . . . and how foreigners came to this land in search of wisdom and instruction, and how we should now have to get them from abroad if we were to have them. So general was its decay in England that there were very few on this side the Humber who could understand their service-books in English, or translate a letter from Latin into English; and I believe there were not many beyond the Humber. There were so few of them that I cannot remember a single one south of the Thames when I came to the throne . . . I remembered also that I saw, before it had been all ravaged and burned, how the churches throughout the whole of England stood filled with treasures and books.

This gloomy picture can scarcely have been an exaggeration, for though the village priests and churches had survived the raids, it was not they who had been learned before them: the dispersed clergy of minsters burned ten or twenty years before 870 would hardly have been known to Alfred. Sherborne, Glastonbury and Winchester had all been sacked, and it took time for Alfred to find, in unravaged Mercia and Wales, scholars who had escaped the general ravaging. Then Alfred, in his letter, recalled to Wærferth how the law had been first made known in Hebrew, how the Greeks translated it, and then the Romans, 'and all other books beside'. Therefore, he concluded, in this dearth of learning, 'it would be better for us also (like the Greeks and the Romans) to translate some books which are most needful for all men to know into the language which we can all understand, and for you to do as we very easily can, if we have tranquillity enough, that is, for all the youth of England of free men, who are rich enough to be able to devote themselves to it, be set to learn as long as they are not fit for other occupations, until they are able to read English writing well: and let those be afterwards taught more in the Latin language who are to continue in learning and be promoted to a higher rank'.

Remembering all this, Alfred says, 'he began to translate the book called in Latin *Pastoralis* and in English "Shepherd's Book"': sometimes word for word and sometimes according to the sense, as he had learned to do from 'Plegmund my bishop, Asser my bishop, and Grimbald my mass priest and John my mass priest'. He meant to send a copy to every bishopric in his kingdom, and in each there was an illuminated or embroidered bookmark worth fifty mancuses; no man must be allowed to take the bookmark from the book, or the book from the monastery. 'There are learned bishops now, thank God, nearly everywhere: they may allow the book to be copied.'

The *Shepherd's Book* was made with a directly ecclesiastical intention; and Alfred's translation of Orosius' world history only less so: for it had been written *Contra paganos*, of the first struggles of Christianity and the ages of persecution; the struggle of Alfred against the Northmen had been no less *Contra paganos*. Even Alfred's translation of Boethius' *Consolation of philosophy* was chosen partly from this angle: for he regarded Boethius as cruelly imprisoned and killed by the Arian king Theodoric, all for his appealing to the Greek emperor. Alfred explains in his preface that Theodoric 'was a Christian, but persisted in the Arian heresy'. Then Boethius the consul, which we should call 'heretoga' (a leader of the host, the 'here'), 'exceedingly wise in knowledge of books and in the ways of the world . . . observed the manifold wrongs which king Theodoric was committing against Christianity and the ancient rights which they had under the Caesars . . . and he secretly sent letters to the emperor at Constantinople, and besought him for help for the Christian faith . . . and king Theodoric gave orders to cast him into prison'.

To king Alfred, Boethius was a Christian who suffered adversity and yet praised God. His consolation in adversity, indeed, in the 'sunless cell' in which he was imprisoned, was no Christian figure, but Philosophy herself: 'Art thou not the man', she cried, 'who was once nourished and taught in my school?' She drew near to his mind, his intelligence, and raised it from its prostrate state: she asked it cheerily whether it knew again its foster-mother. With that the mind turned towards her and forthwith clearly recognised his own mother, that same Philosophy that long before had trained and taught him. But though Boethius found consolation as a stoic and a disciple of Plato, or wrote his book in that sense, to king Alfred he was a good Christian, oppressed by a bad king. And if Boethius wrote the old tale of Orpheus who harped in hell, and was allowed for his harping to bring back Eurydice his wife, losing her only by looking back, what of that? The old pagan story foreshadowed the resurrection. Though Alfred could not know it, they buried the emperor Charlemagne at Aix in a stone tomb with the story of Eurydice carved upon it.

The end of Boethius' book, where his mind, taught by Philosophy, comes to the contemplation of God, must have seemed to Alfred indeed Christian, and the teaching like that of the great Fathers, Gregory and Augustine.

At the end of her teaching, Philosophy taught Boethius[1] that 'We ought with all our might to inquire about God, who is eternal'.

'What is eternity?' I said.

Then said she, 'Thou askest me a thing great and hard to understand' . . . 'we know', said she, 'very little of what was before us, save by memory and asking, and still less of what shall be after us: that only is with certainty present to us which exists at the time. But to God all is present, both that which is before and that which is now; all is present to him. He never calleth aught to mind, for he hath never forgotten aught. He looketh for nought, pondereth nought, for he knoweth all. He seeketh nothing, for he hath lost nothing. He pursueth no creature, for none may flee from him. . . . He is ever giving, yet he never waneth in aught. . . . He needeth nothing. He is ever watching, never sleeping. He is ever equally kind. He is ever eternal, for the time never was when he was not, nor ever shall be.'

'O Lord, Almighty God', Alfred wrote, or commanded to write, at the end of the Boethius book, 'I beseech thee by thy great mercy, and by the sign of thy holy cross, and by the virginity of Saint Mary and by the obedience of Saint Michael, and by the love of all thy holy saints and by their merits, that thou wilt guide me better than I have deserved of thee.'

Another work Alfred chose to translate was the unfinished *Soliloquies* of St. Augustine, which he called 'flowers' or 'blossoms': in them, Alfred explained, 'reason answered the thoughts in his (Augustine's) mind, when the mind doubted about anything'. In a notable preface, Alfred compared Augustine's book to a timber yard: he explained the different kinds of timber and bolts needed

[1] See *King Alfred's Version of the Consolation of Boethius, done into modern English*, W. J. Sedgfield, 1900, 173-175.

for the building of a cottage; we dwell, he said, in a transitory cottage by the wayside, but we have an everlasting home promised us in the sayings of St. Augustine, St. Gregory and the holy Fathers. 'I, he said, have cut and collected the timber, the staves and stud-bolts from the book of St. Augustine: let other men gather timber for the cottage of this life from him too.'

Alfred believed knowledge of their own country's history to be as useful to laymen as that of the general history of Orosius. Tradition has asserted that he translated or had translated Bede's *Ecclesiastical History of the English Nation*, and the work has come down to us in English. Whatever Alfred's personal share was in the work of trans-lation here, it is clear that he must have derived his beliefs on 'what wise men there were formerly throughout England' and how 'foreigners came to this land in search of knowledge and instruc-tion' from a good knowledge of Bede. How easily Alfred could read Bede's good, classical Latin we do not know: it may seem that Alfred's desire to educate Englishmen, clerical and lay, sprang from hearing Asser or another paraphrasing in English Bede's account of those patrons of learning, Oswiu and Aldfrith, Anna of East Anglia and Ine who built the great church for Glastonbury: of bishops Wilfrid of Ripon and Acca of Hexham and, above all, the great Greek scholar, Theodore of Canterbury. It is impossible to believe Alfred had not heard Bede read to him before he wrote: 'what wise men there were formerly throughout England'.

Of even greater use to the historian was his instigation of the compilation of a good set of annals in English: annals not of a par-ticular house, written into a column of an Easter table, but with the year's events written at length for each 'annus incarnationis', for the use of the whole English people. The Carolingian court, years before, had started the keeping of the *Royal Annals*, of course in Latin. They appear, from the close knowledge shown of the life of Charles the Great and his sons, and of events as viewed by the im-perial court, to have been written by a succession of learned scribes at the Carolingian court. The desire for national annals was no new thing in Alfred's day: but to compile and fuse together an English annal dating from Julius Caesar's invasion to his own day, using such local annals and genealogies as were available, and Bede's history, was a considerable and, for the day, scientific work. For the early part, reliance was had on Gildas, Bede, some northern annals (see

p. 167), a set of Mercian annals, and a set of West Saxon annals, possibly written in Latin.[1] Bishop Daniel of Winchester had already passed on to Bede what he knew, or fondly believed true, of West Saxon history, so that no Winchester annals are likely to have added much to Bede's account; nor could much have been learned from the annals of Glastonbury and Sherborne, houses that had been sacked; but with the genealogies and other materials at hand the king's chaplains, perhaps at Sherborne,[2] compiled the Anglo-Saxon Chronicle, bringing it down to the year 891. Alfred had copies made and distributed among his bishops, and the annals so given were, in various centres, kept up to date; contemporary events were recorded down to the twelfth century.

Alfred's insistence on the use of English and the learning of English letters by as wide a circle as possible was revolutionary and one of the foundations of the pastoral work of the late Old English bishops. But Alfred himself had something to work on: the tradition of Old English verse and scriptural poetry handed on to Wessex by Mercia, ultimately from Northumbria. Vernacular verse, sung to laymen after feasts and read in the refectories of minsters, was already part of the Old English social background. Alfred had earned the coveted book of poems by committing its contents to memory. Nor was this, except for his youth, any very unusual feat; poetry is more easily memorised than prose, and many monks, at the time, sang the Latin psalter by heart. Under the Mercian supremacy of king Offa and later, Mercia had carried on the poetic traditions of Cædmon, and there are dialectal signs that many of the poems in Late West Saxon manuscripts came from an earlier Mercian version. The poetry book that Alfred learned off by heart no longer exists: but it would seem to have been in the Anglian tradition.

The greatest name in the Mercian poetic tradition, at least as regards religious poetry, is that of Cynewulf; and it is of interest that the best modern scholarship regards the poem *Beowulf* also as quite possibly coming from Mercia. It was written in the half century 750–800, about a century earlier, that is, than the poems of Cynewulf.[3] Though it deals with the tales of the pagan past, with Beowulf's

[1] See ASE., 15, n. 1.
[2] See Sir F. Stenton on 'The South-Western element in the Old English Chronicle,' in *Essays presented to Thomas Frederick Tout*, 23.
[3] See D. Whitelock, *The Audience of Beowulf*, 24.

fight with the monster, Grendel, the sea-burial of Scyld and the rest, it was written by a Christian poet for a Christian audience, and at a time when the English had been so long converted that paganism was no longer held a dangerous enemy. It is 'first and foremost, literature of entertainment'; it was meant for oral recital and could easily have been delivered in three sittings.[1] It is sophisticated poetry, written down for those who accepted the Christian order of things, who could understand allusions to biblical events and needed no explanation of 'noon' as implying a service at the ninth hour, or 'the great doom' as implying the Christian last judgment. The poet used many of the stock Christian phrases: though his verse had some linguistic features earlier than those found in the Cynewulf poems. The poem *Beowulf*, that is, occurs later than the verse of Cædmon and those who followed him, but earlier than those of Cynewulf and his school. It is later than 'the age of Bede', and it suggests that there was a school of secular poetry in Mercia in the age of Æthelbald and Offa, when Cynewulf was writing.[2]

Cynewulf's verse, and that of members of his school, at any rate, shows a change in scope and character from that of Cædmon. The earliest Anglo-Saxon religious poetry all dealt with the Bible story, and all had the loose, alliterative, epic verse structure: God himself, Christ and his saints were hymned on the harp in the manner of Anglo-Saxon kings and heroes. Songs of this kind included Cædmon's hymn to the Creator and his lost poems: the extant Old English Genesis, Exodus and Daniel, and those continental poems inspired by the Anglo-Saxon missionaries, the ninth century Old Saxon *Heliand* and the Gospel version of Otfrid in Old High German.

Cynewulf's works belong to a later stage, when a beginning had been made at rendering the scripture stories into vernacular verse, and it was now desired to have English versions of edifying Latin works, such as might be read in refectory: the legends of saints, homilies, or special expositions. The structure of the sentences in these later works was clearer and less diffuse: the writers were men used to the greater clarity of the Latin sentence. Cynewulf is the best known writer of this school, and the only one who made known his name to the reader.

---

[1] See D. Whitelock, *The Audience of Beowulf*, 20.

[2] Professor Whitelock is careful to suggest that there may have been a Christian, sophisticated poet and audience also in Wessex or other kingdom: but some slight indications point to Mercia: *ib.* 60.

Apart from his signature in the text of four poems, all inferences about where he wrote and when he wrote have had to be made from the text of the poems themselves: he is not referred to in any outside source. His poems appear in the Late West Saxon dialect of the Exeter Book and the Vercelli Book, but certain linguistic forms show they were written first in an Anglian dialect: and the form of his name, Cynewulf and not Cyniwulf, shows that the Anglian dialect was Mercian and not Northumbrian, and that he certainly wrote not earlier than c. 750.[1] Linguistic and metrical tests, and comparison with the earliest Anglo-Saxon poetry, show that more probably he wrote about 850 or between 850 and 870. Though the Viking raids had been begun, the great minsters were still intact: the learned abbot, Lupus of Ferrières, wrote and asked for a copy of Quintilian's *Institutes* from the great library at York in 850; the monks of Lindisfarne were producing their beautiful *Liber Vitae* (list of benefactors), with its letters of gold and silver, between 800 and 850: they were only forced to abandon their monastery in 875. The Danes ravaged York in 866, and overran Mercia in 867: a scholarly Mercian cleric like Cynewulf might well have written and died in some Mercian monastery like Lichfield, Leicester or Peterborough around the middle of the ninth century. Cynewulf was a competent Latin scholar, basing all his verses on Latin sources though he occasionally enlarged upon some point in the manner of the old, Anglo-Saxon epic poets; like most of our first Christian poets, he made the most of warlike occasions, where he had plenty of good models and stock phrases. He wrote as a man trained to read and write Latin.

He wove his famous signatures into the text because he desired that his audience should pray for him by name; otherwise, like all the other Anglo-Saxon poets, he would have remained anonymous. Æthelwald, bishop of Lichfield from 818–830, like the Carolingian scholars, wrote his name in the form of an acrostic in the Book of Cerne (an illuminated manuscript of the Passion and Resurrection narratives) written at Lichfield, and such a signature would be clearly intelligible to a reader. But for a poem to be read to an audience, a mental combination of the initial letters of lines would be impossible, and Cynewulf adopted a method that could be followed by listeners. In a famous passage in his *Elene*, for instance, he interspersed the

[1] See 'Cynewulf and his poetry', K. Sisam, 1933, in *Proc. of the Brit. Acad.*, vol. xviii, pp. 5-8.

18

description of his own life with the names of the runic letters that spelt his own name, coupling the lines with the request that he should be prayed for by name.

The four poems that are certainly Cynewulf's, as containing his signature, include those on the *Ascension*, the martyrdom of *St. Juliana*, the *Elene*, and the *Fates of the Apostles*. The *Ascension* was an exposition written for the instruction of some great man, his patron, and is one of three poems jointly known as the *Christ*, the other two not being certainly Cynewulf's. The other three Cynewulf poems are all on subjects connected with the martyrology or calendar (see p. 243), as are many other anonymous Anglo-Saxon poems. Clerics following the divine office year in, year out, might well choose as subject the saint's legend as it presented itself for meditation year by year, or some homily occurring in the nocturns of mattins. For some houses, possession of a relic of the holy cross or some martyr would afford a special reason for a poem that might be read, not only in refectory, but to the laity.

The so-called Hieronymian martyrology (see p. 14) from which those of most English houses were derived, begins with a summary of the works and martyrdom of the apostles, and this summary lies behind Cynewulf's *Fates of the Apostles*. The order in which the apostles are taken in Cynewulf's *Fates* is not exactly that of the Roman canon, but, with one exception, that of the Irish-written Stowe missal: his order of the apostles' names is not found in insular documents before 800.

The martyrdom of St. Juliana occurs in the calendar on February 16, and Cynewulf's poem paraphrases a Latin description.

The *Elene*, the most pleasing of his poems, commemorates on May 3 the Invention of the Holy Cross by Helena, mother of Constantine. The description of her voyage, not found in the Latin source, illustrates Cynewulf's willingness to enliven his subject by descriptions taken from the secular English epic poets: he was no sea-goer himself but he here launched into a descriptive passage that seemed to him conventionally fitting:

At once a band of warriors hastened down to the sea. The ships stood ready by the shore, afloat and anchored. Then all might see the Queen's journeying, when she sought the surging waves with her retinue. There on the Mediterranean shore stood many a proud man. Troop after troop in turn marched over the ways and loaded the vessels with mailcoats, shields and spears, with armed warriors, men and women. Then they loosed the tall ships to go foaming over the sea-monsters' home. . . . Never, before or since, have I heard of a lady leading on the ocean-ways a fairer company. . . . The brave warriors were glad and the Queen rejoiced in her voyage, when the ring-prowed ships had passed over the ocean-strongholds to their haven in the land of the Greeks.

A similar description of the Twelve Apostles, where they appear as the fighting thegns of an Anglo-Saxon king, runs as follows:

Lo, we have heard of twelve glorious warriors, thegns of the Lord, who lived in old days beneath the stars. Never did their prowess fail in battle, when standards clashed, after they had separated, as the Lord himself, the high King of heaven, appointed their lots. They were famous men upon earth, brave leaders and keen in war, doughty warriors when shield and hand guarded the helm on the battlefield.

As to the *Advent* poem, not certainly Cynewulf's but usually reckoned as part of the poem *The Christ*; its inspiration is now from the office book, namely, from the 'Great O' antiphons that were sung to the Magnificat from December 17 till Christmas Eve. They run:

O sapientia: O wisdom that goeth forth from the mouth of the most high . . . come and teach us the way of prudence.
O Adonai: O Lord and leader of the house of Israel . . . come and redeem us with outstretched arm.
O radix Jesse: O clavis David: O oriens:
O rex gentium: O Emmanuel: come and save us,
O Lord our God!

Cynewulf's paraphrases are half-Latinised in structure; the Old German scriptural poems of the ninth century approximated rather to the style of Cædmon, who had been the first to use the old, alliterative verse as the vehicle for scriptural narrative. Bede says many singers followed him; some verse of this kind would have been transmitted to the ninth century West Saxon court, though now lost to us. A life of Christ in alliterative verse, in the tongue of the continental Old Saxons, the *Heliand* (Saviour) was composed in the second quarter of the ninth century, and was eventually taken back to England and copied along with scriptural paraphrases in Anglo-Saxon manuscripts:[1] though not probably known to Alfred, it is of interest as inspired by the work of Anglo-Saxon missionaries some fifty years before Alfred's day. A Latin preface and verses, possibly referring to the *Heliand*, states that the work was commissioned by the emperor Louis the Pious: no doubt in the hope of using the missionaries to make Frankish rule more acceptable to the obdurate Saxons. The preface refers to Bede's story of Cædmon's song, and also mentions that the author of the *Heliand* was already well known to the Saxons as a poet. Either the poet was himself a cleric, or his sources were translated for him from the Latin by a cleric; the main source was a Latin version of Tatian's *Diatessaron* or harmony of the four gospels. The commentaries of Bede, Alcuin and Hraban Maur were also used; Hraban Maur, the greatest scholar in Germany and abbot of Fulda from 822 to 840, had been a pupil of Alcuin at Tours, and when he was placed by him at the head of the monastic school at Fulda, he trained a generation of scholars which included the other compiler of a gospel harmony in Old High German, Otto of Weissenburg. Fulda was Boniface's monastery, the head of his mission, and a very learned house, whose library might well have included a copy of Tatian's gospel harmony; Hraban Maur was the premier German scholar of the day, and his circle could have included, or instructed, the writer of the *Heliand*. Hraban became archbishop of Mainz in 847, inheriting the pastoral responsibility of St. Boniface.

In the *Heliand*, Christ appears as a royal figure among his thegns, and though there is less stress on the heroic, warlike character of the apostles than, for instance, in the Anglo-Saxon *Andreas*, owing to the source of the narrative of Christ's life, yet a few minor touches indicate a background different from that of the gospels. The shepherds who came to Bethlehem are replaced by herdsmen guarding their horses, as with the half-nomadic tribes of eastern Germany; a paraphrase of the alliterative verse of the passage might run:

---

[1] It is contained in the tenth century Cotton MS., Caligula, A. vii, and in a ninth century Munich MS. There is, as far as I know, no printed translation into modern English, though several into modern German.

Then 'twas made known to many,
over this world. Keepers first perceived it
who of horses were herdsmen out yonder,
wights on the watch, o'er their needs to keep ward,
animals on the plain. They saw the frowning blackness in twain
cleave asunder in the sky; then came the light of God
with witching beauty, through the clouds, and the keepers there
enfolded on that plain.

The mighty angel of God bids the keepers fear no harm from that light: now, this selfsame night is the Son of God born in Bethlehem's guarded town: the mightiest of the sons of men there lies, wound in swaddling clothes, in the cattle crib. When the angel had spoken, a legion of angels came to join him: they came from the woods and the meadows of heaven, and when they had sung 'let glory be in the highest realm of heaven' they wound their way through the welkin back to the heavenly meadows, and the herdsmen, taught by the clear-shining signs, set forth to Bethlehem.

It is such stuff as an Anglo-Saxon bishop might preach to his people at the feast of Christmas; though he would preach in prose, not verse, yet he might well make use of rhyme and alliteration, as Ælfric did later.

Alfred must have known well the connexion between the monastic life and the maintenance of a learned clergy: but he was able only to found two monasteries in his own day, though he made plans for another in Winchester. He founded a house for men on his own lands at Athelney, at the mouth of the Parret and a nunnery at Shaftesbury for his daughter Æthelgeofu: for these two houses he proposed to devote the fourth part of that portion of his royal revenue reserved for specifically religious uses. The house at Athelney must have been meant, apparently, to follow the example of such Carolingian houses as Corbie or Fulda: that is, to be a Benedictine house, for the recitation of the opus dei and study, as Monkwearmouth and St. Augustine's had once been; from the choice of site, Alfred's intention could scarcely have been to found a house both pastoral and monastic, as most of the ravaged English minsters had once been; he might have hoped it might become a Saint-Denis, learned, and in close touch with his court.

He found no learned English cleric who desired the abbacy,

however. He had sent 'legates' to Gaul, seeking for learned men willing to enter his service, and Grimbald, priest and monk and a very fine singer and skilled in ecclesiastical discipline, had come to him, and John the Old Saxon, a man of fine intellect, priest and monk, and skilled in the literary and many other arts. This John, he made abbot of Athelney: Asser says that no Englishman of noble or free birth wished for the monastic life, for though in that region there were many monastic buildings standing, the regular monastic life was not observed in any of them. John was abbot over a small congregation of foreign priests and deacons, but the community, mainly of monks from Gaul, did not flourish under their German abbot; one monk even tried to murder him.

In view of the difference between Alfred's aim for Athelney and that of the men who had founded the old, half-pastoral, minsters like Ripon or Medehamstede, some understanding is needed of contemporary monastic history.

In England, there are indications that secular and family interests had produced, even in Bede's time, 'sham monasteries'; and that, even in cathedral minsters in the early ninth century the clergy no longer lived together, as in a bishop's familia, but in small houses round the close, and that some were married. In the days of Gregory of Tours, when the giving of the priesthood was delayed, canon law required that a clerk who had married while yet in minor orders should, on attaining holy orders, separate from his wife and children, leaving them to live in his villa in the country, and take up his own residence with the bishop as a member of his familia.

There is no evidence of such a practice in England, or that archbishop Theodore, for instance, countenanced a married priesthood. The large majority of clergy in his day were monastic, and the rural priests who served thegns' churches in the countryside, few. But by the mid eighth century it is likely that many of the rural priests were married, though no canon ever allowed this; whether the clergy who lived round the close in a cathedral minster were as yet customarily married, there is no evidence.

It is certain, however, that St. Boniface tried to pull up the level of church life among the Franks, and to make the bishops' churches less disorderly. His close friend, Chrodegang, bishop of Metz from 742 to 766, drew up a rule for his cathedral clergy, requiring them to live communally with him: the wars of Charles Martel had been largely financed by encroachments on church lands, and many bishops' churches among the Franks were now poor and discipline bad. Chrodegang explained in the preface to his rule that the communal life of the clergy with their bishop was the old and better way, but that it had now lapsed and he wished to restore it. He wished to put an end to the system by which married clergy lived round the close, and which led to a dispersal of church lands because the sons of such clergy expected to inherit their fathers' benefices: as in England the relatives of abbots expected to succeed to the abbacy. The claim to inherit benefices among the clergy would automatically disappear when a celibate clergy lived communally with their bishop, as would the abuses of too secular a style of living. Long ago St. Augustine of Hippo had required his clergy to live canonically with him, and had drawn up a rule for such an 'apostolic' life, and a monastic time-table: but the time-table of offices was old-fashioned, and the fasting, bearable in the hot climate of north Africa, unreasonably severe for that of north France. Chrodegang drew up his own rule, holding it as generally known that the primitive, apostolic life was com-munal: 'No man said that he had anything of his own, but they had all things in common'.

In the preface of his rule, which was to have so much influence both among the Franks and in England, Chrodegang wrote:

> Since the authority of some 310 canons of the holy fathers re-mains inviolable, and shows that a bishop ought to live with his clergy according to the norm of righteousness, it might seem superfluous for us with our own small powers either to treat again or say anything new upon a matter already disposed of in an orderly manner: but since the negligence of both pastors and their subjects has in these times exceeded all bounds, what else can we do, who have come into such grave peril, except, as far as in us lies, if not as far as we ought, we should seek to draw our clergy, by the inspiration of God, back to the line of righteousness?

Therefore, Chrodegang continues, when he began to exercise the pastoral charge over this episcopal see which he obtained, and seen then the neglect into which clergy and people had fallen: he had been driven by necessity to compile this little canonical rule (parvum decretulum), whereby the clergy should be constrained from things unlawful . . . and unanimously and assiduously attend the divine office, always being ready to obey the bishop and the provost (prae-positus) as the canonical order (ordo canonicus) requires.

The rule or canon[1] for his cathedral clergy which Chrodegang thus compiled required that these clerics should make use of a single dormitory and refectory, like monks, but that nevertheless, they should not be monks or wear the monastic cowl. They should receive equal 'stipends' or allowances of food and drink from the bishop (though the canons were not required to give up all their property); attend the night and day offices; go to confession three times a year ('this is our custom: monks go to confession every Saturday'); old or sick canons should be cared for by the bishop; the senior half of the canons should receive new capes and woollen clothes every year, returning the old ones, and the old ones should be given each year to the junior half of the community; those who were called priors under other prelates should now be called provosts, and they should be of service to the whole community and themselves keep the canonical institutes: they should give the canons all that they ought to be given. The community should have a school for the training and education of young clergy, and appoint a brother of good life to have charge of them, teach them ecclesiastical doctrine and the weapons of the spiritual life, and promote them as they become worthy to the various ecclesiastical orders.

Although these canons were required by Chrodegang to lead in many respects a monastic life, they still exercised the pastoral charge over the cathedral parish, which was then large. They received the tithe from the parish, dividing it into three parts, one for the orna-ments of the church, one for the poor, one for themselves. They must pray for and anoint the sick. They must bless marriages, but not attend marriage feastings and drinkings. They may be appointed to a church by the bishop, and each priest thus appointed must have in his church books in which are understandably written masses, or epistles, or the gospel, or the offices for baptism or penance, 'or the cycles of the years' (see p. 85), or the lessons of night offices.

This rule of Chrodegang was to prove influential both on the Continent and in England. From the time of Augustine of Hippo some doctors in the church had seen the apostolic life, the life of the

---

[1] 'Regula' and 'canon' are Latin and Greek words for the same implement: the foot rule of the surveyor. In the Greek version of Justinian's Novels, 'canon' replaces 'regula'.

clergy with their bishop, as necessarily communal, from the sentence in Acts: No man said that he had anything of his own, but they had all things in common. No general church council had ever, in fact, applied this doctrine to the life of the clergy, nor declared it contrary to the canons of the church for the clergy to hold property. But in a time when the lives of the Frankish clergy were often too much assimilated to those of the secular nobles, while in the newly conquered German lands a devoted and ascetic clergy was particularly required, and inspired indeed by the lives of the Irish and Anglo-Saxon missionaries, the demand for a clergy leading the 'apostolic' life was renewed.

The repercussions of this movement were felt in England, when in 786–787 the papal legates presided over synods (see p. 226) which required that 'the bishops take diligent heed that all canons shall live canonically, and all monks and nuns according to their rule'. They were felt moreover on the Continent, when the Benedictine reformer, Benedict of Aniane, succeeded in inspiring the council of Aix-la-Chapelle, 817, to pass canons to regulate the life of canons by the *Regula Aquisgranensis*, which was inspired by the old rule of Augustine of Hippo and the rule of Chrodegang. It was made obligatory on all the cathedral chapters and collegiate churches of the Carolingian empire. Monks were similarly ordered to keep the Benedictine rule.

It was necessary, however, that if a bishop's familia should live communally, it should have communal property separate from the general landed endowment of the diocese; up till this time the bishop supported, or was supposed to support, his familia from the third or fourth of the diocesan revenue which should go to the clergy of the see: the cathedral chapter had no separate endowment. Besides rendering communal life difficult, the system was the more unsatisfactory as the cathedral clergy were liable to go hungry if the bishop's lands were for any reason confiscated by the king, or taken into his hands at a bishop's death. The mid eighth century saw more than one effort to give the cathedral familia an endowment, a 'mensa', of their own.

In England, the over king Offa of Mercia had made one grant of land to archbishop Jænberht of Canterbury, and another grant to Christ Church for the endowment of his familia: from the time of this grant, 774, the familia may be said to have had a mensa, but they did not live communally. In 805 archbishop Æthelheard made a grant expressly to the familia: 'I will grant it to the holy church of Christ as its own possession'; he also recalled to the use of the familia a grant which a lay thegn of Canterbury had made over to the familia for their mensa. The signatures to this charter include those of two 'provosts': probably of other minsters in the see of Canterbury (see p. 202).

The recalling of the Christ Church community to a strictly monasterial life, on the Chrodegangian pattern, was the work of Wulfred, archbishop of Canterbury 805 till 832. He added to the Christ Church endowment in 811, and in 813 he assimilated the life of his familia to the ideals of Boniface and Chrodegang: he made them 'canons'.

> For the honour and love of God I have caused to be rebuilt, renewed, and restored the holy monastery of the church of Canterbury, for the presbyters, deacons, and all the clergy serving God there together. I, Wulfred, give and grant to the familia of Christ to have and enjoy the houses which they have built for themselves at their own cost by the perpetual right of inheritance, during their own lifetimes, or of those descendants to whom each shall have free power to leave or grant them within the said monastery, but not to any external person without the congregation (i.e. the possibly married canons who have received stipends, and lived in their own houses, may bequeath them to sons or relations trained in the Christ Church familia, as the canons had probably received them themselves, but not to their other children). But under this condition, that they sedulously frequent the canonical hours in the church of Christ . . . And that they frequent together the refectory and dormitory, and that they observe the rule of the discipline of life in a monastery. But if any of them . . . dare to gather together feasts for eating and drinking or even sleeping in their own cells (houses), let him know, whoever he be, that he shall be deprived of his own house and it shall be in the power of the archbishop to hold and to grant to whomsoever it shall please him.

Wulfred's charter is signed by eight presbyters, some inferior clerks, and a 'presbyter abbas'. The 'priest abbot' had taken over the whole direction of the community under the bishop. Other charters show that some cathedral clergy had been actually living in little

houses near the cathedral: Wulfred ordered later that the house and
garden where 'Dodda the monk' had been living should now be at
the community's disposal, and that they might allow a sick priest or
deacon to live there 'with due honour'. A grant of Werhard the
presbyter in 832 calls the Christ Church familia 'monks', but clearly
shows that Werhard had received a portion of the Christ Church
endowment as stipend, as well as enjoying means of his own (see
p. 314). It is clear that the intention of reformers like archbishop
Wulfred was not to secure that 'no man said he had anything of his
own', but to ensure the regular life of the cathedral clergy, and safeguard the landed endowments granted to some of them as stipends.
The 'vita canonica' had been established at Canterbury before its
destruction in the raids; how far it was re-established under archbishop Plegmund in Alfred's reign is uncertain.

Of Alfred's foundations, Athelney survived, though precariously,
and the nunnery at Shaftesbury seems to have had a continuous life,
and certainly existed in Athelstan's time. King Eadred's will refers to
nunneries both at Wilton and Winchester, the latter founded by
Ealhswith, Alfred's widow. Alfred's son, king Edward, founded at
Winchester the New Minster, a house of clerks. The new impulse to
the monastic life was to come, however, from the old Benedictine
tradition. The original movement for Benedictine reform dates from
the work of Odo, the great abbot of Cluny in Burgundy from 927:
but Burgundy and the Rhone valley were far from tenth century
England, and no direct effect of the reform can be traced in this
country. But the great Frankish daughter house of Cluny was
Fleury-on-the-Loire: and there had always been direct communication between the west of England and the mouth of the Loire. It was
through Fleury-on-the-Loire that Alfred's yearning cry: What wise
men there formerly were in England! was to find a response: after an
interval of about eighty years.

CHAPTER XIII

THE TENTH CENTURY CHURCH REFORM:
ITS PREPARATION

THE great landmark in the history of ninth century England was the failure of the Northmen, 'the heathen men', to capture all England in Alfred's reign, and their settlements in the north eastern part of it. The great achievement of the tenth century was the restoration of the powers of the English church, and the efflorescence of learning, accomplished largely through the efforts of archbishop Dunstan, and his friends and disciples, Æthelwold and Oswald: in short, the tenth century reform movement. The problems that had to be solved were many of them common to western Europe; the solution in England was found mainly in the restoration and extension of the Benedictine life. Many more strict Benedictine communities were set up in the lifetime of Dunstan than had existed in England before the Viking raids. Such an effort was only made possible by the defence of the country both from outside enemies and the settlers in the Danelaw by the mid tenth century English kings: and even then it was only achieved by a recall of church lands from the thegns to whom they had been leased in the wars, and the granting away of the profits of justice by the crown. Bitter resentment, to the point of civil war, was aroused among such of the earls and thegns who held themselves injured.

As to the political and social background of the tenth century reform, something more may be said of the work of Athelstan (924–939: see p. 253); it had a bearing on the political resistance to the reform. Athelstan, after his reconquest of the Danelaw, had to arrange for the civil government of the regions newly taken over. In the old kingdom of the West Saxons even older sub-kingdoms or tribal territories still existed under the command of the king's 'ealdormen', and these old territories were themselves subdivided into districts of varying size, assessed at the payment of hundred hides (family lands) to the king's 'feorm', districts coming to be known in the tenth century as 'hundreds'. These hundreds in Wessex were sometimes called after the king's estate where the feorm had been immemorially collected. In the southern Danelaw, however, the larger administrative districts centred in 'burhs' or fortresses, under the command of some Danish noble. To these, too, the word 'shire' came to be applied, as to the larger shires of Wessex. In these also, from the reconquest, the administrative subdivisions, territorial units of 120 hides, came to be known as hundreds: the Danes used a 'long hundred' of 120, the English one of 100. Thus the old 'shires' of the ealdormen were equated with the new, fortress-centred 'shires' of the Danelaw: while the hundred moot, meeting from four weeks to four weeks, did justice according to what was now royal and largely written law. The king's reeves presided over the hundred moots, and the administration of justice was profitable to the king, to whom went various 'wites' or fines, and other payments. 'The hundred of the midlands was probably the result of a deliberate remodelling of administrative geography carried out in this region in the tenth century.'[1] The system of local government by hundred moot, which had grown up naturally in Wessex, and which may have existed in the northern kingdoms before the Danish conquest, was now imposed from above on the midlands. It was to be, eventually, the granting away of royal rights over these hundreds to the new minsters of monks that provoked bitter opposition from a large section of the thegn class to the tenth century reform.

In the next reign, Athelstan's brother Edmund (939–946) continued his work. He was only eighteen when he succeeded, and the Danes of Northumbria and Dublin renewed their attempt to make Yorkshire an independent Danish kingdom under Olaf. Wulfstan I, archbishop of York, sympathised with them: when the invading army, led by Olaf Guthfrithson, king of Dublin, took York, he and the archbishop of Canterbury arranged a treaty between him and Edmund, leaving the Danes the rule of a large territory between the Watling Street and the Northumbrian border. Olaf Sihtricson, on the death of the king of Dublin, was in 940 received as king in York, Wulfstan concurring. In 944, however, Edmund reconquered York. In Edmund's reign Oda, bishop of Ramsbury in Wiltshire, was made archbishop of Canterbury: he was of Danish birth, and had been used by king Athelstan on a diplomatic mission to Hugh Capet, duke

[1] ASE., 295.

of the French, count of Paris; Athelstan had heard at a council at York that Hugh was proposing the recall of the Carolingian Louis, son of Charles the Simple, to France. Charles had been in exile in Athelstan's kingdom, and the matter of his return was successfully arranged by Oda: Oda's usefulness to the kings of England as an envoy to men of his own race and speech, in York or Normandy, probably explains his appointment, though a Dane, to the see of Canterbury in 942. He was known there later as Oda the Good, and he was the first English bishop to desire to see the monastic practice of Fleury-on-the-Loire followed in England.

Another political tendency in Edmund's reign important in the political struggle over the tenth century reform was the grouping of two or three of the older shires under a single leader, an earl or duke: or in the Danelaw, a jarl. In Edmund's time there were eight dukes for southern England, three south of the Thames, five for Mercia and East Anglia. Succession to these dukes was hereditary, as it had not necessarily been to the old ealdormanries of the shires, and great family interests became involved in the struggles between the supporters and opponents of the reform.

Eadred, the youngest son of Edward the Elder, succeeded Edmund in 946, ruling till 955. His reign saw a fresh rising of the Yorkshire Danes, and though Eadred marched north and archbishop Wulfstan swore loyalty to him with other northern magnates in 947, Wulfstan accepted the rule of the Norwegian invader, Eric 'Bloodaxe', at York in 952, and appears to have been deposed from his see for a time by Eadred. He was restored before Eadred's death. Eadred died after a long illness in 955, and was succeeded by two sons of Edmund, his brother.

Eadwig (955-959) was only fifteen years of age, and Edgar, the younger son, twelve. The chronicler Æthelweard comments on Eadwig's handsome appearance: and though he was so young a king, he found good counsellors in the ealdormen of Mercia, Essex, East Anglia and Hampshire. For more than twenty years England was free from the threat of foreign invasion, from the Northmen of Dublin or Scandinavia, and the memory of happier days of this reign survived when the Danish raids began again in 980; the work of Dunstan, Æthelwold and Oswald was mainly accomplished in this period of peace. Other work for the law and good peace of the country was contemporary with the building up of the Benedictine houses, and writers of the next generation associated all these measures with the name chiefly of Edgar, Eadwig's brother. For a time in 959 it looked as if a revolt against Eadwig, a revolt by the supporters of the monastic reform aided by the smouldering discontent of the Northmen in York and the great duke of East Anglia, Athelstan Half-King, might split the kingdom between Eadwig and Edgar: but Eadwig died on October 1, 959, and Edgar was at once accepted as king. Archbishop Oda had died in 958, and after a curious interlude, Dunstan became archbishop of Canterbury in 960.

Edgar's reign (959-975) was notable for the coronation oath taken (see p. 304), for the passage of some notable secular legislation, for the reform of the old minsters and foundation of new ones by Dunstan and his friends, and by the grant of great 'sokes' (see p. 319) to churchmen for their endowment. As a sequel to Edgar's anointing and coronation, which was deferred till he was thirty years old, in 973 (probably because Dunstan saw a mystical connexion between the anointing of a king and consecration to the priesthood, which would normally be deferred till that age), Edgar is reported as being accepted as king by all the kings of Britain. There were no less than eight of these, Cumbrians and Scots, who acknowledged his supremacy: some manuscripts of the ASC. state that when, after his anointing, Edgar sailed with his fleet to Chester, six kings came to him and promised to serve him by sea and by land: later chroniclers expand this into the picturesque tale of his being rowed on the Dee by eight kings, while he held the rudder. They rowed him from his palace at Chester to the church of St. John and back again.[1]

Edgar died suddenly in 975, leaving two sons by different mothers. Edward, the elder, was accepted as king after what amounted to a short period of civil war. The difficulties in Edward the Martyr's reign were due partly to the antagonism of the parties supporting the claims to rule of Edgar's two sons, and partly to that between the reformers and their opponents (see later). Edgar died on July 8, 975, before either of his sons was old enough to rule. They were the children of his two wives, the second, Ælfthryth, being the daughter of an ealdorman of Devon and the widow of an ealdorman of East Anglia, a lady with powerful connexions. The elder son, Edward, was still a youth and reported to have been violent in speech and behaviour: the younger, Æthelred, cannot have been more than ten

[1] See ASE., 364.

years old, for Edgar married his mother only in 964. It was a case in which the witan had the right, or duty, to 'ceosan to cyninge' that son who was most fit to reign, for both were qualified by blood, and as it was possible for the witan to choose an uncle in preference to a son under age, so it was possible for them to choose among sons. Succession by primogeniture was not yet, nor for many years, the established practice.

To Dunstan, however, Edward was more acceptable as likely to continue his father's benevolence to the new minsters; the 'sokes' (see p. 320) granted to endow houses in Mercia and East Anglia were very unpopular with the supporters of Ælfthryth, as East Anglian thegns and magnates. Dunstan and Oswald, archbishop of York, secured the acceptance of Edward by the witan and anointed him king; but the thegnage of the country was divided as between the supporters of the two brothers, and a state of near civil war followed in the next few months. Ælfhere, ealdorman of Mercia and very strong in the Severn valley, was accused of driving out the monks of the new houses, and some magnates who considered they had a claim to minster lands once leased to them asserted their rights. Hostility to the monks was not inspired by religious prejudice, but to dislike of a new class of monastic landowners.

In 978, when Edward was visiting his stepmother and her son at Corfe, in Dorset, he was murdered in circumstances of peculiar treachery, and buried without any church service at Wareham. The Peterborough version of the ASC., strong in its reforming sympathies, recorded the murder and broke into indignant verse beginning:

> No worse deed was ever done among the English
> Than this was,
> Since first they sought the land of Britain;
> Men murdered him, but God exalted him.

Public opinion was shocked: had he not been anointed? and beyond that, murder by kinsmen was black treachery, from time immemorial. There was no suggestion at the time that queen Ælfthryth had plotted the murder: but it was held that the household of the younger prince had done so, to secure his succession as king. No one was punished for the crime: but a year later, when Æthelred was safely king, Ælfhere of Mercia for decency's sake had Edward's body transported to the church of the nuns of Shaftesbury. Here so many miracles were announced around it that he was soon reckoned a saint. He had died at the hands of the church's enemies, and his death was accounted a martyrdom. The whole matter of the murder was not only the worst kind of sin, but politically unfortunate, for Æthelred started his reign under a cloud. He was called 'Unræd' or 'No counsel' (a bitter comment upon his name which means 'noble counsel') and he certainly lacked the power of wise decision: but modern historical opinion regards his unwisdom as due to lack of confidence, either in himself or the loyalty of his own supporters. Uncertainty as to whom he could trust came from the circumstances of his accession: he succeeded through a horrible crime. He was not the man to inspire national loyalty; he was incapable as a leader in war; the Danish population of England could not be relied on, not to side with the invaders; the conservative thegns had their own quarrel with the reformers; the outlook for national defence against the Danes was bad. In such a period of misery it might be expected that the reforming movement would lose momentum, or even peter out: but this did not happen.

A factor which further explains Æthelred's failure to deal with the raids was the existence of two or more camps for the professional training of the Danish raiders: for them, fighting had become a full-time profession. Jómsborg on the Oder trained raiders first for penetrating the Baltic and the Russian rivers, later, the North Sea. Trelleborg on the Danish island of Zealand also trained them for passage into the North Sea or along the Frisian and Frankish coasts. Excavation has shown that Trelleborg was a circular or ring fortress, the headquarters of a warrior community, a kind of army training centre, a west Zealand Jómsborg. Young men learned the business of sea voyages and the practice of war. Aggarsborg was a similar centre, and there may have been others; centres from which king Swein Forkbeard launched his attack on England in Æthelred's reign. The young English thegns and sons of thegns learned to fight in defence of their homes, as they learned to hunt, individually, from their fathers; they were amateurs in the business of war, not whole-time professional fighters, like the spearhead of the Danish attack.

As to the landmarks in the secular history of Æthelred's reign (978–1016): Æthelred's minority ended in 980, when archbishop Dunstan retired to Canterbury and took no more part in guiding the

19

counsels of the kingdom. The Danish king, Harold, had by now won for himself Denmark and Norway, and there was the less scope for the fighters of the Scandinavian peninsula in wars at home. Moreover, Harold had imposed Christianity on his subjects and many resented it, and he had earlier organised the Viking community at Jómsborg. There was plenty of Viking material now for raids on England and plenty of motive; the ASC. records a raid on Southampton in 984, when most of the citizens were slain or taken prisoner, and the harrying of the island of Thanet; Padstow was ravaged and three pirate crews landed in Dorset. In 991 Olaf Tryggvason, later king of Norway, came with 93 ships to Folkestone, and harried outside, and sacked Sandwich and went on to Ipswich and harried all the countryside, and so on to Maldon; and they fought ealdorman Byrhtnoth and slew him in battle.

The story of the raids continues in the ASC., and the story of the gelds paid by Æthelred to buy the Danes off. Olaf Tryggvason and Swein, son of Harold of Denmark and father of Cnut, came to London in 994 and thought to set it on fire, but failed, after doing much harm: and Æthelred sent for them to Andover and offered Olaf tribute and had him honourably baptised; but the pirate hosts continued to harry England on all sides. Æthelred, a young and vigorous king, should have fought and defeated Olaf before offering him baptism; as it was, he and the witan paid the heavy geld of sixteen thousand pounds to secure Olaf's and Swein's departure.

Æthelred, in his difficulties, had allowed certain Danes to settle in southern England and given them land, on condition of their fighting for him against his enemies. He had thus bought the services of a Danish jarl, Pallig, who had married Gunnhild, the sister of Swein. Then, in 1002, the Vikings harried Devonshire, and followed their usual tactics, slaying and burning; and great levies of the men of Somerset and Devon were mustered, and Pallig and his men should have come and fought with them, but he did not. The enemy came burning right up to Southampton Water, for the English levies had been defeated with great slaughter: no fleet by sea nor levies on land dared approach them, however far inland they went. 'In every way it was a hard time, for they never ceased from their evil deeds.'

The king and the witan decided to pay tribute: and they paid twenty-four thousand pounds. 'Then in the midst of these events the king gave orders that all the Danish people who were in England should be slain on St. Brice's Day (November 13): because he had been told that they wished to deprive him of his life by treachery.' Pallig and Gunnhild were slain among them: and her brother Swein set about the conquest of the country where she had been murdered. Ten years war between English and Danes followed, from 1002 to 1012.

So much for the English political background for the tenth century reform: but England, in the tenth century was not unmoved by ecclesiastical events in France. While the kingdoms of the Scandinavian north were producing a professional fighting class, the Carolingian empire, or rather, its succession states, still stood for Christianity, learning and the old Greco-Roman tradition. The countries of the Scandinavian north shared a north Germanic culture, the Carolingian kingdoms one that came originally from the Mediterranean: it was not yet certain into which political orbit England would fall. The Danish adventurers were such good fighters: the lack of communications, rendering it so difficult for the English to get their forces in the right places to meet them, made it possible that the North Sea would become a Scandinavian lake. England might have a Danish king and ruling class: heathen, or rather unwillingly Christian. Contemporary with the struggle over the tenth century reform was the political unbalance as between the influence of Scandinavia and the Carolingian Franks. Down till the reign of Æthelred the admiration of the kings of England was for the Carolingian states, with which they occasionally had diplomatic intercourse; Carolingian example, after a certain time-lag, was likely to be followed; Scandinavia was a source of danger as the possible ally of the Northmen settled in the Danelaw. In Æthelred's reign, however, Scandinavian attack threatened to lead to a Danish conquest, and eventually did so.

Since England in the tenth century could not escape Carolingian influence, even as regards the anointing of her kings and the provision for and training of her clergy: what had the efforts of church reformers produced in France?

King Pepin and Boniface had not succeeded in making the Frankish monks keep any one, general rule. Charlemagne, however, had loved and admired uniformity; in the matter of monasticism, he had asked for and obtained from the abbot of Monte Cassino an authentic copy of the Benedictine rule. He had had copies made and sent to the various Benedictine abbeys: but he was not willing to grant to the monks the right to free election enjoined in chapter lxiv of the Benedictine rule; he reserved the right to nominate abbots. Sometimes he appointed learned clerks from the palace; sometimes he used the appointment as a means of rewarding faithful service. He still allowed even the greatest houses of what were popularly called 'monks' (fratres) to reject the Benedictine rule and live as canons; the great and ancient houses of Saint-Martin at Tours, and Saint-Denis near Paris were anomalous foundations, following the Martinian course of psalmody, with most of their members monks, but some of them clergy who served the basilica and were not bound to enclosure; both had 'matricularii', devout poor maintained by the foundation. Both these houses in the reign of Charlemagne adopted the rule of canons, not monks.

Louis the Pious, under the influence of Benedict of Aniane (see p. 273), set about reforming the discipline of both monks and canons, stressing, as Boniface had, the difference between the two lives. While archbishop Wulfred was enjoining that his familia should lead the 'vita canonica' at Canterbury, and providing them with the necessary buildings, Louis had made a speech at the council of Aix, 816, setting forth the need of reforms to the heads of houses of canons there assembled. The abbot of Saint-Wandrille was told to collect passages from the Christian Fathers about the life of clergy living in common, and to draw up a statement about what should be canonically enjoined on them. He drew up, in consequence, the *De Institutione Canonicorum*: which contained certain citations from the Fathers, some remarks on the general principles of the life of the clergy thus living communally, and a rule for canons.

The extracts from the Fathers began with passages from Isidore about the orders of clergy: about the first tonsure, about 'ostiarii', lectors, exorcists, acolytes, subdeacons, deacons, presbyters, sacerdotes (priests and bishops); from Augustine, several citations about provosts, and several about bishops, including one from Prosper of Aquitaine (d. 465) to the effect that bishops should have nothing of their own, but should hold all the revenues (facultates) of the church as common property for which they would have to render an account to God. As to the canons themselves, citations were included about women secretly admitted (subintroduced), about clerks receiving usury, about the reception of pilgrims, that serfs should not be promoted to the ministry without letters (freeing them), that 'convivia' should by no means be held in churches, that no ecclesiastic should eat in taverns, etc., and finally, from Augustine, about the life and customs of the clergy. Though his rule was not quoted entire by reformers, as the Benedictine rule was for those who wished to reform monks, yet Augustine was regarded as the great doctor on the communal life of the clergy with their bishop.

The effective part of the *De Institutione*, the rule itself, contained no explicit reference to the rule of Chrodegang of Metz (see p. 270), but quite clearly followed its teaching. It was also influenced by the Benedictine rule: but it clearly distinguished between things allowed to canons and things allowed to monks. Canons, it was laid down, must live in common: they must have a common dormitory, refectory and 'officia' (departments). Their rule of enclosure within their residence should be strict. It was laid down that for canons enclosure should be diligently maintained: a canon seen prolonging idle conversations in the byways or squares of towns must be reproved, publicly if necessary: women must not be allowed so much as to enter the house or within the enclosure of the canons, except only into the church.

At the same time, in 817, a rule was issued for canonesses, under the title *regula sanctimonialium*. The rule of life was less strict than that for Benedictine nuns, nor were a common dormitory and refectory required. The citations showed, however, that, as nuns living in community, each must receive an equal measure of food and drink, the prioress being allowed double (providing for a guest, servant, etc.), and all must attend the monastic offices. The greatest diligence should be shown in instructing maidens in these monasteries for women; and there should be a hospice for the poor beside the gate of the monastery, supported by the nuns' revenues.

The canonical legislation of Aix, 816 and 817, stressed chiefly that monastic houses must decide whether they should live as houses of canons, or monks. If monks, they must keep the *Capitulare Monasticum* of 817, and be guided by the two treatises composed by Benedict of Aniane, the *Concordia Regularum* and the *Codex Regularum*. If canons, they must keep the *De Institutione Canonicorum*. The imperial *missi* were ordered to enforce this ruling, but the wars and troubles of

Louis the Pious' reign prevented, in fact, any strict enforcement; fresh councils of Aix in 829 and 836 again required their enforcement, a sign that they had not been more than partially successful. Many houses were still too much under lay control for reform to be carried out.

The canons of Aix-la-Chapelle were not, of course, in force in England: they could not be enforced even in the Carolingian states. But the influence of the Carolingian emperors, and of all the Carolingian bishops, were behind them, and they offered a safe-guard against the misappropriation of church lands in England. Here, as with the Franks, the cathedral clergy often received a piece of land as their stipend, and wished to hand it down, like private land, to their sons.

But against the enforcement by canon of the communal life for cathedral clergy the old historical practice of stipends could be quoted. Even after 817 it was still canonical for a priest to 'rule' as rector the landed endowment of a rural church; he might have one or two young clerks to maintain, but the land was his stipend, for the time being. No general church council had ever condemned such stipends: why then should the cathedral clergy only be refused per-mission to have them? Moreover, whatever the emperor of the Franks decreed, the popes made no special effort to enforce the canons of 817 for Italy; Italy was a land of small sees and small chapters: the old practice of individual stipends continued.

One tendency developed in the Carolingian empire, in spite of the difficulty of enforcing the canons of 817: an increased amount of attendance at office was demanded from the cathedral clergy: more saints' days were observed, with their long, three nocturn night offices: it became more and more necessary for the clergy to live quite near the cathedral to attend office. Moreover, the bishop as landowner had now so many quasi-feudal duties that took him from his cathedral city, that there was no longer a continually resident nucleus in his familia for the saying of offices. There had to be another nucleus in the clergy of the cathedral, now generally called 'canons', to say the canonical hours: whether they lived com-munally or separately. To safeguard the livelihood of these clergy from the rapacity of rulers, many bishops gave their canons a 'mensa' (see p. 318), which made them an endowed community; in many sees (as at Reims, Cambrai, Chartres, Toul, etc.) the canons were given separate little houses and a separate prebend, both in money and kind. Nevertheless, the word 'claustrum', a term proper to the enclosed grounds of religious, was used of the land on which the cathedral and the little houses stood, and has survived in 'close'.

The Carolingian reform schemes of Benedict of Aniane were largely blocked from the mid century by the raids of the Northmen, as in England: but in the early tenth century fresh efforts were made to secure a reform, both of monks and canons. The reformed house of Cluny gave its name to the whole movement, and, indeed, spread the ideals of the new Benedictine reformers both in unreformed houses of monks, and in houses originally of canons: but the foundation of Cluny was not originally responsible for the movement for the reform of canons, by Gérard de Brogne in Lower Lorraine, or of John of Gorz in Upper Lorraine. Reform was needed, because wars and pillaging had destroyed monastic buildings, and caused the granting away of abbey lands to laymen; sometimes the 'abbatia' of a house was granted to a layman, as at Saint-Denis, sometimes a noble received the protectorship, the 'tuitio' of a house: the monks or canons were dispersed, or survived only as a small band of clergy, living in separate houses, and treating such share of the abbey property as they received as their hereditary possession. Houses of monks in many cases adopted the canonical rule, not only because it allowed private possession, but because canons, having their own resources, were less expensive to feed for a lay abbot, or even a very good abbot; monks who had renounced their property must be fed. Some of the ancient and honoured houses had never, in fact, been Benedictine abbeys. As a general result of all these causes, strict monasticism and strict observance of the *vita canonica* were at the beginning of the tenth century in the west at a very low ebb: and many canons of councils deplored this.

The study of charter evidence has recently confirmed the view that the first obstacle to reform in France, as in England, was the holding of monastic endowments *quasi propria* by the clerks, or even the *fratres* of the house.[1] The biographer of abbot Odo of Cluny says of the introduction of the reform at Fleury that the monks there

[1] See 'The king and the monks in the tenth century reformation', Eric John, *Bulletin of the John Rylands Library*, vol. 42 (1959), 76 and following.

assuredly did not hold the property of the monastery in common, but divided them among themselves at their own will and pleasure; they also gave estates to their relatives from the endowment. Odo tried to persuade the monks at Fleury that 'to possess nothing of their own' was fundamental to reform, and, indeed, to the monastic status. It has been observed that, in the reform of all these houses in the tenth century, 'communisation of the endowment was commonly the first stage in the reform of the monastery concerned'. Since the office holders and senior members of the community were frequently men of high birth, such communisation of endowment, and expulsion of married clerks, frequently raised violent opposition from the relatives of the well-born abbots, provosts and monks outside the abbey.

The abbey of Cluny in Burgundy was founded in 910 for a stricter observance of the Benedictine rule, taking into account that most monks would now be ordained priests, and that manual work could hardly be required of them, as of the monks very seldom so ordained in St. Benedict's day. Under the first abbot, Berno, the Cluniac observance had spread among the monasteries of Aquitaine and Burgundy, even though under his rule strict communisation of endowments was apparently not insisted on. When Berno died, his nephew, Wido, expected to succeed to the abbacy, as to a hereditary possession, and his rejection was only achieved after a crisis. The election of the great abbot Odo (927–942) saw the monastery of Cluny attain a widespread general influence. He travelled incessantly through Europe, seeking to interest princes, bishops and abbots in reform. He visited the threshold of the apostles at Rome almost yearly, taking the yearly census paid for the patronage of the holy see, and the privilege of being directly responsible to it and exempt from the jurisdiction of the local bishop. He was named 'archimandrite' of all the monasteries in Rome and its neighbourhood: and the houses of St. Mary on the Aventine and Subiaco, the holy place of Benedictine monasticism, were given into his charge, and undertook the Cluniac observance.

In France, many houses were commended to him by their patrons: the one to have greatest influence in England being Fleury-on-the-Loire. The monks there had been indignant when reform was first suggested by Odo, but were won over when he arrived mounted simply on an ass, on Palm Sunday. No definite link was formed between Fleury and Cluny (as at Romainmoutiers, where he was given the abbacy), nor at most of the reformed houses: all depended on the personality of Odo. Cluny had the 'abbacy' directly over her own daughter houses: over a few houses affiliated to her: and a wide general influence over older Benedictine houses where reform on her lines had been undertaken. The Cluniac abbots, moreover, had a strong political influence, for they preached against lay abuses and lay investiture. In England the tenth century kings were the strongest support of the reformers against anti-clerical nobles; but it was in line with Cluniac political thought that Dunstan should stress the quasi-sacerdotal power of kings at their coronation (see p. 304). The English kings were usually, in fact, behind the reformers: but there was the less theoretical objection to a king's giving away bishoprics and abbacies, if his near-priestly character were stressed.

Cluny and her daughter houses are sometimes spoken of as an 'ordo', and in the modern sense of 'Order' they were such: all under one rule and the single government of the abbot of Cluny. Nothing like it had happened before in monastic history. But at the time, in the tenth century, 'ordo' had its earlier sense of 'order': the 'order of Cluny' meant the monastic practice, the customs of Cluny. The earliest surviving manuscripts of the *ordo Cluniacensis* go back to the time of abbot Maieul, the successor of Odo; but a monastic customary would normally be practised many years before it was formally written down, and would not have, even then, an absolutely un-changeable character. The Cluniac 'ordo', followed at Fleury, and not without influence on Oswald and Æthelwold, was inspired by the Benedictine spirit, emphasised monastic silence and modified the Benedictine time-table. The hours of manual work were reduced, and more time given to the singing of the office; the chant as used in Cluniac houses reached a peak of beauty, and one monastic chronicler has a pleasant picture of the oblate boys, collecting themselves in little groups and singing over together the music for the morrow's office. But apart from the beautiful rendering of mass and office, there was a tendency at Cluny to add more and more special offices and psalms. The monks had more time on their hands, with less manual work, and such time should be filled; but in the end the monks' time-table became overburdened.

Intellectual work was not specially provided for or safeguarded by the Cluniac legislators: no chapter of the customary deals with it.

Each monastery had a school for oblate children, and there was a library for adult monks: but there is no sign of much insistence in the early observance in the use of either: for study was not much stressed in the Benedictine rule itself. It nevertheless came about that Cluniac monks copied manuscripts assiduously and illuminated them beautifully.

The giving of alms, on the other hand, was carefully provided for. Each house should have an almoner to care for poor pilgrims. He should feed the poor at the gate, giving them lodging if need be; and once a week he should go through the neighbouring town or village, inquiring into the needs of the sick. Distributions should be made to the poor, as far as the resources of the house permitted.

Meanwhile, the movement to secure a strict observance of the *vita canonica* proceeded in Lorraine. In Lower Lorraine a knight of the count of Namur, Gérard de Brogne, founded a house of canons at Brogne, and then went himself and stayed at Saint-Denis, to study its observance; its members were now again termed 'monks', and had been influenced by the Benedictine rule; it remained, however, by its traditions a learned house. Gérard was much impressed, received the monastic habit and stayed many years; when he at length asked permission to return to Brogne, he became abbot there, and replaced the canonical observance with the Benedictine rule. The abbey became renowned for its holiness and several princes asked Gérard to reform their monasteries, which then adopted the Benedictine rule. These included several Flemish houses, especially the house of St. Peter at Blandinium in Ghent, Saint-Omer, and Norman houses like those of Saint-Wandrille, Saint-Ouen at Rouen, and St. Michael's Mount. His reform affected mainly Benedictine houses, and influenced English reform through Dunstan's stay at Blandinium. Gérard died in 959.

The movement in Upper Lorraine, on the other hand, affected mainly the canons of cathedrals and collegiate churches; it was longer lived than that of Gérard. John of Gorz founded a house of strict canons in the province of Trier c. 933, and bishop Adalbero of Metz reformed his own cathedral clergy, and helped inspire a reform of those of Toul and Verdun, and other churches in his own see. The movement sought to follow the reforming canons of Aix, 817, and was more widespread than that of Gérard de Brogne; 'the Lotharingian reform movement' is generally taken as implying a reform of canons rather than monks. The constitution adopted for the see of Crediton later followed the ideals of John of Gorz and this movement in Upper Lorraine.

The reform of monasteries under the influence of Æthelwold, Oswald and Dunstan is recognised as inspired by the practice of Fleury and Blandinium, and more remotely but fundamentally from the Carolingian reforms of 817. The Carolingian reformers, however, did not content themselves with legislating for monks and canons: within the next decade the general weakness in the pastoral care of the church was considered, and in 829 four great councils were held at the order of Louis the Pious to take the necessary measures. We have no record of the canons passed at Lyons and Toulouse and only limited information about the council of Mainz, 829. But of the canons of the council of Paris, 829, a full record has survived. No less than fifty-four canons were passed: the archbishops of Reims, Sens, Tours and Rouen met in council and compiled this long list of decisions affecting the Frankish church at large. The canons formed, as it were, a book of the pastoral care of the modern church of the Franks; they were headed by an imperial missive and they can scarcely have been unknown to archbishops Oda and Dunstan. There is, apparently, no verbal borrowing in the English codes from the Frankish: but a kind of shape for a complete code of canons emerges. In the Frankish ones of 829 and 843, and in the codes of Oda and Wulfstan, the obligation to hold the Christian faith comes first, then expositions of the church as composed of clergy and laity, then canons about the general defence of Christianity against paganism, then regulations about baptism, penance, sins, other sacraments, and the relations of bishops to local minsters and churches. Both the canons of Paris, 829, and Mainz, 847, were provincial codes, which explains their length and elaboration; metropolitans who attended would in the year or years following convene their own synods and issue to them either the whole code or some summarised or selected version; the bishops who attended were expected in due course to instruct the clergy of their own diocesan synod in whatever version of the canons they chose to give them. The intention of metropolitan and more than metropolitan synods was not merely the imposition, but the publication and eventual popularisation, of the new canons. Some knowledge of the pastoral canons, as of the canons dealing with monks and canons, must have come across the water from the

Franks;[1] the Frankish princes, exiles and envoys who attended the court of Athelstan, for instance, would have brought clerical chaplains with them; and a general knowledge of what reforming opinion held about the pastoral care would have passed to England.

The Danish wars retarded reaction in England: but reforming opinion lies behind the code of Oda, and, less obviously, behind ecclesiastical regulations in the secular laws of the English kings. There was no sharp dividing line in England between the matters dealt with by the king's witan and in metropolitan synod; the canons or laws issued by witan or synod would have the royal authority.

Of interest in comparison with English ecclesiastical laws or canons in the tenth century were the following canons of Paris, 829, and Mainz, 847 (a council held under the presidency of Alcuin's pupil, Hraban Maur):

Paris, 829, laid down that Christians must have the true faith and live according to it . . . the body of the church includes two kinds of people with special qualifications, priests and princes. Bishops must tend the sheep of their sheepfold; the faithful must pray for the emperor Louis, his wife, his children and the kingdom. Catechumens must be well instructed before baptism: parents now have their children baptised in infancy, but they do not have them sufficiently instructed afterwards. (Much about baptism.) Simony is too common in our days and should be rooted out. Bishops must avoid avarice and use hospitality, and not seek to enrich their relations. Bishops ought to exercise much closer supervision of their minsters than they have hitherto. Laymen should not present other than capable clerks to their bishops (for appointment to their own local churches), nor should bishops refuse to appoint without reason given. Two provincial synods used to be held each year: we order that at least one be held annually, priests and deacons attending, as also those who hold themselves injured and desire the judgment of the synod; the bishops should bring to the synod learned persons, well known to all the churches. Bishops should not send their clerks on worldly missions so that they leave their church for a time vacant.

As to parish churches, or rural churches: it was ordered that bishops in travels or visitations must not be a charge on the parish

---

[1] The *capitula* of Theodulf of Orleans, for instance, was one of the sources of the Pseudo-Edgar canons of c. 1004–1006: see K. Jost, in *Anglia*, 1932. The *De vita canonica* was also quoted.

priest or the faithful; although by ancient right, a quarter of the tithes and offerings come to the bishop, they should renounce the right when the revenue of the church is insufficient; they should take only what is strictly necessary: the rest goes to the (local) church and to the poor. Many priests do not impose on penitents the canonical penances, but very small ones, getting authority for this out of little books called 'penitentials'; every bishop should seek out these little books in his diocese and have them burnt.[1] Bishops should fast before administering confirmation, and the time fixed regularly for confirmation should be, as for baptism, at Easter and Pentecost. (Much about correcting priests who are sinful and desert their churches.) Theatrical discourses and farces are not suitable for the clergy. Mass should always be said on Sundays: the emperor is asked to ordain that markets and solemn pleas and agricultural work should not be held or done on Sunday. Great lords and churchmen should see to it that they use only one weight and measure, without trickery and abuse of the peasants; bishops should pay the full market price for cheese and wine. Those who have been admitted to public penance should not be received as godparents, at baptism or confirmation.

Hraban Maur, when he was elected to the metropolitan see of Mainz in 847, at the will of king Louis the German, convened a great synod of the bishops of his province, together with the 'chorepiscopi', great abbots, monks and clergy. They drew up and addressed to Louis a code of thirty-one canons, commending it to him on the ground that they have begun their labours with a three days' fast and the recitation of the litanies, and enjoining on all the parishes prayers for him, the queen and the royal family. The code begins with the necessity above all things of the Christian faith, and repeats many of

---

[1] The penances in the early penitential books (fasting on bread and water, the saying of psalms, upright or with genuflections, etc.) had been severe; but by the ninth century the practice of commuting penances had brought the penitential books into disrepute. Originally the Celtic penitential writers, regarding penance as medicine for the soul, had allowed some modification of the prescribed penance on the grounds of sickness or some disability of the penitent. Then it came to be recognised that a specified number of psalms, or the feeding of a specified number of poor men, might be taken as substitutes for a day's fasting on bread and water, or a year's fasting on bread and water Wednesdays and Fridays, or three week-days in Lent with other fasts; finally, some little books specified a tariff of money alms in lieu of graded penances: or even the performance of the fasting penance by a poor man in return for money alms. See *The Celtic Penitentials*, J. T. McNeill, 1923, 59; *Die Bussordnungen der abendländischen Kirche*, F. W. H. Wasserschleben, 1851, 1958: for commutations in the *Pseudo-Bede*, 229; in the *Pseudo-Egbert*, De pretio anni vel diei: pretium autem diei hoc est, agapem duobus vel tribus pauperibus, 246.

the requirements of Paris, 829. Among new recommendations are found:

That the clergy should read frequently collections of canons, and every bishop should have a collection of homilies, and translate from it clearly 'in the rustic Roman tongue (French) or German', so that all understand what he is saying in the pulpit. Power over church property belongs to the bishops, and the laymen who help them to exercise it ought to obey them: counts and judges should support the bishops. A clerk should give back to the church what he has received from the revenues of the church; he may only use for his own pleasure what he has received as a gift or what he has inherited. Women who kill their children or commit abortion used to be condemned to penance for the rest of their lives: now, for ten years. Marriage between those related in the fourth degree is forbidden (Frankish synods had now adopted the Germanic manner of reckoning degrees).

To come then to the movement for monastic and clerical reform in England, sheltered if not initiated by Dunstan.

This son of a Somersetshire thegn, the nephew of Athelm, first bishop of Wells, was born c. 909; his uncle became archbishop of Canterbury, and he himself was archbishop of Canterbury from 960 to 988. He was outstanding as monk, reformer and pastor in four kings' reigns; those of Eadred, Eadwig, Edgar and Edward the Martyr; he was a statesman with a sense of the possible, and though it would be absurd to equate his position with that of a modern prime minister, with these kings his counsels had great weight. For the day, he was a very learned man: and his desire for ecclesiastical reform in England sought to re-establish the monastic order, not solely for its own sake, but for the benefit of the pastoral service of the church. The Benedictine houses founded in this century did, in fact, become schools of bishops. Dunstan and his friends and pupils, Æthelwold and Oswald repaired the ravages which Alfred had deplored: 'What wise men there used to be in England', he had written; Dunstan and his friends succeeded both in promoting learning and using the vernacular for homilies, saints' lives and verse scriptures, opening to laymen the treasures of Latin learning in their own tongue, according to the mind of Alfred.

It should be remembered that though in Dunstan's day there were many small, private churches, belonging to thegns and bishops, yet these were served by rural clergy who knew little Latin and had no books except the few manuscripts belonging to their church: perhaps one a sacramentary, and one containing the prophecies, epistles and gospels needed for the mass: perhaps also a martyrology or calendar. A rural priest should be able to teach his people the Lord's prayer, the articles of the faith (the creed) and about the meaning of the mass and of baptism. He belonged to a not very numerous class, and by custom he might be married, though the canons forbade it. If Dunstan desired to pull up the level of church discipline, manners and learning, it meant reforming the minsters, and the bishops' households, where the clergy were trained. Learning and good observance would spread downwards to the mass priests of the thegns out in the countryside. Dunstan and the reformers then proposed to reform the minsters, where lay influence was strong, and where the clergy lived in their little houses round the close, often with their family, to one of whom they hoped to pass on their prebend as a family estate: to reform these minsters by substituting for them houses of Benedictine monks, or canons living canonically, as at Christ Church, Canterbury. It was not usual in western Europe to substitute Benedictine monks for an episcopal familia: but in England the passage of an abbacy in the abbot's family, as if by hereditary right, had been customary in very many cases and given rise to abuses. The substitution of a Benedictine familia, whose rule safeguarded the right of the free election of an abbot, seemed more likely to guard against unsuitable, lay-appointed, abbots, than the substitution of strict canons living according to the rule of Aix-la-Chapelle, 817. These might keep their private property: which was a loophole.

Two bishops of an older generation than Dunstan initiated the work of reform in England; they were aware of reform movements among the Franks. Oda, the Danish archbishop of Canterbury appointed by Edmund in 942, had gone to France to negotiate the return of a Carolingian king (see p. 277); when he was appointed archbishop, he sent to Fleury, the strictest Benedictine house in touch with England, and requested to be sent the monastic habit. He had had no monastic training and can scarcely be reckoned a monk; he could hardly have known that the Orthodox required a bishop to be a monk before consecration, and he had actually been bishop of Ramsbury before. His action seems intended as a gesture to set him on the side of the Carolingian reformers. In any event, he sent his nephew Oswald to be trained as a novice at Fleury: to study there and come back and work in England, as a monk.

The other bishop, Ælfheah (Alphege) 'monk and bishop', otherwise called Ælfheah the Bald, was himself a relation of Dunstan, and probably trained, like him, at Glastonbury. He became bishop of Winchester in 934, in Athelstan's reign, and must have been influenced by the Carolingian reform movement, for it was he who eventually persuaded Dunstan to give up the idea of marriage and lead the monastic life.

Dunstan himself, son of the thegn, Heorstan, and akin to the royal house of Wessex, was born at Baltonsburgh, four miles from Glastonbury. He was sent for training and education to the old minster there, the state of whose discipline at the time is exceedingly obscure. The first Life of Dunstan, dedicated to archbishop Ælfric (995–1005) (the Life called B), says only that his parents sent Dunstan to be educated at the ancient and holy place of Glastonbury, and when they found he was good at his studies, they considered it fitting that he should receive the tonsure of clerkship and join the community of the famous church.[1] Now many Irish fratres, living the pilgrim life, had come to Glastonbury and many other of the faithful: for the Irish had a great affection for the place, chiefly on account of St. Patrick the younger, who is said to rest there in peace. Dunstan read their numerous books, treading the path of philosophic (secular) learning in faith, and wisely searching the books of the holy fathers about the scriptures.

There is nothing here to suggest that the Irish 'pilgrims' had made a new foundation at Glastonbury, nor is it suggested in William of Malmesbury's account of the early history of Glastonbury. He speaks as if the abbacy of Glastonbury had not lapsed, even during the raids; he had, for his day, a good knowledge of manuscripts, and when he states that certain kings in the ninth and tenth centuries made land grants to abbots whose names he obtained from the charters, his statements cannot be disallowed off-hand. From the De Antiquitate it appears that a succession of Saxon abbots held Glastonbury, though the list may not be complete: no new foundation by the Irish is

---

[1] See 'Vita sancti Dunstani auctore B', in Memorials of Saint Dunstan, ed. W. Stubbs, 1874, 10, following; the Life of Osbern the Precentor follows. For William of Malmesbury's description of Glastonbury, see the 'De Antiquitate Ecclesiae Glastoniensis', in vol. xv of Gales' Scriptores.

indicated. The house was wrecked by the Danes, and that its lands were mainly sequestrated is suggested by the fresh grants (or re-grants) made by the kings Athelstan, Edward the Elder and Ælflæd his queen. There is nothing in the *De Antiquitate* to show that the Saxon abbacy of the clerks living at Glastonbury lapsed, or that the house became an Irish foundation; equally, there is nothing to show that the clerks in the time of Athelstan and Edward lived communally, or were in possession of all the lands they held before the raids. It is likely that they lived in little houses round the old, ruinous buildings of the minster.

Osbern, the precentor of Canterbury, whom William of Malmesbury said wrote with a 'Roman elegance' (but a less good knowledge of historical material), gave a rather different account of conditions at Glastonbury when Dunstan went there. He said that 'monastic religion had almost completely disappeared there': the abbey's revenue was in the king's hand, 'regalibus stipendiis addicta', and the abbacy was in his gift. But certain Irish monks had taken up their abode there, out of reverence for the second Patrick. They included many eminent scholars; and because they were without the necessities of life, they received the sons of thegns and nobles to teach them the liberal arts.

At Glastonbury Dunstan received the first tonsure and profited greatly from his studies in the liberal arts, in the church chant and, as we are told, in 'the mechanical arts', by which is probably meant the metalwork (horse shoes, ploughshares, bolts, etc.) produced by the village smith, and the gold and silver work produced by finer craftsmen for church vessels, rings and brooches. Dunstan's uncle Athelm (Æthelhelm), bishop of Wells till 923 and then promoted to Canterbury, heard of his nephew's ability and sent for him to join his household. Here also he would lead the clerical life, and when king Edward died in 924, Athelm commended him to king Athelstan, that he might attend his court. Dunstan as a young cleric would have seen the foreign embassies that came to Athelstan's court, the Frankish refugee prince, Louis d'Outremer, the Breton prince Alan, king Athelstan's godson, and the young Haakon from Norway. He would have known Oda the Dane while he was still bishop of Ramsbury: and he knew and admired Ælfheah, bishop of Winchester from 934 till 951. He was at court at a splendid period when it was in touch with the great personages of Flanders and France.

20

He was still leading the clerical life and pursuing his studies, though the first tonsure was no canonical bar to marriage. For the life of a lay thegn he had not been trained: he might become a married canon, but his birth and long training in letters fitted him for high ecclesiastical rank, which was incompatible with clerical marriage; the whole tendency of ecclesiastical thought was against clerical marriage. Dunstan's studies had rendered him unpopular with the young thegns at court, and the story told by William of Malmesbury of how they bound him and threw him into a pond full of black mud suggests perhaps the old penalty for witchcraft. Knowledge of the stars and astronomy, though indeed one of the liberal arts, often provoked suspicion of witchcraft among laymen. Dunstan escaped from the pond covered with black mud.

About 936 Dunstan, who had been considering marriage, though urged by bishop Ælfheah to become a monk, made his decision. He had been ill, and Ælfheah came to him, and at his request, gave him the monastic habit, making him a monk in intention though without training. Soon after he ordained him priest, together with his friend Æthelwold, who had also been a young clerk at Athelstan's court. Dunstan then seems to have lived partly as chaplain to Ælfheah and partly in retirement at Glastonbury, where he built for himself a small cell near the venerated wattle church of Old St. Mary's. He taught those who came to him, and gave the sacrament to the lady Æthelflæd (Ælflæd), who lived in a cottage near the small houses of the clerics serving the church. As far as he could, Dunstan lived the monastic life.

In 939 Athelstan died, and Dunstan returned to the life of a court chaplain to Edmund. He still had enemies, and they intrigued to turn the king's mind against him. He would have had to leave the country when, as the first Life of Dunstan recounts, Edmund's preservation from death out hunting by the Cheddar gorge saved him: Edmund believed his preservation due to Dunstan's prayers and forthwith installed him as abbot at Glastonbury. From that day, in 943 or 944, the foundation of a Benedictine house in the old abbey, beside the monks' cemetery with the great Saxon crosses, became Dunstan's work. Edmund had promised endowment for the new house, and Dunstan built monastic buildings and gathered disciples. The earliest Life of Dunstan relates that in all his studies in holy books and theology, he yet found time to become very skilful in the art of writing and of playing the harp and the illumination of manuscripts (pingendi); he vigilantly inspected also all furnishings and utensils. King Eadred committed to Dunstan's safe keeping in the monastery of Glastonbury the finest of his tapestries and coverings, and very many title deeds of his estates (rurales cartulas), and besides this, the treasures of the kings his predecessors, and sundry treasures he had acquired himself.

Among the young scholars who came to Dunstan, his friend Æthelwold 'learned the grammatical art and metrics and the divine books', and at length received the monastic habit from Dunstan. He had a more severe turn of mind than Dunstan, and at this time desired to go and study monastic perfection at Fleury: king Eadred, however, was dissuaded from allowing this, in the fear that a notable subject might be permanently lost to him. About 954 Æthelwold's desire for a stricter life was satisfied by the royal permission to go off and restore the derelict monastery of Abingdon; three Glastonbury monks accompanied him to make the new foundation. Oswald, trained as a novice at Fleury, also joined Dunstan at Glastonbury; and Dunstan's brother Wulfric, as reeve or provost, took charge of the Glastonbury lands.

For ten and more years Dunstan and his young monks devoted themselves to building up the Benedictine life: but about the monastic time-table there is some uncertainty. St. Benedict's rule, chapter viii, laid down that in winter time, from November 1 till Easter, the night office should be arranged with a long interval between Matins and Lauds; in summer time, when the nights were short, it was to be somewhat shortened and with no interval. Similarly, in the longer summer days, when the climate of south Italy dictated even to peasants a midday siesta, monks also might rest upon their beds for the space of about two hours. Now this provision was hardly necessary in an English summer, especially for the whole period between Easter and November 1. The original Benedictine time-table was in fact difficult to keep in a colder climate and one where there was much greater difference between the variation of the length of days and nights in summer and winter. St. Benedict moreover enjoined that the abbot should order such matters as the appointed times for the opus dei, and for the monks' meals, as seemed to him best: such alteration of detail in no way conflicted with the main provisions and the spirit of the holy rule.

Dunstan may have had the canons of Aix, 817, to guide him: and he certainly seems to have had an old monastic time-table common to the west in the tenth century, the 'Order how the office is to be said', the *Ordo qualiter*.[1]

With all the cares of building up a Benedictine house on his hands, Dunstan was in touch with the court, and often called on to give counsel. When king Edmund was murdered by an outlaw he recognised, sitting as a guest at his banquet at Pucklechurch in Gloucestershire, he had had Dunstan in his train. His body was taken to Glastonbury for burial and Dunstan sang his requiem. Eadred, his brother, ruled for nine years in constant affection with Dunstan; he appears to have wished Dunstan to accept the see of Crediton (a see provided by king Athelstan for the Cornishmen), and when Dunstan refused, desiring to continue his work at Glastonbury, he made Daniel, a monk of Glastonbury, bishop there.

Eadred died in 955, after long illness, and his will is of interest both as witnessing to his friendship for Dunstan and recognition of the reestablishment of Glastonbury's honourable position in the west, and to the manner in which a pious, tenth century king rewarded his servants and provided for the relief of the poor in his different territories.[2]

'In nomine domini', the will begins, and then, in Anglo-Saxon: 'This is the will of Eadred the king. He gives to the place (minster) where his body shall rest two golden crosses and two swords with golden hilts, and four hundred pounds' (of silver, by weight). To the Old Minster at Winchester and to the New Minster (Hyde Abbey) and to the Nunnaminster there, he gives three estates each: and to the three nun minsters, at Winchester, at Wilton by Salisbury and at Sherborne, thirty pounds each.

Also he gives sixteen hundred pounds for the redemption of his soul and the good of his people, to purchase for themselves relief from want and from the heathen army, if they have need. The will goes on to arrange that the archbishop at Christ Church shall have four hundred pounds of this sum, for the people of Kent, Surrey, Sussex and Berkshire, and if anything happen to the bishop, it shall remain in that minster in the charge of the witnesses in the witan who shall be in that shire. The bishop of Winchester is to have four

---

[1] See MOE., 38, 43.
[2] See *Select English Historical Documents*, F. Harmer, 34.

hundred pounds, two hundred for Hampshire and a hundred each for Wiltshire and Dorset. Also abbot Dunstan is to have two hundred pounds and keep it at Glastonbury for the people of Somerset and Devon; and the bishop of Winchester is to have the two hundred pounds left over, for whichever shire may need it. The bishop of Dorchester to have four hundred pounds for the Mercians: bishop Wulfhelm has that sum of four hundred pounds (Wulfhelm II of Bath and Wells).

The king then assigned his gold treasure, in ornaments or bars, for distribution: it was to be coined into mancuses (sometimes a weight of precious metal, but here as elsewhere a solidus as coined in south Italy, with which pilgrims came to be familiar, and which they had brought back); gold to the amount of two thousand mancuses was to be so coined, and a third each to be given to the archbishop, the bishop of Winchester and the bishop of Dorchester, to be distributed throughout the bishoprics 'for the sake of God and the redemption of my soul'.

The king then bequeathed large estates to his mother (he had no children), to the archbishop personally two hundred mancuses, to each bishop one hundred and twenty, to each earl the same, and to his steward (dish thegn), chamberlain (clothes thegn) and butler, eighty gold mancuses. 'And to each of my chaplains to whom I have given charge of my relics, fifty gold mancuses and five pounds in silver pennies.' And five pounds each to the other priests: and certain other money legacies. The king wills that twelve almsmen be appointed on each above mentioned estate, and if anything happen to any of them, another to be appointed in his place.

King Eadred's death in 955 marks the end of the period when the 'old minsters' trained the clergy and bishops of the English church and were not yet held in disrepute because their 'fratres' were not monks. They lived on their prebends and many were married; and in the books of canon law no sanction could be found for married priests. But the gifts of kings and devout ealdormen and thegns continued to be made to the minster churches, which could scarcely have happened if disapprobation of the situation had been general. King Eadred had supported Dunstan in his abbacy of Glastonbury, and Dunstan intended his monks at Glastonbury to train other houses in the Benedictine life: a few intelligent clerics could see, as he did, the good work the great Benedictine abbeys were doing among the

Franks, and wish for such abbeys in England. But Eadred's will planned to reward service and do good works according to the status quo in England: three estates each to the three Winchester minsters, a great sum for poor relief and to buy off the Danes, to be kept and administered by the archbishop of Canterbury, the bishops of Winchester and Dorchester and the abbot of Glastonbury, and his treasure divided among his bishops, chaplains and lay officers.

Many land grants between the days of king Alfred and king Eadred were made to the old minsters: either to the church there, in which case the bishop (if the church were a see church) would control the lands as belonging to the see, or expressly to the familia (hiwan, higan, hired) to the endowment of the community. The lady Ceolwin[1] left land at Alford to the familia (of the old minster at Winchester): land left to her by her husband, which was made over to him with the cognisance of king Alfred. Wilfrith, bishop of Worcester in 922, left land and profits of fisheries to the familia at Worcester; earl Athelstan, in king Athelstan's time, left land to the minster of St. Mary at Stowe; king Athelstan granted and confirmed to 'God and St. Mary and St. Michael' and the Celtic saints 'St. Samson and St. Branwalader' (that is, to the minster at Milborne, Dorset) considerable estates in the neighbourhood; some at Osmington (in modern days a great place for lobsters), 'a weir (for fish) on the Avon at Twyneham' (Christ Church, where the salmon come up river), 'and all the water within the shore of Weymouth, and half the river of Weymouth', and much beside. King Athelstan granted land also to the familia of the Old Minster at Winchester. The thegn Alfred granted land at Stoneham in reversion to the New Minster at Winchester, as freely as king Athelstan had granted it to him.

These and other grants, like the will of king Eadred, show that though reformers like Æthelwold might term the brethren of the old minsters 'lascivious clerks', no general scandal had been caused. On the other hand, no names like those of the outstanding scholars and pastors of the next generation appear among them.

---

[1] See ASChar., p. 31, for this and many other grants throwing light on the endowment and finance of the tenth century church.

CHAPTER XIV

THE TENTH CENTURY CHURCH REFORM :
ITS ACHIEVEMENT

WHEN king Eadred died in 955, general opposition to the introduction of Benedictine monasticism in England had not yet been aroused, and there is no evidence that the hostility of Eadred's successor, Eadwig, to Dunstan was due to a dislike of monks. The reason was personal. Dunstan was present when the handsome fifteen-year-old Eadwig was anointed king; and whether it is true or not that Eadwig withdrew himself from the coronation banquet to disport himself with the lady Ælfgifu (whom he afterwards married) and her mother, and Dunstan and another bishop were sent to recall him to the banquet: it is certain that the elder lady's personal hostility secured the confiscation of all Dunstan's property, and his expulsion from the country in 956.

Dunstan fled first to the court of Arnulf, count of Flanders, then to the monastery of Blandinium at Ghent. The father of the count who gave him refuge had been that Baldwin who had married king Alfred's daughter Ælfthryth, and received with her a marriage portion of land in England; Ælfthryth had then given her lands at Lewisham to the reformed monastery of St. Peter on the height called Mont Blandin. A welcome was thus prepared for Dunstan both at court and in the monastery where Gérard de Brogne had been in charge for some twelve years from 941. It is possible that Dunstan's view of the relative value of the Benedictine and canonical life was influenced by Blandinium's inspiration from Saint-Denis rather than Fleury: that house had for so long been a very learned house of canons, before its assumption of the strict Benedictine rule.

Meanwhile, in England, Eadwig's rule was not acceptable to all, though he granted away much land to try to win support. The old kingdoms of the north and midlands showed themselves not unwilling to break away from the rule of Wessex. In 957 Eadwig's brother Edgar was chosen king of the Northumbrians and Mercians, who withdrew their allegiance from Eadwig. Dunstan was recalled from Ghent, consecrated bishop by archbishop Oda, and given the see first of Worcester and then of London: both Mercian sees. Eadwig's death in 959 ended the division of the country and the ascendancy of Dunstan's enemies; the same year, Dunstan was made archbishop of Canterbury. His monk and pupil Æthelwold, in a vernacular account of the restoration of the monasteries, says that up till now, the time of king Edgar's accession, Glastonbury was the only true monastery in England and there only could monks be found;[1] the lands of the house at Abingdon which he had himself refounded in 954 had been confiscated at Dunstan's banishment, though charters were granted to Abingdon in 956; Æthelwold did not consider his house at Abingdon securely established as yet. Oswald was still a monk at Fleury; archbishop Oda recalled him in 957, but did not live to see his nephew again.

King Edgar was to prove a firm supporter of the monks; he had himself been in the charge of Æthelwold when he was abbot of Abingdon, and had been instructed by him, before his accession to Mercia in 957; as an ætheling, he had stayed at Abingdon and with Æthelwold watched the reconstruction of the monastery. Æthelwold rather than Dunstan became the king's principal counsellor from now on, and received greater endowments for his new monasteries than any founded by Dunstan. Dunstan was archbishop from 959 and in pastoral charge of the whole country; Æthelwold, surnamed Boanerges for his enthusiasm and drive, headed the movement for monastic reform. The refoundation (and endowment) of Abingdon, the two Winchester minsters, Peterborough, Ely, Crowland, Thorney, and probably St. Albans, was carried out by him.

King Edgar's support of Æthelwold is well expressed in his foundation charter to Ely, where the preamble sets forth how God has reduced beneath Edgar's sway Scots, Cumbrians and likewise Britons 'and all that this island contains, so that I now occupy my throne in peace . . . I desire now with God's guidance to fill the deserted minsters everywhere in my dominion with monks and also

---

[1] There is some evidence that Eadwig confirmed earlier grants to the monastery of Abingdon, to retain Æthelwold's support: see E. John, 'Latin charters of the tenth century reformation', in *Revue Bénédictine*, lxx (1960), 342, and BCS. no. 1046.

with nuns . . . and to renew the worship of God, which has been neglected. And the monks shall live their life according to the rule of the holy Benedict.' In Edgar's confirmation of the freedom of Chilcomb, made in witan at the request of bishop Æthelwold, the king decreed that this estate anciently granted to the Old Minster and assessed to geld as from one hide though it was actually worth one hundred hides, should ever continue thus assessed: the king enjoined 'that none of his children as successors should ever again put priests in the minster but it should be occupied for all time by monks, as he had furnished it with the help of Almighty God, when he drove out from it the proud priests for their evil deeds and placed monks there to serve God, according to the teaching of St. Benedict'.

The work of these three great bishops, Dunstan of Canterbury, Æthelwold of Winchester and Oswald of Worcester, all of them monks of Glastonbury, was fundamental for the revival of discipline and the renaissance of learning in tenth century England. Of the three, the monastic reform stems from Æthelwold, called at the time the 'father of monks'. The bitter opposition to their reforms sprang from the diversion to monastic funds of prebendal and even hereditary possessions, and dislike of the creation of a new class of land holders and administrators in the abbots of houses endowed with private hundreds and sokes.

As to Dunstan's work: his care for church discipline and the church at large included the supervision of bishoprics, synods and the maintenance of canonical order, beside the care of his own familia at Christ Church.

In the creation of new bishoprics, Dunstan profited from the work of his predecessors, finding the ground pretty well covered by existing sees. In 909 the great see of Winchester had been subdivided into five, with papal approval: Winchester, Ramsbury (Wiltshire), Wells (Somersetshire), Crediton (Devonshire) and Sherborne for Dorsetshire. In king Athelstan's reign a new see had been set up for Cornwall, either at St. Germain's or St. Petroc's; but it is a sign that the church at Glastonbury was of much more importance than the bishopric of Crediton and St. Petroc, that in king Eadred's will, made in 955, 200 gold mancuses for the relief of the people of Devon and Cornwall were left in the keeping of Dunstan at Glastonbury, and not in the charge of the bishop of Crediton.

Dunstan, therefore, did not increase the number of English sees; he was inclined rather to favour the endowment of new monasteries, as tending to produce better bishops and eventually better clergy. English bishops were, in fact, all chosen from the monasteries, almost down till the Norman Conquest.[1]

As to the passing of new canons: bishops had always used the issue of such canons for the direction of the clergy in their own see or province. A great provincial synod had been convened in 786, to meet the papal legates and deal with reform (see p. 226). The first step in canonical reform in the tenth century was taken, however, by a predecessor of Dunstan.

The work of archbishop Oda at Canterbury (942–958) and Wulfstan I (931–956) at York began the reform of the pastoral work of the church considerably before any beginning could be made of the reform of the minsters. This latter, in the end, would produce well-learned bishops of regular life, able to govern their sees by example, precept and synod: but such reform was expensive. The minster must, as a preliminary, be given a mensa and regular buildings: a few clerics living round the church of a minster close might be living partly on inherited land: it would be more costly to support a body of monks or strict canons. On the other hand, to draw up a canonical code cost nothing, except the bishops' expenses in coming to the meeting, and they would bear those themselves. Oda and Wulfstan began with the issue of direct rulings on ecclesiastical matters in witan or synod. Various matters might be dealt with by the witan, in the Anglo-Saxon tongue; anything like a canonical code must be issued to a meeting with a much larger proportion of bishops, and might be drawn up in Latin; though a translation would accompany it.

The Anglo-Saxon laws known as I Edmund were published and confirmed in a witan held either in 942 or between the years 944 and 946. The preamble to the laws, published in Anglo-Saxon in the witan and given under royal authority states that:

> King Edmund has convened at London, during the holy season of Easter, a great assembly (sinoth) both of the ecclesiastical and secular estates. Archbishop Oda and archbishop Wulfstan and

[1] See Professor Darlington's 'Ecclesiastical Reform in the late Old English period', in EHR., li (1936), 385-428.

many other bishops have been there taking counsel for the welfare of their own souls and the souls of those who have been placed under their charge.[1]

The six laws that follow deal solely with ecclesiastical matters. The preamble implies that they had been discussed by archbishops and bishops, meeting beforehand in a preliminary assembly, an ecclesiastical synod: the actual writing down of the canons (laws) would have been the work of the archbishops or their clerks. No Latin version of canons passed in any such preliminary assembly survives: but there is a set of Latin canons compiled by archbishop Oda for recitation to his synod at this or another time, which can be compared with the English laws.

The laws of I Edmund enjoin that those in holy orders must teach the people by example and observe the celebacy that befits their estate: otherwise they shall be punished according to the canon, lose their worldly possessions and not be buried in consecrated ground: unless they repent.

Every Christian man must pay tithes and church scot and Peter's pence and plough alms. Anyone who kills a Christian (shall be excommunicate) and not go anywhere near the king, till he have done penance, as the bishop or his confessor appoints. Those who have intercourse with a nun, or are adulterers, shall not have Christian burial. Bishops should restore all the houses of God on their property (their private churches): we ask the king that all houses of God shall be well put in order: and there is great need of this. Perjurers[2] and sorcerers shall be cast out from the fellowship of God, unless they do penance.

The clause about the payment of church dues by the laity is of importance as a summary of payments now enforced by the state. As regards tithe, this is the first time its enforcement appears in the law, though Charlemagne had enforced its payment in 782 among the conquered Saxons, and later from all Frankish estates, including the royal vills. In England it appears as an act of piety in Theodore's penitential, and as a pious act which all should make in the legatine synod of 786. Now its enforcement is ordered, together with the old church scot of Ine's laws, and Peter's pence, or Rome fee, which had

---

[1] See A. J. Robertson, *The laws of the kings of England from Edmund to Henry I*, 7.
[2] Justice depended on a man's clearing himself by a solemn oath and oath helpers.

apparently been paid annually since Alfred's reign. Plough alms is mentioned for the first time (see p. 329).

In the code known as II Edmund the preamble states that king Edmund informs all his subjects that he has been considering with his wise men, ecclesiastical and lay, how best he may promote Christianity (Christendomes). All the clauses thereafter deal with the keeping of the peace, with deeds of violence, with homicide, and its consequences. Men must at all costs give up the unchristian custom of the blood feud; if anyone slay a man, he must pay, himself, the slain man's wergeld, according to his rank; if the kindred of the slayer will neither help him pay the wergeld nor give him food or shelter, they themselves shall not be attached by the slain man's kindred in the blood feud; they shall be free of the blood feud. If any of the slain man's kindred take vengeance on the kin of the slayer (except they harbour him), the king shall punish him. If anyone flees for sanctuary to a church or to the king's residence and anyone attacks him there, he shall incur the appropriate penalty. . . . The witan shall put a stop to the blood feud. In short: the blood feud is unchristian: its sanction goes back to pagan time: the king wills to put a stop to it.

For the issue of these laws in Edmund's reign Dunstan was not responsible: he was engaged in building up a monastic community in Glastonbury. They must have been brought about by the counsel of archbishops Oda and Wulfstan I, both of whom desired a canonical reform of church life. Oda drew up a set of canons, intended to be read in synod, for in the preamble he asks those who hear them read aloud to meditate frequently upon them, that they may bring forth the peaceful fruits of harvest; he says that for the consolation of king Edmund he has compared certain documents worthy of the attention of all Christians, and decreed that their contents shall be set forth together 'in this short parchment (*in hac cartula*)'. Canonical compilers usually claim that they are setting forth nothing new, but restating what is already the teaching or practice of the church: but Oda's reference to 'documenta' suggests that he had some canonical collection before him, and not an English one; the excerpts do not suggest a rewriting of the canons of Clofeshoh, 747, or the legatine synod.

Of these canons of Oda, the first declares the immunity of the church of Christ, which should not be violated by the 'interruptions of the wicked'. Princes should obey archbishops and bishops, to whom have been given the keys of the kingdom of heaven. Bishops should visit their sees (parochias) once a year. Priests should lead an exemplary life; clerks should live honestly and canonically; monks should study to fulfil their vows, day and night. Unlawful marriage is prohibited, as with nuns or within the prohibited degrees. All Christians should pay a tenth of all they possess to God, and live and give alms on the remaining nine parts.

It is curious that no canons of Edgar's reign, issued by archbishop Dunstan, have come down to us: those given in Anglo-Saxon in a Cambridge manuscript, and for long believed to have been his, have now been shown to have been the work of archbishop Wulfstan II of York (see p. 340). But the counsel of Dunstan lies behind the ecclesiastical provisions of the law of Edgar.

The code known as II Edgar, apparently published at Andover, and before 962, deals only with ecclesiastical matters;[1] the preamble calls the law a 'gerædnis' or ordinance that king Edgar has enacted with the advice of his witan, for the glory of God and his own kingship and the good of all his people. No mention is made of bishops attending: but the exclusively ecclesiastical matters dealt with suggest a similarity of procedure with Edmund's synod of London; Dunstan, in any case, was at hand. The code is of great importance for its directions as to the recipients of tithe and church dues; it begins:

> This is the first provision: that God's churches shall be worthy each of her own rights. And all tithes shall be paid to the old minsters to which obedience is due: payment shall be made both from the thegn's demesne land and of his tenants' land: all land that is under the plough. (In all south country villages, wheat and barley crops were grown in two or three great open fields, some acre strips belonging to the thegn, some to the individual villagers. The village had also its hay meadow, woodland and waste; but tithe should be paid only from crops grown on ploughed land, and the amount automatically varied with good or bad harvests. The old minsters, which would include the bishops' see churches and also non-episcopal minsters such as Lyminge and the Kentish minsters, Beverley, Chertsey, Glastonbury, and the other old foundations from which the countryside had originally been

[1] A. J. Robertson, *Laws*, etc., 4, 21 and 302.

converted, must not lose their old means of support: what should be done, however, about the private, rural churches now built in considerable numbers about the countryside? The code continues.)

If, however, a thegn has a church built on his bookland (land held by written title deed), and the church has a graveyard, he shall pay the third part of his own tithes to his church. If the church have no graveyard, he shall pay what he will to his priest out of the next tenth part. (The division of the corn crops was the easier, in that a 'tenth' was every tenth sheaf, which the officer, reeve, of the old minster would take away; the thegn might allow his priest to take that number of the sheaves of the next set of tenth sheaves that he thought fit.) And the church scot from every free household shall be paid to the old minster. Plough alms shall be paid 15 days after Easter (perhaps because the payment would not be made on a Sunday).

The tithe of all young animals shall be rendered at Pentecost and that of the fruits of the earth at the Equinox (often used as equivalent to 'harvest') and each church scot at Martinmas, or else the full fine (wite) which the doom-book (written law) reckons.

If, however, anyone refuses to pay tithe as we have decreed, the king's reeve and the bishop's reeve and the mass priest of the minster shall go to him, and take against his will the tenth part to the minster to whom it is due, and the next tenth shall be allotted to him (from which to pay his own priest), and the eight remaining parts shall be divided in two and the lord of the land (the thegn, earlier) shall take half, and the bishop half.

And every hearth penny shall be paid by St. Peter's mass day (the penalties for non-payment a first, second and third time are exceedingly heavy, culminating in 'the loss of all he possesses'; such payment would be exceedingly hard to enforce in the Danish and near pagan part of the kingdom, and harshness of penalty usually points to extreme difficulty of enforcement).

Finally: every Sunday shall be kept as a festival from noon on Saturday till dawn on Monday (no work being done): and each other mass day according to the rule about it. Appointed fasts must be kept (and each Friday unless it be a festival). And soul's scot shall be paid for each Christian man to the minster that gives him burial (this would apply to any church with a graveyard).

And each church-peace (right of sanctuary) shall be maintained according to the highest standards of the past.

This code marks the point when not only the landed class, but all villagers are legislated for as responsible for the economic mainten-ance of the church. The thegn who had built the village a small church might use a part of his own tithe to pay his priest; but all the villagers must let the officers of the old minster take their tenth sheaf. They had paid 'church scot' immemorially; there is nothing to show how long before, or how regularly, villagers had given their tenth sheaves. To the villager, however, who had found it easy to steal a sheep from the open down, or some smaller object from a man's house, and who had been pursued by his fellow villagers of the hundred, knowing that if he were taken 'hand having or back bearing' he might be hanged from the nearest tree without any trial in the moot at all: or be taken by pursuers under strong suspicion: the sanctuary of the nearest church was a valuable right; it gave him a chance of life.

It is accepted that the code known as III Edgar was promulgated at the same meeting of king and counsellors as II Edgar. It deals with secular subjects: mainly, the securing that each man shall get justice (folkright) and the holding of the hundred, the borough and the shire moot, where justice is done. But it is laid down that the shire bishop (the diocesan) and the ealdorman shall attend the shire moot, held twice a year: strict canonical opinion demanded that cases between churchmen, or involving churchmen, should go before a bishop. The law here enjoins that the two, bishop and ealdorman, should teach (tæcan) God's law and worldly law; 'teach' would be Anglo-Saxon for 'docere', which is an expression found in collec-tions of canons; every clause begins 'docemus'.

The preamble of IV Edgar begins, 'Here is notified in this written order, that king Edgar has been considering what remedy (bote: the legal word for the emendation for an offence) can be found for the plague' which has been afflicting his people. The ASC. records a year of plague in 962. The king and his witan have thought that this mis-fortune has befallen because Christians have often disregarded his commandments, and specially by not paying their tithes: laymen have been audacious in this. I and the archbishop (Dunstan) enjoin that you pay your tithes, as set down in my ordinance at Andover. My reeves shall deal with such failure in the manner prescribed. And the servants of God who receive the dues shall live a clean life. The rights of the laity shall not be infringed, and my own royal rights shall remain as in my father's life-time: the Danes shall maintain the rights of the laity by good law as best they may: among the English, the additions I and my witan have made to the laws shall be observed. (Which may be taken to mean that the king enforces the payment of tithe among the English: but the Danes must make their own law about it.)

In the reform of the minsters, the chief driving force was Æthelwold rather than Dunstan, though every effort of his friends to replant Benedictine monasticism in England had Dunstan's support. His sanction lay behind the *Regularis Concordia*, though its author was actually Æthelwold.

Nevertheless, the foundation of certain Benedictine houses, above all Glastonbury, was Dunstan's work, and after his return from exile in 957 he refounded, or reformed, the houses of Malmesbury, Bath and Westminster; Benedictine houses at Milton and Exeter were also newly founded at this time,[1] with the help of monks from Glastonbury. The small houses of Athelney and Muchelney in Somerset appear from this time as daughter houses of Glastonbury. Four other houses in the west were founded towards the end of Dunstan's life, and had some connexion with himself or Glastonbury: Cerne, Tavistock, Horton and Cranborne. The bishop's familia at Sherborne became monastic under Wulfsige, who had possibly been a monk at Glastonbury, then abbot of Westminster and finally bishop of Sherborne. William of Malmesbury says of the small house of clerks at Thorney, to which Æthelwold had once thought of retiring as to a hermitage, that Dunstan when bishop of London made Wulfsige abbot at 'the west monastery' to build up a small Benedictine house with twelve monks.

The opposition to the foundation of Benedictine houses and the forcing of the Benedictine rule upon houses of clerks sprang not only from the diversion of royal endowments, but the unwillingness of many of the English magnates and thegns to change the custom by which the endowments of a church were divided into prebends, to one duly supporting a body of clergy living the common life. To

[1] MOE., 49.

the tenth century reformers, the essence of the monastic life was that the monk had nothing of his own, not even that which had come to him by hereditary right. Yet at some time in the past it had become customary for a portion of minster property to be assigned to the individual fratres of the minster; they should, by right, return it at death, but many hoped to pass it on to their children, or at least to one son who might himself become a member of the monastic chapter. Apart from the abuses alleged against some of the clerical prebendaries, as that they lived luxuriously or immorally, the reformers held that prebends themselves were uncanonical, while the conservative minded clergy and laity regarded the practice as tolerable. Archbishop Wulfred at Canterbury had not forced his cathedral clergy to give up their little houses, though he provided a common dormitory and refectory. King Edmund, even after he had made Dunstan abbot of Glastonbury and given him endowment for a monastery there, gave the lands of the abbey of Bath to clerks who had fled from the monastery of St. Bertin in Flanders, because they would not undertake the reformed life which Gérard de Brogne was seeking to enforce there. Similarly, many English clergy, married and with prebendal portions, were men of high birth, whose kindred refused to acquiesce in their expulsion and who detested the new class of abbatial landowners, whose officers presided over the new courts or sokes with which the new foundations were endowed. Such ealdormen and thegns supported the older ecclesiastical practice almost to the point of civil war, in the reigns following Edmund's.

The evidence of English land grants shows that the 'families' of many of the 'old minsters' had separate endowments by this time, and therefore the means of living the canonical life; possibly various Anglo-Saxon terms in the grant, all of which may be translated 'refectory' (beodland, beodern, etc.), may indicate that they had refectory buildings and common meals; they may equally well indicate that separate food allowances from the endowments were dealt out to the fratres. The lady Ceolwin (see p. 302) made a grant to the 'beodern' of the familia of the Old Minster; king Athelstan in 934 granted estates to its refectory and wardrobe (beodlande and hrægel-talu). These and the many grants to the 'families' of minsters point to a state of things similar to that found by Dunstan, on his accession to Canterbury.

The familia at Christ Church in 960 when he became archbishop

21

was clearly one of clerks, some of whom at least were awarded individual prebends. Nor is it recorded that he installed Benedictine monks there or aroused the opposition that such a course provoked at Winchester, and in other sees. Even before the Viking raids, however, though Wulfred had provided a common dormitory and refectory, the prebendal system was in use: in 832 Werhard the priest in his will restored 'to the monks my brethren serving God there (at Christ Church) all the lands which I have held within Kent and without, at the gift of the archbishop (Wulfred, his relative) and with the consent of the familia, together with 22 hides of land of my own patrimony'. He asks for the brethren's prayers, for he has restored what he ought to give back, and also given freely what was his own. How far the landed endowment of Christ Church had been diminished in the period of the raids we do not know; but it is certain that when Dunstan became archbishop, his familia was composed of clerks, not monks. They were replaced by monks by archbishop Aelfric (995–1005) at the papal command.

There is, further, no evidence that Dunstan took any steps to ensure a strict following of the Benedictine rule at St. Augustine's. Monastic practice may have been stricter there already than at Christ Church; Dunstan appointed Sigeric, a disciple of his own from Glastonbury, its abbot.

It was Æthelwold, however, from the time he was appointed abbot of Abingdon, who took the lead in the monastic revival. He was bishop of Winchester from 963 till his death in 984, and through the twelve prosperous years of Edgar's reign, and the wars and alarms of those of Edward the Martyr and Æthelred, he pursued this one object: the establishment and building up in England of Benedictine houses; where the monks should have no prebends, no wives, no luxury and the right to choose their own abbot according to the Benedictine rule. The Peterborough version of the Anglo-Saxon Chronicle under the year 963 says of bishop Æthelwold that he established many monasteries; after he had driven out the secular clergy from his own cathedral, 'he came to king Edgar and asked him to give him all the minsters the heathen had destroyed, because he wished to restore them: and the king cheerfully granted it. The bishop went first to Ely . . . and had the monastery built, giving it to one of his monks whose name was Byrhtnoth . . . afterwards he came to the monastery called Medehamstede, which had been destroyed by the heathen, and found nothing there but old walls and wild woods . . . Medehamstede too he restored.'

The chronology of the replacement of the secular clerks by monks in the see churches of Æthelwold and his friend, bishop Oswald, is difficult to ascertain exactly. Land grants and leases were now often dated by the 'annus Incarnationis', and the entries made in the different versions of the ASC. were made under years, as 'annals': but narrative sources, even good ones like the anonymous lives of Dunstan and Oswald, seldom gave dates. Even the statement that an event occurred in a certain annus Incarnationis is not always conclusive: for though in England the year began on Christmas Day, and the scribes of the Anglo-Saxon kings used this reckoning, other systems of year-beginnings were in use on the Continent. In the old Gregorian sacramentaries the year began on January 1, as in the Julian calendar: and uncertainty whether a chronicler were using this system of time reckoning, or the reckoning from December 25, might affect such a statement as, for instance, 'the king had held a great witan at the Christmas feast in this year'. Fortunately, the scribes of charters used the Christmas reckoning, if they gave the annus Incarnationis at all: as one Worcester charter in Old English put it: 'this was done in the year that was away from Christ's birthtide nine hundred winters and ninety-one winters': A.D. 991.[1]

The anonymous life of St. Oswald,[2] for instance, written as it was by a Ramsey monk likely to be well-informed about Oswald, who had founded and loved his house, is not easy to reconcile in chronological detail with the dating in the long series of charters made at Worcester in Oswald's episcopate, or with the account of the expulsion of the married clerks at Winchester as given in the Peterborough Chronicle. The main outline, however: the fact that clerks were replaced by Benedictine monks in most of the minsters of southern England, and the ruined minsters of Mercia refounded as Benedictine houses, is clear. That the expulsion of the clerks at the Old Minster, Winchester, took place at a given point is clear; the

---

[1] KCD. no. 676. Anglo-Saxon reckoning was always by winters because the year began at Christmas. See for time reckonings: F. M. Powicke, *Handbook of British Chronology*, 1939, 373; for year-beginnings in the ASC., D. Whitelock in an appendix to C. Plummer's ed. of *Two of the Saxon Chronicles Parallel*, originally by J. Earle.

[2] See the *Vita Sancti Oswaldi, auctore anonymo*, ed. J. Raine, in *The historians of the church at York and its Archbishops*, 3 vols., 1838: vol. I, pp. 399 ff.

question whether a sudden expulsion or a gradual transformation took place at Worcester and other sees is not clear.

Æthelwold's see church in Winchester was the Old Minster. Its familia of clerks were of noble birth, married, and having *sua propria*: the reformers said they lived lascivious and disreputable lives, leaving one woman for another. Æthelwold was made their bishop in 963, and desired to replace them by monks: young king Edgar desired that all clerks in minsters should be replaced by monks. Æthelwold brought monks from the monastery he had founded at Abingdon, and on the first Saturday in Lent, February 21, 964,[1] they waited outside the church of the Old Minster, and heard the clerks within singing the Communion verse: 'Learn discipline lest ye perish from the right way'. This seemed to give the sanction of God and the monks entered; the king's thegn, Wulfstan of Dalham, standing at the church door with drawn sword, bade the clerks begone, or prepare to accept the Benedictine life. Men were used to seeing the king's reeves enforcing the collection of tithe, and the enforcement of decrees of the witan, or simply the king's will, and royal intervention would not have seemed strange to contemporaries: the Winchester clerks, as a body, preferred to go (all except three), rather than accept the Benedictine rule. Æthelwold had prevailed over the most highly born and strongly entrenched cathedral chapter in Wessex: it was unlikely that other cathedral clergy would offer much resistance.

It is not quite clear whether the expulsion of clerks at Winchester was made with the sanction of a council of bishops and abbots as well as that of the king. The monk, Florence of Worcester (d. 1118), writing long after, but apparently with the help of a Worcester version of the Anglo-Saxon Chronicle not now extant, speaks of a great synodal witan held at Christmas, 963, at Gloucester, which enjoined the replacement of clerks by monks. Æthelwold had been consecrated on November 29, 963, and if he attended the king's Christmas feast at Gloucester, soon after, he could have expelled his own clerks in February 964, after this body had given its pronouncement. The Anonymous Life of St. Oswald, however, relates that a great assembly of bishops and nobles met to consult with king Edgar after Easter, and the king, rejoicing to see the great assembly of bishops, abbots and abbesses, ordered that forty monasteries of

[1] MOE., 41.

monks should be established. It is unlikely that two great ecclesiastical councils should have been held very close together: and it appears that Æthelwold and the king expelled the Winchester clerks first, and then sought to secure the foundation of monasteries of monks and virgins elsewhere by the holding of one or more ecclesiastical witans.

By the end of 964, not only had the Old Minster been furnished with monks, but the conversion of the New Minster at Winchester, of Chertsey and Milton had followed. Monks trained by Æthelwold made a foundation in 966 at Peterborough, in 970 at Ely, and 972 at Thorney; Croyland, St. Neot's, Chertsey and possibly St. Albans are reckoned as Æthelwold's at his death, in 1005; Eynsham was founded with his most famous pupil, Ælfric the homilist, as its first abbot.

Oswald, the third great bishop of the reform, was consecrated for the see of Worcester in 961, and to the archbishopric of York in 972: he ruled both sees till his death in 991. He found his episcopal familia in 961 one of clerks living on their prebends, some probably married, some quite young and in the minor orders. He had himself passed some years as a monk at Fleury, and desired to plant the monastic life at Worcester. He at first, in 961, planted a small colony of monks at Westbury, 'a parochia of his see', which must imply that it had a church, glebe land and such right to church dues as would support a small minister, if slenderly. The Anonymous Life of St. Oswald says that the monks spent four years there or more: but Oswald was uneasy for their future if he should die, and begged king Edgar for another site and endowment for them. In the event, duke Æthelwine gave him a site at Ramsey, in the fens, and Oswald made his greatest foundation there with the Westbury monks. A Worcester postulant or monk, Wynsige, joined the community of Ramsey, which was headed by the priest Agelnoth from Westbury.

At some time, not earlier than 969,[1] Oswald brought back a contingent of monks from Ramsey headed by Wynsige the priest and monk, planted them within the precincts of the old minster dedicated to St. Peter, and built within the minster a new church dedicated to St. Mary. Florence of Worcester speaks of an expulsion of some of

[1] BCS. no. 1243, a Latin grant of 969, has an Anglo-Saxon note at the end attesting that this was done by the witness of Wynsige and the monks: but the note, copied in Hemming's cartulary as part of the grant, may have been an early endorsement.

the clerks of the familia:[1] Oswald 'expelled those refusing to receive
the monastic habit', while he 'monachized those who consented,
setting over them Wynsige, a man of great monastic devotion'.
Certainly the names of some clergy who signed Oswald's early
charters appear after the point of 'monachization': at least a partial
absorption of the earlier familia in the monastic one, of which
Oswald was abbot and bishop, seems indicated: the year of mona-
chisation is very difficult to determine.

Certainly the communalisation of the funds of the community
must have followed the adoption of the Benedictine rule at Worcester, for this was of the essence of the tenth century reform;[2] there
is no charter evidence to show that the minster had its own mensa
before Oswald's time, as had the Christ Church familia. The exact
apportionment of the bishop's revenue (from lands or jurisdiction)
as between himself and the community is not known: while Oswald
lived as abbot and bishop no such exact apportionment may have
been made. Oswald granted leases of three lives to a few of his
thegns from minster lands, with the consent of the community, and
he made a land grant for three to Æthelstan, the primus (mona-

---

[1] The two post-Conquest chroniclers, Florence of Worcester and William of
Malmesbury, differ as to the fate of the 'married' clerks under Oswald: the former
saying the clerks were expelled, the latter that Oswald used 'holy guile' in using both
monks and clergy for a time together. The late J. Armitage Robinson's argument, that
Oswald for a time maintained two separate communities, is not now accepted: but
his careful study of the Worcester charters in St. Oswald and the Church of Worcester is
of value: see Brit. Acad. Supp. Papers, no. v (1919). See also for the charter evidence
relevant to the Worcester familia the useful discussion in ASWills, pp. 321, 360-
361, 371. Mr. Eric John, in his article on 'St. Oswald and the Tenth Century
Reformation', JEH. ix (1959), 159-172, holds that Oswald expelled the clerks in 964,
holding that some old grant lies behind BCS. no. 1135, which is dated as given in 964,
and which states the expulsion of the clerks as already made and confirms to the
monks in a long and detailed document all the liberties and privileges in the great
triple hundred of Oswaldslow. Hemming, however, the monk who copied the
Worcester charters into his famous cartulary towards the end of the eleventh century,
had no knowledge of this charter and, in order to quote some written authority for
rights long exercised by the church of Worcester, quoted the relevant passages from
Domesday Book. Comparison of the charter with Florence of Worcester's chronicle
suggests rather that Florence was known to the compiler of the charter than vice
versa; and king Edgar's claim in the proem to have conquered part of Ireland and the
most noble city of Dublin suggests the twelfth century rather than a pre-Conquest
source. The date and the reference to a Christmas witan or synod at Gloucester may
have been borrowed from a Worcester version of the ASC.; but it is difficult to set
much reliance on this charter (no. 1135), as it appears to be a twelfth century compilation, of which no portion exists in Hemming; and specially difficult to accept
Wynsige's arrival as a monk trained at Ramsey as early as 964. For Hemming's work,
see T. Hearn's Chartularium ecclesiae Wigornensis, 1723. BCS. no. 1135 itself exists
only in a twelfth century copy: Harl. MS. 7513. See also Mr. Eric John's Land tenure
in early England, 1960, 80-112.
[2] See Eric John, 'The king and the monks', supra, 72.

chorum), and to a later head of the community under him, and to his deacons, diocesan officers. The monastic 'primus', however, and deacons, both needed horses and servants: it is not incongruous that such grants should have been made to monks (see p. 288). The whole question, however, whether bishops with a monastic familia normally used a monk as deacon, or not, is obscure.

Oswald's use and extension of the Benedictine rule was as permanent and successful as that of Æthelwold, though the sites and endowments given him by Edgar were not quite so extensive and valuable as though bestowed on his personal friend and counsellor, Æthelwold. Worcester was very well administered under Oswald, to judge by the careful records of his deacons; the neighbouring sees of Wells and Crediton were 'monachized'. Ramsey became a flourishing and strict Benedictine house, with Winchcombe and Pershore as daughter houses. Germanus, Oswald's friend and also a monk of Fleury, became the first provost of Ramsey under Æthelnoth, and latter abbot of Winchcombe.

The most dangerous opposition to these new Benedictine foundations was aroused, not only from support of the old prebendal system, but antagonism to the new church sokes. The well-born relatives of the dispossessed clerks disliked equally the share in local justice and administration given to the abbots and abbesses. The abbots exercised it through their reeves who presided over certain hundreds of Wessex and Mercia, and the sokes of East Anglia and the Danelaw: and they received the fees and fines which had once gone to the king: the profits of jurisdiction.[1]

The royal grant of jurisdiction had preceded the endowments of the reform under Æthelwold: but not the grant of the whole jurisdiction over a moot. King Alfred granted to the convent of Shaftesbury where his daughter Æthelgeofu 'took the veil on account of bad health' the jurisdiction (soke) over certain separate estates amounting to 100 hides 'as he had held it himself': the right to the fines of obstruction and attacks on a man's house and breach of a man's peace. This did not give the right of holding a court, but only of receiving fines going to the king from certain cases brought up in the moot, presided over still by the king's reeve. But in the

---

[1] Cf. for the effect of the grant of a hundred, Eric John, *Land tenure in early England*, 1960, 113-117.

later grants, the old royal servants who administered justice in the moots, the ealdormen and the king's thegns, were excluded from exercising their old rights and duties over the estates now granted to the new monasteries:[1] the bishop or the abbot were 'burdened with certain judicial and even military obligations formerly discharged by the lay *ministri*'. This seems to have been done by making the bishops (or abbots) in question the heads of hundreds: in the tenth century the principal Anglo-Saxon unit of local government. In later language, the king granted away hundreds to the churches of Worcester and Winchester, etc. In the case of Worcester, bishop Oswald was granted the royal rights over all his tenants, whose separate estates (some of them outside the county of Worcester) amounted to a district half as large as the county itself; it was known later as the 'triple hundred of St. Oswald' or 'Oswaldslow'. The abbot of the re-founded abbey of Medehamstede (Peterborough) on the other hand was granted jurisdiction over eight hundreds in Northants, where more than half of the estates were owned by the abbey. The Peterborough version of the Chronicle, under the year 963, quotes the foundation charter of Medehamstede conferring the eight hundreds, 'with market and toll so freely that neither king nor bishop nor earl nor sheriff shall have any authority, nor any man but the abbot only and his officers'. Similarly, in king Edgar's foundation charter to Ely, he said that as a result of the frequent admonitions of bishop Æthelwold, he had it in mind to endow the monastery at Ely with its own freedom and special honour; he alluded gracefully to Bede's account of the holiness of St. Etheldreda, who lay there to this day in her pure white marble tomb, enumerated the estates granted now to the minster, and 'all the jurisdiction over the fenlands included in the two hundreds, and at Wicklow in East Anglia likewise all the jurisdiction over five hundreds, and the fourth penny of the public penalties paid at Cambridge'. When all accounting was done with sums written in Roman numerals, the processes of division and addition and subtraction were difficult, and not to be worked out by written sums on parchment. From fines going to the crown, the ealdorman took, normally, every third (silver) penny, as payment for his services; it would seem that henceforward at Cambridge, the abbot of Ely's reeve would take every fourth penny.

Active opposition to the new monastic policy was led by Ælfhere,

[1] Eric John, 'The king and the monks', 83.

ealdorman of Mercia, a very great nobleman, and aggrieved because bishop Oswald had handed over the minster at Winchcombe to Germanus, once his fellow monk at Fleury, to train the community as monks. Dispossessed canons from Pershore and other houses in the Severn valley also appealed to Ælfhere; they regarded abbacies and prebends as hereditary. Ælfhere was strong enough to drive out the monks from Evesham, and he is accused of ejecting others from houses in Worcestershire and Gloucestershire. When similar efforts were made to contest the rights of the new monks of Ramsey, Ely and Medehamstede, Ælfhere brought an armed force to support the contestants; but Æthelwine, ealdorman of East Anglia, and Byrhtnoth, ealdorman of the East Saxons, brought their armies against him, and he had to retire. The confusion was resolved when king Edward was murdered at Corfe in 978, and Dunstan withdrew to Canterbury. But though the supporters of the young king Æthelred were hostile to Dunstan, the new Benedictine foundations remained.

To assess the advantage or disadvantage to the English church of the establishment of Benedictine abbeys as the see churches of many bishops, and the great mother churches of many areas, is not quite simple. The religious life by which England had been converted, both in the north and in the south, had been restored, and it was a very potent agent for good. Learning was pursued and cherished, better clergy were educated, a whole vernacular literature was produced for the benefit of lay people. Many small churches were built out in the countryside, and the giving of alms to the poor taught as a foundation virtue. But the price of all this was the pressing of the abbots of great houses into the business of local government. Bishops had had already to concern themselves with the management of their estates, what the charters call their 'hams', and abbots were bound to do this to keep their community fed and clothed; they began now to administer what, after the Norman Conquest, was to be called 'feudal justice'. No one could have called Columba or Benedict Biscop 'a country gentleman': but the way was now open for the Benedictine abbot to become one. It took him about six centuries to become one: and not all Benedictine abbots, then.

The literary memorial which marks the climax and peak of the monastic movement in Edgar's reign: the years when king, reforming bishops, monks and magnates were working closely together and with as yet no open dissentients: was the document published to secure unity of observance in the new monasteries. It was drawn up by Æthelwold and entitled the *Regularis Concordia Anglicae nationis monachorum sanctimonialiumque*, a document of great importance in the history of monks, of the liturgy, and even the pastoral care and education of laymen.

At Æthelwold's desire, and under Dunstan's guidance, the king took over the authorisation and issue of the document, apparently in a year near to 970. Precedents were studied, particularly the royal holding at the palace of Aix, under Louis the Pious, of the great reforming synod of 817, when the canons for the reform of monks and canons had been issued under the imperial authority. The preface to the *Regularis Concordia* (monastic agreement) relates the occasion of its compilation: king Edgar has learned that all the holy communities (coenobia) of his dominions are wasting away and neglected and set about restoring them to their former good estate; he has driven out the negligent clerks with their abominations, and while he himself in fulfilment of his royal office will be as the Good Shepherd to the monks, queen Ælfthryth shall be the protectress of the communities of nuns. He has held a synodal witan (synodale concilium) at Winchester, and sent a letter splendidly written on parchment to the assembly (which implies that, after they have heard it, they will debate as abbots and abbesses among themselves) wherein he humbly advises them all to be of one mind as regards monastic usage, 'lest by an unequal and various use of one rule in one country their holy life shall be brought into disrepute'.

The preamble continues that bishops, abbots and abbesses give thanks that they have had so good a teacher (in the king); they remember the letters of pope Gregory the Great instructing them to use the seemly customs as well of the Gallic churches as the Roman church, and they have summoned monks from St. Benedict's abbey of Fleury and the renowned monastery at Ghent, and gathered much that was good from their praiseworthy customs; and tempering them by the subtle judgment of reason have embodied them in this little book. The whole assembly then, lest they should incur the sin of the Sarabaites (a reference to the Benedictine rule) made a solemn vow to live under the yoke of the rule and carry out these selfsame monastic customs with one uniform observance.

Dunstan the archbishop has confirmed the council of this aforesaid synodal assembly (*praefati synodalis conventus conciliabulum*), adding that no monk of high or low degree should presume to enter the private dwelling places in nunneries (they would celebrate in the nuns' churches). It was further added that the election of abbots and abbesses should be carried out 'with the consent and advice of the king, and according to the teaching of the holy rule', and wherever monks serve a bishop's see church, the election of the bishop shall be carried out in the same way as that of the abbot; the bishop shall then live the monastic life with his monks.

At the time, in England, the king was indeed the defender of the reform against the conservative policy of many of the magnates; the preamble continues at once, after conceding gladly that abbots and abbesses shall be elected 'with the king's counsel', to state that the assembly has forbidden monasteries to acknowledge the over-lordship of secular persons (saecularium prioratum), and this under pain of anathema. (The king has come to be regarded as having a quasi-sacerdotal character, as is indicated in the coronation rite practised by Dunstan: see p. 279.) This distinction between the secular power as exercised by the king and by the ealdormen and thegns, and acceptance of the shield of the royal power, is further indicated in the preamble by the direction that the prayers of inter-cession that are said for the king and benefactors, according to the custom of our forefathers, are not to be chanted too quickly, but distinctly, so that the mind may follow what the voice says, as our father Benedict exhorts us. The *Regularis Concordia*, cap. 18, further lays down that after nocturns (which must end at daybreak), two psalms must be said for the king, and, in later chapters, two more psalms after lauds and after compline.

The body of the *Concordia* is full of detailed regulations about the performance of the opus dei, first (as in the Benedictine rule) in the winter months when the nights are long, then in the summer months (without reference to the monks resting on their beds for the siesta). There are also liturgical directions for the celebration of certain feasts: for the great procession with palms on Palm Sunday, from the church where the palms are kept to the church where the passion is sung and the Palm Sunday mass celebrated; for Holy Thursday, when the antiphon 'Christ the Lord was made obedient even unto death' is sung by the clear voices of two children set on the right hand side of the choir and two on the left hand side, and again by the whole choir of brethren, and when also the Maundy shall be carried out, at which the brethren, singing the proper antiphons shall wash, dry and kiss the feet of poor men, food also being given them. The same day, and on Good Friday, as at the secret sign of a mystery, 'the brethren shall vest and go to the doors of the church bearing with them a staff with the representation of the serpent: there fire shall be struck from flint and blest by the abbot, after which the candle which is set in the mouth of the serpent shall be lit from the fire, and one candle only in the church from the serpent's candle. And so, the staff being borne by the sacrist, all the brethren shall enter the church and one candle shall be lit from that fire.' This ceremony is to be repeated on Good Friday, the dean bearing the staff, and on Saturday, the provost bearing it. (The Old Testament symbol of Christ the Saviour, the serpent raised on a pole by Moses, was regarded with much devotion in these centuries, and a picture of it was brought back by Benedict Biscop for the adornment of the church at Jarrow.) On the three great days of Holy Week, when the New Testament account of the Resurrection could not yet be announced or meditated on, the Old Testament foreshadowing of the redemption could be reverenced by symbolic act. Only one candle may be lit in the church, for in this procession with the mysterious prefiguring symbol of Christ we are still in the half darkness of the Old Testament: the light of Christ has not yet risen.

At the mass said on Holy Thursday, which may be said by a bishop when he consecrates the chrism, communion shall be given to the brethren and to the faithful, and sufficient hosts reserved for all to communicate on Good Friday. After mass the abbot shall carry out his own Maundy, washing the feet of all the brethren, and a senior monk washing his feet. After the washing, the deacon and other ministers shall vest, the deacon wearing a dalmatic and bearing a book of the gospel and preceded by acolytes and thurifer; they shall go in procession to the collation (light meal) in the refectory, where the gospel book is set on a pulpit and the deacon reads the gospel of St. John about the foot washing, with the verse, 'Mandatum novum do vobis'.

The directions for Good Friday include the veneration of the cross, set up before the altar and held by two deacons; the reproaches beginning 'Popule meus' are sung, two sub-deacons singing in Greek, 'Agios o theos, Agios yschiros, Agios athanatos eleison ymas', and the song school singing in Latin: 'Sanctus deus'. They sing 'Pange lingua', the verses of Fortunatus, the cross is unveiled, and the abbot prostrates himself thrice before it, and so the brethren.

On Holy Saturday when the burial of Christ is celebrated, 'if any-one should care or think fit to follow in a becoming manner the practice of certain religious men, which is worthy to be imitated to strengthen the faith of unlearned, common people and the newly baptised: on that part of the altar where there is space for it there shall be the representation of a sepulchre, with a veil hung around it, in which the holy cross, when it has been venerated, shall be placed in due order, during the singing of "I will lay me down in peace" (the words of the compline psalm) and "my flesh also shall rest in hope"; and in imitation, as it were, of the burial of the body of our lord Jesus Christ, they shall sing the antiphon, "When the lord was buried, they sealed the sepulchre". And in that same place the holy cross shall be guarded and watched by the brethren, till the night of the lord's resurrection.'

On the holy day of Easter, the seven canonical hours are to be celebrated by the monks in the manner of canons, out of regard for the authority of blessed Gregory, pope of the apostolic see. . . . The sacrists shall set the cross in its proper place. . . . While the third lesson at nocturns is being read, four of the brethren shall vest; one of them, in an alb, shall go stealthily to the place of the sepulchre and sit there quietly, holding a palm in his hand. And while the third respond is being sung, the other three brethren, in copes and holding censers in their hands, shall enter and go to the sepulchre step by step as if searching: this is in imitation of the angel seated on the tomb and the women coming with sweet-smelling spices to anoint the body of Jesus. When he that is seated shall see the three drawing nigh, he shall begin to sing, softly and sweetly:

'Quem quaeritis'.

And the three shall answer together:

'Jesum Nazarenum'.

Then he that is seated shall say that 'He is not here, he is risen, as he said. Go, say that he is risen from the dead.'

At this command the three shall turn to the choir saying:

'Alleluia. The lord is risen.'

When this has been sung, he that is seated, as though calling them back, shall chant the antiphon: 'Come, see the place', and then he shall rise and lift the veil surrounding the sepulchre, bare now of the cross, but having the linen in which the cross has been wrapped. And the three shall lay down their censers in that same sepulchre, and take the linen and hold it up before the clergy, and, as if showing that the lord is risen and no longer wrapped in it, they shall sing the antiphon, 'The lord is risen from the sepulchre'.

In this act of liturgical devotion, for the benefit, as the *Concordia* says, of the simple and illiterate, the whole series of medieval drama begins. It begins at the night office of a Benedictine monastery, but it becomes part of the Easter vigil of all churches with clergy to celebrate it: the laity watch the three women approaching the angel of the tomb, and for them too the earliest mystery plays and moralities will soon be celebrated.

There is another prescription in the *Concordia* which will, and perhaps even now had, become a rite of concern to all laymen: the prayer when the church bids the Christian soul go forth from this world. As early as the council of Toledo, 399, it had been ordained that only the bishop could bless the holy oil for anointing the sick: so that the final anointing of the dying was made, as it were, by the Twelve themselves; now, the church commended the dying person with the beautiful words: 'Subvenite, sancti dei': 'Come to his help, ye saints of God, hasten to meet him, ye angels of the lord, offering his soul in the sight of the Almighty: may Christ who called thee receive thee, and angels lead thee to Abraham's bosom'. The commendation is here enjoined for a sick monk.

The first Life of Dunstan, written by a scholar who claimed personal knowledge of him, but who wrote seventeen years after his death, is of interest as giving a contemporary estimate of Dunstan's share in the movement for monastic reform, and for a general estimate of his character: even though he professedly wrote in eulogy of his subject.

'The servant of God, Dunstan,' he says, 'shone as the first abbot of the English nation.' While he spent laborious and tedious days at work, his chief energy was given to holy prayers and reciting the psalms of David 'upon a psaltery of ten strings; he conquered sleep to keep vigil in church or zealously gave himself to ecclesiastical business; or even, at the first light of day, he corrected erroneous books, washing out or erasing the misreadings of the scribes. Or with sagacious ability he discerned the false from the true in judging between man and man: or with quiet word he set the implacable and the struggling at one. He gave kindly assistance to widows, orphans, pilgrims and strangers in their necessities, or parted those foolishly and unjustly married with a just separation.... He endowed churches: he seasoned with the salt of his teaching the uninstructed of both sexes, men and women. The whole land of England is enlightened with his holy teaching. Whatever distractions beset him beforehand, he gave his whole mind to singing the mass of the day, as if he spoke to the Lord face to face. On the feast of the Ascension (988) he completed the celebration of mass, and preached three times to the people committed to him, how the Lord, having set free his people, was seen by them to return to the heaven from which he came; and on the following Sabbath day (Saturday), which means the day of rest, the old man went to his everlasting rest in Christ.'[1]

[1] 19th May, 988. The Life quoted is known as B, and described earlier.

CHAPTER XV

RELIGION AND LAY PEOPLE IN THE LATE OLD
ENGLISH PERIOD

FOR all lay people, ealdorman, thegn and peasant, in the late Old English period, the Christian faith and the practices of religion were a built-in part of society. It made no difference whether the layman had any personal sense of possible contact with God or not; whether he was a good man or a bad man: whether he were stupid or intelligent: whether he hung round the ale house and disliked his wife and contemplated pushing her into the mill stream some day (which was, after all, the easiest way of getting rid of a wife), or paid his tithe and followed the procession of the litany and hoped that his five-year-old little Æswige would one day be a little clerk; for to all these men the Christian faith was sure and certain. He might not, like pope Gregory, ever hear time's wingèd chariot echoing near, but certainly before him lay deserts of vast eternity. But this did not depress him, whether he were good or bad: doomsday, the parson said, when the Lord came with fire, and the sun shone seven times brighter than now it shines, would be very alarming; but the saints were kind, all men knew the mild-heartedness of our Lady: there was always confession, for wife-murderers and men going to be hanged, and though no man wanted to be hanged, death was over in a minute, whether you died on the gallows or in your bed; all was not lost, ever.

In a sense, civilisation as well as the Christian faith came to the English peasant in his little wattle and daub house, and the thegn in his hall, through the church. There was, almost certainly, no stone building in the village except the church. Even the church might be of wood; but the inside would be plastered, the walls painted with pictures, the saints and Bethlehem, and the Last Judgment over the rood screen: and embroideries on the altar, and fine coloured silk for the priest's mass-hackle, and a silver dish and cup, well carved, for the housel, and a fine gospel book. The thegn in his hall had plenty of carved wood, for his beam-ends, and perhaps the bench ends for his settle, and his wife had a brooch and bracelets: but the church had the best of it, with its altar furnishings, and the priest could read English books and sing the service in Latin, and the thegn might not be able to read at all. Colour and the beauty of skilled craftmanship were shown to the villager mainly in the village church.

The seasons were measured to him too by the church. Certainly, he could watch the moon wax and wane, and, if he lived by the sea or river mouth, the tides rise and fall; sunset fell earlier and earlier each day till mid-winter's mass night: and then the sun rose earlier and earlier till it up-went to its highest at midsummer; but it was the feasts and fasts of the church that measured time to him in small, manageable portions. From vespers of Saturday till the end of Sunday night was holiday; the Saturday half holiday, as well as the Sunday, were laid down by the church, for a feast day began with its first vespers, the day before. The snow came, and Christmas brought rejoicing till Epiphany; the Lent fast came when food was short enough in any case, and the salt bacon nearly finished, and enough seed corn and beans needing to be kept for the next sowing. The Lent fast was hard: but then, some men starved and died always in a village after a bad harvest; and after a very bad one, men starved all over England. Of the year king Edgar died, 975, the ASC. wrote that 'soon in the autumn of that year appeared the star known as cometa: and the next year came a great famine and many disturbances throughout England'. Little could be done in face of plague and tempest: in 1014, 'on St. Michael's Eve, the swollen, incoming tide swept far and wide through many places in this land; and it ran further inland than it had ever done before, and submerged many homesteads and drowned a countless number of human beings'. Food was, to our minds, perennially short.

Easter came with great rejoicing, and plough alms must be paid, and midsummer with St. John's feast, and our Lady's second feast in mid August. Few men indeed owed a money rent for their holding and therefore quarter days as such meant nothing to them: but the king's chamberlains collected his dues at Michaelmas and after Easter, and Lady Day and St. John's feast and St. Martin's were dates that reeves and the king's officers and the bishop's, too, remembered, for business reasons.

But more than that: the Christian sanctions were built into society

22

by way of oath and ordeal, the ordeal, indeed, being merely one way of using the oath. In a society of villages and small towns, where men's living depended on the crops harvested, the fish caught, the birds snared or hunted with the hawk, and the cloth woven by the women, the national income was very small. There was certainly no margin for a police force in every village, to safeguard law and order. Ploughing was hard bodily work, and reaping even harder: there was no power to be used for any purpose except that of the ox for ploughing, the horse for riding, and the water mill for grinding corn. Because bodily toil was required for so much agricultural work, and indeed nearly every other kind of work, there was no royal or local revenue to supply policemen or prisons, and some means had had to be devised for the keeping of law and order and protection from theft. Prison was only for those who were being swiftly brought to justice: and since there were very few specific 'prisons' (the sheriff might have a cellar or an outhouse he kept for the purpose), such brief imprisonment meant, generally, to remain with hands and feet tied in an outhouse. No sentences of imprisonment for a term of years were, or could be, given: punishment of those convicted of civil or even criminal offences consisted of some sort of composition by money payment, hanging, outlawry, or (in the case of royal justice) the loss of eyes or of a right hand. Beatings were frequently prescribed for offences by slaves (servi).

The difficulty of catching criminals, the normal brutality of punishment, and the lack of any system for the scientific proof of crime by evidence, must all be taken into account in the attempt to understand the importance of the oath in English pre-Conquest society, and the provision of an ordeal rite by the church. To modern minds, the ordeal was shockingly brutal: but it was an age of brutal punishments, regarded then as not unjust, because they left a man alive who probably deserved to die.

In a society without police, the punishment of murder among the Germanic nations used to depend on the blood feud: a man's kin sought out and punished his murderer. This had been prohibited in favour of a money composition in the earliest English laws: a man's 'worth' rested on his 'wer', the price to be paid for killing him. Yet still, in this late Old English period the blood feud was met with, for it was denounced as unchristian in the canons. But in the case of murder or violent injury the criminal would usually be known; what was to be done when a man was accused in the gemot, but denied that he was guilty?

The system of weighing evidence, for and against the accused, had not been devised.

The method of determining guilt actually used was to obtain the affirmation, on oath, of witnesses who declared a man guilty, or innocent; and the value of the oath depended on the status of the oath giver. The oath of a thegn was worth more than the oath of the 'gebur' of the village: the oath of a priest was worth more than the oath of a deacon, that of a deacon more than the oath of a layman. One of Cnut's laws enjoined that everyone, over twelve years of age, should take an oath that he would not be a thief or a thief's accomplice: a trustworthy man, who had never failed in oath or ordeal, was entitled to clear himself when accused within the hundred gemot by a simple oath of exculpation: that is, the accused man must find two men within the hundred ready to take the oath with him that he was innocent. An 'untrustworthy man' with a bad reputation, accused in the hundred gemot, must make the triple oath of exculpation: he must find five oath helpers to swear with him that he is innocent: or else he must go to the ordeal. Before he could be sent to the simple ordeal, three solemn oaths that he was guilty must be made to the hundred moot; six solemn oaths before he could be sent to the triple ordeal.

That is, in the case of certain specified and grave offences, when the oaths of the accusers and the defendants were equal in value, recourse was had to the ordeal to obtain the judgment of God as to who was lying.

The ordeal itself was of pre-Christian origin, as oath-taking itself was pre-Christian: the church accepted the institution and sought to Christianise and regularise it.[1] The rough and popular ordeal of witch ducking and probable drowning had no sanction or authorisation in law or from the church: there are no ecclesiastical forms for it and no secular law mentions it; it was an old, popular piece of mob violence, directed to the ascertaining if a woman were a witch, at a time when the efficacy of a witch's spells was accepted.

A simple and pre-Christian ordeal was offered on lesser accusations to prove truth-telling: a kind of 'This I swear and if I swear falsely may this food choke me'. A piece of trial food (corsnæd), a

[1] See T. F. T. Plucknett, *A concise history of common law*, 1956, 113.

small piece of bread or cheese was offered, and if the oath taker ate it freely and without injury, he was declared innocent. The holy housel was used for this purpose in Christian times, if a priest or clerk could find no oath helpers.

The form for carrying out the simple or triple ordeal is found written out in that Rochester gospel book (the *Textus Roffensis*) which was written between 936 and 1000 and has preserved the text of the earliest laws of the English kings. The ordeal of lifting a stone from a vessel of boiling water and carrying it three paces before dropping it: or lifting a bar of iron from the fire and carrying it the three paces, is understood in the description: as is the carrying out of the terrible rite under the presidency of the priest of the church. The description in the *Textus Roffensis* is in Old English and runs:[1]

And of the ordeal, we enjoin in God's name and in the name of the archbishop and of all the bishops, that no man enter the church after the fire has been brought in with which the ordeal of hot (water or iron) shall be made, except the priest and he who is to go to the ordeal. And there shall be measured nine feet from the stake to the mark, by the measurement of his feet who is to go to the ordeal. And if the ordeal is single, he shall plunge in his hand for the stone up to the wrist, and if the accusation is threefold, up to the elbow. And when the ordeal is ready, two men of either party shall enter and be assured that the water is boiling; as we have said before. And there shall enter the church an equal number of men from both parties to the ordeal (his accusers and his supporters) from outside the church, and they shall be fasting. And the priest shall sprinkle them with holy water, and each shall bow as he receives the holy water, and he shall give them all the book of the holy gospels to kiss and the sign of the cross. And no one shall make up the fire after the blessing has begun; but the iron (of the ordeal) shall lie upon the coals until the last collect; then it shall be laid upon the bars (stapelan). And there shall not be there any word spoken, but busy prayer to God the father almighty that he would deign to make known the truth. (The Latin version adds: And the accused shall drink holy water, and holy water shall be sprinkled on the hand with which he shall carry the ordeal, and so shall he go to it. Three steps shall he take to

[1] See *Die Gesetze der Angelsachsen*, F. Liebermann, 3 vols., 1903, i. 386-389.

cover the nine feet, and then cast down the iron and hasten to the altar.)

And after (the Old English version continues) his hand shall be wrapped and sealed, and on the third day examined whether it be clean within the wrapping. And he who breaketh these laws (lagu), the ordeal is broken, and he shall pay the king 120 shillings fine (wite).

The *Textus Roffensis* has further directions as to the offences for which men shall be sent to the ordeal. For arson and murder (death working), men shall go to the triple ordeal, that weighs three pounds, the ordeal of water or the ordeal of iron, which the accuser wills. If he cannot support his oath (by the ordeal), it shall be left to the judgment of the elders who belong to his town (byrig) whether he shall have his life or not. A long list of further penalties, not involving the ordeal, follows.

Terrible as the ordeal was, it showed an effort of the church to control the procedure. It was not simply 'open to the public' intent on viewing horrors: only those who swore the oath of accusation or exculpation, the priest, and him who went to the ordeal were admitted; two men of either party to be assured that the water was boiling: then an equal number of accusers and oath helpers, 'from outside the church'. Then, the decision whether the hand or arm which had endured the ordeal were 'clean' or not at the unwrapping, rested with the priest.

The solemnity of oath-taking, as a foundation of social order, was further enhanced by the taking of the oath 'on the relics', and therefore in the special presence of the saint whose relics rested there, and with the likelihood that he would punish perjury. Every oath sworn before the altar was sworn by the relics that lay beneath it: and an oath taken (with the hand resting on the capsa or shrine containing the saint's relics) was a very solemn attestation that a man spoke the truth. The precursor, in Old English society, of the feudal oath, was the oath of personal loyalty (the hold oath), taken upon the relics. The *Textus Roffensis* has a direction:

How a man shall swear. By the Lord, before whom these relics are holy, I will be true to (name) and love all that he loveth and shun all that he shuns (ascuniath).

The value set on the sanctity of the oath sworn on the relics, as in the presence of God and the saint, was one outcome of the veneration of the saints, and expectation of help from them that was part of every layman's religion at the time. It was popular veneration indeed that led to canonisation, now only enacted with the approval of the local bishop, and still without confirmation by the papal see.

Canonisation of the martyrs in the first ages of the Church's history had been a spontaneous act of the local community,[1] operating automatically. The faithful buried the martyr's body in the cemetery outside the town, or even by the wayside, and met there afterwards annually, to celebrate the martyr's anniversary, his birthday in heaven (dies natalicius). The action was purely popular, for the martyr's heroic death was known to all, and no inquiry was needed.

It was in the African church, of wide territorial extent, and divided by schism, that inquiry by the church, involving legislation and authorisation, began. Fifth century African councils condemned those who venerated the relics of uncertain martyrs and declared that authority for dealing with the veneration of relics rested with the bishop of the see; some investigation should be made as to the identity of the supposed martyr's body and the cause for which he had died: dreams and vain revelations should not be accepted as evidence. The church was not hostile to the cult of the martyrs, but Roman prudence demanded to be assured that it was in fact the body of a martyr that was venerated, and that he died for Christ in the catholic faith and not as a schismatic. Another African canon laid the foundation of the future office of the martyr in the words: 'Let it be lawful to read the passions of the martyrs when their anniversary days are celebrated'.

Before the Peace of the Church, two more classes of saints were added to those whom the faithful might venerate: confessors, tormented in the persecutions but not killed, and those who practised heroic virtue, as, for instance, ministering to the sick in the plague, 'seeming in no respect to come behind martyrdom'. It is possible that some Welsh place names embodying the equivalent of 'martyrium' commemorate the burial place of a saint 'ad martyras', a phrase meaning simply, the cemetery. Gradually, many types of Christian virtue

---

[1] See E. W. Kemp, *Canonization and authority in the western church*, 1948, for the history of canonisation.

came to be regarded as meriting veneration: great asceticism, defence of the faith, and the pastoral work of a good bishop. For the veneration of the relics of such saints, no formal authorisation was needed in the Merovingian period, though bishops, as earlier, sometimes investigated and gave decisions.

The Germanic invasions and migrations in the fifth and sixth centuries were responsible for many translations of a saint's relics, and for the breaking down of the stricter Roman discipline about veneration. The practice began of 'elevating' a saint's relics from the ground outside the church, or a humble position within it, to some altar tomb, or shrine in some connexion with the altar: a movement important in the architectural development of churches. Such a solemn 'raising to the altar', as in the case of the raising of St. Ætheldreda (Æthelthryth) of Ely (see above, p. 205), was made with or without a bishop's blessing. Episcopal inquiry and authorisation before such a raising became necessary, however, among the Franks in the later Merovingian period, when church building and missionary effort, dependent on financial advantage, were found to follow the discovery of the relics of some hitherto unknown martyr in the vicinity of the new church. In such cases, the bishop was sometimes asked to inquire and bless; he usually, in fact, investigated with a hopeful mind! At other times, the dream of some anchorite or holy lady that the bones found were indeed those of a saint was held a sufficient guarantee.

By the end of the ninth century, the actual translation of the body of the saint may be regarded as the formal act of canonisation, whether the bishop had sanctioned and, on occasion, the diocesan synod had been consulted, or not; but episcopal blessing was now usually obtained. The Carolingian reform had brought with it a revival of the older Roman discipline. As one of Charlemagne's capitularies, of 805 or 806, put it:

About churches, or saints newly found without authority: they shall by no means be venerated without the bishop's authority.

Which amounted to a refusal to authorise the discovery of an unknown saint in the vicinity of the church whose building was proposed: a practice which had been very useful in the reconversion of Muslim Spain from the north, or even among the eastern Franks. The council of Mainz, 813, again, had summed up the requirements for the authorisation of a translation: the advice of the prince, and the leave of the sacred synod of the bishop. Up to the time of the issue of Gratian's Decretum (the great code of canon law) in 1140, and even in the Decretum, canonisation was still regulated by the local bishop, his synod and the synod of the metropolitan.

This can be seen in the case of English canonisations. Celtic place names embodying a saint's name are not evidence of any formal canonisation, but only that the 'llan' or minster, or its small cell, had been founded or used by the saint. St. Augustine was venerated from the time of his death at Canterbury, as were the relics of Aidan, Hilda and other early Anglo-Saxon saints, all without process. Archbishop Cuthbert and his metropolitan synod decreed the veneration of St. Boniface in England in 755. When Swithun's miracles were reported to king Edgar, it was he who took the initiative in requiring bishop Æthelwold to have the relics raised to the altar.

All the saints canonised in England in the pre-Conquest period, were, as elsewhere, venerated without any papal authorisation or confirmation of the act. There were, of course, early cases of papal canonisation on the Continent: but requests for papal canonisation only became frequent in the pontificate of Urban II (1088–1099).

The history of canonisation is thus mentioned, as a response to a lay desire to venerate a saint's relics, and a belief in a saint's power to help and heal. The ASC. wrote under the year 994:

> In this year on the Nativity of St. Mary (Sept. 8) came Anlaf and Swein to London with ninety-four ships, and they were there attacking the city (borough) ceaselessly and they even intended to burn it down: but there they met with greater harm and evil than ever they thought the townsfolk could have done them. For God's holy Mother on that day showed the townsfolk her mild-heartedness, and saved them.

This was, to the chronicler, a miraculous deliverance: but often the miracle was to the individual, who might indeed expect it, as a Christian invoking a Christian patron.

Kings were as devout to the saints as peasants, and cherished their relics. They visited the famous shrines of saints, as Athelstan, when he went north, visited St. Cuthbert and made offerings. The priests who accompanied them (for an Anglo-Saxon king seldom stayed more than a fortnight in one place, and often only a night or two) were called their chaplains (capellani), a word derived from the 'capa' or cloak of St. Martin of Tours, the most famous relic in France. The 'capellanus' was the guardian of a relic chest or portable shrine, for both the Frankish and English kings always had their relics with them on their journeys, and even when they went into battle.

For the Anglo-Saxon kings, their relics were their 'halidom' (haligdom): the first duty of the bishops or priests who accompanied them as their chaplains was to guard their relics.[1] Asser for some years accompanied king Alfred as his chaplain, and he relates how Alfred, having apportioned his revenue to secular and sacred uses, desired also to divide his time, giving half of it, as far as business and bodily infirmity permitted him, both by day and by night, to the service of God. Time was divided in those days naturally between the night, which ran from sunset to sunrise, and the day, which ran from sunrise to sunset: but Alfred desired to have a day of twenty-four hours, divided into six equal portions. He ordered his chaplains to have made six wax candles, weighing '2 pounds of silver pennies', so that the six candles might burn in succession before his relic shrine and last for twenty-four hours: a fresh candle was to be lit at the end of each four hour period, day and night, by the chaplains. They became the guardians of the king's time as well as his relics. The most precious of Alfred's relics would seem to have been the relic of the holy cross sent him by pope Marinus (see p. 257). It has been suggested that the famous Alfred Jewel, with the eastern design of king with rod and sceptre, was a reliquary for wearing on the breast: it may, on the other hand, be merely a secular ornament.

King Athelstan, a great military commander, ardently desired the support and prayers of the saints behind him, and he was a great collector of relics. He founded the new minster at Exeter, and the Anglo-Saxon account of this foundation states that he sent true and discreet men over sea and they travelled as far and wide as they might, and obtained the most dearworthy treasure that might be gathered together on earth, for it was a halidom the greatest that might be gathered from places far and wide. He then bestowed the

---

[1] The word 'shrine' is derived from 'scrinium', originally a desk and pre-eminently the desk of the notaries. The king's chaplains would travel round with a 'scrinium', using it in his various halls. They would keep documents in it: king Æthelred's confirmation of Æthelric's will (997) implies that documents and relics were both kept in the 'scrinium': the confirmation ends: 'There are three of these documents: one is at Christ Church, another at the king's halidom, the widow has the third'. ASWills, no. 16 (2).

third part of this halidom upon the minster of St. Peter at Exeter.
And the most precious of these relics was a relic of the holy cross.
The Anglo-Saxon and Latin list of relics was written into the great
Exeter book of bishop Leofric, and it includes relics of Celtic saints,
Breton and Cornish, as well as the great saints of Italy and western
Europe.

The Peterborough version of the ASC. again illustrates the value
attached to obtaining the protection of the saints through possession
of their relics. Under the year 1013, after a long account of the
miseries suffered from Danish attack, when Swein had so disastrously
defeated the English earls and ealdormen that even the citizens of
London 'submitted and gave hostages, because they were afraid he
would destroy them'; when king Æthelred and his queen fled to
Normandy and 'at this time nothing went right for this nation,
neither in the south nor in the north: Ælfsige, abbot of Peterborough,
who had accompanied the queen to Normandy, went to the
monastery called Bonneval, where the body of St. Florentine lay'.
He found the house poor, for it had been pillaged by the Danes: and
he bought from the abbot and monks the body of St. Florentine for
five hundred pounds (a very great sum): and he gave it on his return
as an offering to Christ and St. Peter.

The history of St. Gudwal, and that of the translation of his relics,
and the passage of his cult to England in the tenth century, illustrates
the long story of the veneration of saints in England. The parish
church of Finstall in Worcestershire is today dedicated to 'St. God-
wald', a Flemish form of the name of a Breton saint; and it is
significant that it was the cathedral of Worcester, a great focus of the
tenth century reform, that received a relic of the saint from Ghent
and made the dedication of the church at Finstall.

Gudwal[1] was a great Celtic monk-bishop of south Brittany: he
was a contemporary of St. Cadoc and St. Samson of Dol. His Celtic
monastery (in Wales it would have been called a llan) was at Locoal-
Mendon: he was venerated chiefly at his place of burial at the
adjacent Plec, and also throughout the see of Vannes. His name
Gudwal goes back to the same Celtic root as the common Welsh
personal name, Idwal, and occurs in the genealogies of both the

[1] For the best modern study of his life, see Max Förster's *Zur Geschichte des
Reliquienkultus in Altengland, Sitzungsberichte der Bayerischen Akademie der Wissenschaften*, 1943, Heft 8, p. 47, which has much information about Celtic saints. For a
more popular study of Gudwal, see G. H. Doble, *Saint Gudwal or Gurwal*, 1933.

kings of the Isle of Man and a line of Welsh kings: but it occurs also
in a line of Breton kings, where a king Judwal was the friend of St.
Samson of Dol (d. 565). All the dedications to St. Gudwal are in
south Brittany, and his Life states that he was of royal birth: but his
exact relationship to king Judwal is not known. He and his followers
lived partly in a monastery on the island of Locoal, in the sea of Etel,
off the south Breton coast, and partly on the adjacent mainland; he
had no territorial see, but travelled as a Celtic bishop from preaching
station to preaching station. He was buried at Plec, where he had once
lived as an anchorite: and the 'fratres' of his monastery must have
read some short account of his life and miracles at the night office of
his dies natalis for at any rate the name Plec was preserved by such
means.

When the tenth century brought a renewal of the Danish raids, the
fratres of his monastery took up the saint's coffin and bore it away
for safety. They travelled eastwards through north France. It was a
dangerous age and, just as in Æthelred's reign in England, men fasted
and went in procession to the church, singing the litany and imploring the help of the saints, so in Brittany they called for help to the
great apostles and the saints of the martyrology, and to the Celtic
saints, who were, no doubt, nearer at hand. They cried aloud:

Sancte Samsóne (who had come from Britain to Brittany)
    Ora pro nobis
Sancte Gílda (who wrote history and died in his Breton
    monastery)
    Ora pro nobis
Sancte Cadóce (who worked in Cornwall and Brittany)
    Ora pro nobis
Sancte Maclóue (St. Malo)
    Ora pro nobis
Sancte Paúle (St. Paul Aurelian)
    Ora pro nobis
Sancte Guidgále (who was St. Gudwal)
    Ora pro nobis.

The journey of the fratres with Gudwal's bones took years, just as
the Lindisfarne monks wandered for years with St. Cuthbert's coffin.
Gudwal's fratres were received at length by the great reforming
abbot, Gérard de Brogne, at the monastery of Blandinium in Ghent,

and on June 6, 955, the relics of St. Gudwal were solemnly raised to the altar. The monastery of Blandinium was dedicated to St. Peter, but St. Gudwal and St. Bertulf, whose relics were received at the abbey at the same time, became the two special patrons of the abbey, and many miracles were worked. The fratres of Gudwal could tell the monks of Ghent very little about their holy founder's life: but a sermon was preached at the translation and a Life was composed soon after; one of the stories of Gudwal's Life, characteristic of the Celtic sense that to the Christians all nature and all animals were helpful and friendly, was that when a great storm threatened to wreck his cave monastery, the fishes built a barrier of sand to protect it.

The year of Gudwal's translation, 955, was also the year of Dunstan's visit to Blandinium, and whether or not he was present, he certainly knew that Gudwal was now the holy patron of the great reforming abbey. Relics of St. Gudwal were at some time procured, and venerated later at Exeter and Worcester. The sermon at Gudwal's translation related how king Athelstan had sent a certain thief called 'Electus' to steal Gudwal's coffin during its journeying: that he succeeded, but when count Arnulf of Flanders heard of this, he pursued the robbers and recovered the relics. This story is unlikely to be true: for the earliest relic list of Athelstan's minster of Exeter does not include a relic of St. Gudwal: but it shows that the mission sent by Athelstan to acquire relics was remembered in Flanders, and not with pleasure.

The saintly bishop, Wulfstan II of Worcester (1062–1095), had, however, acquired a relic of Gudwal: he dedicated his episcopal hospice at Worcester to him, when he rebuilt his cathedral. The stone, basilican, church which Oswald had built at Worcester had been plundered and burned in the Danish raids: though the halidom may have been saved. Wulfstan had to clear the ground of the ruins of Oswald's church, and he stood and wept tears of regret for the great men whose work he was clearing away. He dedicated the chapel of the hospice he built beside the church to St. Gudwal, and such dedication implies the possession of a relic. The devotion was now, not so much to a Celtic saint, as to the patron of the reformers at Ghent. Gudwal's name occurs in the Worcester antiphoner,[1] and the chapel at Finstall which preceded the present parish church

[1] See the 'Antiphonaire monastique de Worcester', in *Paléographie Musicale*, xii (1922).

and was dedicated to St. Gudwal, was on the lands of Worcester cathedral.

The cult of St. Gudwal at Exeter existed from the time of bishop Leofric, the Lotharingian chaplain of the Confessor. The name of Gudwal, at any rate, occurs in the Latin relic list written into the Leofric Missal in the time of bishop Osbern. It was usual to recite the list when the relics of the cathedral were carried in procession, and possibly some of the names of the earlier Anglo-Saxon list were difficult for the Norman priests to chant aloud: a new Latin list was prepared.[1]

The veneration of relics then, and the solemnity of the oath taken upon them, had become by the mid eleventh century a national institution, part of the religious background. In view of this, the story of how Harold swore oaths of loyalty to duke William of Normandy on the relics of the saints, and broke them in opposing William's claim to succeed Edward the Confessor, was a most useful diplomatic justification for the Norman invasion and conquest. In the climate of opinion of the day, Harold was an oath breaker. The Bayeux tapestry represents Harold as taking the oath upon the relics; and the magnificent piece of work was designed to hang upon the walls of the relics' chapel at Bayeux.[2]

Of even greater popular importance than supplying a sanction for oath takers was the belief that prayer before the saint's relics, or some sort of physical contact with the relics, might be followed by a miracle of healing. Scientific medicine was in its infancy and those who had recourse to physicians were unlikely to receive much benefit; but there was good hope that the saints would effect a cure. The lessons read about the saint at the night office preceding his feast would record, above all, his miracles, and they were commonly miracles of healing. There were endless stories of how the poor and indigent were healed of their diseases: for here the rich man had no advantage: crowds of the poor, the sick and the needy sought the shrines of the saints and hoped for healing. Of the saints it was told that they had healed the sick in their lifetime: it was confidently hoped that after death they would obtain from God the cure of their suppliants.

[1] See F. E. Warren, The Leofric Missal as used in the cathedral of Exeter, 1883; Förster, Reliquienkultus, 50.
[2] See Sir Frank Stenton, 'The historical background', in the Phaidon ed. of The Bayeux Tapestry, 1957, 9.

St. Swithun of Winchester had been the great healer of Æthel-wold's day; the martyred archbishop Ælfheah became the great hope of those seeking a miracle in the first half of the eleventh century. The ASC. relates, under the year 1012, how the Danes were enraged with the archbishop, whom they had seized at Canterbury, and who would not offer them money or ransom; 'they led him to their tribunal on Saturday evening, within the octave of Easter . . . and one of them smote him on the head with an iron head of an axe, so that he sank down and his holy blood fell upon the earth, and his holy soul went to God's kingdom'. Then the bishop of London and the citizens received his body and buried it in St. Paul's church, 'where now God makes manifest the miracles of the holy martyr'. In 1023, when Cnut was king and times were better, the lady Emma and her son Harthacnut, had the body of Ælfheah borne with great honour to Christ Church, Canterbury, and buried on the north side of Christ's altar, 'with great pomp and rejoicing and hymns of praise . . . to the glory of God and the honour of the holy archbishop and eternal salvation of all those who daily resort there to his holy body with devout heart and all humility'.

Another Christian feature of Anglo-Saxon life was the practice of almsgiving. Society as a whole was poor: even the king's revenue sufficed only for defence and justice, and not very adequately for these. There was no organisation for social relief, apart from the duty of feeding the hungry, caring for the sick and burying the dead, taught by the church to men of all ranks. On bishops the duty of caring for widows and orphans and the poor in general was specially enjoined. Kings and ealdormen and thegns were expected to give some food alms at every meal: the village priest had a special duty to the poor: to give alms to the poor was enjoined as a duty to every individual: but the alms were given by distribution, or in individual cases, rather than in permanent institutions on any large scale.

Almsgiving was thought of as almost solely needed for the sick, the aged and bedridden and child orphans: of work there was no shortage. Most men worked on the land, and the land in this peasant society was always in need of labour. While the lord's demesne had been worked of old by the rent-labour of the gebur, it had now become fairly common for the lord to hire men at a money wage to supplement their labour: for the whole and healthy, work was to be had. But the lot of the injured, the maimed, the helpless, was very precarious. The church taught that Christian men owed a special duty to the poor.

The secular laws, as well as canonical teaching, enjoined alms-giving in general, and on particular occasions. The code known as VII Æthelred was drawn up (bet. 1000 and 1006) at a time when 'the great army of the Danes came to the country', and a great effort to obtain divine help against them was ordered. All men must go out in procession singing the litanies: they must 'go out with the relics (halidom) and call earnestly to Christ'. They must keep a three days' fast, eating no meat, 'and all the food which each would enjoy if this fast were not prescribed for him shall be zealously distributed after the fast, for the love of God, among the needy and the bedridden and the afflicted'. Those who did not observe the fast should pay a heavy fine (30 pence for each householder was a heavy fine) and that too should be distributed. In another clause the code enjoined that all the king's friends should ever 'comfort and feed the poor of God (Godes thearfan)'; and that if money payments had to be made for religious offences, as fixed by the secular law, it was proper that such pay-ments should be made for the relief of the poor (thearfena).

Back in the days of pope Gregory and Augustine it had been accepted that a third of the offerings made by the faithful at mass should go to the poor, and a sixth century bishop would expect to use a large part of such a third in the maintenance of a 'xenodochium' or 'hospitium', where strangers and pilgrims could be received and food distributed at times to the poor. It is likely that some such hostel was maintained from the earliest times at Canterbury, for it was in accordance with canonical practice: but there is almost no evidence for the maintenance of episcopal hostels in early England, and when the bishop himself and his familia lived in small huts adjoining the church and procedure was informal, it is hardly to be expected that we should know whether the bishop maintained a special guest-hut or guest-barn, or put up pilgrims and distributed food in his own quarters. It is likely that by the tenth century reform good bishops had some special building for alms and strangers, and that monasteries of monks and nuns had some such arrangements. The Chrodegangian rule laid down that nuns must have such an almshouse at the gates of the monastery. There is some evidence that monks and nuns and even the larger parish churches maintained bedesmen or 'matricularii':

'almsmen' (ælmesmann) were such poor; but there is little direct evidence as to which churches maintained them, or how many. Most of the alms given to the poor must have been in food: given by the individual or distributed by the parish priest.

Casual references in homilies and saints' lives witness to the value ascribed to generous almsgiving. The ASC. for 1021 describes Ælfgar the bishop as 'the charitable: the almsful'. 'We may tell by a man's almsgiving how good his soul is', says one writer, and the story of how St. Martin gave as alms to the beggar his own cloak was frequently told. To the Anglo-Saxon Christian, the beggar had, as it were, the right to ask for alms. Bishops, it was said, should daily deal alms to the hungry: no greater blame could be laid on any man than to say: 'Almsgiver was he never'.

The homilies of Wulfstan are full of exhortations to almsgiving: with so many homes wrecked by the Danes, and the battles between pro-Danish thegns and the forces of the English ealdorman, there must have been many homeless and hungry to feed. 'I will', wrote Wulfstan, 'that ye daily deal alms to almsmen and the poor'; and he exhorted that a third part of the people's alms should be given to the poor. 'Each alms-right that man owes to God should be paid.' 'I bid that ye daily deal alms, even if it be but a fourth part of an alms-loaf'; priests should exhort men to give alms, and they themselves should distribute them, and exhort the poor to pray for them that gave the alms. The Blickling Homilies exhorted: 'Break thy loaf to the needy', and elsewhere 'alms work' is enjoined: 'It is a good act to set one stone in a muddy place, that the almsmen may pass over on dry ground'. The almsmen would be, it is implied, old or feeble or in some way disabled.

Apart from individual food giving and the common distribution of part of the cooked meal to the poor crowding at the back of a thegn's hall (and much more, of the king's hall), certain feastings, of a modest sort by modern standards, accompanied ecclesiastical occasions. The word 'bride ale' speaks for itself: and a canon ordered priests who attended a wedding feast not to attend the drinking afterwards. Various public acts were ordained to take place at the church door, among them, the giving of the marriage promises and the blessing by the priest: king Alfred's *Pastoral care* speaks of marriages as made 'before the church door'. The feasting and drinking would seem to have been done at the ale-house afterwards; the hanging out of a 'bride bush' before the door for such a feast may have been as early as this period.

Funerals, too, had their appropriate feast, for those who had said mass for the dead man, or said the psalter for him, if they were laymen. Wills frequently mention also the feeding of so many poor men, as an act of charity which the testator desires to provide for, for the good of his soul.

The wills of the period not infrequently include among the alms to be given for various purposes the feeding of a certain number of poor men. The ætheling Athelstan in his will of 1014–1015 granted certain property to the monks of Ely, and a hundred pence to be given to that monastery and a hundred poor people to be fed there ever on St. Etheldreda's mass day.[1] The royal lady Ælfgifu in her will made between 967 and 975 granted the surplus of her property after great legacies to the bishop and abbot (of Winchester) 'for the repair of the foundation and for them to distribute (deal) for me among poor men'.[2] Brihtric and Ælfswith his wife bequeathed between 973 and 987 great estates to Christ Church, their kinsmen, etc.: certain lands went to the brothers Wulfstan Ucca and Wulfsige, and also 'forty mancuses of gold to distribute (deal) for us and our ancestors, and the same for Wulfsige to distribute: and may they have to account with God, if they do not do it'.[3] Other wills provide ale and meat clearly intended for the funeral feast: Wulfgeat of Donington, probably before 994, bequeaths with his burial fee to Worcester a brewing of malt; and four or two bullocks each to Hereford cathedral, St. Guthlac's, Leominster, Clifton, Wolverhampton, Penkridge and Tong. The feast would be for the priests who said mass, clerks who said the psalter, and almsmen who prayed.[4]

Another Christian practice enjoined by the church was the freeing of 'servi', literally, 'slaves', and very different in social scale from the 'geburs', who were the freemen of the village, holding their land and their rights by virtue of their labour services on the lord's demesne. Labour service, when the supply of coined money and the precious metals was so very small, was not held degrading: the eldest son of the gebur inherited his father's holding as a valued right. But the 'servus' was in a quite different category. Originally, he had been a war captive, the property of the warrior who might have taken his

[1] ASWills, no. 20. [2] Ib. no. 9. [3] Ib. no. 11. [4] Ib. no. 19.

23

life, but had saved it: he and his children became the property of his personal conqueror.

But by this time slavery, the state of being a servus, was usually acquired as a severe legal punishment, or inability to pay a very severe wite or legal fine. The wife and children of the new 'servus' shared his status; all of them became commonly the household servants or the estate servants of their new lords. To sell a Christian into slavery to a heathen was condemned by the church; to own servi was tolerated, though to free them was an almsdeed, a good act. The punishment indeed, compared to the modern one of imprisonment for a long term of years, was for the criminal or defaulter himself much preferable: he lived with his wife and children and as part of a household and a village community; his wages and food allowances were laid down by the custom of the estate or the household. But to be born of servile birth was very hard.

The lady Wynflæd made a will about 950, freeing certain serfs by name.[1] She may possibly have been a lay-abbess connected in some way with the nunnery of Shaftesbury: she may have been a widow who had taken a vow of chastity, for she refers once to her 'nun's clothing': she had considerable estates. One paragraph of her will runs:

> And Wulfwaru is to be freed and she is to serve whom she pleases ... and Wulfflæd is to be freed ... And she bequeaths (i.e. they are not to be freed) to Eadgifu a woman-weaver and a seamstress, the one called Eadgifu and the other called Æthelgifu. . . .

Then follow the names of 29 other men and women, with the villages where they live, who are to be freed; and the paragraph ends: 'And if there be any penally enslaved man besides those whom she has enslaved, she trusts to her children that they will release him for her soul's sake'.

Bishop Ælfsige of Winchester (951 to 958) freed in his will each penally enslaved man on the episcopal demesne.[2] The lady Æthelflæd in her will ordered that 'half my men in every village be freed for my soul'.[3] Archbishop Ælfric in his will similarly enjoined that 'after his day every penally enslaved man who was condemned in his time be set free'.[4] The lady Wulfwaru's will, drawn up after 984, provided

[1] ASWills, no. 3. [2] Ib. no. 4. [3] Ib. no. 14. [4] Ib. no. 18.

that twenty servi should be freed, half in the east and half in the west, of her estates.[1]

To come back from Christian activities and features of society to the local churches, where the Christian faith was taught, and the Christian sacraments received. The church that had a parish, a shrift shire, would also have a churchyard for burial: 'church hedge' (church 'haga' is sometimes found for cemetery). By this time, a church might well have small transepts, and a central tower, not very lofty, with a bell. The village priest, who had earlier lived in many cases in a chamber over the porch, would now have his own small house, no grander than the wattle and daub cottages of the villagers, and his glebe land (acre strips in the common fields) would be worked for him by a villager; he might well do some field work himself, and help with the haymaking or harvesting. It was his duty to keep his church in repair, and particularly the roof, and to see that the altar vessels and altar books were properly kept. The distinction between repairing the chancel and repairing the body of the church was not yet laid down; the thegn of the village might be expected to help with maintenance of the church, particularly as he or his ancestors had probably built it, and he regarded it as his family property.

Unless the village were in the shrift shire of a large or small minster, the village church would in most cases have been built by the thegn or his ancestors, and the church would be, as it were, part of the estate. The church might, of course, be in the patronage of the distant bishop or king: but most of the smaller churches belonged to the local thegn. Even a small minster of one or two priests might be, as it were, the property of the thegn or ealdorman who had built it: and since secular and spiritual matters were dealt with in the king's laws, and the laws enforced by secular and spiritual officers: so, in village life it was equally the duty of priest and thegn to see that secular and spiritual obligations were fulfilled. No offence was given, at the time, at the lay 'possession' of churches. Villagers and priest and thegn lived together and got on with the business of keeping themselves alive (a very tiring enterprise at the time) and serving God and his saints. It would arouse no surprise, even after all had

---

[1] ASWills, no. 21. It is not clear that in some later wills, such as no. 32, which require that 'half the men are to be free', the clause refers to the freeing of 'servi'. Cf. no. 34.

been said about hereditary minsters in the tenth century reform, that a good lady should 'set free' her minster, her family possession, in her will: or that the will should transfer ownership from the lady's family to the clergy of the minster. The lady Leofgifu, for instance, confirmed the grant of a small minster at Colne to Æthelric the priest, Ælfric the priest and Æthelsige the deacon: Ælfric the priest to have the position in which Ægelnoth was, 'so that he may be the guardian of the minster who is above all others'. The lady Leofgifu's husband had not only 'possessed' the small minster at Colne; she herself had a domestic chaplain as well: she made a bequest to Ailric, 'my hird priest'.[1]

When ealdormen, thegns and their ladies had so much church property as a private possession (and with normally no complaints about misuse), it was natural that bishops should draw no very clear line between the landed estates of the see and land they might have bought, or inherited. On lands of the see where earlier bishops had built churches, possession of both would pass to the succeeding bishops. The will of Ælfric II, bishop of Elmham (or East Anglia) from 1030–1038, is of interest as showing the dispositions made by an eleventh century bishop. Ælfric made an oral statement before witnesses as to how his property should go, and, as was normal, caused an Old English 'noticia' to be written down of his wishes. He left considerable property to the monks of Bury St. Edmunds and an estate to 'Leofstan' the dean there, and, among other bequests, five pounds to his kinsman Wulfweard the monk; 30 acres at Egmere to Ælfwine, his priest at Walsingham, 'and Ufi the provost is to have the rest'. Edwin the monk was to have the mill at Guist; 'the fen which Thurloe gave me' was to go to the refectory of the priests at Elmham, and 'the priests at Hoxne' were to have other fenland. 'And I grant the haga in Norwich to St. Edmunds', and the haga in London to St. Peters. (Haga was the term lawyers translate 'messuage': a fenced plot, with the single-roomed frontage of the house on the street, and a small yard at the back.) The bishop had a house, that is, in Norwich and in London, but they were apparently his own property and he did not leave them to his successor, but to the minsters of St. Edmundsbury and Peterborough.[2]

To the villager, or the burgess of Norwich or Elmham, it made little difference whether it was the king or the bishop or the abbot of

---

[1] ASWills, no. 29. Hird = familia.   [2] Ib. no. 26.

Ramsey or his own local thegn who owned his church. He heard his news from the inn, owed certain services to his landlord the thegn and his reeve, and depended for the welfare of his soul and much of the interest of life on the village church and its priest. Many hints in literature and a few architectural survivals show that the walls of churches were often painted, for the exposition of the faith. The commonest subjects would be Bethlehem and the Last Judgment: for the unlearned, the beginning and the end of the Christian dispensation, and nowadays a fine carving or painting of the Crucifixion was becoming common.

The church at Breamore (Hants) may be instanced as an example of a medium-sized church, built in the late Old English period with a certain lavishness of structure and decoration: to the villager, a very fine church. Breamore is on the western edge of the New Forest, north of the present Fordingbridge. There is no record of its original building, but the fact that village and church were bestowed by the conqueror William on one of his followers suggests that Breamore had earlier belonged to the crown: it had been in the Forest area, though the place name suggests moorland on the edge of the Forest. The church was complete by 1040 (the date accepted by experts for the painting of the crucifixion over the south door),[1] and was cruciform in plan, with a narrow, lofty nave, a short chancel and a north and south porticus at the east end of the nave; the crossing was marked by four rounded arches, narrower than nave or porticus, and stone supports remain to show that a wooden bell tower surmounted the arches. Above the main entrance door on the south side of the nave at the west end was carved a singularly beautiful figure of Christ on the cross, in the style of the Winchester illuminators, with the extended arms arched, the body curved, and the pose suggesting the head drooping or bending to the side, as if to gaze at the church-goer entering beneath. The carving has been at some time cut away, so that only the outline of the figure, light against the dark, broad cross, remains.[2] The Virgin and St. John stand at a little distance beside the cross. The building of a porch outside this west door obscures the importance of the original design: but it is clear that the intention of the 'artifex' of the church was to present to those who entered the, as it were, welcoming figure of the Redeemer.

The inner side of the stone arches under the tower received at some

---

[1] Rice, 99. [2] See Rice, fig. 16a.

time an interesting inscription in Anglo-Saxon lettering, characters which might as regards their form be pre-Conquest, but equally may have followed a manuscript tradition and be somewhat later. At some point in Henry I's reign (i.e. before 1135), the patron of Breamore church, sir Baldwin de Redvers, and his uncle Hugh bestowed the church of Breamore in alms upon the canons regular, and the king confirmed the grant, further bestowing on the canons certain rights of pasture within the New Forest and pannage for pigs without payment.[1] The actual record of royal confirmation was retained by the king's chancery: but a 'Noticia' of the grant of the church seems to have been carved on the central arches within the church. When the round Norman arches, which much constricted the view of the chancel, were taken down in the fifteenth century, wide, flat perpendicular arches being substituted, one arch, with the beginning of the inscription, was left;[2] and one stone with three Anglo-Saxon letters was used in rebuilding the chancel arch. It is clear that one arch of the original four was allowed to remain because it had the opening of the original inscription, which was not meant as an aid to worship (the worshippers, indeed, could not read), but as a legal record.[3] The inscription runs:

Here is notice given of the agreement which
(HER SWUTELATH SEO GECWYDRÆDNES THE)

'Swutelath' is the technical legal term for 'notice given', 'swutelung' for evidence or proof, and the recording of a 'noticia' normally uses one of the words in the opening sentence: as in the following cases.

Her swutelath on thison gewrite . . . swa his cwythe (will) swutelath (a confirmation of the will by king Æthelred).

The document goes on: theos swutelung wæs thærrihte gewriten.

[1] *Monast.* vi, pt. i, 329.

[2] See plate x in Mr. P. Hunter Blair's *An Introduction to Anglo-Saxon England*, 1959; Baldwin Brown, *Arts in Early England*, ii, 351.

[3] Mr. Hunter Blair, *op. cit.* plate x, gives a different interpretation of the words, which would, if accepted, have been a most interesting example of church teaching. The wording, however, seems to me entirely legal: see Prof. Whitelock's ASWills, no. 13, n. i, where she discusses the 'noticia' as an evidence document, the record of an oral contract, sometimes ordered to be entered into a church book. In one case, the gemot ordered that such an entry should be made; it is possible that here the offer of the church to the canons was made in the hundred, and the noticia inscribed on the arch in consequence. Prof. Whitelock instances further, no. 30, n. 2, the oral will of Eanwen, KCD. 755, announced to the gemot and recorded in a noticia.

Her is on sio swutelung (another will records).
Tha boc . . . to swutelung (the title deed as evidence).
To fulre swutelung (as a sufficient proof).[1]

The villager at Breamore, then, as elsewhere in England, had the church as solidly a part of his daily life as the fish in the Avon, the long-legged crane in the water meadows and the bucks for the king's hunting in the Forest on the hill above. He had been baptised in the church, and so had his children; the bishop had confirmed the youngest the last time he rode through the village, he and his chaplain getting down from their horses and sitting in Godeman the priest's little house and talking with him, while Tidhelm, who was the priest's man, ran round the village and collected the children. His own boy, Osric, was a bit young, but he could say his paternoster, and the priest said it was all right. The villager and his family went to mass on Sundays, under the picture of the Crucifixion over the door: even when there was the hay to get in, they all went to mass first. Mass was about three hours before noon: you could feed the beasts first. They stood through the mass, looking towards the altar through the narrow chancel arch, and watched till the priest blessed the housel, which was the very Paschal lamb and Christ himself, as the abbot had once said in his sermon.

If you had asked the villager what it meant to him, the church and the litanies and the mass and all that went with them, he would have found it difficult to understand your question. God made the world and there were churches for his service everywhere; the king himself had built many of them. The laws enjoined the service of God. Mercy and pity and the service of God went together, and keeping one's oath and being trustworthy. The king's reeve did justice in the shire moot, where he himself had once been called as a witness, and the bishop was at the moot, too, that day, and he spoke up when a man

---

[1] ASWills, nos. 16(2); 12, 5, 30. Cf. also, for the opening sentence of a noticia: ASChar. no. 26, Her swutelath; 31, This is seo gerædnes (the word 'gecwythrædnes' is unique, but appears to mean 'agreement'); 37, Her swutelath on thyssum gewrite; 38, Her is geswutelod; 40, towards end, This is seo swutelung the Ælfweard on Dentune wrothte; 45, Her is geswutelod on thysum gewrite; 49, Her is geswitulod. 'Swutelung' in some form appears also in nos. 51, 53, 54 ('this noticia, swutelunge, archbishop Oswald made orally and had it written down'), 62, 66, 69, 70, 71 (a noticia written into a gospel book), 73, 74, 75-79, 80 (another noticia in a gospel book), 83, 85, 86, 92, 97, 99-103, and many others, where 'Her swutelath' is used as the normal beginning of a noticia. 'Gerædness' for 'agreement' occurs in nos. 7, 19, 31, 32, 94, etc. I have to thank Prof. Whitelock and Dr. Harmer for much help about this inscription.

was going to be hanged (and justly too), and said, 'Mercy pleadeth against judgment', and so the man was outlawed and not hanged; men said he had taken ship to go and fight for the emperor. 'Mercy pleadeth against judgment': it was useful that the church should plead that, for the guilty man had been his wife's cousin and she was very upset.

As to the church, of course there was a church at Breamore, for the king had a mill on the river, just by the bridge, and that brought folk to the village, and it was a fine village, with a fair at Michaelmas, and food seldom lacking. Of course there was a church. There had to be, for the service of God. God made the world as all men knew, and he willed everything that was good, and he willed that all men should be good themselves, but naturally, not everybody was. At times, he wasn't himself. The abbot said once in his sermon that this world was very unsteady, and we lived in it as in a transitory cottage: but we had a home in heaven:[1] where else should he have heard that, but in the church at Breamore? You, sir, must know that God's son came down from heaven, to be our Saviour and Redeemer, and some day he will take us up to be with him, to the fine country of heaven, where are no storms nor icy cold, nor hunger nor thirst, but the fine park of Paradise, with Christ and his saints walking in it? Which is what 'in saecula saeculorum' means, as all men know. To which, the villager said as he turned away to bring your horse round, may Christ bring us all in the end.

[1] See frontispiece, for a representation of heaven more like a walled city, or a fortress. The picture illustrates Gen. 5. 24: And Enoch walked with God: and he was not, for God took him. In the coloured original, the sky is blue, and God stoops over a wall to pull up Enoch within.

BIBLIOGRAPHICAL NOTE

MOST general histories of the English church allow very little space to the pre-Conquest period and are not here mentioned. For reference to the background of pre-Conquest church history the two relevant volumes in the Oxford History of England should be noted: R. G. Collingwood and J. N. L. Myres, *Roman Britain and the English Settlements*, 1936; F. M. Stenton, *Anglo-Saxon England*, 1943 and 1947.

For an extremely valuable discussion of sources and bibliography, together with selected translations of the more important sources, narrative and documentary, see Professor Dorothy Whitelock's section in Part iii of her *English Historical Documents*, pp. 567-854; and for an exhaustive bibliography which lists under subjects both books and the relevant articles in periodicals: W. Bonser, *An Anglo-Saxon and Celtic Bibliography (450–1087)*, 2 vols., 1957.

CONTRACTIONS

ASC. *Anglo-Saxon Chronicle*: the Everyman's Library ed., no. 624, ed. by G. N. Garmonsway; for text, C. Plummer, *Two of the Saxon Chronicles parallel*, 1892–1899.

ASChar. A. J. Robertson, *Anglo-Saxon Charters*, 1939.

ASW. F. E. Harmer, *Anglo-Saxon Writs*, 1952.

ASWills. D. Whitelock, *Anglo-Saxon Wills*, 1930.

BCS. W. de G. Birch, *Cartularium Saxonicum*, 4 vols., 1885–1889.

BHL. *Bibliotheca Hagiographica Latina*, ed. Soc. Bollandiani, 2 vols., 1898–1901, with Supplementum, 2nd ed., 1911. (For saints of whom there is a written Life: for Celtic saints, of whom there is often no Life, see Gould, S. Baring, *infra*, p. 356.)

Darlington. 'Ecclesiastical Reform in the late Old English period', in EHR. li (1936).

EBC. *Studies in the Early British Church*, ed. Nora K. Chadwick, 1958.

EHD. *English Historical Documents, c. 500–1042*, ed. D. Whitelock, 1955.

EHR. *The English Historical Review*.

Ellard. G. Ellard, *Ordination anointings in the western church before 1000 A.D.*, Med. Acad. of America, Publications no. 16, 1933.

HE. Bede's *Historia Ecclesiastica Gentis Anglorum*: for Latin text and notes, see ed. of C. Plummer, 2 vols., 1896; for English translation, the Everyman ed., no. 479, with introd. by Prof. David Knowles.

HS. A. W. Haddan and W. Stubbs, *Councils and ecclesiastical documents relating to Great Britain and Ireland*, 3 vols., 1869–1878.

JEH. *Journal of Ecclesiastical History*.

KCD. J. M. Kemble, *Codex Diplomaticus Anglo-Saxonicus*, 6 vols., 1839–1848.

MGH. *Monumenta Germaniae Historica*.

MOE. *The Monastic Order in England*, Dom David Knowles, 1940.

Monast. W. Dugdale, *Monasticon Anglicanum*, 6 vols., 1846, *seqq.*

PL. *Patrologia Latina*, ed. J.-P. Migne.

Plummer. *Venerabilis Baedae (historia ecclesiastica)*, ed. C. Plummer, 2 vols., 1896.

Rice. D. Talbot Rice, *English Art 871–1100*. 1952.

BIBLIOGRAPHY

Åberg, N. *The occident and the orient in the art of the seventh century*: the British Isles, 1943.

Acta Sanctorum, ed. Johannes Bollandus, 1643 *seqq.*

Addleshaw, G. W. O. *The beginnings of the parochial system*, and *The development of the parochial system from Charlemagne to Urban ii (768-1099)*, nos. 3 and 6 of St. Anthony's Hall publications, York.

Anderson, A. O. 'Ninian and the southern Picts', in *Scottish Historical Review*, xxvii (1948), 25.

Anderson-Arngart, O. S. *The Leningrad Bede*, 1952: in *Early English manuscripts in facsimile*, eds. B. Colgrave, Kemp Malone, Knud Schibsbye, 2.

Ashdown, M. *English and Norse documents*, 1930. (See for some references to barbaric cruelty of the Northmen.)

Atchely, E. G. C. F. *Ordo Primus Romanus*, 1905, in Library of Liturgiology and Ecclesiology, vol. 6.

Attenborough, F. L. *Laws of the earliest English kings*, 1922.

Bethurum, D. *The homilies of Wulfstan*, 1957. See for text and introduction.

Blair, P. H. *An introduction to Anglo-Saxon England*, 1959, for much information about the later Anglo-Saxon church, diocesan boundaries, etc.

Brechter, S. *Die Quellen zür Angelsachsenmission Gregors des Grossen*, 1941.

Brown, G. Baldwin. *The arts in early England*, 6 vols. (in 7), 1903-1937; *From schola to cathedral*, 1886.

Bruce-Mitford, R. L. S. ed. *Recent Archaeological Excavations in Britain*, 1956, for articles on Mithraic remains at Carrawburgh and on the Walbrook and on Lullingstone; *The Sutton Hoo Ship-Burial*, 1949.

Chadwick, N. K. *Studies in early British history*, 1954, specially for the Bernicians, and early dedications in the Welsh church; 'St. Ninian', in *Trans. of the Dumfriesshire and Galloway Nat. Hist. and Antiq. Soc.*, vol. xxvii.

Chadwick, O. *John Cassian*, 1950, and see for variant view of Cassian, Münz, P., 'John Cassian', in JEH. xi (1960), 1-22.

Chavasse, A. *Le Sacramentaire gélasien (Vaticanus Reginensis 316): sacramentaire presbytéral en usage dans les titres romains au VIIe siècle*, 1958.

Clapham, A. W. *English Romanesque Architecture before the Norman Conquest*, 1930.

Clemoes, P. *The Anglo-Saxons: studies presented to Bruce Dickins*, 1959; specially for pre-Conquest churches.

Colgrave, B. *The life of bishop Wilfrid by Eddius Stephanus*, 1927.

Collingwood, W. G. *Northumbrian crosses of the pre-Norman age*, 1927.

Cook, A. S., and Tinker, C. B. *Select Translations from Old English Poetry*, 1926.

Crawford, S. J. *The Old English version of the Heptateuch, Ælfric's treatise on the Old and New Testament and his Preface to Genesis*, E.E.T.S. O.S.160, 1922; *Byrhtferth's Manual*, vol. i, 1929.

Cruden, S. *The early Christian and Pictish Monuments of Scotland*, 1957: for the Whithorn stones.

Darlington, R. R. *The Vita Wulfstani*, Camden Soc., 3rd Ser., 1928; 'The Anglo-Saxon Period', in *The English Church and the Continent*, ed. C. R. Dodwell, 1959.

Davis, G. R. C. *Medieval Cartularies*, 1958; useful for charter material.

Deanesly, M. 'The Canterbury Edition of the Answers of pope Gregory I to St. Augustine', in JEH. x (1959), 1-49; 'The archdeacons of Canterbury under archbishop Ceolnoth', EHR. clxv (1927), 1-11.

Dekkers, E. 'Were the early monks liturgical?' in *Collectanea Ord. Cist. Ref.* April-July, 1960, for Cassian's monastic aim.

Dickins, B., and Ross, A. S. C. *The Dream of the Rood*, 1934.

Dix, G. *The shape of the liturgy*, 1943, and for more recent work on the evolution of the liturgy, A. Baumstark, *Comparative Liturgy*, English ed. of F. L. Cross, 1953.

Doble, G. H. *The Lanalet Pontifical*, 1934; see for the 'Pontifical of Egbert', Surtees Soc., 1853; and many short tracts on Celtic saints.

Douglas, D. C. *Domesday monachorum of Christ Church, Canterbury*, 1944: for information about Kentish parishes.

Duckett, E. S. *Anglo-Saxon saints and scholars*, 1947: *Saint Dunstan of Canterbury*, 1955; *Alfred the Great and his England*, 1957.

Ekwall, E. *The concise dictionary of English place names*, 3rd ed., 1947; and for place names also, Smith, A. H., *English Place-Name Elements*, 2 vols., 1956.

Evans, A. W. Wade. *Welsh Christian Origins*, 1934; *Vitae Sanctorum Britanniae et Genealogiae* (with trans.), 1944; *The Emergence of England and Wales*, 1956, valuable, but controversial in parts. (See Wade-Evans, A. W.)

Förster, M. *Zür Geschichte der Reliquienkultus in Altengland*, Sitzungsberichte der Bayerischen Akad. der Wissenschaften, Heft 8, 1943.

Fowler, J. T. *Adamnani vita S. Columbae*. 1894.

Gamber, K. *Wege zür Urgregorianum*. Beuron. 1956.

Gifford, D. H. *The parish in Domesday Book: a study of the mother churches and rural chapels in the late Saxon and Norman period*. (Thesis accessible in the Univ. Library, Univ. of London.) 1952.

Gildas. *De excidio et conquestu Britanniae*: Eng. trans., see J. A. Giles, Gildas and Nennius, 1842-1845; and also in A. W. Wade-Evans, *Nennius' Hist. of the Britons*, 1938, 122-153.

Gordon, R. K. *Anglo-Saxon Poetry*, 1954.

Gould, S. Baring. *The Lives of the Saints*, 16 vols., 1897, 98.

Greenaway, G. W. *Saint Boniface*, 1955.

Grieve, A. *Willibrord*, 1923, with a translation of Alcuin's Life of Willibrord; for Willibrord see also W. Levison, 'St. Willibrord and his place in history', *Durham Univ. Jour.* (New Ser. 1), 1940.

Grosjean, P. 'Confusa Caligo', in Zeuss memorial vol. published by Celtica, Dublin, 1955, for the Hisperica Famina and the inflated Latin in the period between Aldhelm and 1066; 'Notes d'hagiographie celtique' in the *Analecta Bollandiana*, lxxv (1957), 158-226, for St. Patrick and his stay at Auxerre under Germanus; *ib.* lxxviii (1960), 'La Date du Colloque de Whitby'.

Harmer, F. E. *Select English Historical Documents of the ninth and tenth centuries*, 1914.

Henry F. *Irish art in the early Christian period*, 1940; useful for comparison with Celtic art in Britain.

John, E. 'St. Oswald and the tenth century reformation', in JEH. ix (1958), 159-172; 'An alleged Worcester charter in the reign of Edgar', in the *Bull. of the John Rylands Library*, 1958; 'The king and the monks in the tenth century reformation', *ib.* 1959; 'Some Latin charters of the tenth century reformation in England', in *Revue Bénédictine*, lxx (1960), 333-359: *Land tenure in early England*, 1960.

Kemp, E. W. *Canonization and authority in the western church*, 1948.

Kendrick, T. D. *Anglo-Saxon Art to A.D. 900*, 1938; *Late Saxon and Viking Art*, 1949.

Ker, N. R. *Catalogue of manuscripts containing Anglo-Saxon*, 1957.

Leeds, E. T. *Celtic ornament in the British Isles*, 1933.

Levison, W. *England and the Continent in the Eighth Century*, 1946.

Liebermann, F. *Die Gesetze der Angelsachsen*, 3 vols., 1898-1916.

Lloyd, J. E. *History of Wales to the Edwardian Conquest*, 3rd ed., 1939: for early Welsh saints.

Lowe, E. A. *The Bobbio Missal: a Gallican mass-book, MS. Paris 13246*, 1917.

Maclagan, Sir E. R. D. *The Bayeux Tapestry*, 1949.

McNeill, J. T., and Gamer, H. M. *Medieval handbooks of penance*, 1938; J. T. McNeill, *The Celtic penitentials*, 1923.

Malmesbury, William of. *De antiquitate Glastoniensis Ecclesiae*, in Adam of Domerham's ed., 1727.

Meates, G. W. *Lullingstone Roman villa*: also Reports in 'Archaeologia Cantiana', lxiii (1951) and lxv (1953).

Mortimer, R. C. *Western Canon Law*, 1953.

Nordenfalk, C. *Beyond the Book of Durrow*, 1947.

Oleson, T. J. *The Witenagemot in the reign of Edward the Confessor*, 1955.

Plucknett, T. F. T. *A concise history of Common Law*.

Powicke, Sir F. M. *Handbook of British Chronolocy*, 1939 (for lists of bishops).

Raby, F. J. E. *A history of Christian Latin poetry, from the beginnings to the close of the middle ages*, 2 vols. 1957.

Renwick, W. L., and Orton, H. *The beginnings of English literature*, vol. i, 1952. See for manuscript sources, etc.

Rice, D. Talbot. *The beginnings of Christian Art*, 1957.

Richmond, I. A. *Roman and Native in North Britain*, 1958.

Robertson, A. J. *The Laws of the kings of England from Edmund to Henry I*, 1925.

Robinson, J. A. *St. Oswald and the church of Worcester*, 1919; *The Saxon bishops of Wells*, 1918; *Somerset historical essays*, 1921; *The Times of St. Dunstan*, 1922.

Saxl, F. *Memorial Essays*, 1957, for 'Implications of the term *Sapiens* as applied to Gildas', M. Deanesly.

Schramm, P. E. *History of the English Coronation*, 1937.

Searle, W. G. *Anglo-Saxon Bishops, Kings and Nobles*, 1899.

Sedgfield, W. J. *King Alfred's version of the Consolation of Boethius*, 1900.

Serjeantson, M. S. *A history of foreign words in English*, 1935.

Simpson, W. D. *The Celtic church in Scotland*, 1935.

Sisam, K. 'Cynewulf and his poetry', in *Proc. of the Brit. Acad.*, xviii, 1933.

Stenton, F. M. *The early history of the abbey of Abingdon*, 1913. 'The South-Western element in the Old English Chronicle', in *Essays presented to Thomas Frederick Tout*, 1925; *The Latin Charters of the Anglo-Saxon period*, 1954; Introduction to the Phaidon ed. of *The Bayeux Tapestry*, 1957.

Stevenson, J. *The historical works of Simeon of Durham*, trans., 1855: useful for northern church history.

Stutz, V. 'The proprietary church as an element of medieval Germanic ecclesiastical law', in *Medieval Germany, 911–1250*, vol. ii of *Essays by German historians*, trans. G. Barraclough, 1938.

Sweet, H. *Selected Homilies of Ælfric*, 1922.

Symons, T. *The Monastic Agreement of the monks and nuns of the English nation* (Regularis Concordia), 1953.

Talbot, C. H. *The Anglo-Saxon missionaries in Germany*, 1954.

Thompson, A. Hamilton. 'Diocesan Organization in the Middle Ages: Archdeacons and Rural Deans', 1943. *Proc. of the Brit. Acad.* xxix; *Bede: his life, times, and writings. Essays in commemoration of the twelfth centenary of his death*, 1935; *Liber Vitae Ecclesiae Dunelmensis*, Surtees Soc., vol. 136, 1923.

Thompson, E. A. 'The origin of Christianity in Scotland', in *Scottish Historical Review*, xxxvii (1958), 17-22.

Thorpe, B. *Ancient laws and institutes of England*, 1840; *Homilies of Aelfric*, 2 vols., 1843–1846.

Toynbee, J. M. C. 'Christianity in Roman Britain', *Jour. of the Brit. Archaeol. Assoc.*, 3rd S., xvi (1953), covers all the archaeological evidence.

Victoria County History. Each county has an early volume with a section dealing with ecclesiastical and monastic history.

Wainwright, F. T. *The problem of the Picts*, 1955.

Walker, G. S. M. *Sancti Columbani opera*, 1957, with trans.

Wardale, E. E. *Chapters on Old English Literature*, 1935.

Wasserschleben, F. W. H. *Die Bussordnungen der abendländischen Kirche*, ed. 1958.

Watkin, Aelred. *The Great Chartulary of Glastonbury*, 1947.

White, Caroline L. *Aelfric: a new study of his life and writings*, 1898: Yale Studies in English, ii.

Whitelock, D. *Sermo Lupi ad Anglos*, 1939; *The audience of Beowulf*, 1951; *The beginnings of English society*, 1952; *English historical documents*, vol. i, 1955.

Wilkins, D. *Concilia Magnae Britanniae et Hiberniae*, 4 vols., 1737.

Wilson, H. A. *The Gelasian Sacramentary*, 1893.

Wormald, F. The miniatures in 'the Gospels of St. Augustine', Corpus Christi College MS. 286. (The Sandars Lectures in Bibliography, publ. 1954.)

Wrenn, C. L. 'The poetry of Caedmon', 1946: *Proc. of the Brit. Acad.* xxxiii (1946).

[As we go to press, the publication of H. P. R. Finberg's *The Early Charters of the West Midlands* is announced.]

ARCHBISHOPS OF CANTERBURY

Augustine, 597
Laurentius, 604–609(?)
Mellitus, 619
Justus, 624
Honorius, 627
Deusdedit, 655–664
Wighard, abp. elect, *c*. 665
Theodore, 668
Berhtweald, 693
Tatwine, 731
Nothelm, 735
Cuthberht, 740 or 741
Breguwine, 761
Jænberht, 765
Æthelheard, 793
Wulfred, 805
Feologils, 832
Ceolnoth, 833

Æthelred, 870
Plegmund, 890
Æthelhelm, 914
Wulfhelm, 923
Oda, 942
Ælfsige, 959
Berhthelm, 959
Dunstan, 960
Æthelgar, 988
Sigeric, 990
Ælfric, 995
Ælfheah, 1005
Lyfing, 1013
Æthelnoth, 1020
Eadsige, 1038
Robert (of Jumièges), 1051
Stigand, 1052

ARCHBISHOPS OF YORK

Paulinus, 625 (resigned 633)
vacancy, 633–664
Chad, 664 (resigned 669)
Wilfrid I, 669
Boisil, 678
Wilfrid I (restored 686)
Boisil (restored 691)
John of Beverley, 705
Wilfrid II, 718
Egbert, 732 or 734
Æthelberht, 767
Eanbald I, 780
Eanbald II, 796
Wulfsige, 808
Wigmund, 837
Wulfhere, 854

Æthelbald, 900
vacancy
Hrothweard, 904–928
vacancy
Wulfstan I, 931
Oscytel, 956
Eadwald, 971
Oswald, 972
Ealdwulf, 995
Wulfstan II, 1003
Ælfric, 1023
Æthelric, 1041
Ælfric (restored?), 1041
Cynesige, 1051
Ealdred, 1062

INDEX